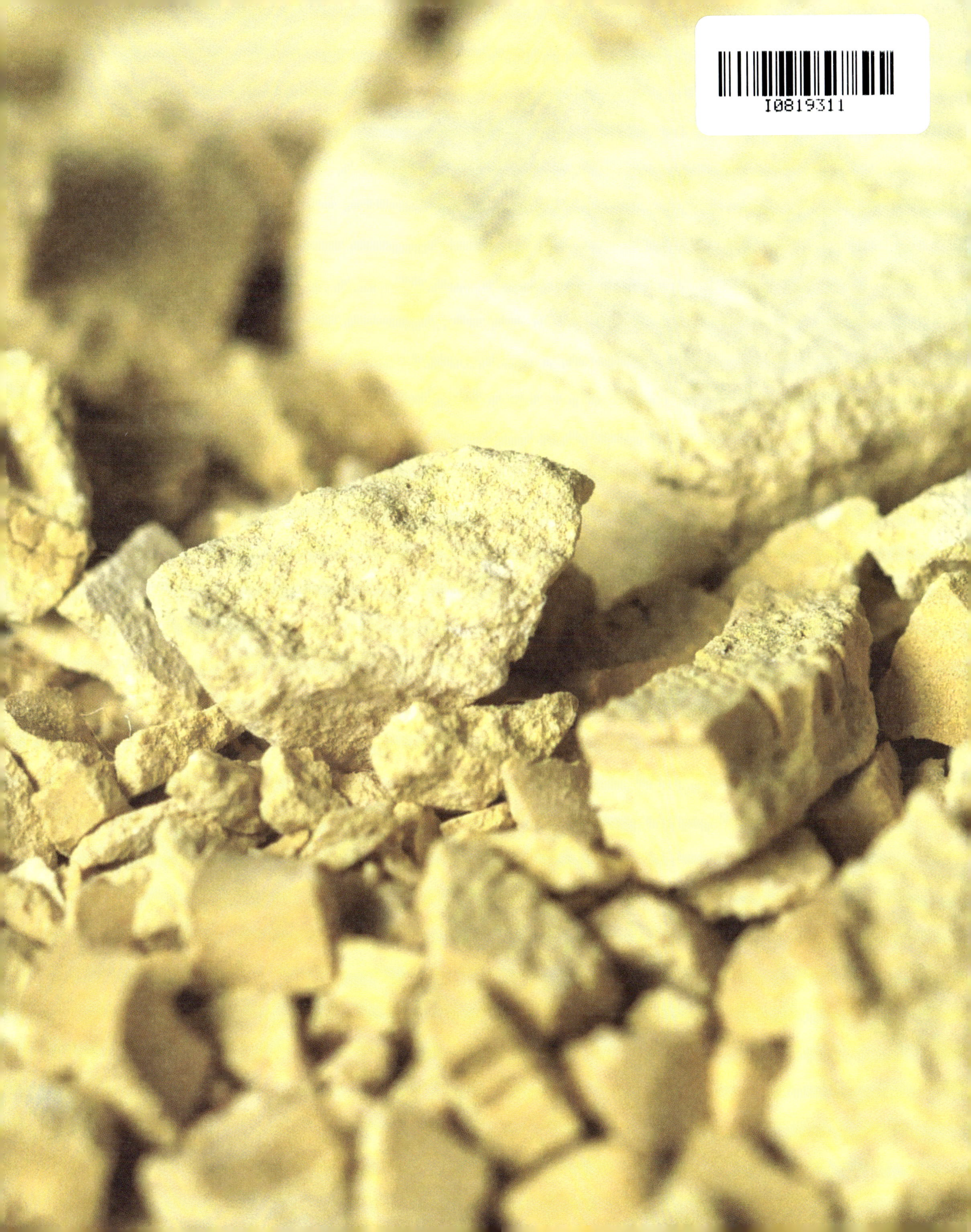
I0819311

FROM **PLANT** TO **PRINT**

Using natural dyes and pigments in printmaking

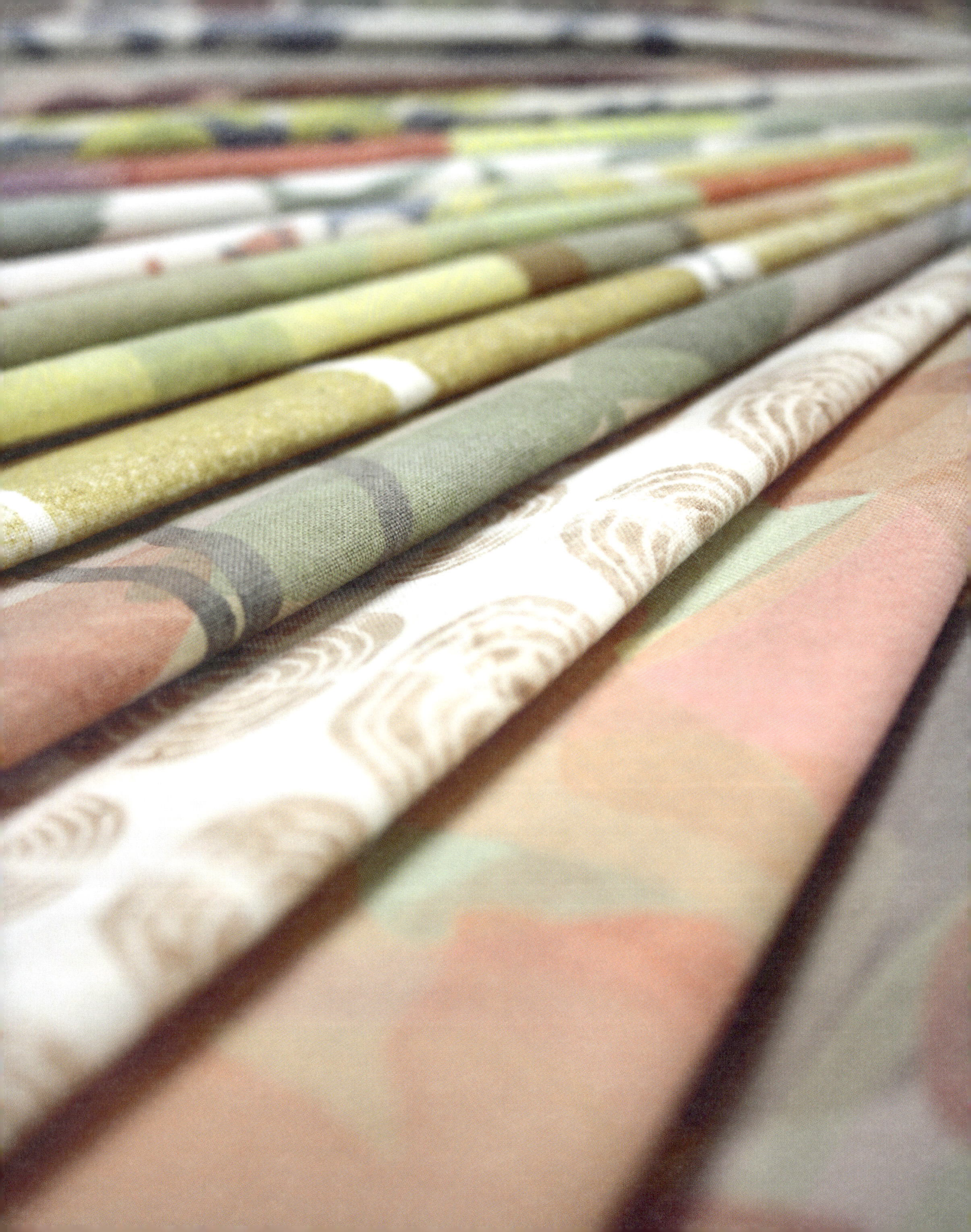

Jacqui Symons

FROM **PLANT** TO **PRINT**

Using natural dyes and pigments in printmaking

THE CROWOOD PRESS

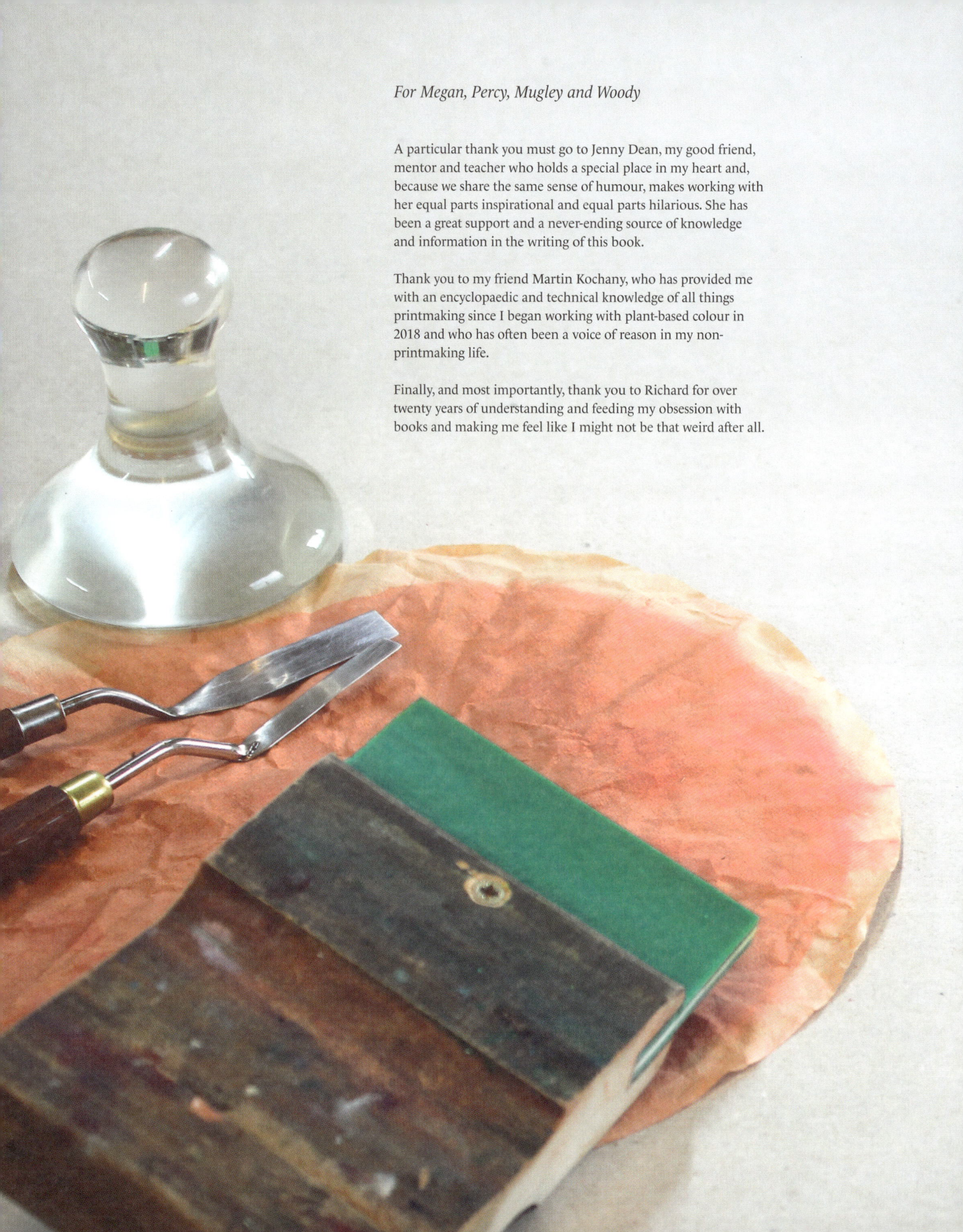

For Megan, Percy, Mugley and Woody

A particular thank you must go to Jenny Dean, my good friend, mentor and teacher who holds a special place in my heart and, because we share the same sense of humour, makes working with her equal parts inspirational and equal parts hilarious. She has been a great support and a never-ending source of knowledge and information in the writing of this book.

Thank you to my friend Martin Kochany, who has provided me with an encyclopaedic and technical knowledge of all things printmaking since I began working with plant-based colour in 2018 and who has often been a voice of reason in my non-printmaking life.

Finally, and most importantly, thank you to Richard for over twenty years of understanding and feeding my obsession with books and making me feel like I might not be that weird after all.

CONTENTS

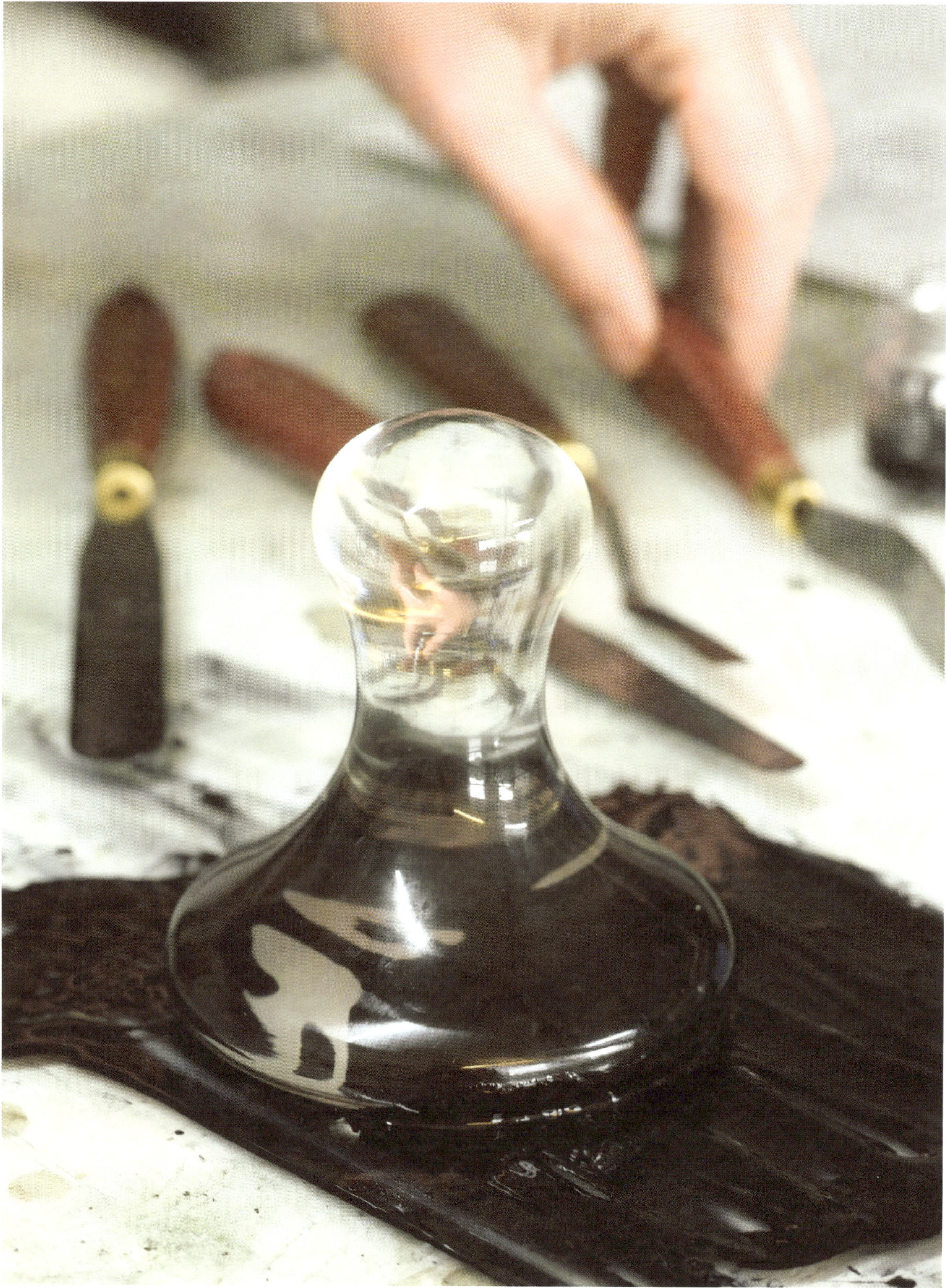

Introduction

Who knew that plants could hold such a magnificent variety of colour within their leaves, their stems, their roots and their flowers? When I first discovered natural colour and plant dyes, I had a vague sense that in the past, people might have used plants to dye their clothes various shades of muddy browns and beiges (mostly informed by watching costume dramas, it has to be said) but other than that, my knowledge of natural colour was non-existent. I knew that the umbers, ochres and iron oxides in my paints and inks were based on, or even were, colours from the earth but that was the extent of my knowledge.

In 2018, I completed a month's residency at KIRA, part of Kingsbrae Gardens in Canada. Whilst there, a local artist asked me if my linseed oil printmaking inks were environmentally friendly. For a printmaker with a love of colour and an artistic practice that centred on climate change, biodiversity and nature, I was shocked to realise I didn't know. I'd given no thought as to where the inks had come from or how they were made. I'd always been sparing in their use, disposed of them properly and used non-toxic cleaning materials so why hadn't I thought about the inks' journey before I purchased them?

On my return, I started to research artists' colour, where the pigments came from and how I might use natural and plant-based resources to produce my own printmaking ink. At the time, there was a surprising lack of information available regarding the use of plant colour for artists' materials and specifically printmaking. In the last few years, more information has become available but when I first started researching the subject, the only advice I could find concentrated on either natural dyes and dyeing fabric or was from the pre-synthetic pigment era. As it turns out, both of these subjects were incredibly important starting points and provided a wealth of information but there wasn't a 'recipe book' that I could use to make plant-based printmaking inks.

Thus followed 'Dyeing (not Dying)', a successful grant application and a year of research and development into the use of plant-based pigments within printmaking. I initially concentrated on making oil-based ink to use for my leaf-printing series on paper but this soon developed into creating water-based inks and paints for screenprinting, watercolours for woodcuts and experiments with printing onto fabrics. Whilst I still feel I'm merely at the beginning of a long, richly diverse and fascinating journey, I've gained a wealth of knowledge that I'm thrilled to share with other people.

I hope this book provides you with the inspiration, information and knowledge to dip a toe into printmaking with plant-based colour. Use it as a starting point to develop an exploratory practice and an investigative approach to using natural materials. Possibly, once that toe has been dipped, a complete immersion into the world of plant-based colour in printmaking will follow.

USING THIS BOOK

The use of plant-based colour for printmaking opens up a whole new world of exciting colour, processes, techniques and recipes for both the printmaker and the natural dyer. This book provides a starting point for using plants as a source of colour and is suitable for both textile and paper printmaking processes. It splits the recipes into sections, depending on what substrate will be used, and offers an introduction to different printmaking techniques for both paper and fabric.

Not all processes and approaches have been covered, but you should find enough information in these pages to exchange your purchased relief inks, intaglio inks, screenprinting pastes and block-printing inks with your own hand-crafted art materials. Be careful – it's an addictive, enthralling and exciting ride – you may never go back!

Recipes: Weight or Volume?

Roughly speaking, one litre of water is equal to one kilogramme of water and therefore 100ml (millilitres) of water weighs 100g (grammes). Whilst measuring out one litre of water is relatively easy, it can be harder to measure smaller amounts such as 20ml, especially without a small measuring beaker or jug. It is often easier to weigh out 20g of water.

The recipes in this book primarily use weight rather than volume to specify liquid amounts. This is purely a practical decision to aid the reader when making up the pastes, liquids and dyes.

If you prefer to use volume, just change the grammes to millilitres for any water in the provided recipes. Be conscious that additional ingredients (such as metallic salts) will add weight even when dissolved, but if you are consistent with always using weight or volume, the recipes will still work.

Most recipes in this book will provide you with approximately 100g of plant-based colour to work with. This is the same as about half a pot of houmous and should be enough for trying out different techniques and recipes. The amounts are very easy to scale up when you're ready but remember not to feel restricted by them – use your instincts and experiment!

Health and Safety Guidelines

Both printmakers and natural dyers will be familiar with standard health and safety rules for working in a studio environment, at a kitchen table, outside or anywhere in-between. However, it is always useful to revisit this advice before trying a new process and familiarise yourself with recommended approaches to working. Most guidelines are common sense and have not been included here. However, I thought it might be useful to mention:

- Plants can be toxic too – make sure you know exactly what you're using and check for allergies.
- Keep kitchen equipment and dye equipment completely separate. Once something has been used for natural dyes, it should never be returned to the kitchen for food use.
- Always ensure equipment, dyestuffs and other materials are labelled.
- Always use a respirator mask when working with fine powders such as lake pigments or mordants.
- If unsure about the disposal of any chemical or liquid, consult your local authority and ask them for advice.

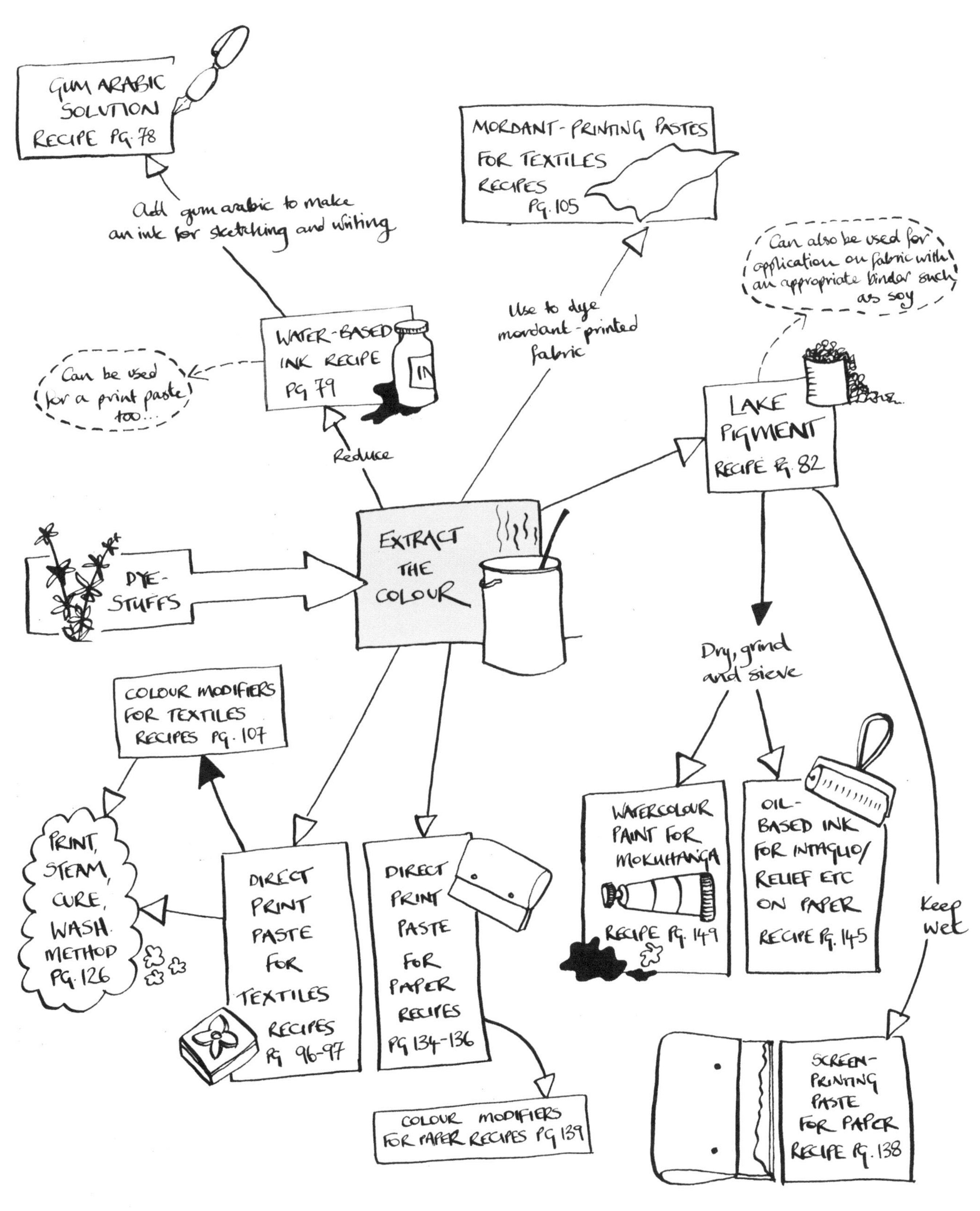
GUM ARABIC SOLUTION RECIPE PG 78
Add gum arabic to make an ink for sketching and writing
MORDANT-PRINTING PASTES FOR TEXTILES RECIPES PG. 105
Use to dye mordant-printed fabric
Can also be used for application on fabric with an appropriate binder such as soy
WATER-BASED INK RECIPE PG 79
Can be used for a print paste too...
Reduce
LAKE PIGMENT RECIPE PG. 82
DYE-STUFFS
EXTRACT THE COLOUR
Dry, grind and sieve
COLOUR MODIFIERS FOR TEXTILES RECIPES PG. 107
PRINT, STEAM, CURE, WASH METHOD PG. 126
DIRECT PRINT PASTE FOR TEXTILES RECIPES PG 96-97
DIRECT PRINT PASTE FOR PAPER RECIPES PG 134-136
WATERCOLOUR PAINT FOR MOKUHANGA RECIPE PG. 149
OIL-BASED INK FOR INTAGLIO/RELIEF ETC ON PAPER RECIPE PG. 145
Keep wet
COLOUR MODIFIERS FOR PAPER RECIPES PG 139
SCREEN-PRINTING PASTE FOR PAPER RECIPE PG. 138

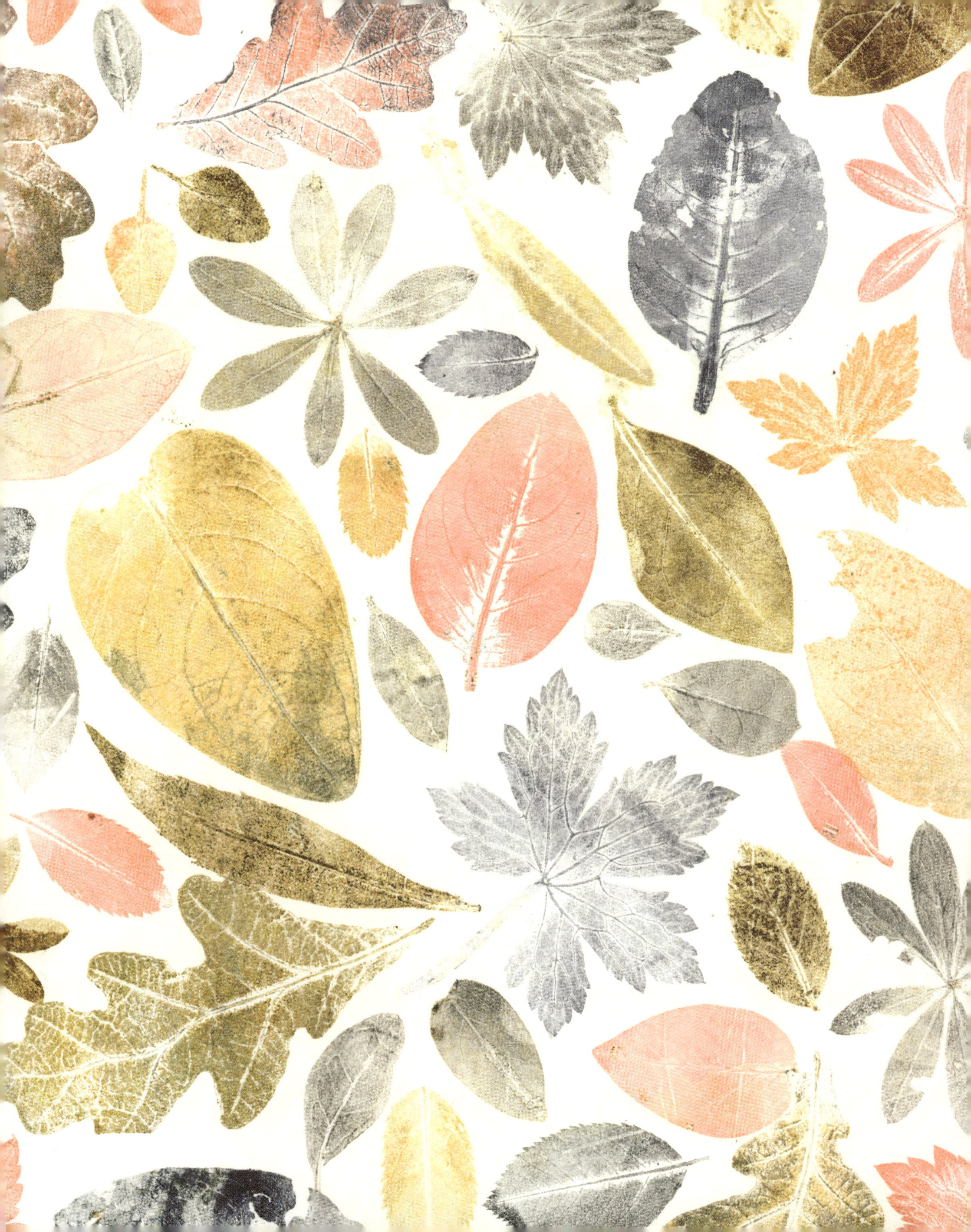

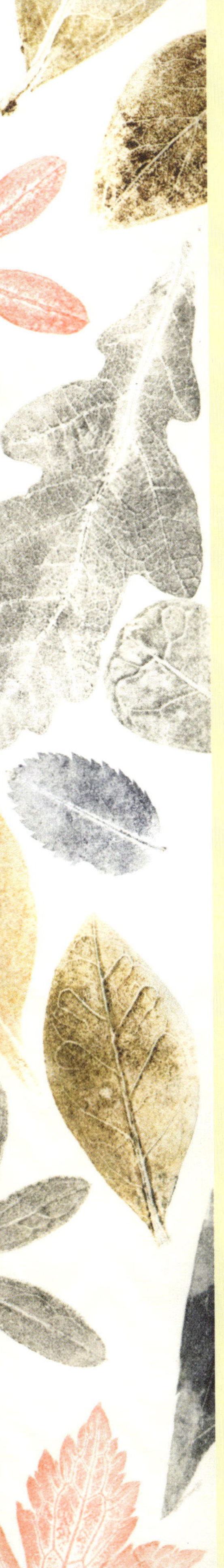

Chapter One

THE WONDERFUL WORLD OF PLANT-BASED COLOUR

FACING PAGE
Where it all started – end paper of the *Dyeing (not Dying)* book of plant-based inks.

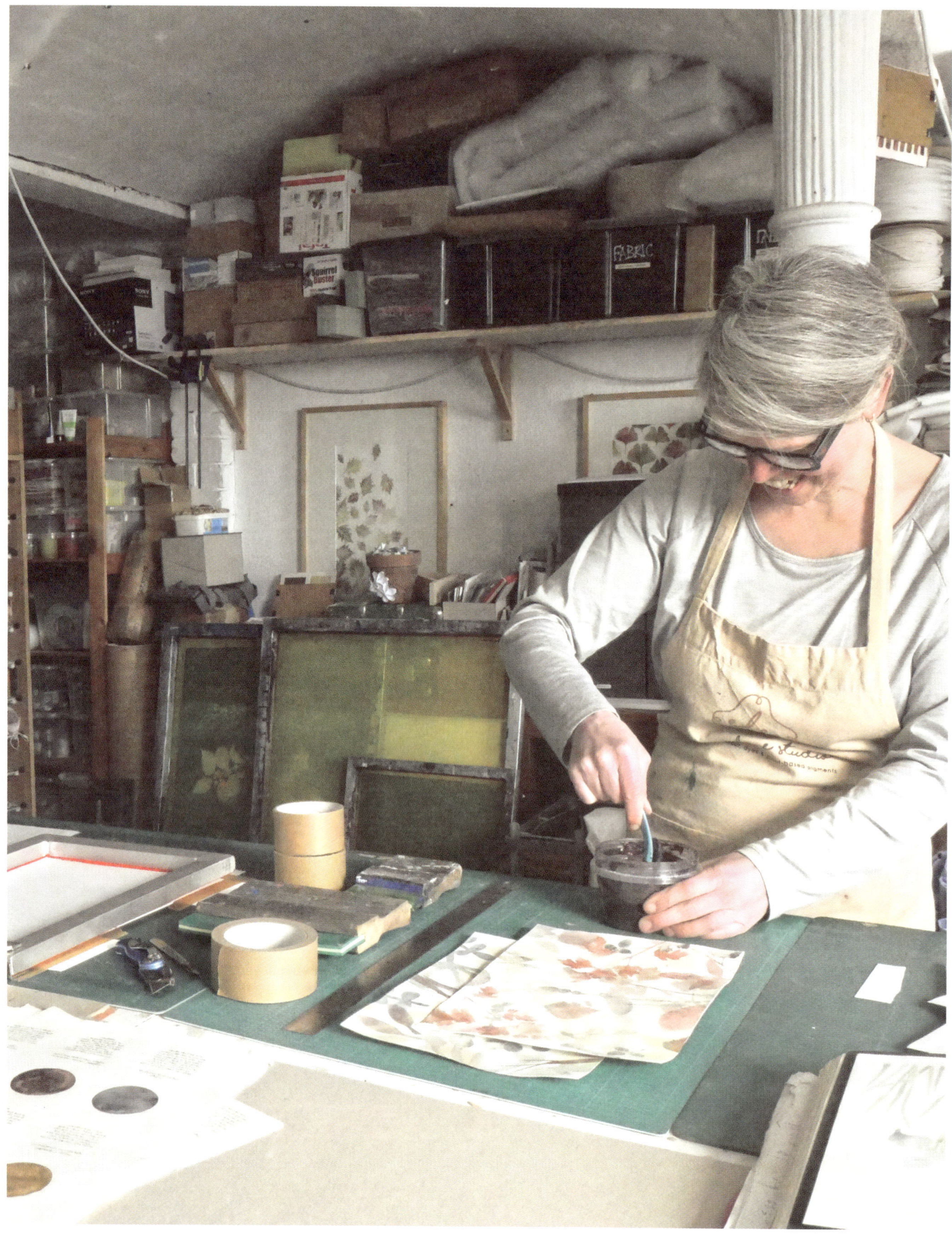
FABRIC
Squirrel Buster

USING PLANT-BASED COLOUR

Creating your own colour from plant-based materials isn't quick, easy or particularly simple. However, it is hugely rewarding, enjoyable and creates a deeper appreciation of nature, plant-life and our environment. The yearly seasonal cycle from new growth in spring and flourishing plants in summer through to harvest time in autumn and the hibernation of winter imposes an enduring and cyclical structure into your practice and requires you to slow down and observe the different seasons more closely and intimately than you might have done previously.

Using plants to create your own inks, paints and pigments will encourage you to adapt and change your practice and your timescales accordingly. Whilst many dried plants are available to purchase and are a good place to start, it is a satisfying and sustainable practice to use what grows in your region's climate and is available locally. However, it should be understood that using materials directly from nature and local to where you live will influence the colours available and the opportunities you have to gather and then use these items in your work. This first became apparent to me when I had gathered some goat willow (*Salix caprea*) pollen to experiment with as a pigment. Whilst wearing a black coat, I brushed past a goat willow tree heavy with flowers in the first flush of spring and the sleeve of my coat became covered in the fine bright yellow pollen of the flowers. I collected a minimal amount, not expecting it to be a useful pigment in any form, and yet it created a strong yellow oil-based ink that whilst difficult to manipulate and use, became a favourite, possibly because of the oddity of using pollen as a pigment. However, by the time I had got around to using the pollen and discovering its qualities, the weeks had passed and the flowers had died and dropped to the ground, making any further pollen gathering impossible until next year – goat willow pollen is not something you can readily buy. Now, each spring I look forward to seeing the trees covered in bright yellow flowers that noticeably stand out from trees that have yet to burst into leaf. Similar to the ethos of eating seasonally, the anticipation and expectation of a plant coming into flower or fruit, to be able to gather and use it in your pigment-making is something to celebrate and enjoy. Materials can also be gathered, dried and stored to be used at a less fruitful time of year just as previous generations used to collect, preserve and store food for use in the winter.

Handmade and homemade inks all have their own qualities and using them is a different experience from using shop-bought products. However, it just requires experimentation and learning and this soon becomes part of the process and part of your practice. When using a new commercial product, you often need to experiment and find the best way of working with it. Using your own inks, paints and art materials is just the same; however, don't expect every product you make to act in the same way or even produce the same exact colour each time.

The willingness to experiment is a vital part of my work and something that has been instrumental in building up my knowledge and skills in creating plant-based colour. Reading, online research and talking to experts gave me a good background knowledge of which plants were likely to provide a useable colour but actually carrying out experiments and tests led to the discovery of unexpected sources and a deeper understanding of plant-based colour. The discovery of one plant that makes

FACING PAGE
The Slow Lane Studio: part science lab, dye house, kitchen, haberdashery, greenhouse, paper store and print studio.

BELOW
Goat willow (*Salix caprea*) pollen: a surprising source of colour.

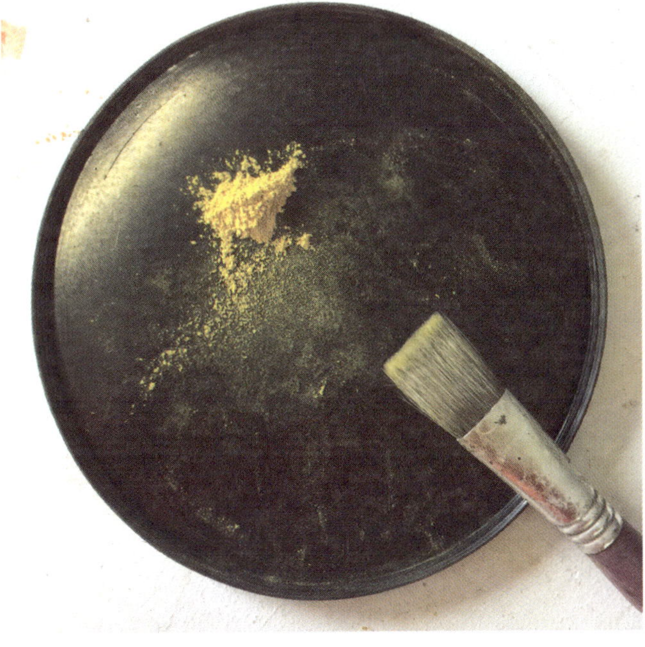

a good lake pigment creates an impetus to try others and I now quite happily try any plant – especially those that are numerous, considered invasive or are being pruned. Himalayan balsam (*Impatiens glandulifera*) is a plant that was introduced in 1839 as a garden plant for its large and showy white and magenta flowers. It is incredibly invasive in this country – once ripe, it flings its seeds out in all directions and they are carried along rivers and streams, spreading quickly once the plant establishes itself. The large leaves and tall habit quickly crowd out light and space from our native plants and take over large swathes of ground. 'Balsam bashing' (a method of removing plants by pulling them up by their shallow roots before they flower and set seed) in areas where the plant grows is encouraged so it seemed a good opportunity to try it as a dye and pigment. In certain parts of North America, a variety of goldenrod (*Solidago canadensis*) is listed as an invasive weed and goldenrod flowers produce the most wonderful yellows as both a pigment and a dye.

Experiencing outdoor environments, be that a cultivated garden, a remote moorland, urban scrubland or the grass verges along a lane, is a source of inspiration and I am constantly looking at plants and considering their potential both as a dye plant and as a lake pigment. Noticing colour in the landscape and thinking about plants is a part of my practice that is now as natural to me as putting one foot in front of another when walking.

Mapping and recording where I have seen interesting plants or potential dye sources is an important part of my work process. Whilst it doesn't mean that I will necessarily return and collect items, it becomes a record of thoughts about a particular plant or the habitat it grows in, the growing conditions, similarities to other plants and ideas about how to use it. Cones from the common alder (*Alnus glutinosa*) tree, once ripe, are a recognised source of rich brown colour and, whilst little and fiddly to collect, are numerous in winter, often lasting through to spring. On a dog walk through my local town, a chance passing of a tree that looked strangely like a common alder 'but different' led to the discovery of the Italian alder (*Alnus cordata*) and its comparatively huge cones. Following testing, I discovered they created a great lake pigment and the size of them means I don't need to collect so many.

My knowledge of plants, trees and flowers has developed through my practice, originally as a necessary requirement for my leaf print series and later on as my interest and curiosity in all things botanical grew. I also spent a year creating *The Dovestone Doomsday Vault*, which is a collection of seeds of all the plant varieties growing

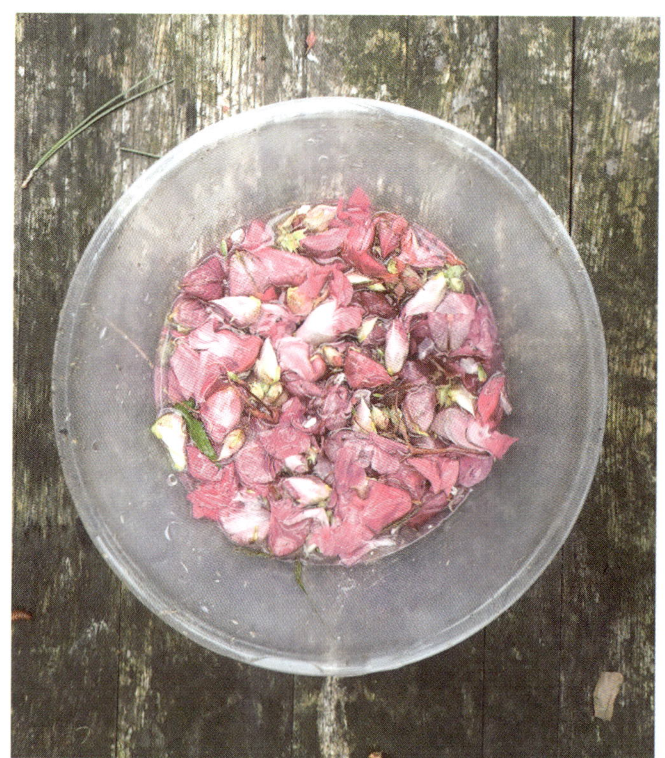

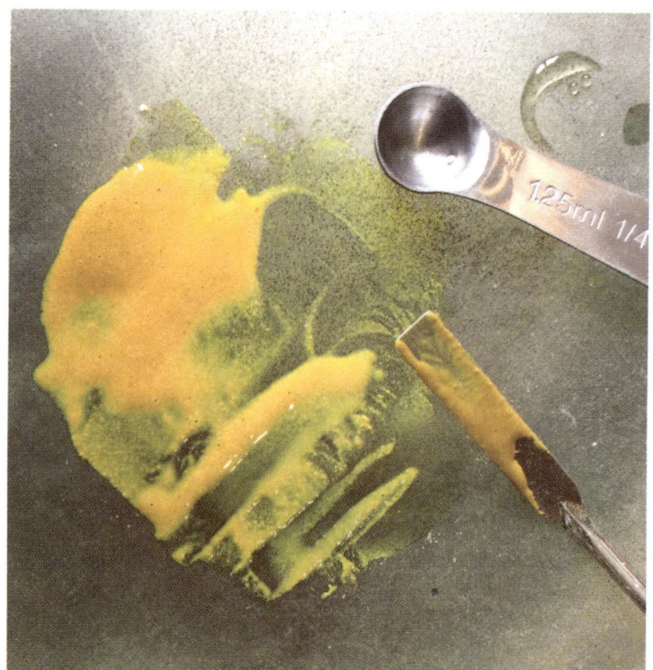

TOP
The flowers of the invasive Himalayan balsam (*Impatiens glandulifera*) plant.

ABOVE
Making goldenrod (*Solidago canadensis*) lake pigment into watercolour paint.

at the RSPB Dove Stone Reservoir on the edge of the Peak District in the UK. Recognising and identifying plant species became a fascination as I strove to create a complete collection and database for the Reserve and this knowledge has benefitted me greatly when searching for potential sources of plant-based colour.

However, as I gain more experience, I have a tendency to return to just a few plants as reliable sources of colour, chiefly indigo, woad, madder, weld, rhubarb and buckthorn, though I don't limit myself to these. This seems to be usual and very typical for many users of natural colour and may be something to do with the desire to use dye sources that have a good reputation for lightfastness and washfastness. For me, part of the attraction in using just a few sources of colour is developing a greater understanding of those specific plants, their many varying attributes and a realisation that within those sources, a great many more colours are available to the experienced user than just the most well-known or obvious one.

Consuming less is an important part of my philosophy. As humans, we are consuming every minute of every day but if we can consume less, we are reducing our impact on the planet and on our environment. Even if it is as seemingly insignificant as using fewer alder cones in my dye; by not using as many, I am leaving more for others, for insects, for wildlife, for new alder trees. Just one alder cone is part of a larger eco-system that is interconnected and has an effect on its surroundings and the local biodiversity.

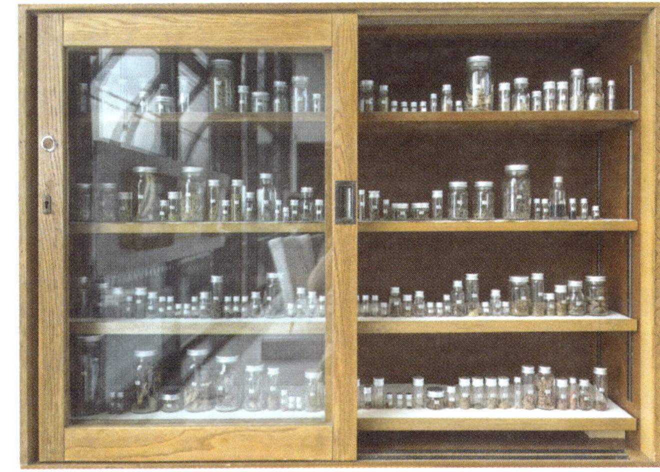

Splendour Awaits in Minute Proportions (The Dovestone Doomsday Vault) or, '272 seed specimens displayed by colour'. Seeds, glass vials, wooden cabinet; 2,300 × 1,000 × 250mm; 2018. This and nature printing started an interest in the trees and plants that surround us.

These pinks, reds and purples screenprinted onto cotton fabric show just a few of the remarkable number of colours that can be extracted from madder.

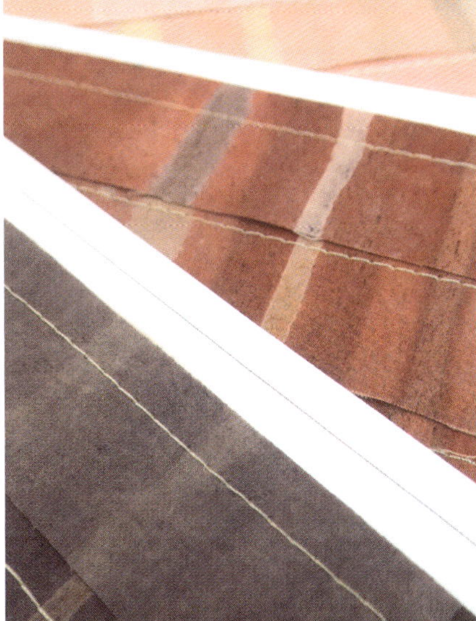

Alder cones are a wonderful source of rich chestnut brown, especially for inks and pigments. The Italian alder (*Alnus cordata*) bears much larger cones than the more frequently seen common alder (*Alnus glutinosa*).

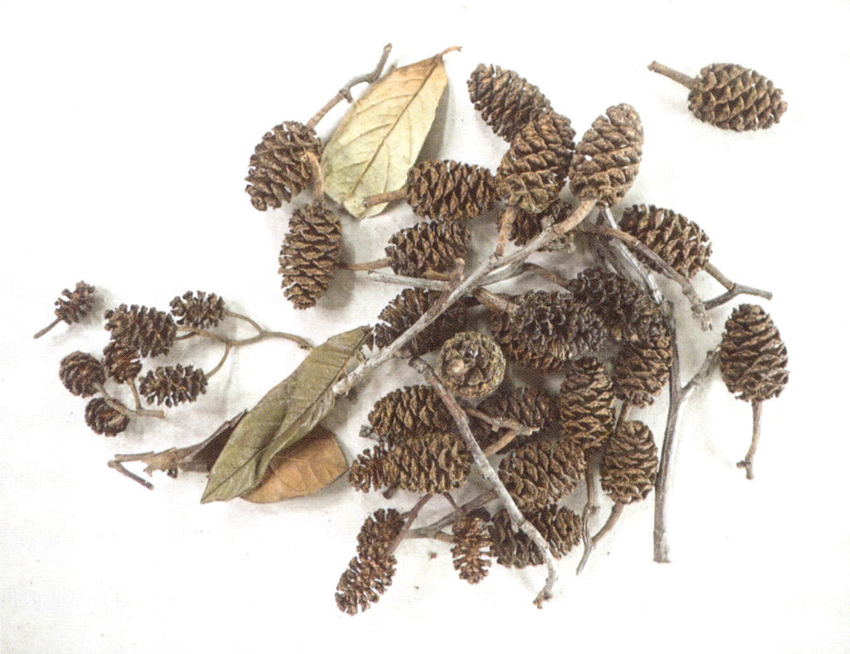

A BRIEF HISTORY OF NATURAL COLOUR

It wasn't until 1856 that the first synthetic dye was patented by William Henry Perkin. That's less than 200 years ago. Prior to this date, all colour was natural and obtained from minerals, animals and plants including pigments, paints and inks used by artists. The cave paintings in Lascaux, France are considered one of the earliest examples of art by humans and, at 40,000 years old, make the last 150–200 years of synthetic colour pale into insignificance. The paintings used chalk, soils and charcoal as sources of colour and these are still as effective today as they were over 1,500 generations ago. Since that date, the use of natural colour, particularly dyes used for colouring fabric and textiles, has become almost completely obliterated by synthetic colour, reduced to a craft activity and cottage industry when previously it was one of the most valued and important sectors of textile production. Synthetic colour is ubiquitous in our daily lives and adorns almost everything we see, use, buy and make.

Before the nineteenth century, it was common to create your own paints and other materials for artists' use, particularly using minerals, rocks and soil for colours such as ochre, umber and green earth. Blacks were made using carbon from a variety of sources, such as deposits from a flame or candle, hence the name Lamp Black. Whites were sourced from bones or chalk. The use of plants as a source of colour wasn't solely the territory of the textile industry and of artisan dyers; they were also used by artists and can be seen in many classical paintings and artworks.

The specific plants used as both dyes and pigments were dependent on global location, immediate habitat, relative wealth and the importance or value of the ultimate use of the dye. Indigo is a good example of this – until the seventeenth century, woad was the only source of plant-based blue (indigo) in Europe. In fact, woad was used as body paint by ancient Britons to intimidate the Romans when they invaded Britain about 2,000 years ago. When *Indigofera tinctoria* began to be imported as a source of indigo, woad quickly became superseded by this more intense blue and quickly fell out of favour. Woad producers consequently tried to outlaw the imported indigo, as their crops and industry lost value.

Some colours, such as orpiment or lead white, were extremely poisonous to both the maker and the user. Nowadays there can be a tendency to associate the word 'natural' with being healthy and non-toxic (mainly as a result of contemporary marketing and greenwashing) but it is important to remember that natural isn't always good for you.

Printmaking with Plant-Based Colour

To look at where printmaking with natural colour began, we merely need to research the history of printmaking. As mentioned, synthetic colour was invented less than 200 years ago, so any printmaking done before that time, either on textiles or paper or other substrates, would have been created using natural colour sources.

Unlike today where printmaking with natural colour is customarily a mindful decision by the printmaker or artist, before the mid-nineteenth century it wouldn't have been a conscious choice, just a utilisation of the available ingredients and materials of the region. These were often particular to the local vicinity, using pigments and dyes that were available to the artist. An area's geography, its climate and its habitat would have influenced the sources used, just as in dyeing and colouring cloth.

Whilst the origins of printing onto fabric and papers are hard to date due to the fragile nature of these substrates, some of the oldest examples surviving today date back to a printing block from Egypt from the fourth century and woodcuts on paper from around the seventh to eighth century in China. Whilst exact dates are uncertain, it is highly likely that some form of printing was carried out before that, with estimates dating back to around 4000 BCE. That's just a short 6,000 years before the first synthetic colours were invented. There are descriptions of printing in ancient texts but any evidence of these must have long since disintegrated.

Paper was being made, used and printed on in the East long before it became common in the West and only made its way to Europe in the eleventh century. Prints made on hemp paper date back to 650 CE and the earliest known printed and dated book, the *Diamond Sutra*, was produced in China in the mid-ninth century using the woodblock technique. Whilst movable type had been used for printing in China for at least 400 years beforehand, Johannes Gutenberg invented the first movable type printing press in the mid-1440s and it very quickly made books widely available, as they could now be mass-produced. Johannes Gutenberg is also credited with being the first to develop an oil-based ink for printing text; before that water-based inks made with mineral pigments and carbon blacks would have been used.

Hundreds of years before these developments, Pliny the Elder (23–79 CE) refers to a technique that seems to describe mordant printing onto fabric, or at least mordant painting. This technique was being used hundreds of years later with overwhelming skill and detail on 'calicoes' imported into Europe from India in the early 1600s, though it's thought they originated in the eleventh century. The printed cottons or chintzes (from the Hindu word *chint*, meaning coloured, spotted or speckled) were so instantly popular that new laws were created banning them from use to protect European wool and silk weavers. In Edward Bancroft's book *Experimental Researches Concerning the Philosophy of Permanent Colours; and the Best Means of Producing Them, by Dying, Callico Printing, &c.* (1794), he refers to a published letter by a Father Coeurcoux, which describes the process:

> *... and afterwards, by pressure and friction, [the cotton cloths were] made smooth enough for being drawn upon by the pencil, with the different mordants. The first of these was an iron liquor (acetite of iron), familiar to that since employed by the calico-printers of Europe, excepting only that, instead of vinegar or alegar, the iron was dissolved in a mixture of four palm wine, and of water in which rice had been boiled. This liquor was applied to the figures or spots intended to become black, and afterwards the aluminous mordant was applied, commonly by children, with the pencil, to the parts intended to be made red.*

He later goes on to describe how a little sappanwood was added to colour the solution so that it might be visible on application:

> *To colour this solution, so that the strokes of the pencil in applying it might be visible, a little sappan or sampsan wood (Coesalpinia Sappan, of Lin.) in powder was steeped in the solution, which being afterwards strained, was thickened with gum, and applied as before mentioned; after which the cotton so penciled was exposed to the hottest sunshine, in order that the parts to which the mordants had been applied might be dried as much as possible; and then the cottons were thoroughly soaked in large pits of water, to cleanse them from the loose superfluous parts of the different mordants, as well as from the buffalo's milk, &c.; and this being done, they were dyed in water, with certain roots answering nearly in their effects to those of madder.*

There is a further description of how the cottons were dyed in a madder dye bath producing red where alum had been applied and black where the iron had been applied. Those familiar with the technique of mordant printing will recognise the process described here.

This piece of chintz, dated to the first quarter of the eighteenth century, is from the Coromandel Coast in India and was made for the export market. It is a beautiful example of the skill of artisans from that era in using mordants, resists and natural dyes to create patterned textiles. The Metropolitan Museum of Art, New York. Purchase, Rogers Fund, and Gerald G. Stiebel and Werwaiss Family Charitable Trust Gifts, 2005.

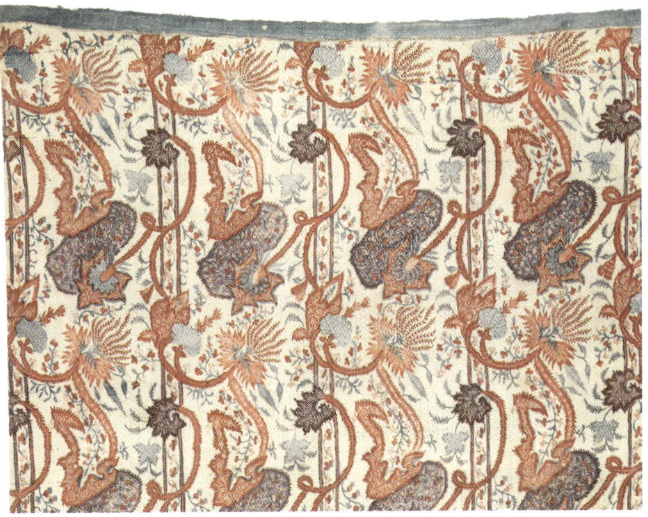

A NOTE ABOUT TERMINOLOGY

The language and terminology used around the subject of natural colour can be, and often is, very confusing. Lots of terms can be used interchangeably, frequently have different definitions depending on the writer and their understanding of the word (without being necessarily right or wrong) and can easily be misconstrued by the reader. Therefore, I have included some words below that I believe require clarification and a definition of how I will be using them within this book. This isn't to say I have the definitive answer; merely that this is my understanding of how a particular word or phrase should be used. However, definitions of words can also be problematic and might often require explanations, side notes and exceptions that aren't particularly helpful – I have tried to avoid this and keep definitions as simple as possible.

We're quite used to words changing meaning depending on their context but sometimes this context doesn't make it clearer. For instance, if ink is mentioned, the intaglio printmakers amongst you might instantly think of a thick viscous oil-based ink whilst writers may be thinking of their dip pens and their water-based writing ink and then natural dyers will be considering a reduction made from a dye bath. Even the term 'natural colour' isn't particularly accurate for this book on plant-based colour, encompassing as it does any colour that is sourced from nature, not just from plants.

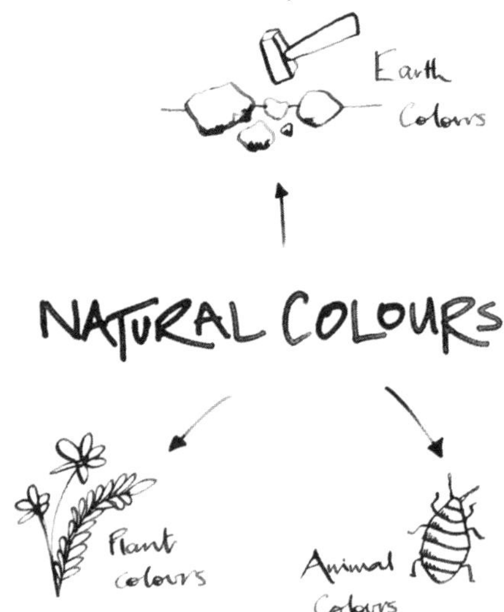

Natural colours are not just sourced from plants but can be extracted from the earth, such as ochre, and from animals, such as the cochineal beetle.

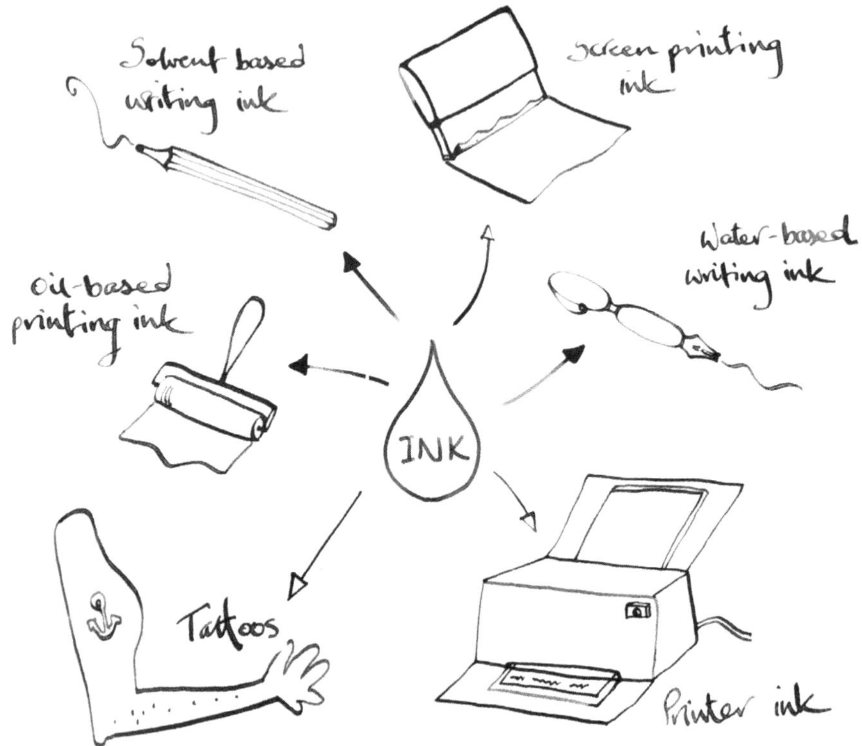

Ink: a substance that is used to transfer an image or is used to write with. Clarification of the type of ink meant is often both helpful and necessary.

Colourant (also colorant) – a dye, a pigment or other substance that imparts colour. It is used within this book when describing colour that can be both a dye and a pigment.
Compound – a substance made up of two or more different chemical elements joined together with a chemical bond. Water is a compound of hydrogen and oxygen.
Dye – a compound or substance that can permanently colour something else by chemically bonding with the substrate it is applied to.
Dye bath – a liquid solution made by immersing plantstuffs (or other dyestuffs) in water to extract the colour. The water is often heated to more effectively extract the colour from the plant.
Dyeing – to permanently colour something using a dye. Shouldn't be used interchangeably with 'dying', which means something more permanent but in a different way.
Dye liquid – the resulting solution made from immersing or steeping plantstuffs (or other dyestuffs) in water or other liquid. The use of the word dye implies that the liquid has dyeing potential. The liquid might still contain the plantstuff. This liquid is also often referred to as dye liquor, a dye bath and dye solution.
Dyestuff – a plant or other source of colour that has dye potential or is used as a dye. It is often useful to refer to a 'dyestuff', rather than 'dye material', which can be confusing if textiles or materials are used within a description. *See* also 'plantstuff' which is used when necessary in place of 'dyestuff', though they are often interchangeable.
Inks – catch-all term for a substance that is used to transfer an image or to write with. Think about water-based ink, oil-based ink, inks for writing, painting, printmaking, ink in a printer, ink in a biro, fountain pen ink, paint that is called ink, ink that is called paint. Ink can also be used as a verb – to ink something would mean to apply ink ready for printing. Within this book, the term ink will always be clarified with the precursor of water-based or oil-based if it is not immediately obvious.
Inorganic – pertaining to a substance that doesn't contain carbon, such as iron or sodium. It may be used to describe something that has been produced with the use of pesticides but this is unlikely. The term non-organic is more likely to be used. However, it may be used to describe something not created from natural growth, so something that is artificial.
Lake pigment – a lake pigment is an insoluble pigment that has been made from a soluble dye derived from different sources such as plants (for example madder) and animals (for example cochineal). The soluble organic dye is bonded onto an inorganic substance (usually an aluminium) and the remaining liquid, called a supernatant, is removed by filtering and drying the pigment.
Liquid – a substance that is not solid or a gas and flows freely. Most usually refers to water or a dye liquid within this book.
Materials – the word material can refer to a substance or matter from which something can be made, things needed for an activity (for example an artist's materials) or pieces of cloth or fabric. In this book the word material most often refers to cloth, fabric or textiles but might occasionally be used for artist's materials. In this case it is always clarified. To avoid confusion, the word 'stuff' has been used when referring to plant materials.
Natural colour – any colour or colourant that is directly sourced from nature, not just from plants, as opposed to synthetic colour. This might include rocks, minerals, plants, fungi and insects.
Natural dye – a colourant derived from a plant, animal or mineral rather than one derived synthetically from substances such as petro-chemicals.
Organic – nowadays most commonly understood as describing food, production or farming methods that don't use chemical fertilisers, pesticides or other artificial chemicals. However, the word organic also means (most often within science) things that are derived from or consisting of living matter, so contain carbon. This can be confusing as an organic (carbon-containing) pigment might have been produced inorganically (using chemical fertilisers). However, a more usual term for something produced with the use of a pesticide would be non-organic, or the word organic would be missing from the description. *See* also inorganic.
Paste – used within this book to describe a thickened water-based solution for printing (most often screen-printing or block printing). Used in place of ink to more easily differentiate from the catch-all word 'ink'.
Pigment – the word pigment is used to indicate a colourant that is insoluble in liquid. It is useful to understand the difference between a dye (soluble in liquid) and a pigment (insoluble in liquid) especially when using to colour textiles and fibres that must be washfast. Pigments won't dye (chemically bond with) fibres, but they may be attached as a surface treatment by binding with a 'glue' (such as soy liquid). Indigo in its dry powdered form is a pigment and, whilst a highly effective

one, can't dye fibres until it has been reduced in a dye vat.

Plantstuff – parts of a plant used within a recipe. In this book most often used to describe the bits of plant going into a dye pot or being used to extract colour. For example, 'add 50g of plantstuff to 500g of water'. Plantstuff avoids having to describe all parts of a plant that might be used each time such as roots, flowers, stalks and/or leaves or using plant material, which can be mixed up with cloth or fabric material. Used in place of 'dyestuff' when the meaning is not clear.

Printing and printmaking – often used interchangeably but printmaking implies a handmade approach (to make a print) rather than a machine-made approach (to print a document). Therefore I have used 'printmaking ink' for oil-based inks rather than the less clunky 'printing ink' purely because it feels more accurate.

Soluble (solubility) – the ability of a substance to form a solution with another substance. For example, instant coffee is soluble and will dissolve into water to make a brown drink whereas ground coffee is insoluble and won't dissolve (but it will make a lovely beverage).

Solvents – a liquid in which other materials dissolve. Common examples of solvents include water, acetone, ethanol and methanol.

Supernatant – the liquid remaining above precipitated or settled sediment, such as when making a lake pigment. It is from the Latin terms *super* (above) and *natare* (to swim), so the liquid 'swimming above'.

Vat dyes – vat dyes are usually those that require an extra process to make the colourant available to dye fibres. Thought to be called vat dyes because they were traditionally prepared using some form of fermentation, the only natural plant source that fulfils this characteristic is indigo or the indigo-bearing plants. Vat is a very specific term and shouldn't be used to describe other plant dyes or dye baths.

From dyeing fabrics and yarns through to printmaking, painting and paper-making, natural colours can be used for most applications where colour is required.

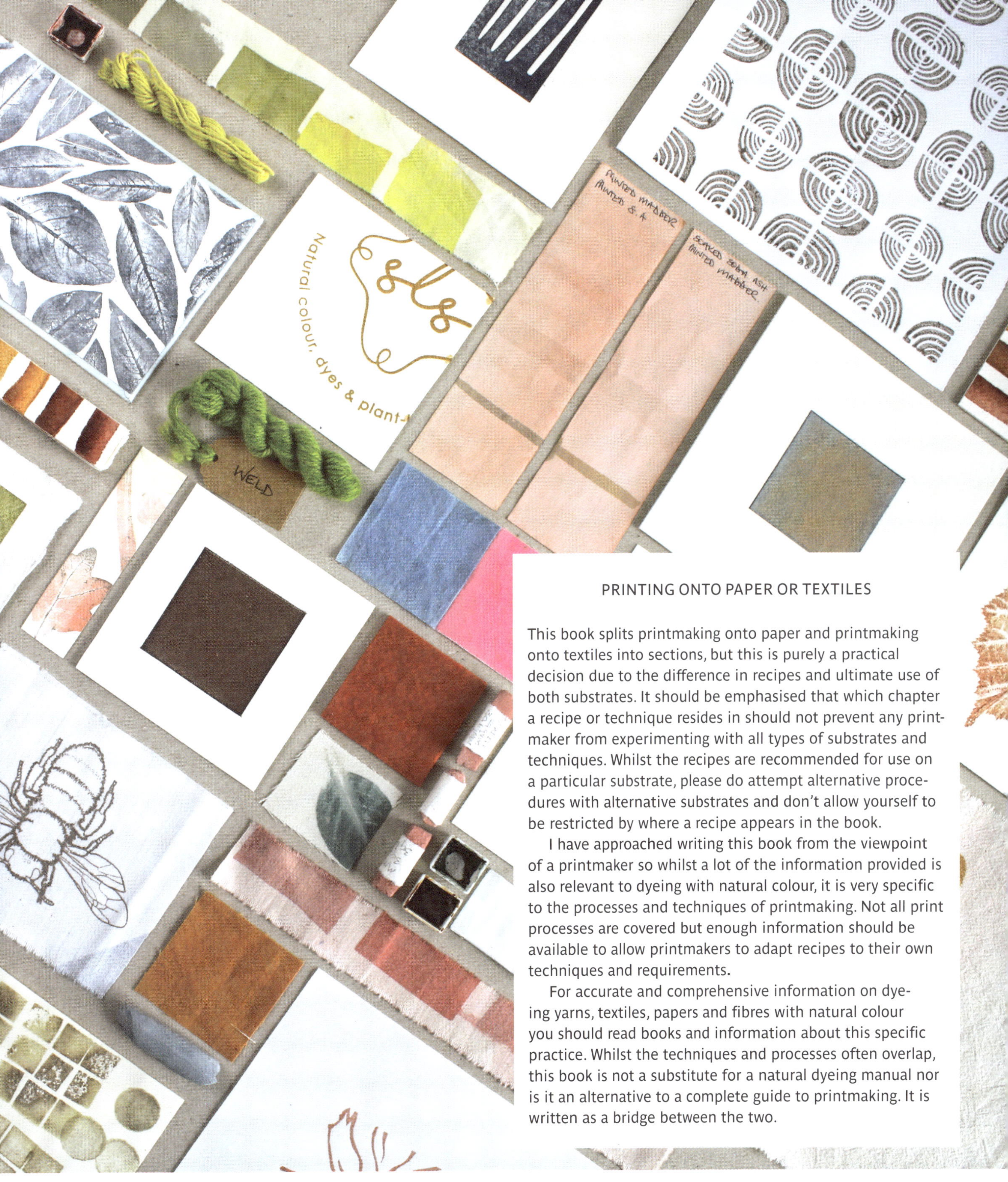

PRINTING ONTO PAPER OR TEXTILES

This book splits printmaking onto paper and printmaking onto textiles into sections, but this is purely a practical decision due to the difference in recipes and ultimate use of both substrates. It should be emphasised that which chapter a recipe or technique resides in should not prevent any printmaker from experimenting with all types of substrates and techniques. Whilst the recipes are recommended for use on a particular substrate, please do attempt alternative procedures with alternative substrates and don't allow yourself to be restricted by where a recipe appears in the book.

I have approached writing this book from the viewpoint of a printmaker so whilst a lot of the information provided is also relevant to dyeing with natural colour, it is very specific to the processes and techniques of printmaking. Not all print processes are covered but enough information should be available to allow printmakers to adapt recipes to their own techniques and requirements.

For accurate and comprehensive information on dyeing yarns, textiles, papers and fibres with natural colour you should read books and information about this specific practice. Whilst the techniques and processes often overlap, this book is not a substitute for a natural dyeing manual nor is it an alternative to a complete guide to printmaking. It is written as a bridge between the two.

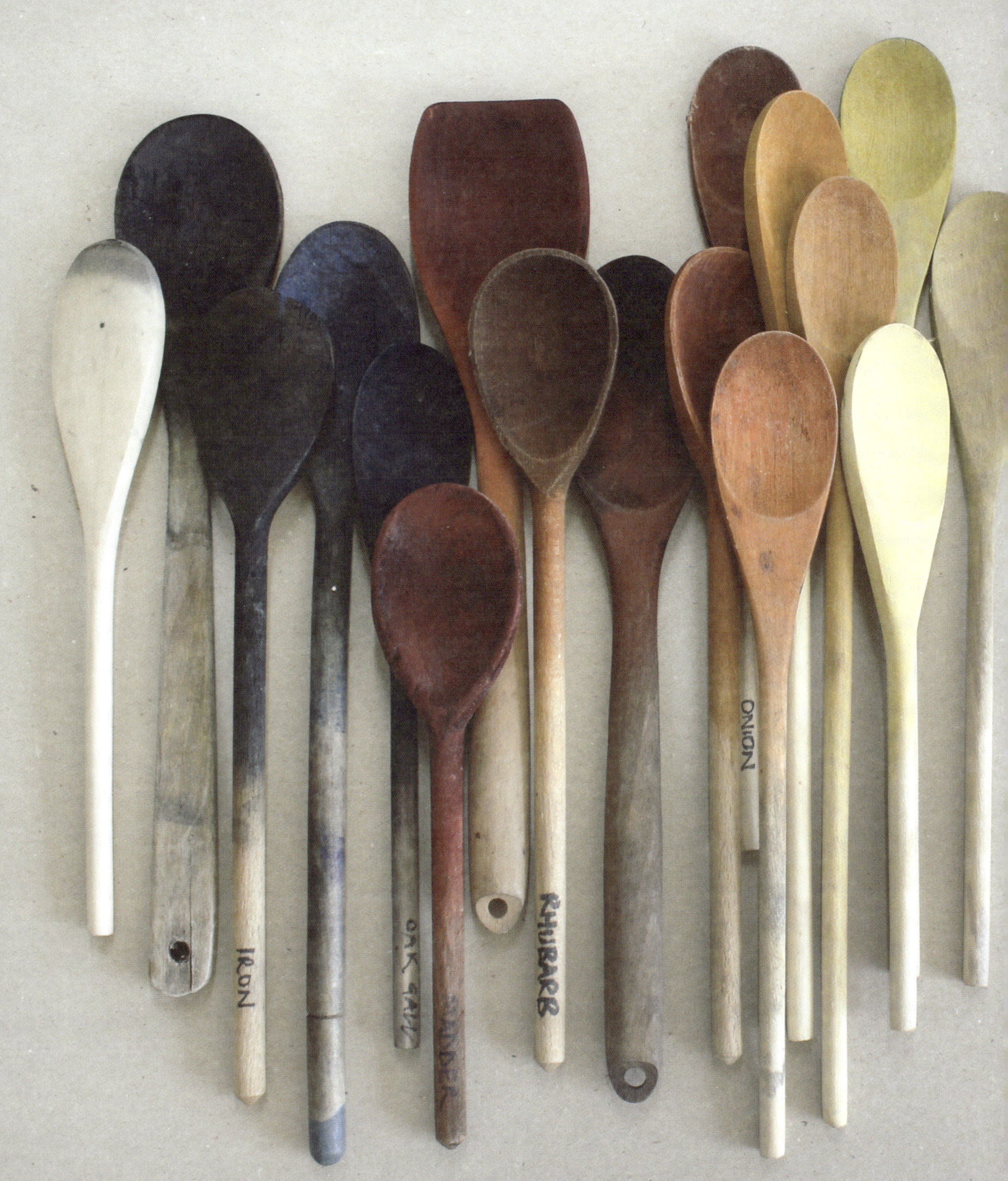
IRON
OAK GALL
RHUBARB
ONION

Chapter Two

UNDERSTANDING PLANT-BASED COLOUR

FACING PAGE

Wooden spoons soon take on the colour of the dye. Keep spoons for similar colours or even individual dyes.

Natural colour can be found in and extracted from many sources including minerals, rocks, various insects and numerous plants, although this book solely focuses on colours that can be sourced from plants. Any part of a plant might contain useful colour and different parts of the same plant may contain different colours. Flowers, bark, roots, seeds, leaves, stems, wood, fruits and berries can all contain useful colour depending on the particular plant, yet some plants may contain hardly any colour at all or may hold colour in just one part.

The colour of the plant or plantstuff is very often a completely different colour from the dye or pigment extracted. For example, indigo blue is extracted from the green leaves of indigo plants and a strong yellow is made from purple buddleia flowers. The season and time a plant is harvested can also result in different colours. Buckthorn berries are a good example of this, as unripe immature berries can produce a very strong yellow dye and mature berries might produce anything from a pink to a deep green colour.

These variable factors might seem overwhelming to start with but it is very easy to quickly learn about the main dye plants, the correct parts of these plants to use and how best to extract colour from them. The other variables become part of an exciting adventure into colour and the natural dyer or user of plant-based colour will quickly learn to enjoy and then embrace the potential surprises in their practice.

Most plant-based colour is extracted from the plant using water (think of how a cup of tea is made), thus making a dye liquid or a dye bath. Dyes are colourants that are soluble in water or other liquids including alcohol and solvents. Some plant-based colour is extracted as a pigment, which is a colourant that is not soluble in water, and some can be both a pigment and a dye depending on certain environmental conditions. Dyes can also be made into non-soluble pigments (called lake pigments) once they have been extracted from the source material.

LEFT
Coreopsis tinctoria. Two-colour screenprint on paper.

RIGHT
Coreopsis tinctoria. Two-colour screenprint on fabric. Compare the same artwork printed onto paper and fabric. The different substrates affect the final quality and colour of the print.

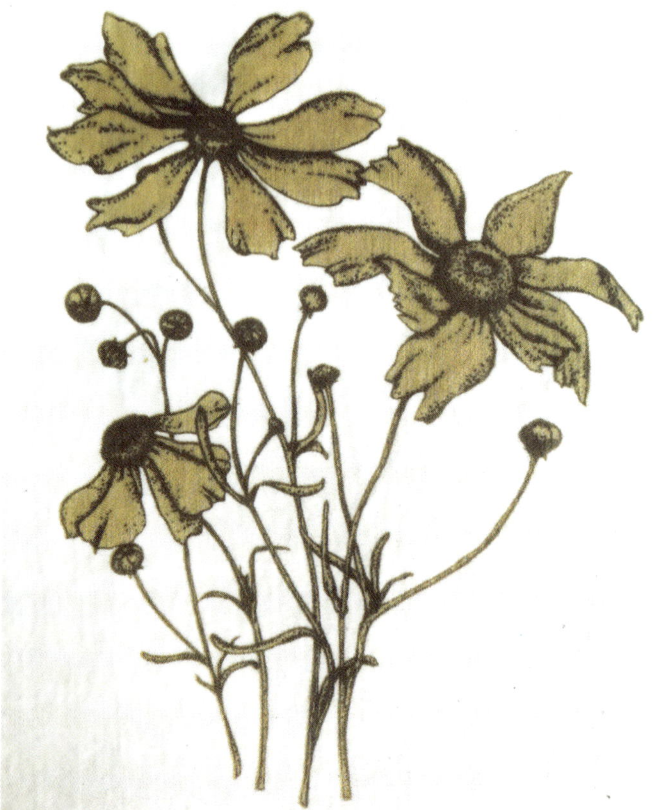

Using plant-based colour for printmaking requires a slightly different approach from that used in simple immersion dyeing, depending on whether the printing is onto textiles or paper. However, the colours achieved when dyeing fibres are generally also available to printmakers for their inks, pastes, paints and pigments. When it comes to using plant-based colour in printmaking, printmakers also have the luxury of easily being able to mix colours before application, either by combining lake pigments before making into an oil-based ink or a watercolour paint or perhaps by mixing print paste colours before screenprinting.

In conventional printmaking practices, the paint or ink chosen depends on the technique being used and commercial products have been carefully formulated to suit different requirements. Exactly the same requirements apply when using plant-based colour, although the characteristics of the paint or ink are controlled by the artist (as the maker of the ink). Therefore an understanding of the particular requirements of different techniques is useful.

One of the other major differences when using plant-based colour and plant-based ingredients is the need to differentiate between printing onto fabric and printing onto paper. With paper, the colour can easily be applied with a suitable binder and/or thickener and doesn't need to be washfast. Therefore, the use of insoluble pigments that won't actually dye the substrate but will just sit on the surface of the paper is perfectly acceptable. However, as most printed textiles will at some point need to be washed, the colour must ideally dye the fabric, in a similar way to how fabric is coloured by immersion dyeing but just in localised areas (exactly where the colour is being applied). This makes the use of insoluble pigments inappropriate without the use of an insoluble binder. Within katazome and other Japanese techniques of colouring cloth, insoluble pigments mixed with soy liquid (milk) are in fact used for colour application onto textiles, though this is beyond the scope of this book.

Perhaps the most useful colour (or shade) to highlight the difference between printmaking onto paper and printmaking onto fabric is black. A black 'pigment' is very easy to make by just using carbon. Any finely ground burnt wood (charcoal) or soot is ideal for making into an ink or a paint and is in fact the origin of the paint names Lamp Black or Vine Black. However, achieving a strong black 'dye' can be challenging, especially as a carbon pigment can't be used to dye a fabric. The best way to achieve a black dye is to use a tannin and iron complex.

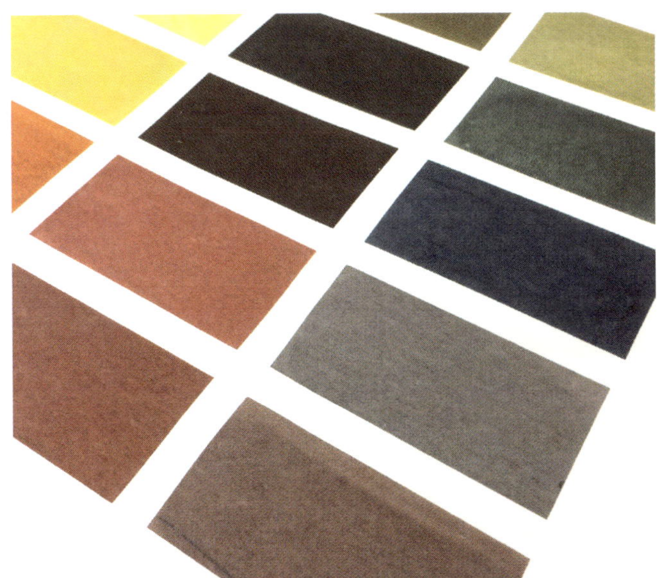

Chroma Flora 01. MMXXI. Fifteen-colour screenprint using plants that can be grown in the UK climate.

When these two elements mix in the dye pot, they form a strong dark colour that ranges from a grey through to a purple black depending on the substrate, the tannin used and the amount of iron used. A dye extract made from the fruits of the myrobalan (*Terminalia chebula*) tree also provides a strong black for use on fabrics when used in a concentrated form.

Dye Plants

Dye plants are those that can be considered to contain useful colourants and that are used in the practice of natural dyeing. Whilst most plants contain some colourant of one type or another, not all contain enough concentration of the colourant, or are lightfast or washfast enough to make them worthwhile to dye or print with.

In seventeenth-century France, laws were passed that specified which plants could and could not be used for dyeing. These dye plants were classified as '*grand teint*', and this term is still used today to describe some of the most colourfast dye plants. The Latin name of a plant will often reveal the properties for which it was known, with many of the dye plant names ending in '*tinctoria*' or a version of this word, such as '*tinctorum*' or '*tinctorius*'. Look out for plants with a Latin name including a version of this word as a clue to their dyeing properties but don't concentrate solely on these – it is purely a suggestion of a plant's properties.

Where to Start

The best place to start with plant-based colour in both printmaking and natural dyeing is to use those plants that are considered to contain good amounts of colourants, are relatively lightfast and from which colour can be fairly easily extracted.

Plant dyes are available to purchase in various formats including a dried (whole, chopped-up or chipped) format, a dried ground format, a dye extract (which is a highly concentrated water-soluble powder) or you can grow your own plants and use them fresh or dried. Think of the differences as you might think of different types of coffee that are available. Coffee beans are the whole and dried format, ground coffee is the dried and ground-up format (that we might use in cafetieres) and instant coffee is the extract format (that dissolves in hot water). It is important to note the difference between the ground dyestuff and the dye extract. The ground dyestuff will not dissolve in water so, whilst it will release colour very well, it will still remain as a gritty substance in any solution whereas the extract should completely dissolve in water.

If you have no knowledge of natural dyes before deciding to print with them, it is advisable (but not essential) to carry out some general reading and research into natural dyes by looking at some specialist books (of which there are a plethora) or potentially going on a course to learn about natural dyeing first. This should provide a good grounding in the theories and basic processes of the craft, introduce the different dye plants and the colours that can be achieved from them.

However, most reference books and texts available on the subject concentrate on using plants as dyes to colour fibres by immersion into the dye liquid. Whilst some of the techniques contained within this book include immersion dyeing, most focus on a slightly different approach to using plant-based colour for printmaking processes. When immersion dyeing with natural dyestuffs, the amount of liquid is important only in allowing the fibres to move freely within the vessel during the dyeing process. For most printmaking techniques, the solution should be as concentrated as possible. Therefore there is a fine balance between too much water and not enough to allow the colourants to leach from the dyestuff into the liquid. This is covered in more detail in subsequent chapters.

1) Dried madder root, grown outside the Slow Lane Studio.

3) Dried and ground madder root.

2) Dried and chopped madder root.

4) Madder extract.

1

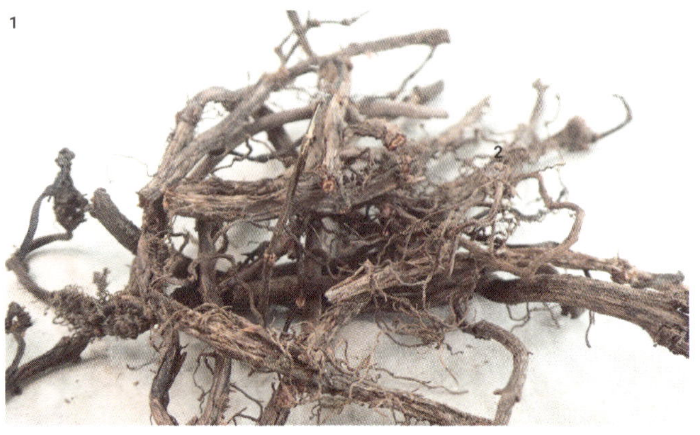

2

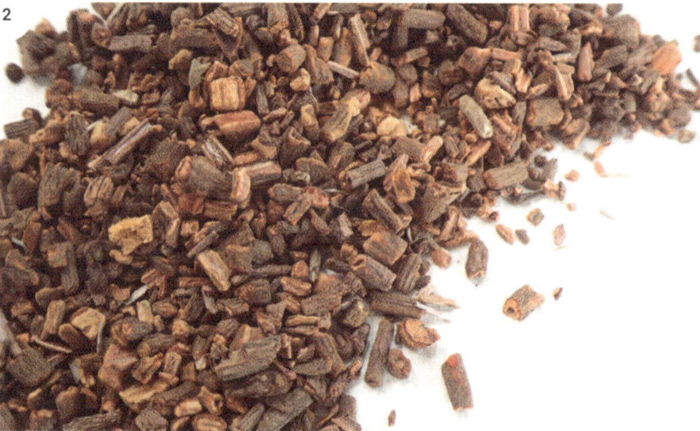

3

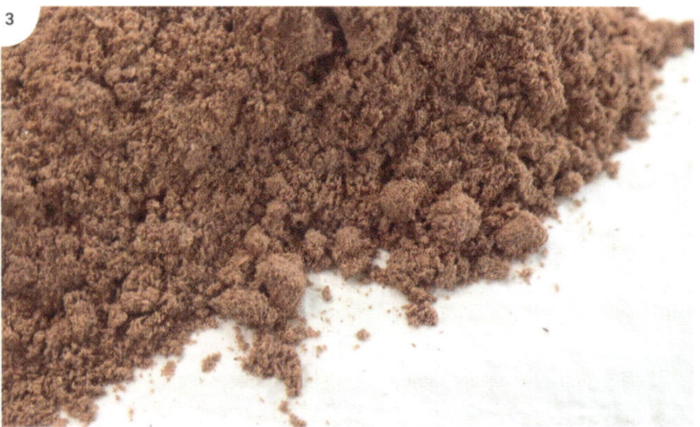

4

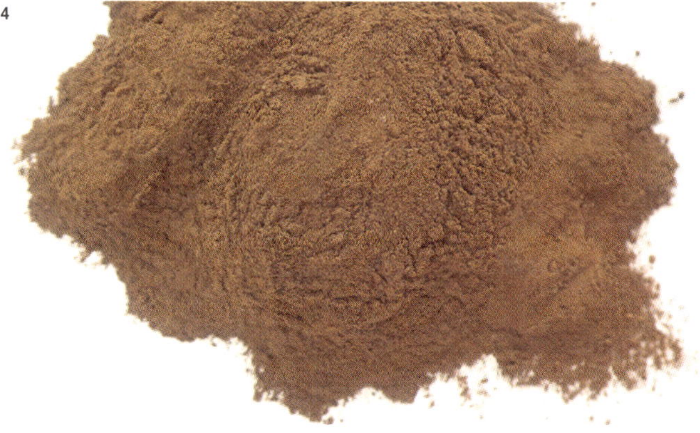

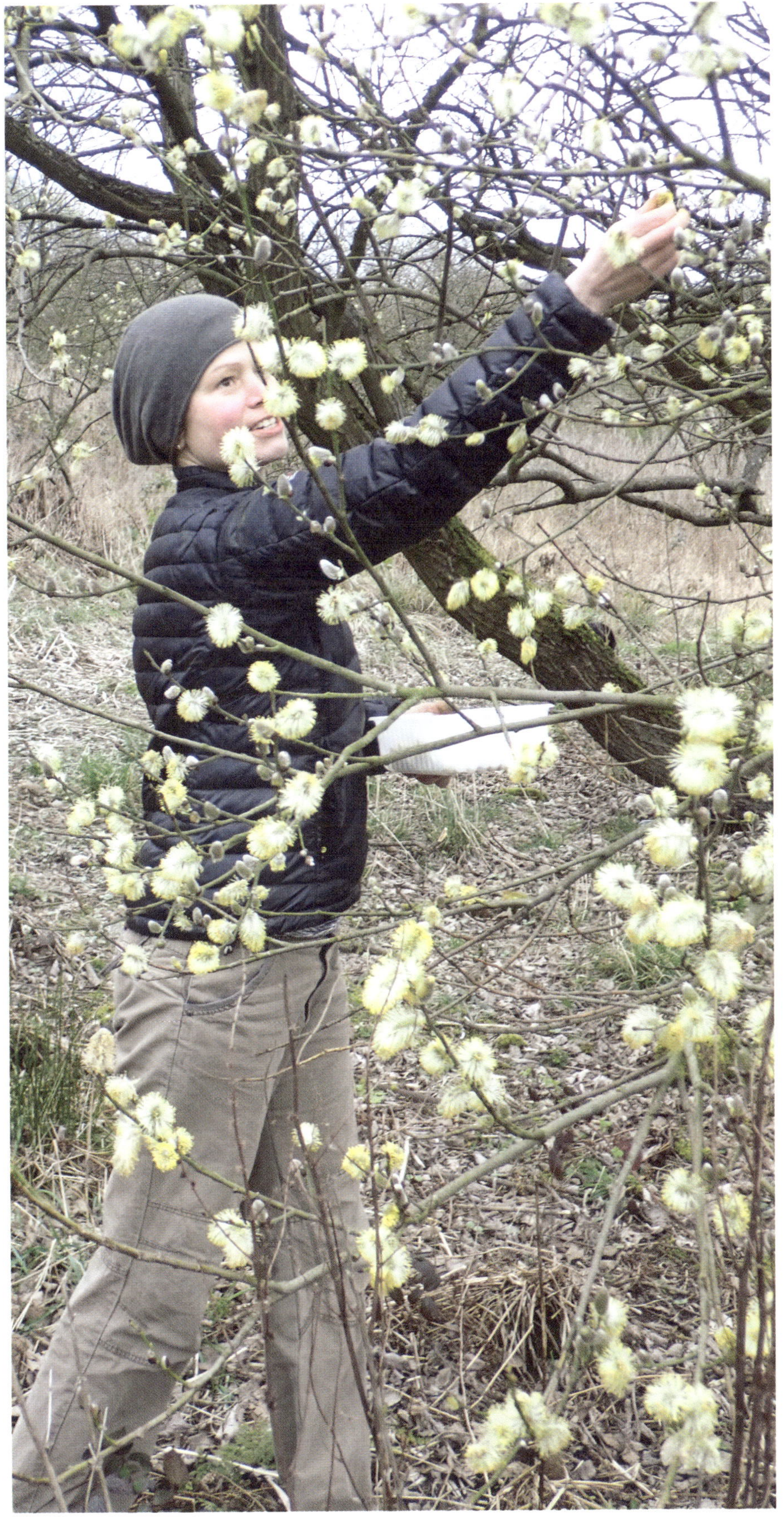

Harvesting goat willow pollen in early spring.

Sourcing Plant-Based Colour

It is up to the individual where to source natural colour from. Some people might want to only use foraged materials, some might not agree with foraging for dyestuffs, some may want to use only what they can cultivate themselves and some might want to purchase all their dyestuffs.

Unless you have access to a dye garden or have experience foraging for local resources, it is easier to purchase dyestuffs from known dye suppliers, at least to start with. As mentioned previously, these will come in the form of dried plants and chopped-up or ground plant pieces, although you can also buy dye extracts, which will be a dried powder or occasionally a highly concentrated liquid. Look for local growers and suppliers of plant dyes, which is by far one of the most sustainable ways of purchasing dyestuffs if there is little opportunity (or time) to grow your own.

THE PLANT-BASED COLOUR WHEEL

The colours shown in this colour wheel are all from plant sources that can be grown in the UK, either outside or with a little protection but with no extra heating. The wheel is also limited to plants with a reputation for having good colourfastness as a natural dye. Each colour shown is from a single origin where possible, although some have been altered using colour modifiers such as iron, soda ash and vinegar. Some mixed colours are also included where it is difficult to achieve this colour from a single plant. Most colours in the artist's colour wheel can be achieved using a single source of plant-based colour although some, like fresh greens, are best achieved using a mix of dye plants. In a natural (immersion) dyeing process, this is most often done by using a two-step method of dyeing with a yellow and then over-dyeing with indigo (or the other way around). Indigo requires a different method of dyeing from that used with most other plant dyes, making it easier to overlay colours without affecting the other colour.

Some plants have also been excluded because of the difficulty of reproducing the colour as a lake pigment or a printing paste. Safflower (*Carthamus tinctorius*) for example can dye the most astonishing luminous pinks, but the colour is lost when creating a lake pigment from the dye due to the changes in pH levels. It is also not a particularly lightfast dye.

It should be mentioned that many other plant-based or natural colours are available to the printmaker and natural dyer, but they don't align with my own practice or beliefs. Cochineal extracted from beetles gives brilliant magentas, pinks and purples whilst lac or stick lac is a red dye made from resin secreted by the scale insect, *Kerria lacca*. *See* 'Using Other Sources of Plant-Based Colour'.

FACING PAGE
A full spectrum of colour can be achieved from a limited number of plants including madder (for example *Rubia tinctorum*), coreopsis (*Coreopsis tinctoria*), weld (*Reseda luteola*), buckthorn (*Rhamnus* spp., *Frangula alnus*), indigo (for example *Persicaria tinctoria*), woad (*Isatis tinctoria*) and rhubarb (*Rheum* spp.).

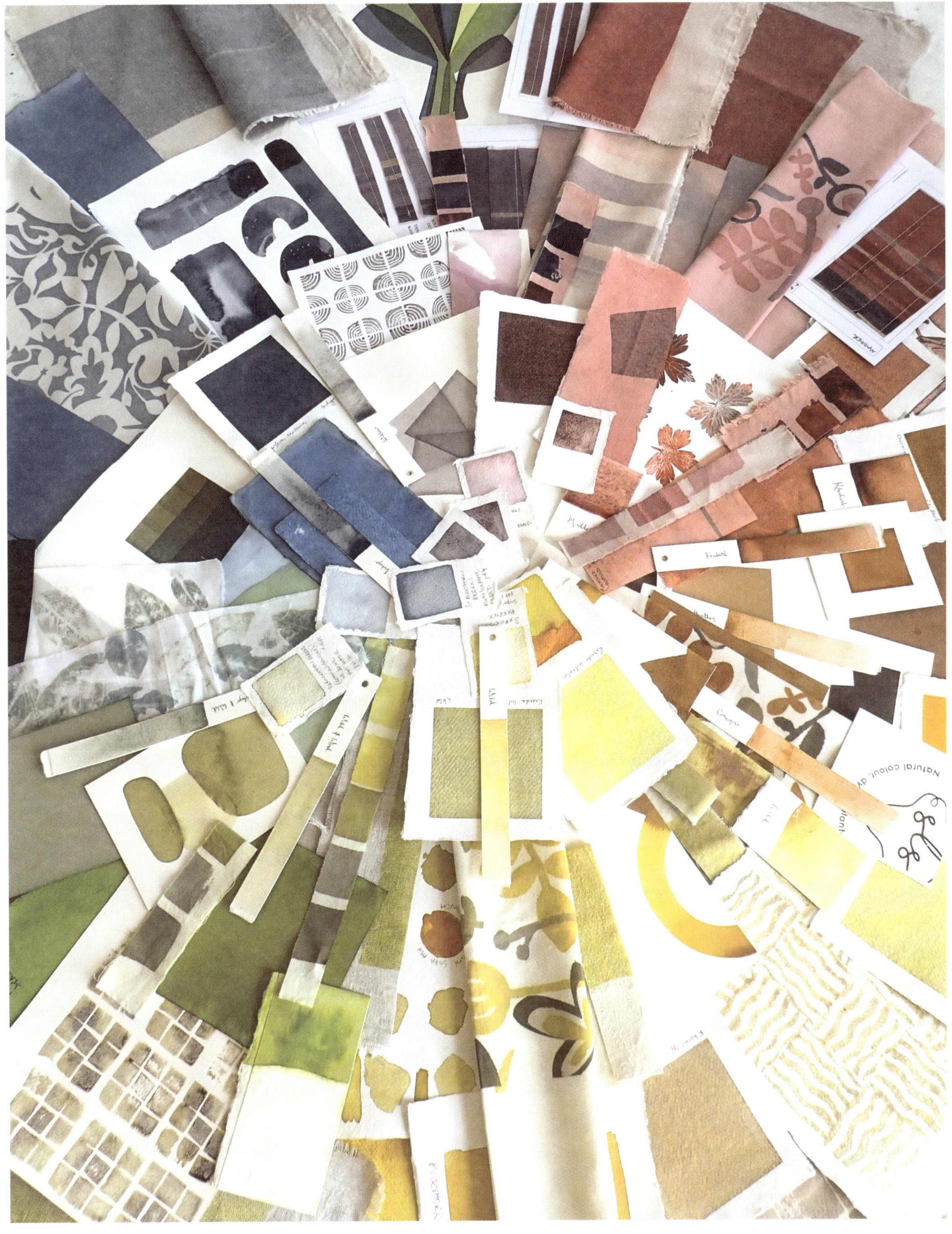

Colours for Different Techniques, Substrates and Recipes

Some plant-based colours only work as water-based pastes, or as a lake pigment or on a particular textile or paper or with a change in recipe. Due to the complexities and individual chemistry of plant-based colours, this variability and unpredictable character should be accepted and celebrated rather than seen as a disadvantage or shortcoming. Madder is an effective dye to highlight the variability in colour achieved depending on process, ingredients, recipes, modifiers and substrate preparation. Purple, pink, red, brown, orange, burgundy, scarlet, crimson, rose and everything in between can be realised from the magnificent madder plant.

USING OTHER SOURCES OF PLANT-BASED COLOUR

It is of course up to you how you approach the use and consumption of plant-based colour. I try to limit myself to the use of plants that can be cultivated in our climate or responsibly foraged in the UK, so no logwood (*Haematoxylum campechianum*) or sappanwood (*Caesalpinia sappan*) for example, but I do use dye extracts purchased from India. There are arguments both for and against using dye sources from other countries, especially those that require transportation by air. Purchasing dyes from responsible organisations can support trade and communities in other countries, especially as many natural dyes are now farmed commercially, but you are also purchasing something with a lot of air miles. Whilst I don't have an answer, perhaps the best thing to do is to stay as informed as possible and make conscious decisions about your own practice and sources of materials.

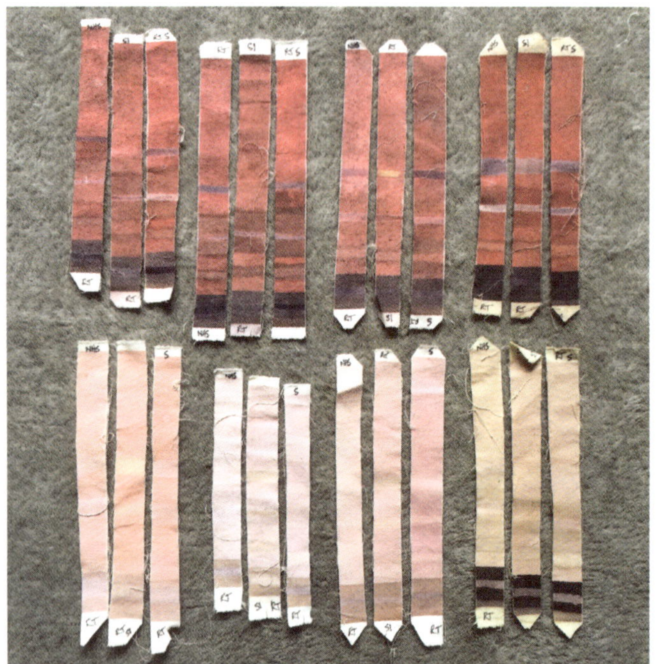

Madder extract water-based screenprinting paste. Top row: madder extract with alum sulphate, vinegar, guar gum and water. Bottom row: madder extract with guar gum and water.

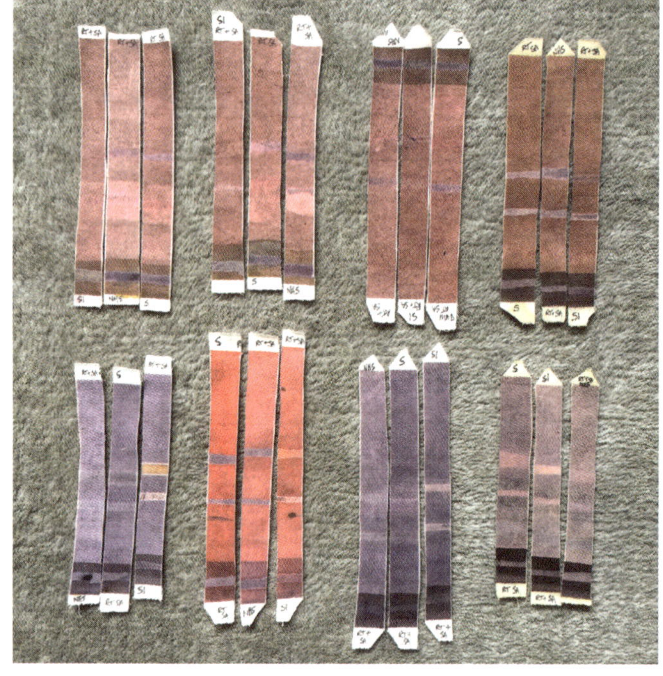

Madder extract water-based screenprinting paste. Top row: madder extract with alum sulphate, vinegar, guar gum, water and soda ash. Bottom row: madder extract with guar gum, water and soda ash. These results show how changing a recipe can dramatically change the colour of a dye.

The Colours

RED: MADDER *(RUBIA TINCTORUM)*
Madder contains a complex set of colourants, of which the most well known is alizarin, which is also the name and colour of numerous paints and inks available commercially. These many and varied colourants (Cardon's *Natural Dyes* lists 15 that are present in the madder plant) are what gives madder its variability in colour: anything from a soft pink to a strong red, a burnt orange or a deep purple can be coaxed from its roots. When creating lake pigments or water-based media, the colours are relatively easy to manipulate by changing the pH of the mix, the concentration of the dyestuff or how much the solution is heated. The addition of iron can bring out purple tones, tannins can help with the take-up of the colour, improving the saturation of the red, and the textile or paper substrate used will also play a role in determining what colour outcomes are achieved. Madder is available as an extract though it can be highly variable in colour. This colour variation seems to make no difference to its use as a dye but does affect the result when used within a print paste for paper, where the original extract's colour is apparent.

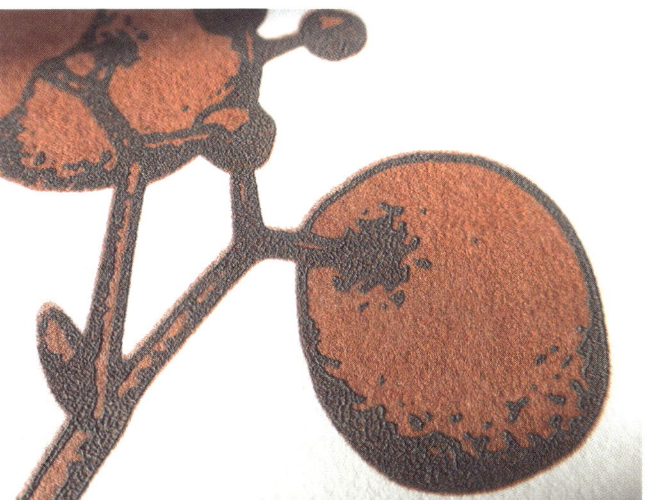
Madder red, screenprint on paper (detail).

ORANGE: COREOPSIS *(COREOPSIS TINCTORIA)*
Coreopsis flowers contain flavonoid colourants called anthoclors (chalcones and aurones) and will give lovely strong yellows and oranges, similar to Cadmium Orange. Clearer, brighter oranges will be accomplished by keeping temperatures low when extracting the colour and when making a pigment or print paste. The flowers can be used both fresh and dried. Coreopsis is also available as an extract, although this is not particularly common, perhaps because it is a very easy plant to cultivate.

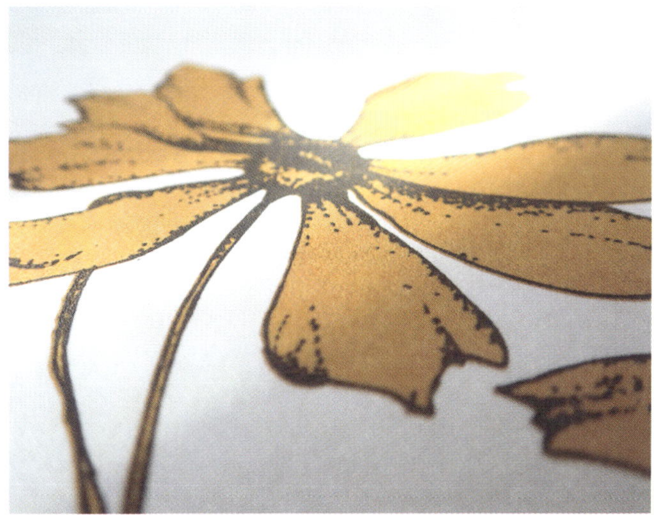
Coreopsis orange, screenprint on paper (detail).

YELLOW: WELD *(RESEDA LUTEOLA)*
Considered the most lightfast of the yellows, weld contains the colourant luteolin, from the flavonoids chemical group, although the colour actually darkens over time. Weld lake pigments are often precipitated onto chalk, although they can appear lighter than weld lake pigments precipitated onto alum. A weld dye bath can be deceiving in appearance, seeming pale and watery but strong yellows can easily be obtained. Weld is available as an extract but is a pale yellow unless used as a print paste onto fabric, which upon washing will develop into a bright yellow colour.

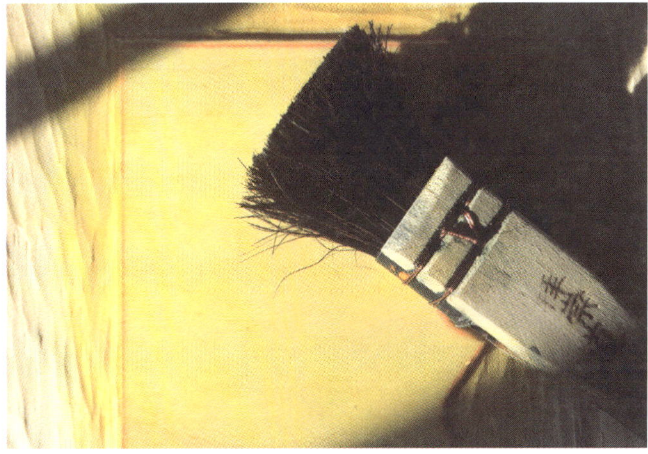
Weld yellow, watercolour paint on mokuhanga block.

YELLOW TO GREEN: BUCKTHORN BERRIES (*FRANGULA ALNUS* OR *RHAMNUS CATHARTICA*; OTHER *RHAMNUS* SPECIES)

Immature and mature buckthorn berries can create strong yellow hues through to greenish tints visible depending on the pH, mordant and modifiers used. Buckthorn berries contain anthraquinones and some flavonoid colourants and are often used instead of weld, though are not considered quite as lightfast. An attractive green can also be extracted from berries and is, in fact, the original source of Sap Green, first used in 1704 and now a common name of a synthetic paint colour.

GREEN: WELD (*RESEDA LUTEOLA*) & INDIGO (FOR EXAMPLE *PERSICARIA TINCTORIA*, *INDIGOFERA TINCTORIA*, *ISATIS TINCTORIA*)

Mixing weld lake pigment and an indigo powder together will make a range of greens through to petrol blue depending on the percentages of both pigments. Indigo, especially if using purchased *Indigofera tinctoria*, is highly pigmented and just small amounts can greatly affect the colour, so use sparingly. A more gentle option is to use woad (*Isatis tinctoria*) powder, which also contains a form of indigotin (the active ingredient in indigo-bearing plants) but in lesser quantities. Anything from a soft turquoise through to a saturated grass green can be achieved as a lake pigment or as a dye, especially if overdyeing a weld yellow in an indigo vat.

GREEN: WELD (*RESEDA LUTEOLA*) & IRON

This produces a very different green from the fresh grassy colour of weld mixed with indigo and is often described as a khaki or olive green. Care must be taken with the addition of iron, which can be damaging to fibres of both paper and fabric. Iron added to a weld dye bath before making a lake pigment can produce a similar green pigment colour to the colour achieved when modifying dyed fabric.

BLUE: INDIGO (*PERSICARIA TINCTORIA*, *INDIGOFERA TINCTORIA*), *SEE* ALSO WOAD (*ISATIS TINCTORIA*)

Indigo is in a special class of its own within natural dyes and requires a certain knowledge of chemistry to understand its method of use. When extracted as a pigment it makes an incredible blue colour, but its chemical make-up means that the blue colourant is only available for dyeing fibres in a highly alkaline environment. If using purchased indigo pigment, it will likely be *Indigofera tinctoria*, a deep, highly pigmented blue that can be extremely dominant when used as either a pigment or a water-based paste. A few suppliers also sell *Persicaria tinctoria* indigo pigment, which can be a lighter and less intense blue but is still a beautiful shade. Indigo can also be used to make Maya Blue, a pigment made by heating indigo powder with a sepiolite clay, which produces an extremely lightfast petrol to turquoise blue depending on how much the mix is heated.

BLUE: WOAD (*ISATIS TINCTORIA*)

The woad plant was the traditional source of indigo blue in Europe and the UK until indigo from India began to be imported in the seventeenth century. Woad contains the same indigo pigment as the indigo plants *Indigofera tinctoria* and *Persicaria tinctoria* but in lesser quantities. Just like indigo, the amount of blue available in the plant's leaves is reduced once the plant has flowered. It can also be used to make a form of Maya Blue, though traditionally this would only have been made with indigo.

PURPLE: MADDER (*RUBIA TINCTORUM*) & INDIGO (*PERSICARIA TINCTORIA*, *INDIGOFERA TINCTORIA* OR *ISATIS TINCTORIA*)

Mixing madder lake pigment and an indigo powder together will make colours from a burgundy to a deep purple depending on the percentages of both pigments. Indigo, especially if using purchased *Indigofera tinctoria*, should be used sparingly or it will dominate the mixed colour. Use woad (*Isatis tinctoria*) powder instead which also contains indigotin but in lesser quantities.

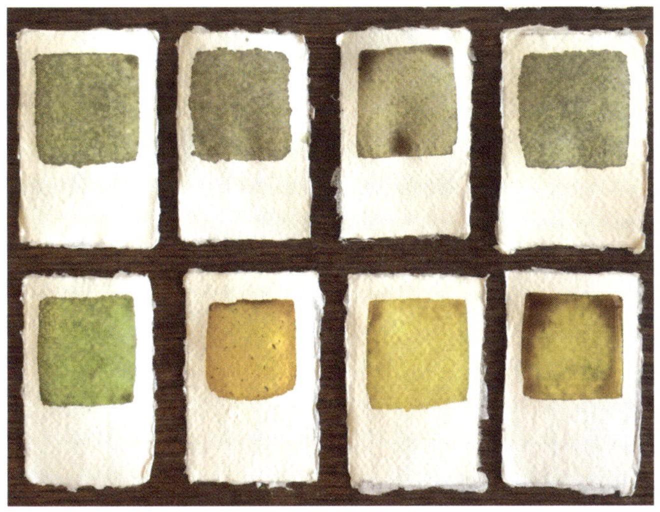

Buckthorn berry yellows and greens, water-based inks.

Woad blue, screenprint on paper (detail).

Weld and indigo greens and teals, oil-based printmaking ink made with (L–R) weld, 1:100 indigo to weld, 1:10 indigo to weld, 1:4 indigo to weld, indigo.

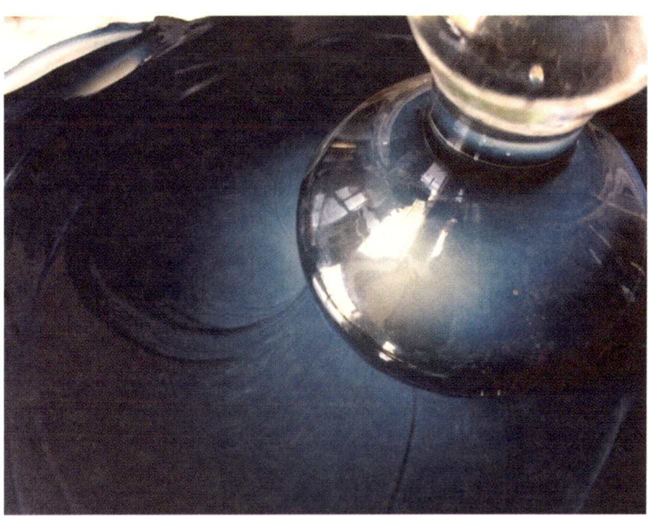

Indigo Maya Blue, petrol blue pigment made by heating indigo powder and sepiolite clay.

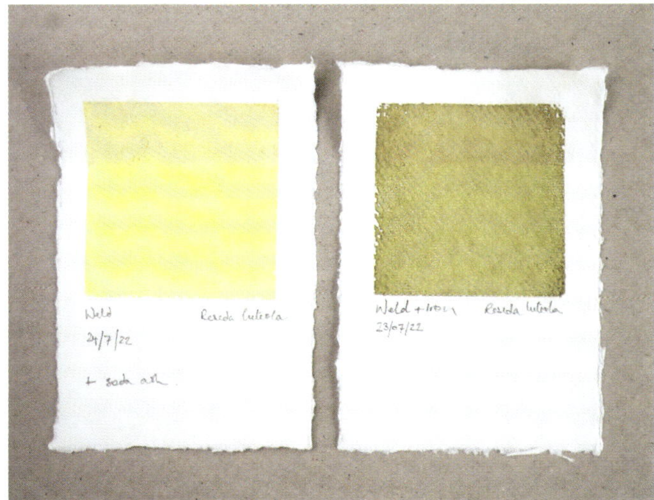

Weld with iron olive green: lightfastness tests of screenprints on paper. Weld (left) and weld with iron (right).

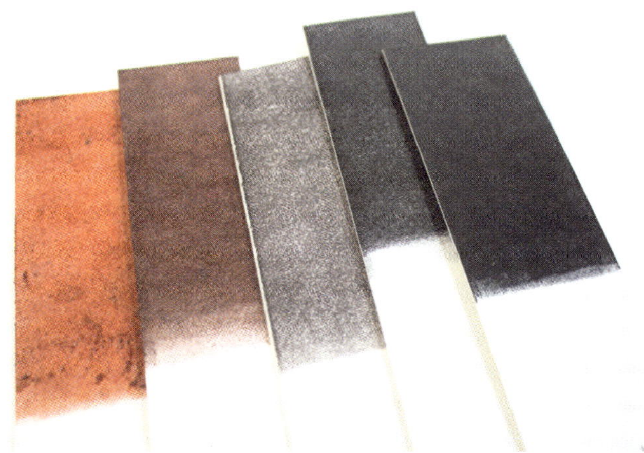

Madder and indigo purple, oil-based printmaking ink made with (L–R) madder, 1:100 indigo to madder, 1:10 indigo to madder, 1:4 indigo to madder, indigo.

PURPLE: OAK (*QUERCUS SPP.*) GALL & IRON

A deep purple-grey dye can be made from an oak (*Quercus spp.*) gall and iron solution. It will easily dye papers, yarns and textiles but it is harder to achieve the purple colour in printmaking inks, whether oil-based, water-based or for textiles or paper. The amount of iron required to achieve the purple-grey shade must also be a consideration, because of the damage iron can cause to fibres (both in paper and in textiles).

PURPLE: MADDER (*RUBIA TINCTORUM*) & IRON

A range of purples can be made using madder and the addition of a little iron. Experiment with amounts to achieve the desired shade. When used for mordant printing, a concentrated purple can be achieved by printing with iron and dyeing with madder.

PURPLE: MADDER (*RUBIA TINCTORUM*) & SODA ASH FOR TEXTILE PRINTING

Using a madder extract paste with added soda ash but without the addition of alum or vinegar can produce shades of purple on textiles after curing and steaming. Pre-mordanting textiles will turn the colour pinky-red and the purple will not be achieved.

PINK: MADDER (*RUBIA TINCTORUM*)

Various shades of pink can be made by using a weaker madder mix. Pinker tones can also be achieved with the addition of an alkali or the addition of chalk in a lake pigment.

PINK: RHUBARB (*RHEUM SPP.*) ROOT & SODA ASH

Rhubarb root usually gives warm yellow to brown shades but can be persuaded to turn a pinker shade when used with an alkali, such as soda ash. The stronger the yellow to start with, the stronger the pink will be. Similar tones can be achieved with buckthorn bark, which contains some of the same colourants.

PINK: HAWTHORN (*CRATAEGUS MONOGYNA*)

A much browner pink can be extracted from hawthorn twigs and leaves for a dye and a lake pigment, while the white flowers make a yellow dye. This is a useful colour in a natural palette though not particularly strongly pigmented.

A Three-Colour Palette

If using plant-based colour for printmaking onto paper, only three plants are theoretically required for the primary colours: madder for red; indigo for blue; weld for yellow. These can then be mixed for secondary and tertiary colours. Add in a little carbon for shading and some chalk or ground eggshell for tinting to obtain a full palette of colour, particularly for printing onto paper. In reality, some colours can be difficult to achieve with just these three pigments but this limitation could be considered a worthwhile exercise, especially if only a small outside space is available and you wish to cultivate all of your own plant-based colour.

If using dyes within your printmaking practice for textiles, you can also limit yourself to the primary colours of red, blue and yellow though, as discussed earlier, blue can be problematic for printing onto fabrics if they need to be washfast.

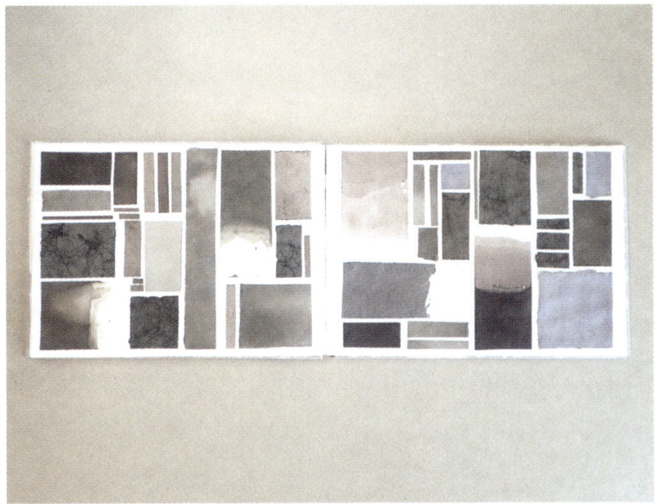

Oak gall with iron purple, immersion-dyed papers.

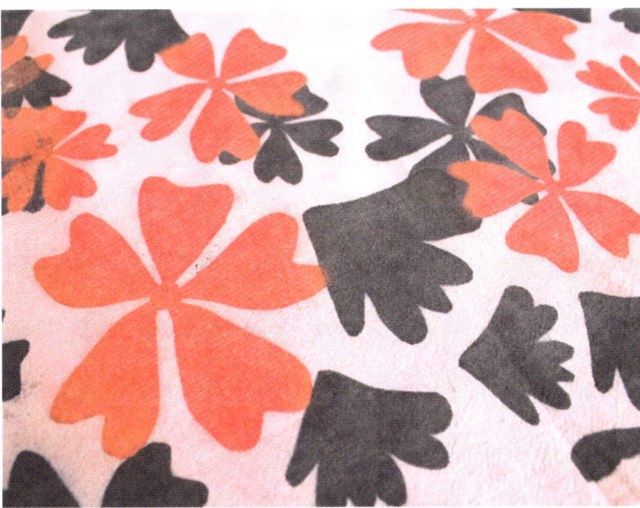

Madder with iron purple, mordant-printed alum (pink) and iron (purple) on fabric, dyed with madder.

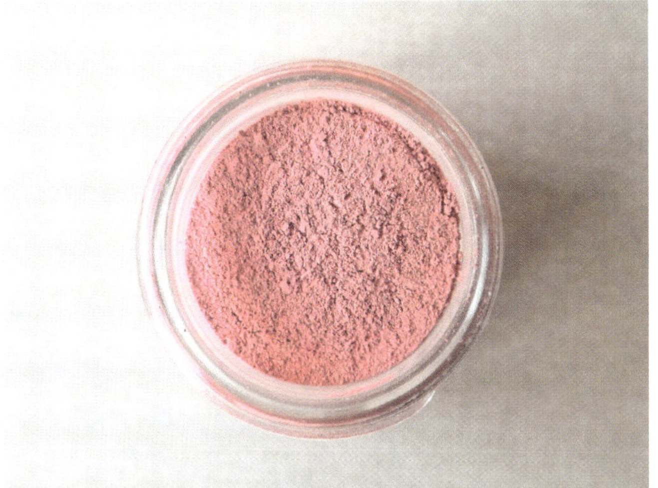

Madder with chalk pink, lake pigment.

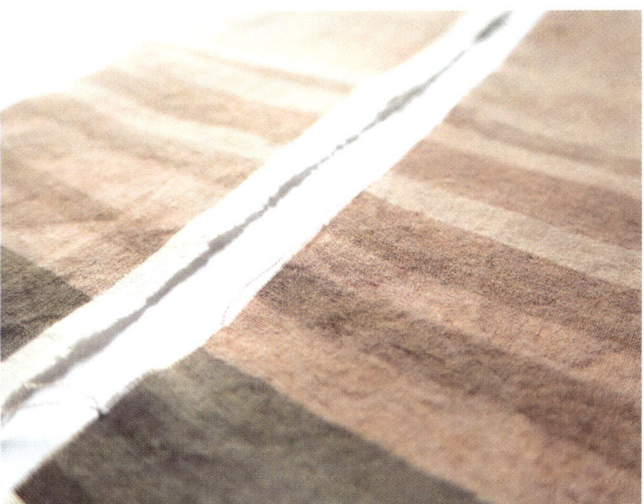

Rhubarb root with alkali pink: screenprinted textile samples.

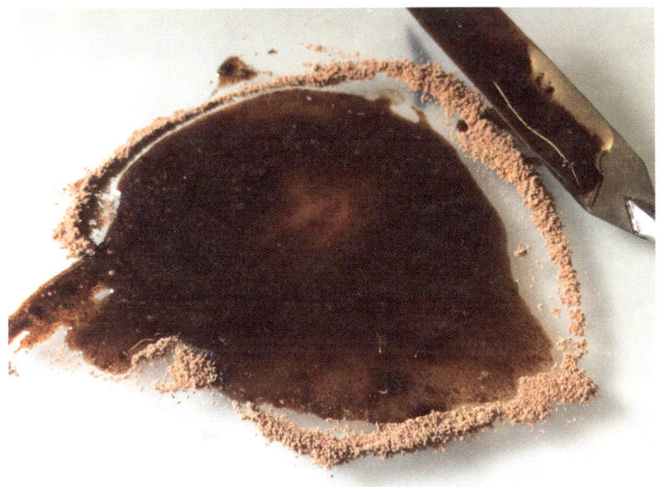

Hawthorn pink, mixing lake pigment and watercolour binder to make paint.

GROWING AND CULTIVATION

If you have space in your garden or possibly an allotment, you might want to grow some of your own dye plants. Some people do so (after all, using plants as a source of colour within your art practice and growing the plants yourself seem to go hand in hand) but some people have neither the time nor the inclination. Don't feel pressure to grow your own plants if you have no interest in gardening! I do cultivate some of my own dye plants – it was an interest and love of plants that sparked my interest in natural colour. The yearly cycle of natural colour growing and production is an incredibly rewarding process to be part of and I find great satisfaction and contentment in it.

The Dye Garden

A dye garden for printmaking might look very different from a dye garden grown specifically for immersion dyeing. Furthermore, one printmaker's dye garden may look very different from another printmaker's garden. The point being that a single list of plants or one garden design will not suit everybody. It is worth trying out some dyes and also trying to grow a variety of dye plants before deciding on which ones you like and which will suit your growing space.

The plants I grow on a regular basis, which include both annuals and perennials, are madder (*Rubia tinctorum*), weld (*Reseda luteola*), indigo (*Persicaria tinctoria*), goldenrod (*Solidago canadensis*), coreopsis (*Coreopsis tinctoria*), saw-wort (*Serratula tinctoria*), meadowsweet (*Filipendula ulmaria*), rhubarb (*Rheum spp.*) and woad (*Isatis tinctoria*).

Slow Lane Studio's trees and bushes include oak (*Quercus spp.*), hawthorn (*Crataegus monogyna*), alder (*Alnus glutinosa*), alder buckthorn (*Frangula alnus*), silver birch (*Betula pendula*) and apple (*Malus spp.*).

If I only had space for two or three plants, I would grow madder, coreopsis and weld. I would also try to squeeze in a couple of alder buckthorn bushes and possibly some rhubarb, but that's because all parts of the rhubarb plant are useful (and I love to eat rhubarb). Some dyers may be confused by the lack of an indigo plant included in this list. This is purely because cultivating indigo or woad for pigment extraction can be a disheartening business with incredibly small yields. Most people don't have the space to grow enough to extract a worthwhile amount of pigment, although growing it for dyeing is recommended. If you plan to use indigo for resist-dyeing or a similar method that requires an indigo vat, grow indigo-bearing plants such as *Persicaria tinctoria* or *Isatis tinctoria*. It is a magical process to extract a blue colour from green leaves and both plants are easy to grow. Woad is also a particularly beautiful plant in its second year.

Depending on where you live, you should acquaint yourself with the rules and laws of your region when it comes to planting and growing dye plants. Some plants are considered invasive in some countries and it is illegal to cultivate them.

An A–Z of Dye Plants for Printmaking

BUCKTHORN (*RHAMNUS SPP.*)

Confusingly, there are buckthorns in different genera that can be used: the *Rhamnus spp.*, which includes purging buckthorn (*Rhamnus cathartica*) in the UK and other species in North America. There is also alder buckthorn (*Frangula alnus*), which grows in the UK and is very similar to *Rhamnus cathartica*. Either can be used though it might be useful to refer to Dominique Cardon's *Natural Dyes*, which has a section on the plants and their differences. Planted as a hedge or grown as a small tree, they are a very versatile source of dye with both the bark and the berries used for colour. The berries can provide different tones and colours depending on whether they are used as immature or mature berries. Colours ranging from rich reds, greens, saturated yellows and chestnut browns can be extracted from the plant and sometimes a pink and a purple from fresh ripe berries, when the pH is modified. The bark contains colourants from the

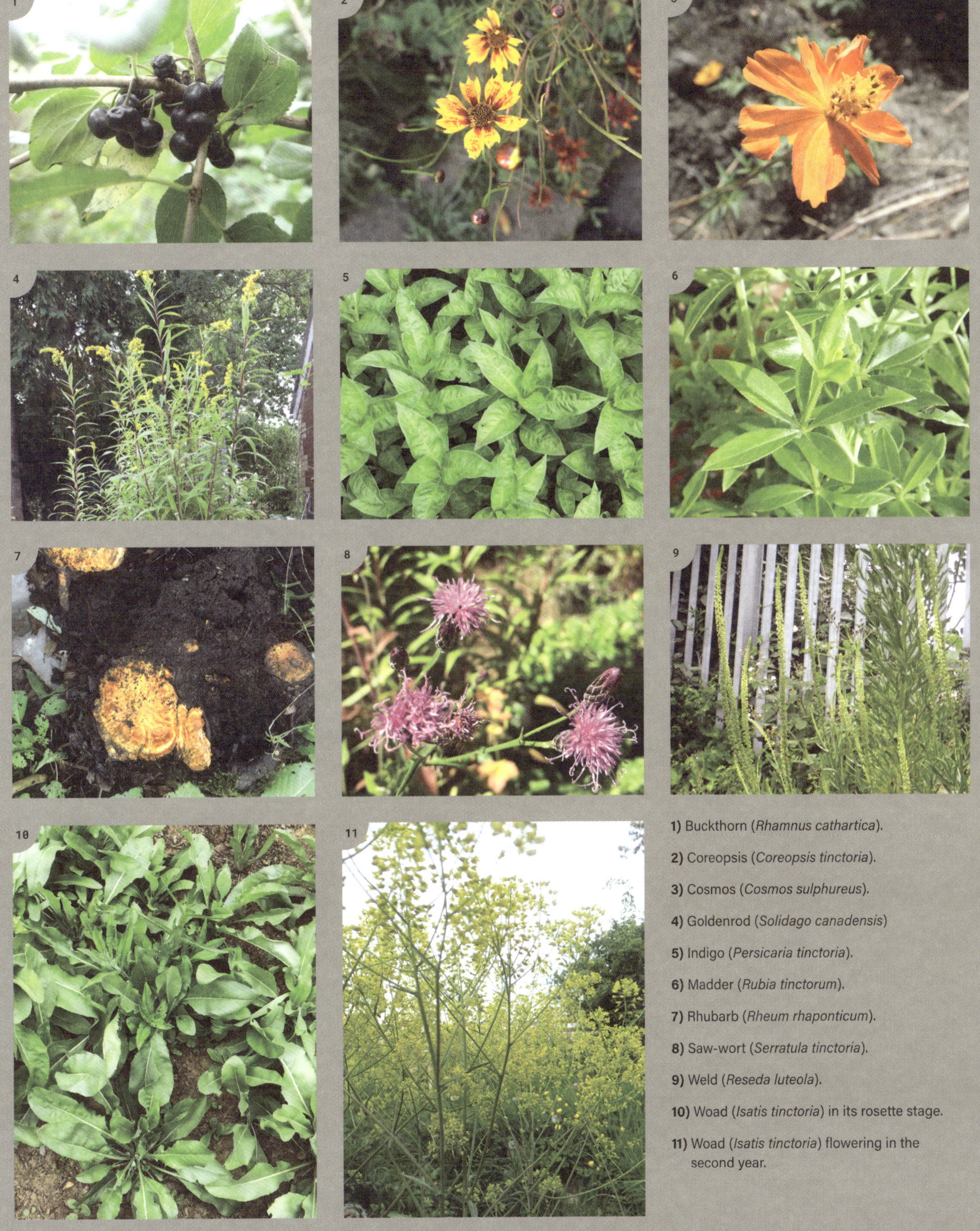

1) Buckthorn (*Rhamnus cathartica*).

2) Coreopsis (*Coreopsis tinctoria*).

3) Cosmos (*Cosmos sulphureus*).

4) Goldenrod (*Solidago canadensis*)

5) Indigo (*Persicaria tinctoria*).

6) Madder (*Rubia tinctorum*).

7) Rhubarb (*Rheum rhaponticum*).

8) Saw-wort (*Serratula tinctoria*).

9) Weld (*Reseda luteola*).

10) Woad (*Isatis tinctoria*) in its rosette stage.

11) Woad (*Isatis tinctoria*) flowering in the second year.

anthraquinone and naphthalene chemical groups, whilst the berries contain anthraquinones and some flavonoid colourants. In parts of North America, some types of buckthorn are considered invasive and it is illegal to grow them.

COREOPSIS (*COREOPSIS TINCTORIA*)

Coreopsis (also known as dyer's coreopsis, tickweed and plains tickweed) plants produce masses of small orange and orange-red flowers during the summer season and until there is a hard frost. The more flowers that are picked, the more flowers the plants produce. Therefore a large patch of coreopsis plants can be quite a commitment during their most prolific months. If only growing a small patch, the best way to harvest them is to pick constantly and dry the flowers until enough of them are saved to use within a project. The flowers can be picked as they begin to turn rather than at the height of their beauty and usefulness to insects. Coreopsis is very easy to grow and will look after itself with just a bit of watering. Allow some flowers to go to seed and collect the seeds for growing next year. Some varieties are perennials and still give good colours, although the annual *Coreopsis tinctoria* plants are traditionally used. I have yet to test the different species in a direct comparison of colour, lightfast properties and yield.

COSMOS (*COSMOS SULPHUREUS*)

Cosmos sulphureus (also called orange cosmos) produce lovely orange or yellow flowers that are an attractive addition to a dye garden and give similar colours to coreopsis. I find these more challenging to grow than coreopsis (primarily because the slugs seem to love them!) but this may be due to many factors including soil type and condition, location of plant beds and how much sun they get. I recommend trying both coreopsis and cosmos to see which grow and produce flowers most successfully.

GOLDENROD (*SOLIDAGO CANADENSIS*, ALSO *SOLIDAGO VIRGAUREA*)

Goldenrod is really easy to grow and, as a perennial, you can plant it and almost forget about it. Though dye books say to use the complete plant top to dye with, I have separated out just the flowers and got the most amazing yellow lake pigment from them. It's a really strong yellow though reputedly not as lightfast as weld. You should carry out your own tests although my own screenprinted paper samples have held up well so far. Whilst *Solidago canadensis* is easily identifiable from pictures, be careful with *Solidago virgaurea* whose flowers look very much like those of the poisonous ragwort. *Solidago virgaurea* is easily identified by the leaves, which are very different from a ragwort's frilly, finely divided leaves. Refer to a plant identification book to see the difference.

INDIGO (*PERSICARIA TINCTORIA*)

Persicaria tinctoria is one of several indigo-containing species but the one most often grown in the UK together with woad. It is very easy to grow and during a warm summer you may get several harvests from the same plants. The blue colour is extracted from the leaves, though once the plant has flowered the amount of indigo present is reduced. The fresh leaves can also be used for fresh-leaf dyeing, tataki-zomé and stencil printing to produce a range of blues. However, the blue pigment is quite hard to extract and involves a complex set of steps to achieve a strong blue powder. I would still grow it though – it is very satisfying to extract blue from green leaves. Try saving some of the plants to allow them to go to seed for next year's crop – the seed is only viable for a year and after that the germination rate will drop considerably. Seeds should be sown indoors and seedlings only planted outside once all danger of frost has passed. Cuttings will root very easily and those with flowers can be cut and brought inside to finish seed production if late in the season.

MADDER (*RUBIA TINCTORUM*)

Grow madder in a pot or raised bed, especially if you don't have much space. Madder is sometimes hard to contain and can become invasive with the right conditions. It can take three years for the roots to develop enough colour to produce the full range of colourants worth using so it's a long-term commitment. It might be useful to plant three pots or containers of madder so the harvest can be rotated over a period of three years. The easiest way to grow madder is by obtaining some bare roots – either find somebody who can donate some or purchase them from a supplier. They take hold very easily and you will soon have fresh green shoots coming up from the roots.

RHUBARB (*RHEUM SPP.*)

Rhubarb plants are hardy perennials that require little maintenance and are very easy to grow. They should also be divided every few years so digging up some of the root to use for colour will also improve the health of the plant. It can be grown from seed but is very easy to buy as a young plant or just ask a friend to donate some when it is being divided. The leaves can be used in a pre-mordant bath but this should be done outside as they contain oxalic acid, which is poisonous.

SAW-WORT (*SERRATULA TINCTORIA*)
Saw-wort is a perennial plant with purple thistle-like flowers and superficially similar to knapweed. The leaves can be used as a yellow dye comparable to weld and actually contain the same colourant, luteolin. It is a fairly slow-growing plant but is a colourful addition to a dye garden. However, if growing purely for colour it may be better to just grow weld.

WELD (*RESEDA LUTEOLA*)
Weld can be a tricky plant to establish. Seeds germinate easily but can soon start to look sickly and wilt if they are in the wrong conditions or the roots are disturbed. However, if the right conditions and environment are provided, weld will grow quite happily, self-seeding and looking after itself. It is considered a ruderal (or pioneer) plant, growing first in areas where there has been disturbed soil such as building sites and roadsides. It is often seen growing on the edge of motorways – keep an eye out in the summer and you're very likely to see it and also rue the lack of a hard shoulder or somewhere to stop on many of the UK's roads. Weld prefers a very well-draining soil and won't tolerate having its roots in a heavy water-logged soil. It also has a very long tap root that shouldn't be disturbed, so growing it directly in the ground is best. Consequently, I grow mine in a gravel bed where they seem to be quite happy.

WOAD (*ISATIS TINCTORIA*)
Woad is a biennial, which doesn't flower in the first year but produces low-growing rosettes of leaves. As with other indigo plants, the leaves can be harvested and used either fresh or to extract the blue pigment for use at a later date. The leaves should be used before the plant starts to flower. Early in their second year, woad plants will send up tall spikes that produce masses of yellow flowers in late spring, closely followed by large pendulous black seeds that can be harvested and sown or left to self-seed. Woad is an easy and attractive plant to grow and is a striking addition to the garden.

FORAGING AND LOCAL RESOURCES

Our local green spaces, hedgerows, waste ground and countryside can be a great source of colour but a knowledge of the rules about gathering plantstuffs and, more importantly, responsible foraging is an absolute must. All wild plants are protected by the Wildlife and Countryside Act (1981), which means you cannot dig up, damage or remove a plant from the land it is growing on without permission from the landowner. Some plants, including rare and protected species, are legally protected and should not be touched at all.

Some older sources mention a 20 per cent rule (don't take more than 20 per cent of a plant), but in the contemporary world, this is surely far too much. Take as little as possible and only ever for individual use – use your common sense and be considerate.

ASK YOURSELF:

- Can I only see one plant or a limited number of this variety in the area?
- Has it been grown or planted for an obvious reason?
- Is it part of a crop or has it been cultivated for a specific use?
- Is it providing useful habitat and food resources for invertebrates and other wildlife?
- Is it providing shelter for invertebrates, other wildlife and other plantlife?
- Is it a plant that is likely to be attractive to other users of natural and plant-based colour?

If you are working on a scale that requires large amounts for production, this isn't responsible foraging – perhaps cultivation of the plant should be considered or find a partner who can do this for you or can provide a source of the plantstuff.

Of course, there are always exceptions to the rule – during my courses, I always tell my students the story of running along the canal towpath by my studio, wielding my secateurs and gathering as much of the flowering meadowsweet as I could possibly carry. This sounds shocking when you think about all the wildlife and pollinators that would have been using the plants until you know that I was in front of contractors who were strimming everything down to a couple of inches in height for safety. I felt fully justified in taking as much of the meadowsweet as I could.

The hedges around me are also regularly cut and trimmed (far too often in my opinion) but this means that I can take prunings and off-cuts of hedging such as hawthorn and oak for use in my dye pots.

Don't be tempted by the berries of most plants as they generally give only fugitive colour and are not worth the effort. One of the exceptions to the rule is the buckthorn berry (from the *Rhamnus* species and alder buckthorn).

Also consider plants that are thought of as weeds such as dock, nettle and bramble. Nobody is going to mind if you help yourself to a plant that is invasive or taking over though always take into consideration the insects and other wildlife that might be using the plants as food, habitat, shelter and places to lay eggs. Nettles are an important food source for the caterpillars of several butterflies and moths. Check under leaves for eggs and choose another plant if you see any.

Also research the best time to forage certain items – oak galls shouldn't be gathered until the oak gall wasp inside has emerged from the gall. This is easily checked by looking for a small, perfectly round hole in the side of marble galls. With knopper galls, it can be more challenging but these galls drop to the ground in autumn and can be gathered from lanes where they will otherwise likely be squashed by cars. They can also be gathered and kept outside (ideally near the source tree) until the gall wasp has emerged in spring.

Useful Plants

Plants and dyestuffs to consider collecting from your local green spaces, hedgerows, verges and wastelands:

OAK (*QUERCUS SPP.*) GALLS

Oak galls are a useful source of tannin, which can be used in a number of ways when working with plant-based colour. Oak galls create a strong brown ink that turns to grey or a deep purple-black with the addition of iron and this makes a beautiful writing ink. Tannin solutions are also useful when printing on textiles.

Marble galls (*Andricus kollari* gall wasp) – hard, spherical growths on the side of twigs (where leaf buds were growing) that are bright green in spring and eventually turn brown. They generally remain on the tree and can be easy to spot in winter once the leaves have fallen.

Knopper galls (*Andricus quercuscalicis* gall wasp) – knobbly, deformed growths that are in or on acorns. Sticky and green to start with, they drop off the tree in autumn and quickly turn brown.

ACORNS AND ACORN CUPS

Also a source of tannin, they contain a lower percentage of tannic acid than galls so produce useful silvery grey tones rather than black with the addition of iron. Try experimenting with different acorns and acorn cups.

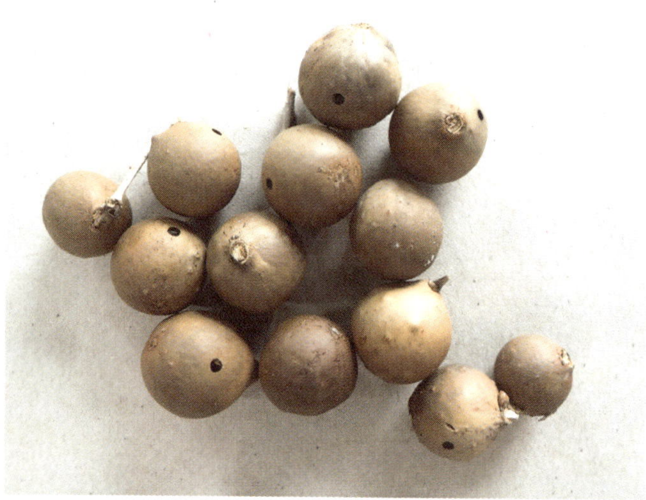

Marble galls.

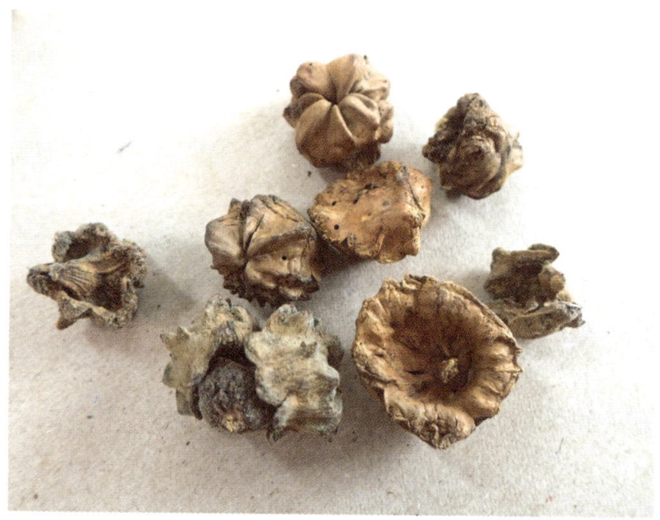

Knopper galls.

ALDER (*ALNUS SPP.*) CONES
Alder cones produce a rich chestnut brown when used for a dye, ink or lake pigment. Plentiful in winter, they can be gathered, dried and stored indefinitely. Alder cones are also tannin-rich so can be used in a similar way to oak galls. The common alder (*Alnus glutinosa*) is the usual species to find in the UK, though the Italian alder (*Alnus cordata*) is a good find as its cones are extra large.

BRAMBLE (*RUBUS FRUTICOSUS*)
Bramble is a common plant and the leaves and stems can be used as a source of tannin. Bramble will also dye fibres yellow though I suspect the colour is not strong enough to bother with as a colourant for printing pastes and inks. Again, don't be tempted to try using blackberries as a source of purple – the colour is highly fugitive and will soon turn to grey. Tolerable if that's what you wanted but disappointing if you were hoping for a long-lasting berry purple shade.

MEADOWSWEET (*FILIPENDULA ULMARIA*)
A large leafy perennial with white frothy flowers in summer, meadowsweet is often found on roadsides and wet verges or in ditches. The plant tops will produce a strong yellow-green as a dye which turns to a dark grey-green with the addition of iron.

HAWTHORN (*CRATAEGUS MONOGYNA*)
The hawthorn tree produces a lovely pinky-brown colour. Collect leaves and twigs from prunings and steep them in water for a few days to soften the woody parts before heating to extract the dye.

WELD (*RESEDA LUTEOLA*)
Weld is included in the foraging section as well as in the cultivation section as it can be found growing on wasteland, motorway verges, building sites and car parks in the UK. I recently found some taking over the edge of a hotel car park after running a natural dye workshop. It was November so the plants were brown and had finished their season, but they still contained useful colour.

BUDDLEIA (*BUDDLEIA SPP.*)
Any flowers from a butterfly bush produce a lovely yellow dye. The flowers can be harvested once they are past their best or even dead, though I haven't tested them once they have gone to seed. Buddleia (also spelt buddleja) plants aren't particularly common where I live but in some places are considered a weed.

WALNUT (*JUGLANS REGIA, JUGLANS NIGRA*)
Walnut husks can be used to create deep brown dyes. Whilst black walnut (*Juglans nigra*) gives the best colours, common walnut (*Juglans regia*) can be used as a source of colour too. The green husks give the deepest browns so if possible, collect them from the ground before they start to dry and turn brown.

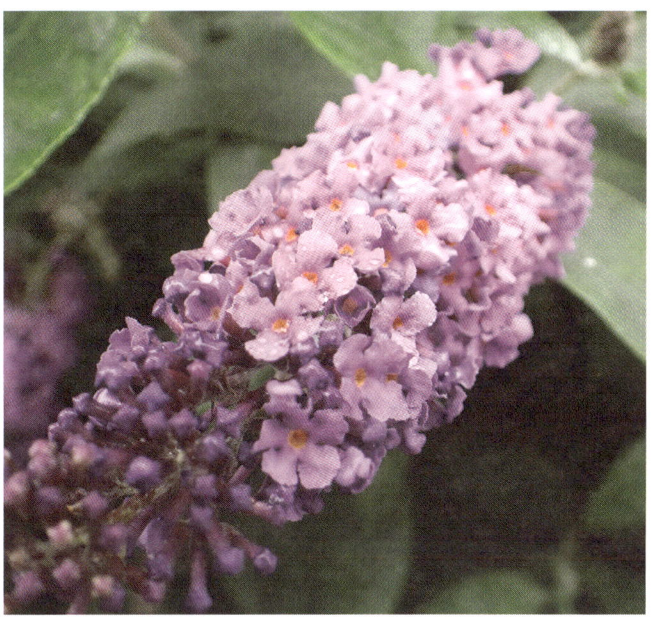

Buddleia (*Buddleia davidii*).

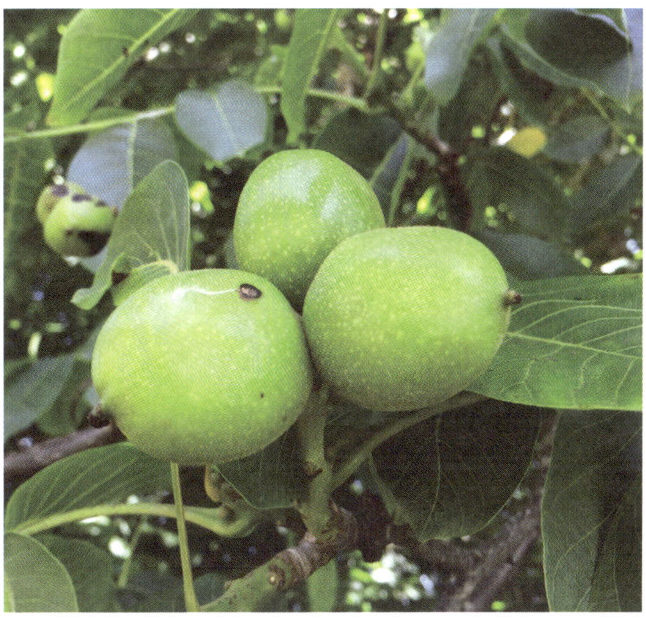

Walnut (*Juglans regia*)

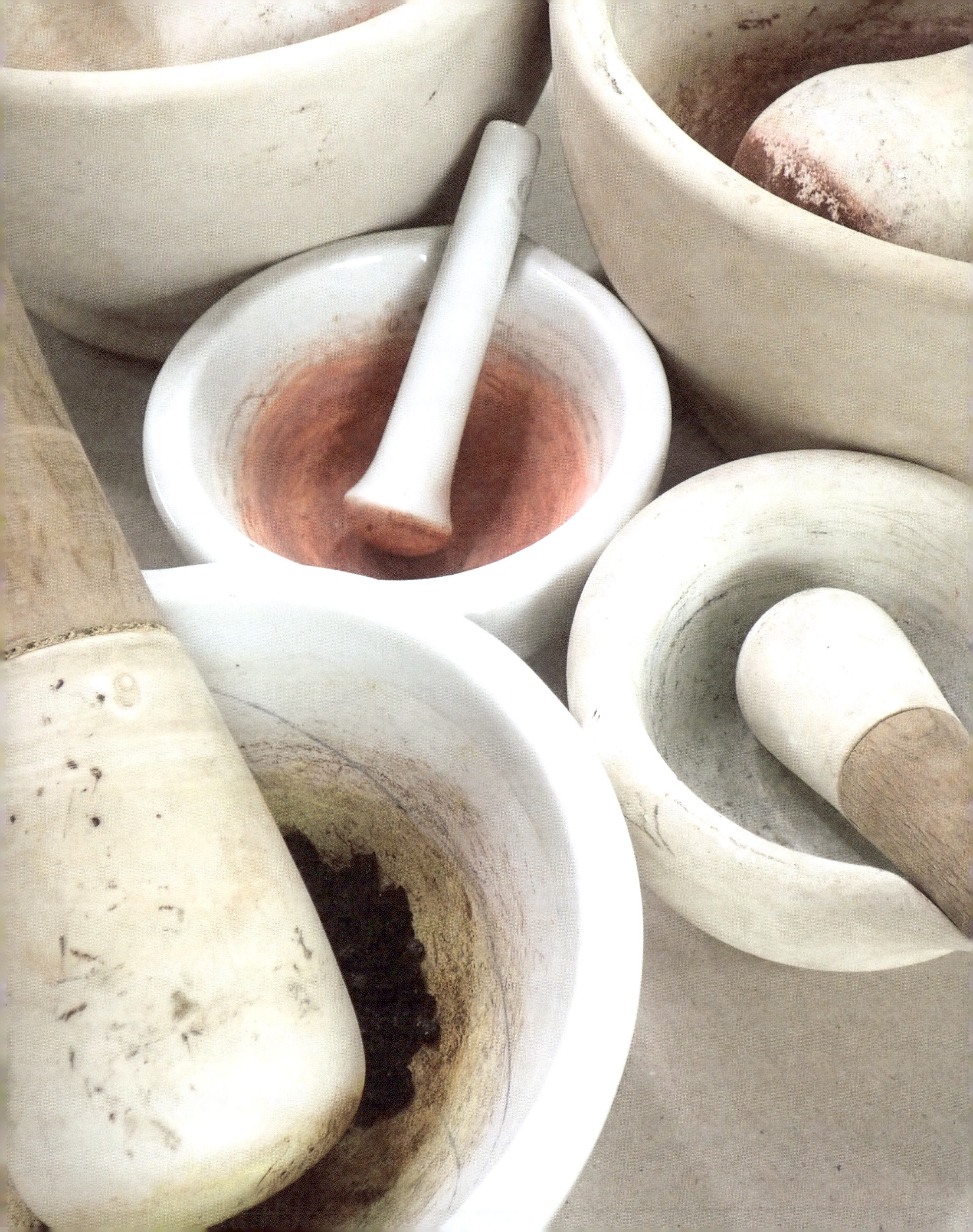

Chapter Three

TOOLS, EQUIPMENT AND MATERIALS

FACING PAGE

Pestles and mortars for grinding pigments.

There are so many different tools, materials and pieces of equipment necessary when using plant-based colour for printmaking that a warehouse might be completely filled and you could bankrupt yourself before buying everything you think you might need or buying the list of items I might advise you to purchase. However, this isn't practical and it wouldn't be particularly useful advice. Therefore I have tried to break down this section into general items that you really would struggle to do without, items that would be useful to invest in but you don't need to rush out to buy and the tools I consider vital for different techniques included in this book (some of which you may have already).

Whilst I do not provide a complete list of tools and equipment for each printmaking process, I have listed some items that may be considered particular to a specific specialism and have decided that their inclusion is necessary. It might be useful to refer to printmaking books that specialise in particular techniques if you are unsure about which tools are required. I have also tried to include cheaper substitutions, make-dos and hacks that will work until you are sure you want to take your practice further and invest in a proper tool or piece of equipment, or until you find a better alternative, or decide the hack is working perfectly well.

In each section I will also list the tools and equipment necessary for the processes mentioned so you may prefer to look at the section you are interested in first and then refer back for further information and advice.

And, as a final note on tools and equipment: don't assume that items listed here are the only option. I encourage you to look within other industries and specialisms for items that might work for you in your practice. Catering is an obvious choice but also equipment from science laboratories, gardening, farming, education and mechanics might yield something worthwhile. As a lifelong skinflint I reason that if you can make or adapt something, or buy it second-hand, why not? At the same time you'll also be reducing your consumption so it's a win-win.

GENERAL TOOLS

Scales

To start with, some general kitchen scales will suit you perfectly. Either buy a set that you specifically keep for your natural colour practice or (and this is not recommended but will work at a pinch) use your own digital kitchen scales sealed inside a clear zip-lock plastic bag. This will ensure they are kept clean for a return to the kitchen. At some point you are going to find the limitations of scales that weigh a minimum of 1g challenging. You don't often need to measure less than 1g but will find that basic scales will stubbornly remain at a figure whilst you add more and more of an ingredient and then they will suddenly jump to 2–3g above what you wanted. This can make it difficult to accurately record your recipes so I would recommend investing in a set of scales that will weigh in increments of 0.1g or even 0.01g.

Measuring Jugs

Borosilicate (or Pyrex) glass measuring jugs in a variety of sizes are the most practical as they will not stain and can be used for hot liquids. Look for second-hand ones or chipped ones donated from friends and family to reduce the cost. I also have many plastic measuring jugs from 250ml up to 3 litres as they are a cheap and useful addition to the studio. They are stained and generally a bit grotty, but I find them handy for holding water and transferring liquids.

Glass Beakers and Containers

I was lucky enough to inherit some laboratory glass beakers and containers from a university department years ago and they have proved invaluable. It's worth investing in a few of them in different sizes if you can.

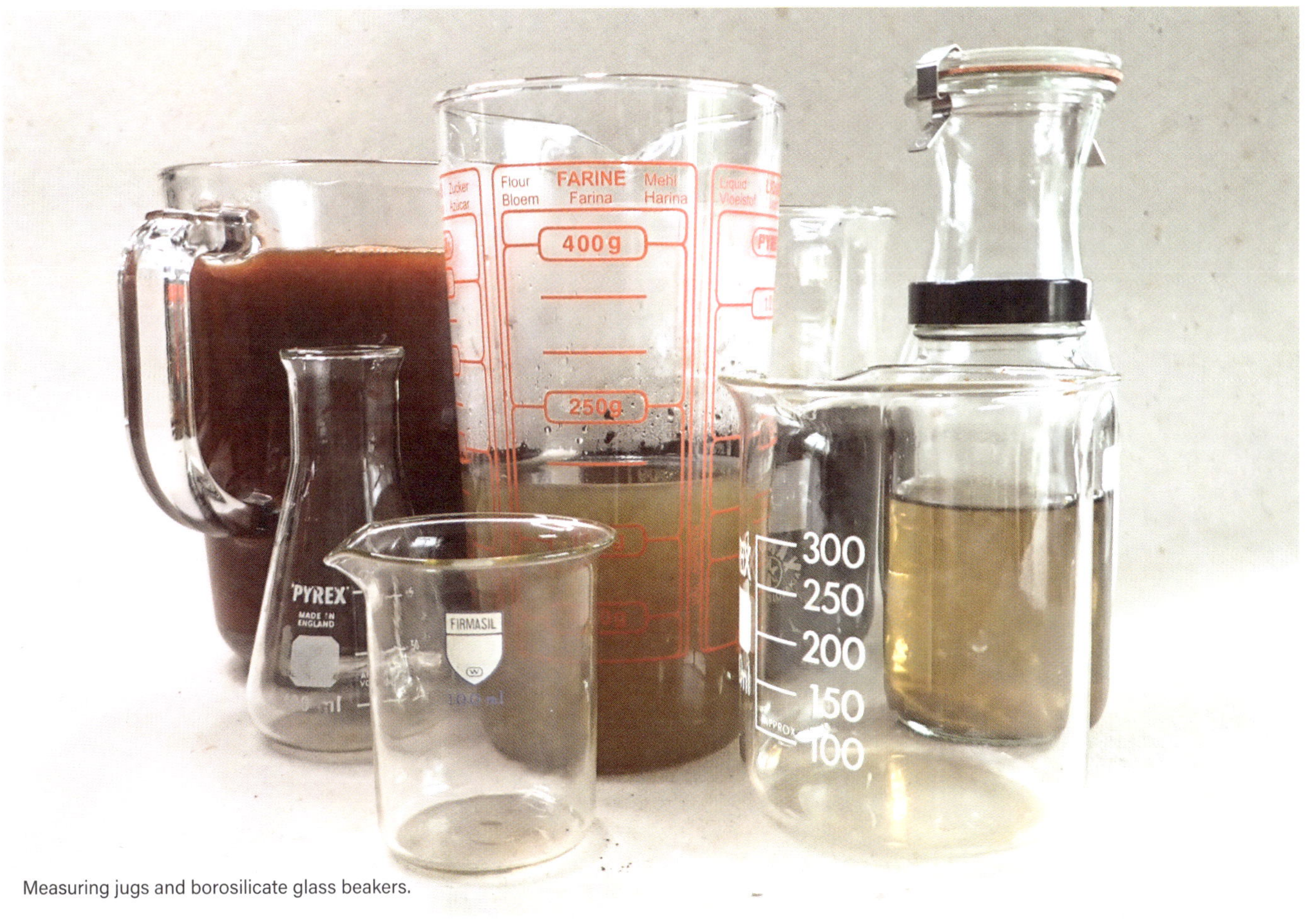

Measuring jugs and borosilicate glass beakers.

Measuring Spoons

Measuring spoons are an invaluable addition to the plant-based colour printmaker's studio. Invest in a stainless-steel set that will last for years and are much easier to clean, rather than a plastic set that will stain and break. I most often use them for measuring small amounts of liquid or oils when weighing is not practical – imagine trying to scrape 1g of linseed oil from your scales.

Wooden Spoons and Other Stirrers

Buy a few and keep them for different dyes and uses and make sure you label them. Wood is porous so it is important to keep some spoons completely separate from others, especially those you have used for iron and strongly pigmented dyes such as indigo. My home kitchen never has any wooden spoons as I am always nicking them for an experiment or two and, once used in a dye pot, they can never go back. I mention other stirrers as it is useful to have as many as possible, of all different shapes and sizes. Wooden lolly sticks, old paintbrush handles, bamboo canes, broom handles (for larger work), pencils, rulers and tongs are all part of my stirring equipment.

Plastic Spoons

I buy sets of plastic picnic cutlery that supermarkets sell during the summer months – they are much more robust than standard plastic cutlery, which is far too thin and shatters easily. The spoons from these sets are exceptionally useful in all areas of the workshop and the knives and forks generally go into my stirring collection. Having lots of small spoons enables you to label them and keep them for different uses – again, remember to keep those used for iron completely separate.

Collect spoons and stirrers such as wooden lolly sticks, old paintbrush handles and bamboo sticks.

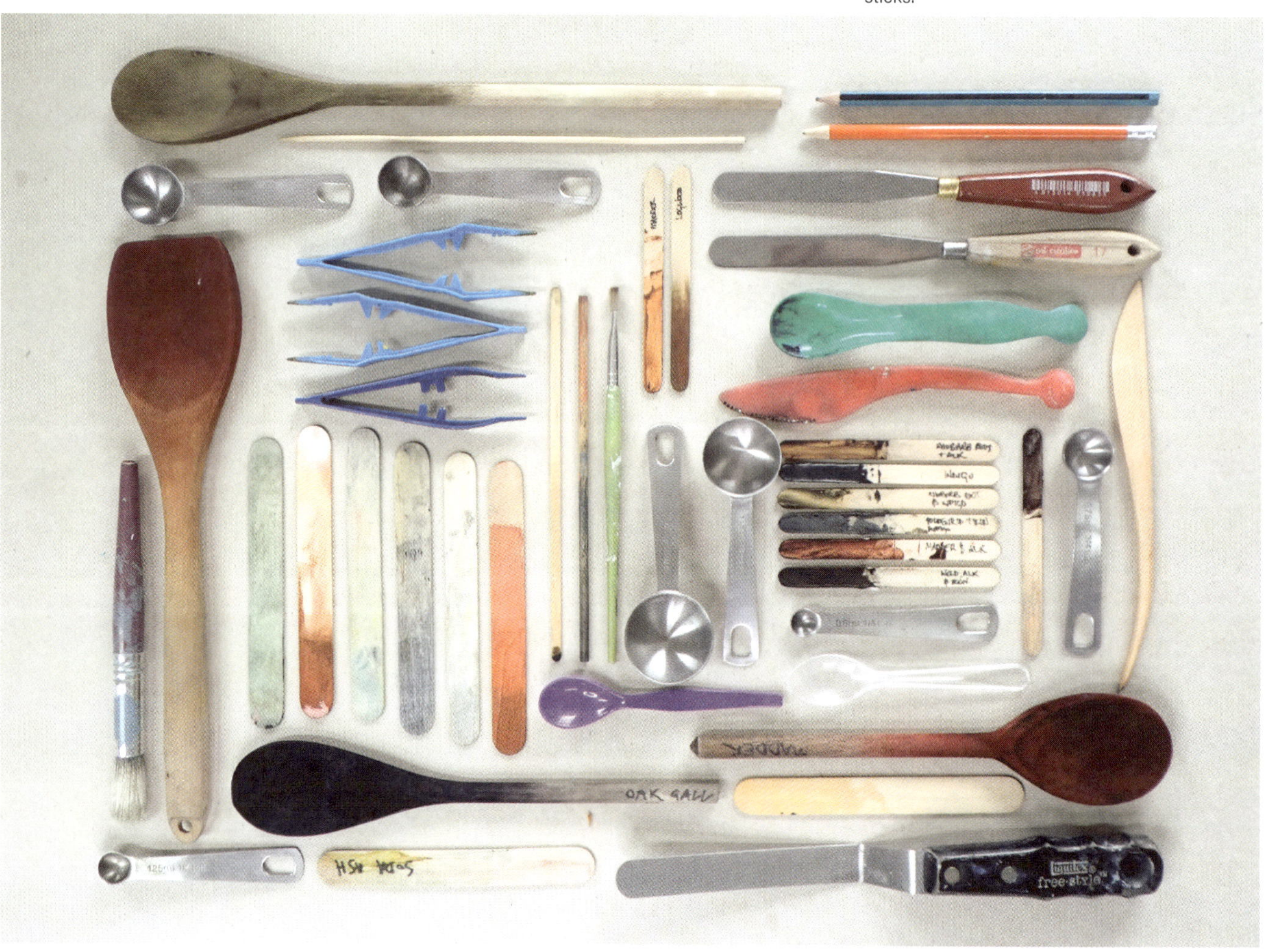

Glass Jars and Other Lidded Containers

Keep your jam jars and any plastic pots with lids – you'll use them. Keep an eye on glass jars with metal lids that have liquids inside or have contained acids. The lids can go rusty and you don't want bits of iron falling into whatever is inside. For my screenprinting pastes, I purchased a set of round plastic pots with screw lids that are easy to wash and re-use. Think about the shape of pots if you do invest in any – you don't really want anything with a neck or rim that is narrower than the main part of the pot or jar. This makes it difficult to access whatever is inside and more difficult to wash.

Stockpots and Saucepans

A couple of domestic saucepans with lids should be enough to get started for creating your own plant-based colour for printmaking. They should be non-reactive; stainless steel or enamel are ideal and they should be suitable for whatever heat source you plan to use. Remember that pans should be well labelled and kept away from any kitchen equipment. Low-cost pots and saucepans big enough for dyeing textiles are often one of the most problematic pieces of equipment to find but they are not necessary for most of the procedures included in this book. You'll only need bigger pans (for example 10 litres and above) if you are mordant-dyeing or plan to dye larger pieces of fabric. In these cases, choose pans that are big enough to allow your fabric to move freely within the liquid. It is much easier to source large aluminium stockpots but fabrics dyed within these may absorb small amounts of aluminium, which as a mordant, might produce areas where more dye has bonded with the fibres. Other artists and natural dyers have reported that this doesn't cause too many problems, although it may be an issue when undertaking mordant printing techniques.

An alternative to a large stainless-steel stockpot is to heat a concentrated dye liquid in a smaller pot, add it to a large plastic trug or container with more hot water and add your textiles to this container. The heat will be enough to get your dyeing started – it may just take a little longer for the textile to reach a deep enough colour. Most natural dyes can be used cold as the heat merely speeds up the process. Whilst not ideal, this is a better approach than squeezing your fabric into too small a pot so it can't move around.

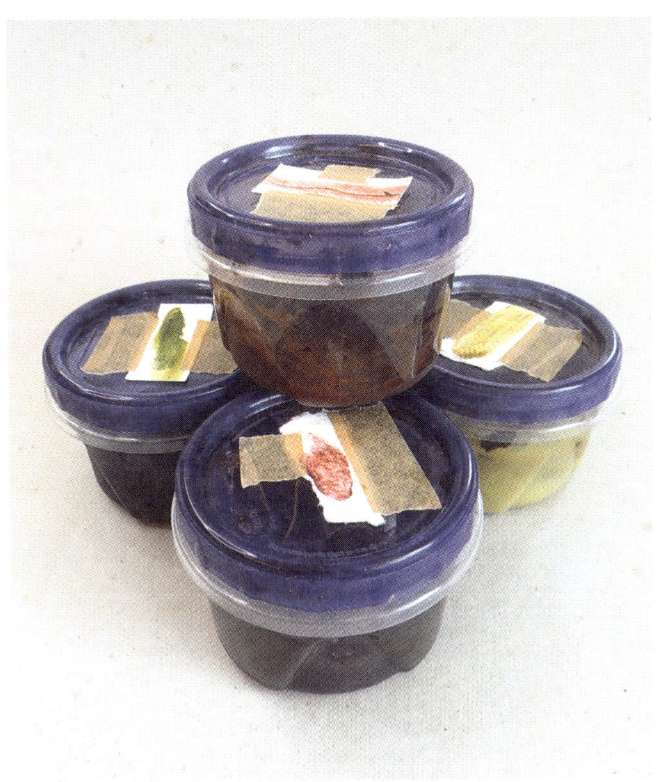

Screenprint paste lidded containers.

Pestle and Mortar

A pestle and mortar are used for grinding pigments into smaller particles. If you are going to make your own lake pigments, you need at least one. A small one is fine for grinding smaller amounts or grinding larger amounts of pigment bit by bit. Mine are all ceramic but marble ones are acceptable if that is all you have. I have several pestles and mortars, which I keep for different pigments so the colour doesn't transfer. The pigments will often become stuck to the sides of the pestle and mortar, which means washing after use and then drying completely if you need to grind a different-coloured pigment.

Respirator Mask

This is essential if you are working with powders and dusty products. Working in a well-ventilated area is not enough. I wear a half-face respirator mask with changeable filters – I have both a gas and particulate filter attached. Grinding pigments is messy and potentially dangerous, so take the necessary precautions. It is up to you to decide what type of face mask to use but it is worth investing in a proper one with replaceable filters if you are going to grind a lot of dry pigments.

Strainers and Kitchen Sieves

A couple of sieves are useful for removing the plantstuff from the dye liquid. They are sometimes not fine enough, so I often place either a folded-up piece of muslin inside the sieve or place the sieve inside a couple of fabric mesh bags which act as a further strainer. Micro-perforated colanders are also useful, but you may still need a cloth filter. Coffee filter papers can be used but they quickly clog up and the liquid will take a long time to drain through. It is important to remove all pieces of organic matter from your liquid, especially when making a lake pigment but also when making a screenprinting paste or water-based inks. If left in the liquid, the plant pieces will go mouldy very quickly.

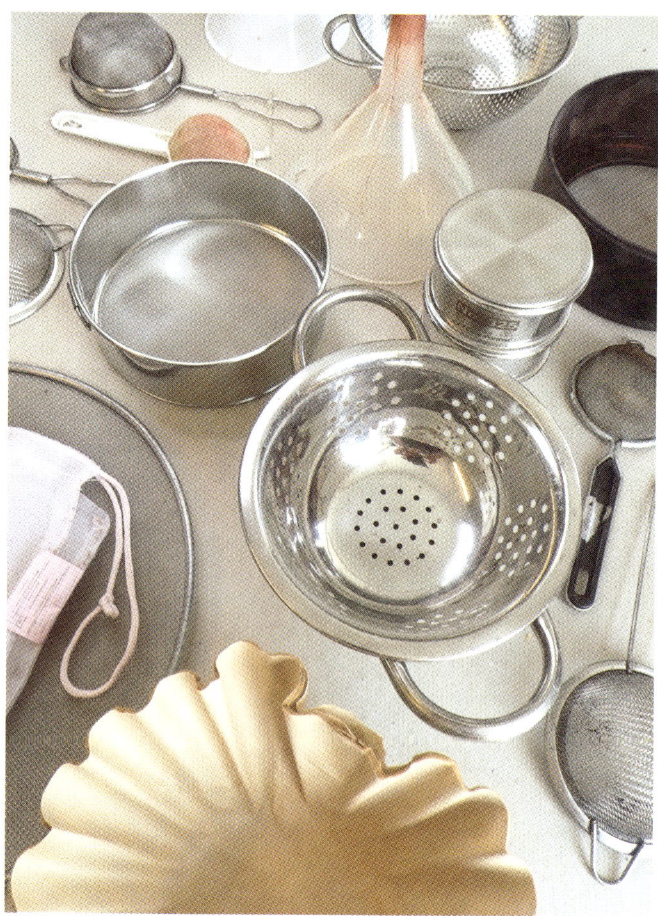

Funnels, filter papers, sieves, colanders and mesh bags are all useful in a plant-based colour toolkit.

Funnels

Plastic, glass or micro-perforated funnels are generally worth having in the studio. I use large plastic funnels to strain excess liquid from lake pigments, although sieves with paper filters are perfectly adequate.

Filter Papers

These are essential for straining liquid from lake pigments and readily available from the supermarket, though you'll probably find you need bigger catering-size filters. Alternatively you can use a finely meshed or woven material, which has the advantage of being washable.

Fabric Mesh Bags

A low-cost and essential item used for keeping dyestuffs contained in a dye bath, washing small samples in the washing machine and as a quick strainer. Most supermarkets now sell reusable mesh bags for fruit and vegetables – these are ideal.

Crank-Handled (Offset) Spatulas

A crank-handled spatula or painting knife is exactly the same as a flat spatula except that the handle is off-set from the blade. This makes it far easier to use when scraping up ink, pigment or paste. I recommend investing in some metal knives or spatulas rather than plastic ones, which will snap with applied pressure or will eventually degrade, becoming brittle and then shattering. I use smaller painting knives for initial mixing of pigments into inks or watercolours and find that the parallel-edged blades are the most efficient for this.

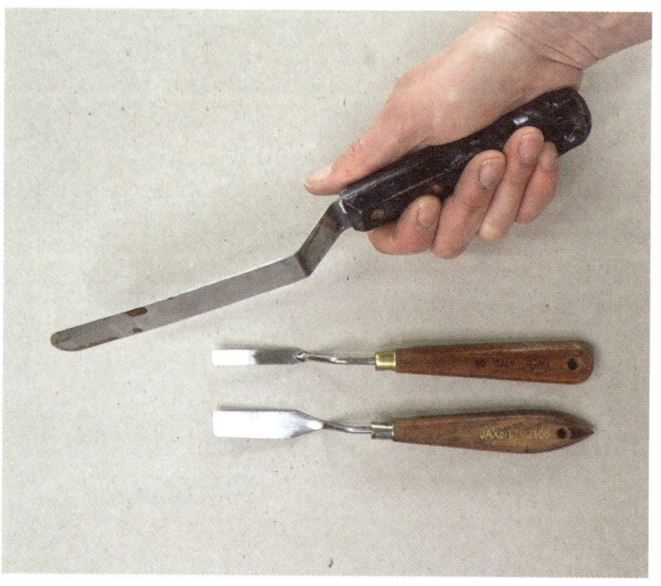

Crank-handled (or offset) spatulas and painting knives.

INVESTMENT TOOLS

Scientific Sieves

Invaluable for sieving pigment particles for making oil-based ink. Oil-based printmaking ink requires very small particles and without a scientific sieve this is near impossible to achieve. I use a 45-micron (or 0.045mm) sieve to sort the smallest particles for printmaking ink and a 100-micron (0.1mm) sieve to sort pigment for watercolour paint. Sieving your pigment also removes any impurities, such as bits of filter paper or dried pieces of plant. You will need a sieve, a lid and a receiving pan, although the lid and receiving pan will be inter-changeable with other particle size sieves you invest in. The one shown here is a 3in diameter stainless steel sieve and though small, is perfectly adequate for an individual's needs.

Muller and Slab

A muller and slab is essential for making your own ink, watercolours and water-based pigment inks and is one of the most useful pieces of equipment when using plant-based colour for printmaking.

The easiest mullers to find for sale are made of glass, though you can also get stone mullers, which are ideal for making oil-based inks. Mullers are an investment so it might be worth trying to borrow one before purchasing to see if making your own paints and inks is something you'd like to do more of. A glass slab is a thick ground or sand-blasted piece of toughened glass that is used as a base when mulling. The surface is slightly roughened rather than being 'glass smooth', which aids in the mulling process. Glass slabs can usually be purchased from the same place as the muller, although it is relatively easy to make your own – *see* later in this chapter for instructions on how to do so.

Solid pieces of glass such as a glass candlestick, a chess piece or a very heavy-bottomed drinking glass also make a viable alternative to a muller. It should be relatively easy to hold and will need a very flat base that has ideally been ground to a flat surface. I have two drinking glasses that I use for lighter mulling, such as mixing water-based pigment inks or for making watercolours. I had the bases ground flat on a slow-speed grinding wheel and they make ideal mullers. Remember that care should be taken when using a hollow glass and applying a lot of pressure – you don't want the glass to shatter in your hand.

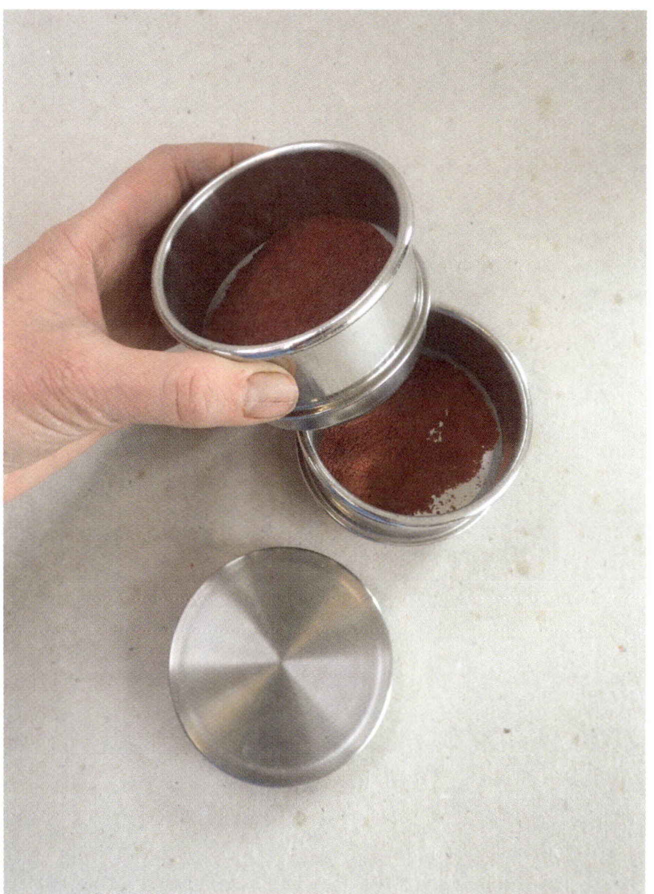

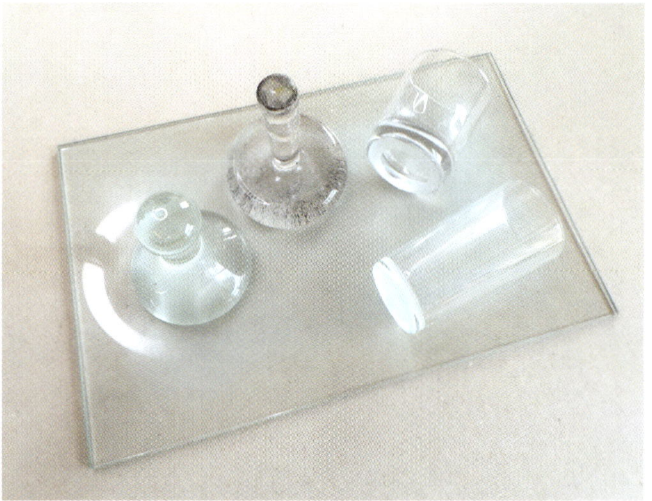

TOP
0.045mm scientific sieve, receiving pan and lid. Sieves are available in different mesh sizes from 0.037mm to 4mm in this range.

ABOVE
Glass mullers and flat-bottomed ground glasses on a glass slab.

Making a Glass Slab for Mulling

YOU WILL NEED:

- A thick piece of toughened glass
- Carborundum (silicon carbide) grit
- Tape
- A muller or a flat-bottomed glass

Most printmakers will be familiar with carborundum as it is often used in making collagraph plates – you can purchase it from specialist print supply shops and some art supply shops. Find or buy a thick piece of safety sheet glass – I got mine from an old cabinet with glass shelves.

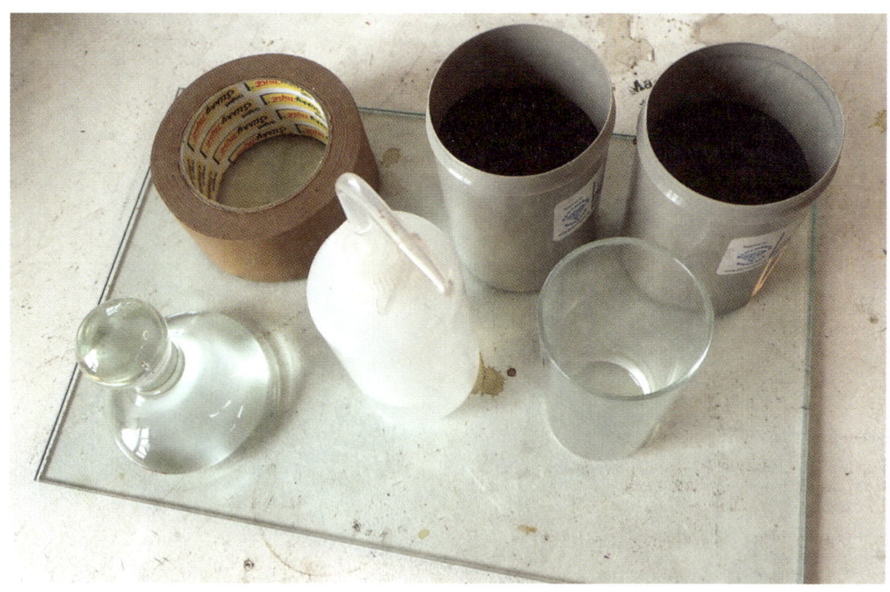

A toughened glass sheet, carborundum grit, water, brown paper tape and a muller or thick-bottomed glass.

Step 1: Tape the glass to the surface you are working on or use a damp cloth to hold it in place. Pour a small amount of fine carborundum (I use 220 grit) onto the surface.

Step 2: Add some water to the carborundum powder and mix to make a paste.

Step 3: Using a glass muller, gently rub the gritty paste over the glass surface in a circular motion, which will grind away the smooth finish and create the slightly roughened surface you need for successful mulling. Make sure you cover the whole slab, using an even pressure the whole time and adding more water if needed.

The water will aid the movement of the muller but it will also keep the ground bits of glass in suspension rather than becoming airborne so more rather than less water is advisable. Add more grit or water as needed.

Step 4: You can periodically check the progress by wiping a small area of the slurry away with a rag. The glass should appear frosted. It can be quite hard to see so be prepared to wash off the grit and start again if it needs further grinding.

Step 5: Once finished, use a bowl to wash the slab in so that the grit and ground pieces of glass are contained. This can be left to settle and the excess water poured off before disposing of the remaining slurry carefully. Wrap it in newspaper, tape it up and dispose of it according to local regulations – do not wash it down the sink.

A note of caution – the carborundum will be grinding your muller at the same time as the glass slab. This shouldn't matter, especially if you are careful to keep the muller absolutely flat whilst grinding, but you may prefer to use a less valuable tool. It might be a good time to make a spare 'muller' from a flat-bottomed glass by using this in place of your muller.

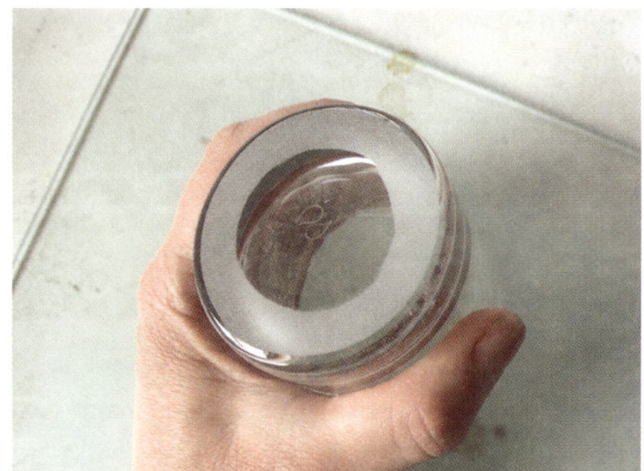

The bottom of the drinking glass after grinding the toughened glass sheet.

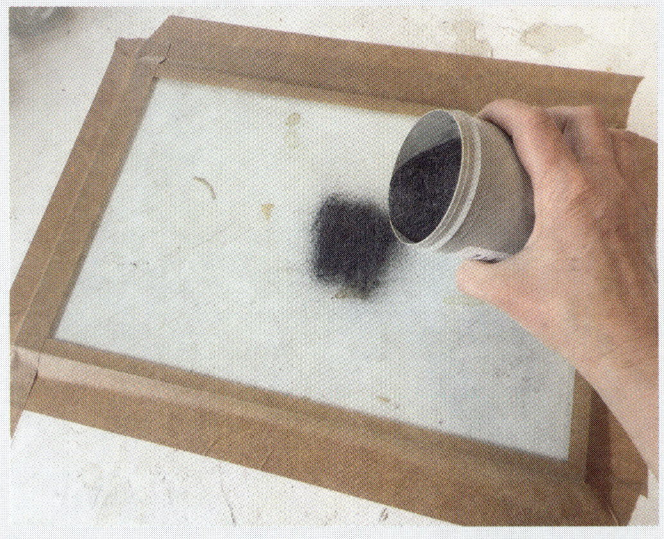

Pour some carborundum grit into the centre of the glass.

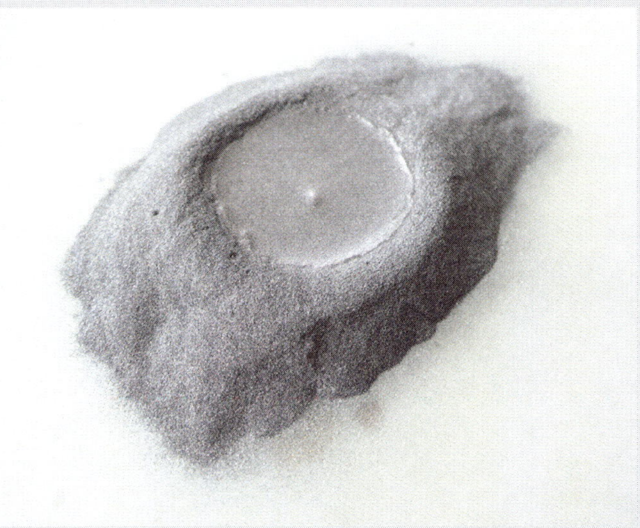

Make a well in the grit and add water.

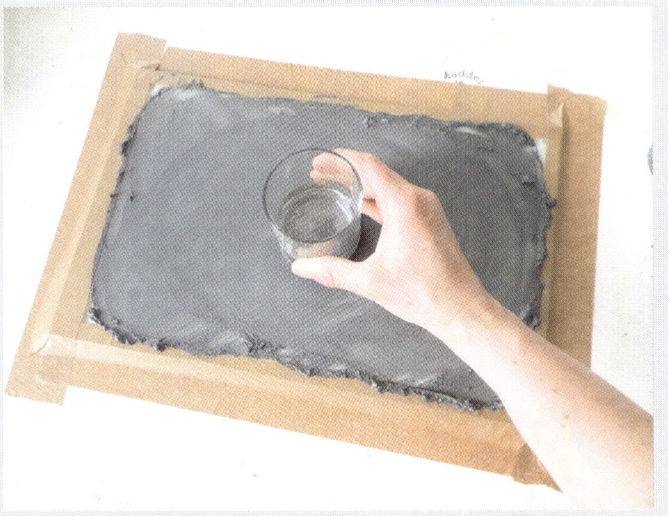

Grind the water and grit slurry with a muller or flat-bottomed glass.

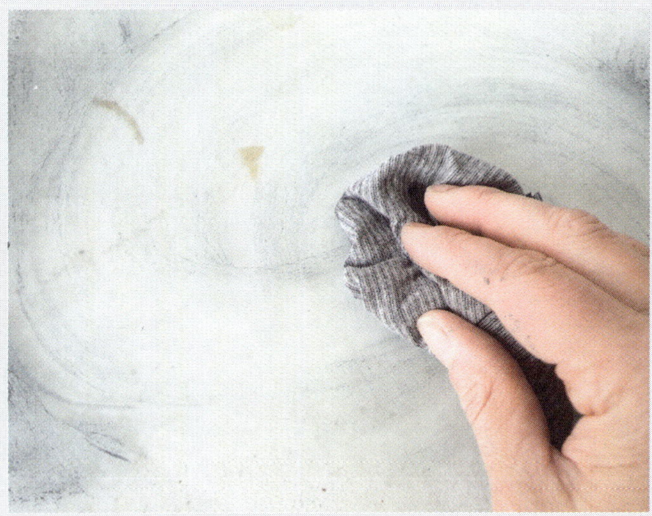

Occasionally wipe the glass slab to check on progress.

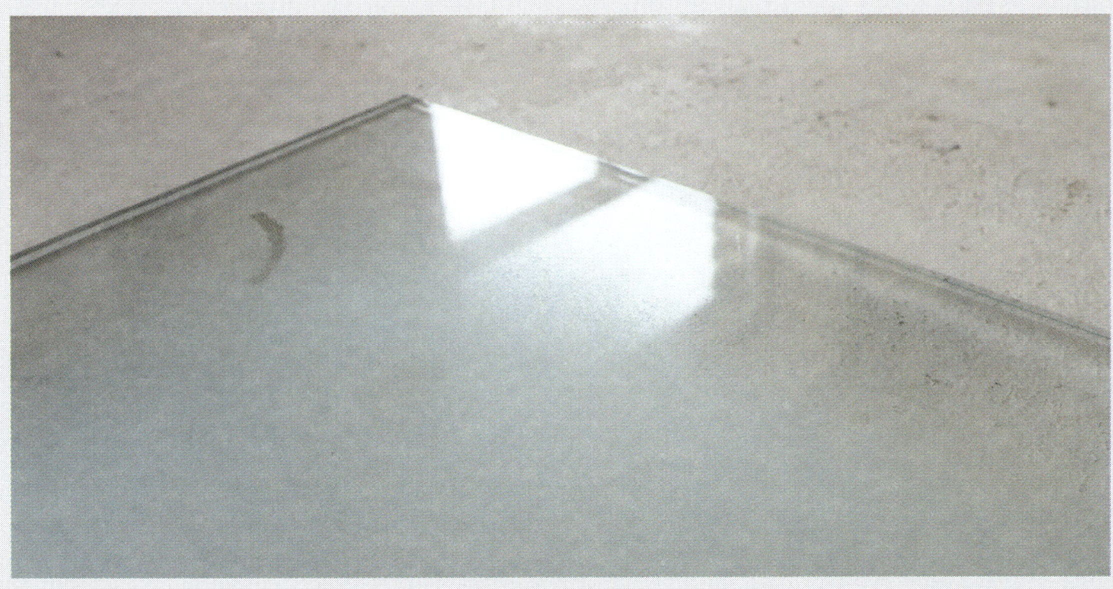

The toughened glass sheet after grinding.

Stencil Cutter Machine

A useful but not essential addition to a screenprinter's workshop, a stencil cutter such as a Cricut will quickly cut a design into paper for paper stencils, saving you the labour of cutting by hand. Good for more intricate designs or those that you might want to use again.

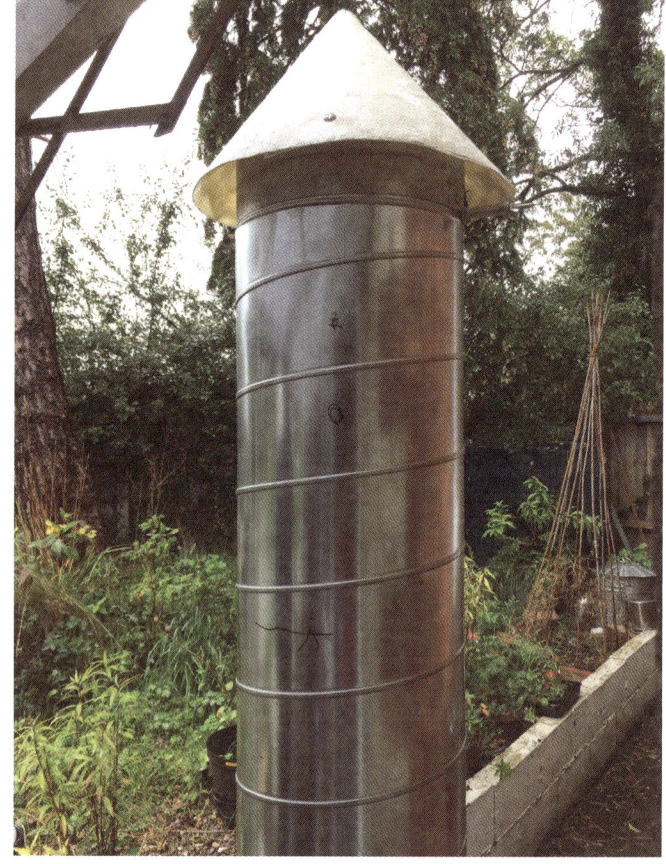

Steamer and/or Steaming Facilities

Invaluable for textile processes, a steamer helps to set the colour within the fabric. A small stove-top or electric steamer is fine for smaller projects, although larger textile pieces are impossible to steam effectively in these. Bullet steamers or steam cabinets are prohibitively expensive but have a look at how they are built and consider making one of your own from a random kit of parts. If you really don't have the facilities to steam fabric, I have run comparison tests by steam-ironing pieces and it works moderately well but be cautious – the application of direct heat onto an acid-based paste can damage the fibres. Using a steam iron, together with time to allow prints to cure, can be serviceable in place of large-scale steamers.

Electric Grinder

A coffee grinder is useful for making chopped-up plantstuffs even smaller. I use mine for grinding oak galls into powder. Not particularly useful for grinding lake pigments as coffee grinders are impossible to wash and previously ground pigment colour will contaminate any future pigment added.

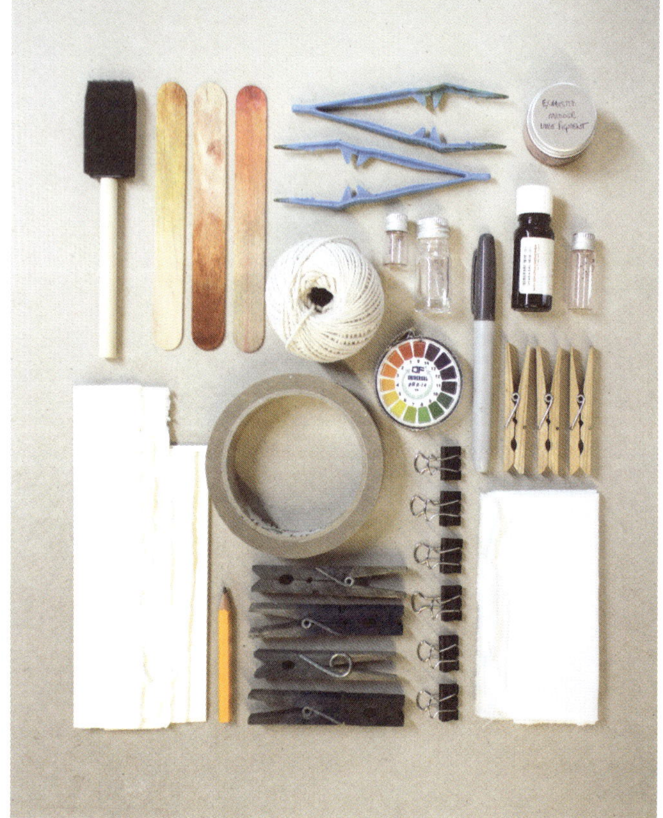

TOP
A homemade version of a bullet steamer.

RIGHT
Workshop consumables and useful random items include pH paper, pegs, bulldog clips, brown paper tape, empty jars and vials, essential oil, string, Sharpies, scrap paper and rags.

SCREENPRINTING

Screens

Screens come in lots of different sizes and differing qualities and can even be made from an old picture frame or embroidery hoop with tautly stretched fine gauze attached. However, small 12in × 16in aluminium screens are relatively inexpensive so buying one is a worthwhile expenditure. Screens use mesh with different thread counts, which affects the level of detail and the amount of ink that can pass through the screen. In the UK, the number of the mesh refers to how many threads (T) there are in each linear centimetre – the fewer threads there are, the bigger the gap between them will be. Screens with a mesh count of 43T or lower are generally used for printing onto textiles because cloth will usually take less fine detail and requires more ink whilst screens with a higher mesh count are generally used for printing onto paper, which has a more consistent texture. I like to use 77T screens as a good general purpose 'middle ground' screen, although I would recommend 43T mesh if printing solely on to cloth. I do also have screens with mesh sizes up to 120T, which are useful for exposed screens with a large amount of fine detail. However, the bigger mesh sizes (those with the lower numbers) allow bigger pigment particles to pass through the screen if printing with pigment-based pastes.

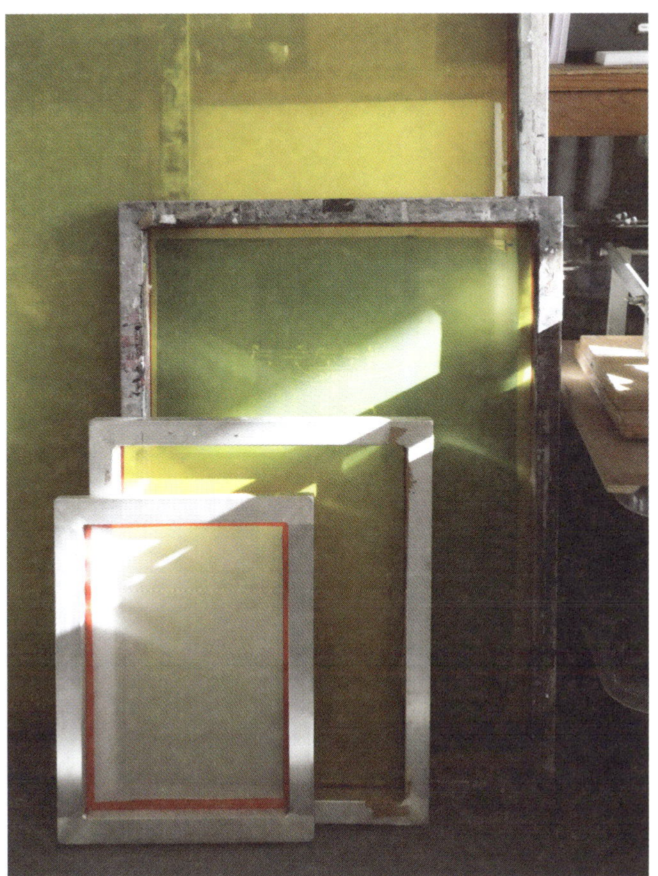

Screens of various sizes and meshes from 43T (for textiles) to 120T (for paper). US mesh sizes are different.

Squeegees

Use standard squeegees or buy some small vinyl applicators that have a rubber edge. These are useful for printing with little stencils and for small details, but they don't have the strength to manage larger areas. The applicators can be cut into smaller sections with a Stanley knife if required. Round-bladed squeegees are best for printing onto textiles as they force more of the paste through the screen, but square-bladed squeegees will work adequately and are much easier to source. Blades also come in different hardnesses or shores. To start with it is not necessary to buy one specifically for textiles.

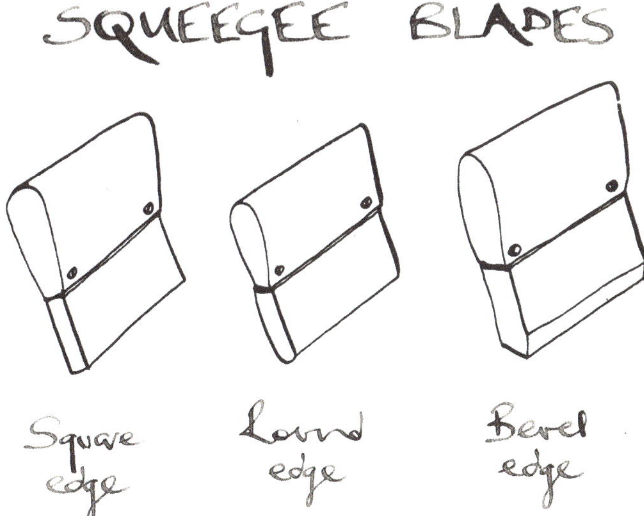

Squeegees can be fitted with different blade shapes including square edge, round edge and bevel edge. The most common is the square edge blade.

Hinge Clamps or Screen Bed (for screenprinting onto paper)

Hinge clamps are a low-cost, space-saving alternative to a screen bed. They can be attached to a piece of plywood or MDF, which can be moved as and when needed. Screenprinting onto paper without the use of a vacuum screen bed can either cause the paper to stick to the underneath of the screen or it can create a bloom on the printed colour as the screen mesh peels slowly away from the paper, especially if it is a large flat shape. To avoid this, make sure your screen has a good 'snap' on it by ensuring the mesh is not directly touching the print surface. I also use small tabs of card taped to the print surface to slot my paper under. This creates sufficient force to pull the paper away from the screen as it lifts.

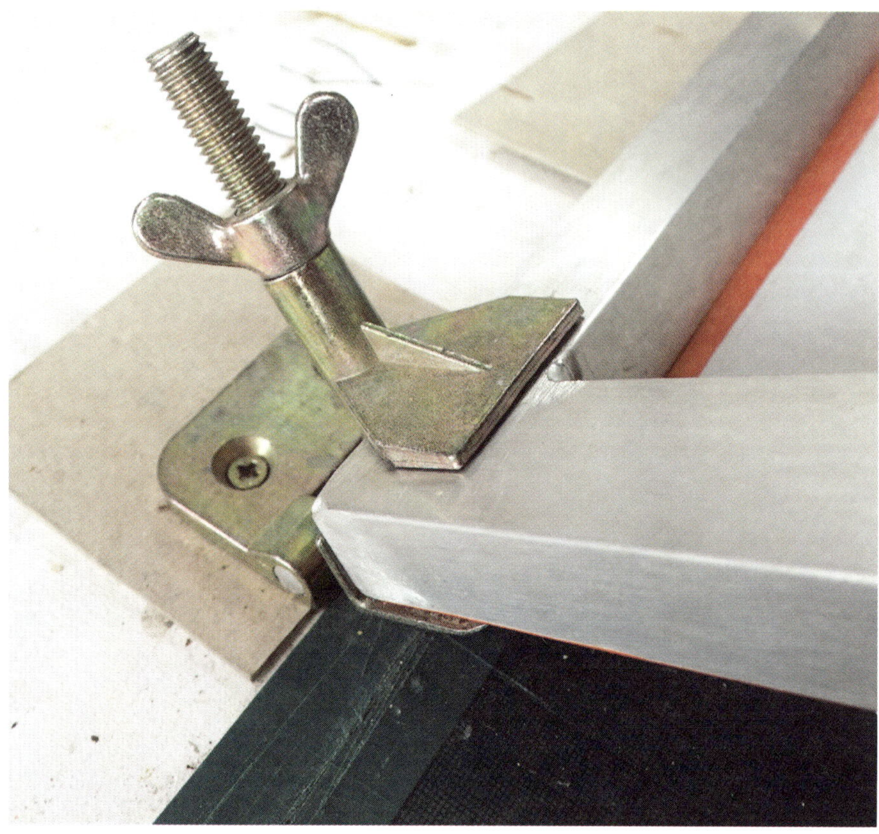

Hinge clamps can be used in place of a vacuum screen bed or table for screenprinting onto paper.

Make your own printing pad

YOU WILL NEED:

- A sheet of MDF or plywood
- Some thick foam (or an old yoga mat)
- Some smooth mid-weight calico
- A staple gun

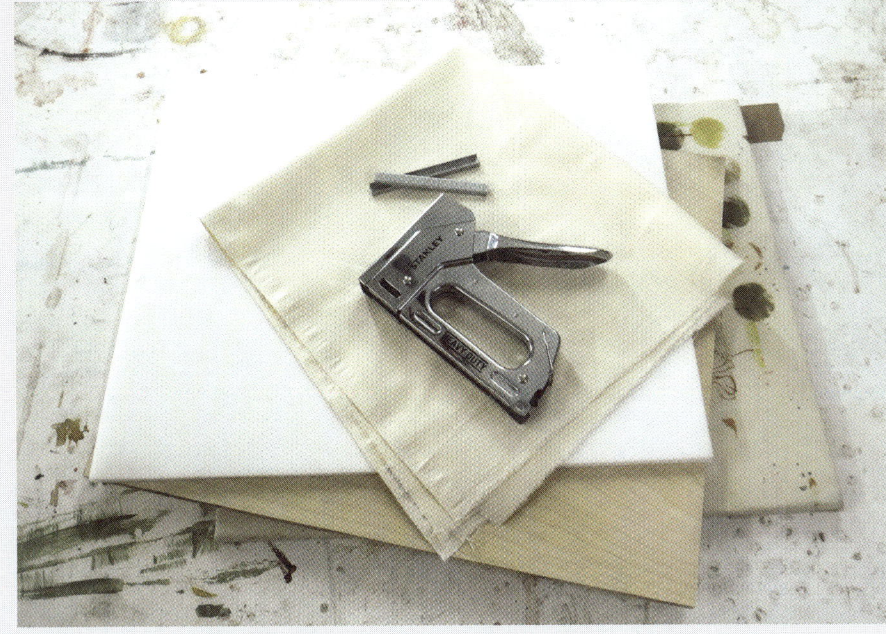

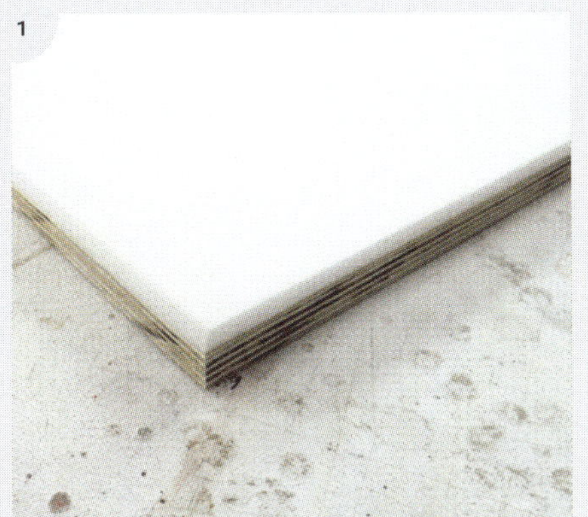

1

Cut the MDF and foam to the same size then stick the foam to the MDF.

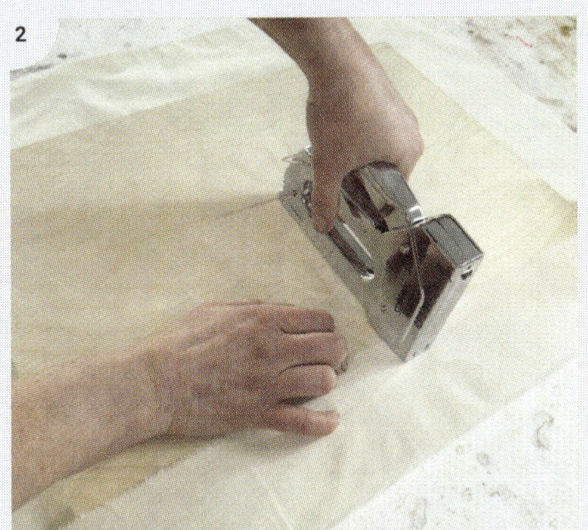

2

Cover the foam with the piece of calico and staple it tightly to the back.

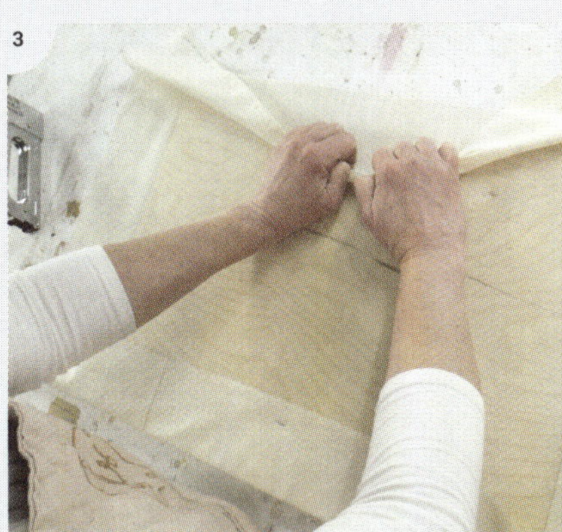

3

Ensure the fabric is pulled as tightly as possible for every staple.

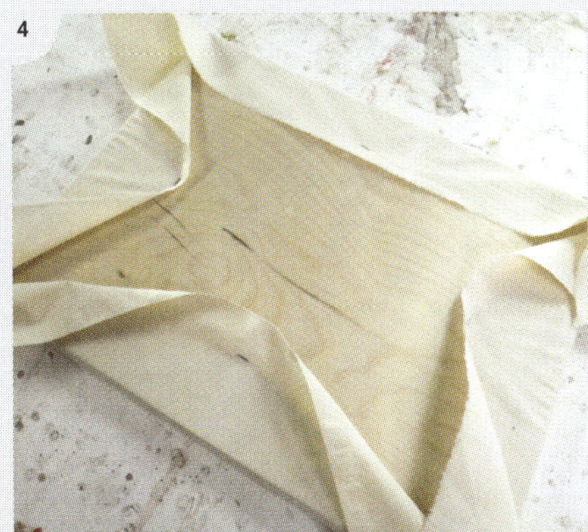

4

Start at the centre of each side then work towards the corners.

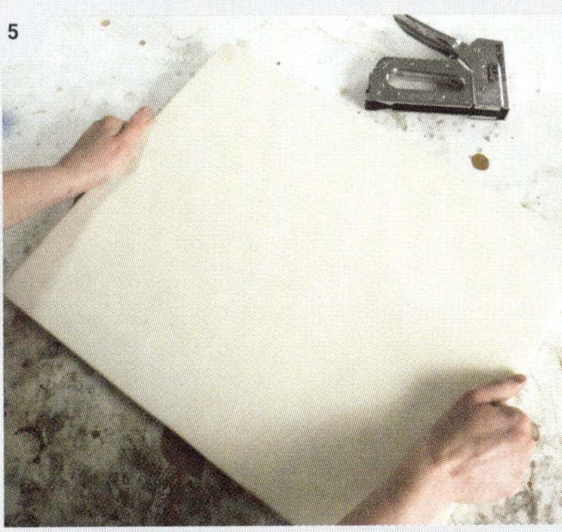

5

The completed printing pad – it won't stay this clean for long!

MAKING A PRINT PAD FOR TEXTILES

Make your own textile print pad using a sheet of MDF (12–18mm thick) cut at least 100mm bigger each side than the biggest screen you'll be using. Cut a sheet of EVA or Plastazote foam or similar (two layers of an untextured old yoga mat are ideal) to the same size and stick to the MDF with adhesive or similar. Cover this with a piece of calico or old cotton sheeting and staple it firmly to the back.

Printing Pads or Textile Print Table (for screenprinting and/or block printing onto textiles)

Printing onto fabric requires a certain amount of give in the support surface. This is achieved with the use of 'printing pads' or a textile print table, which is a long table designed specifically for printing onto textiles. The choice will probably be determined by the project – printing lengths of a repeating pattern will require a table to lay fabric onto, whereas smaller, one-off projects such as totes, T-shirts, patches or squares of fabric will fit on a small print pad. It is probably easiest to start off with a pad that is portable and can be put away when you are not using it.

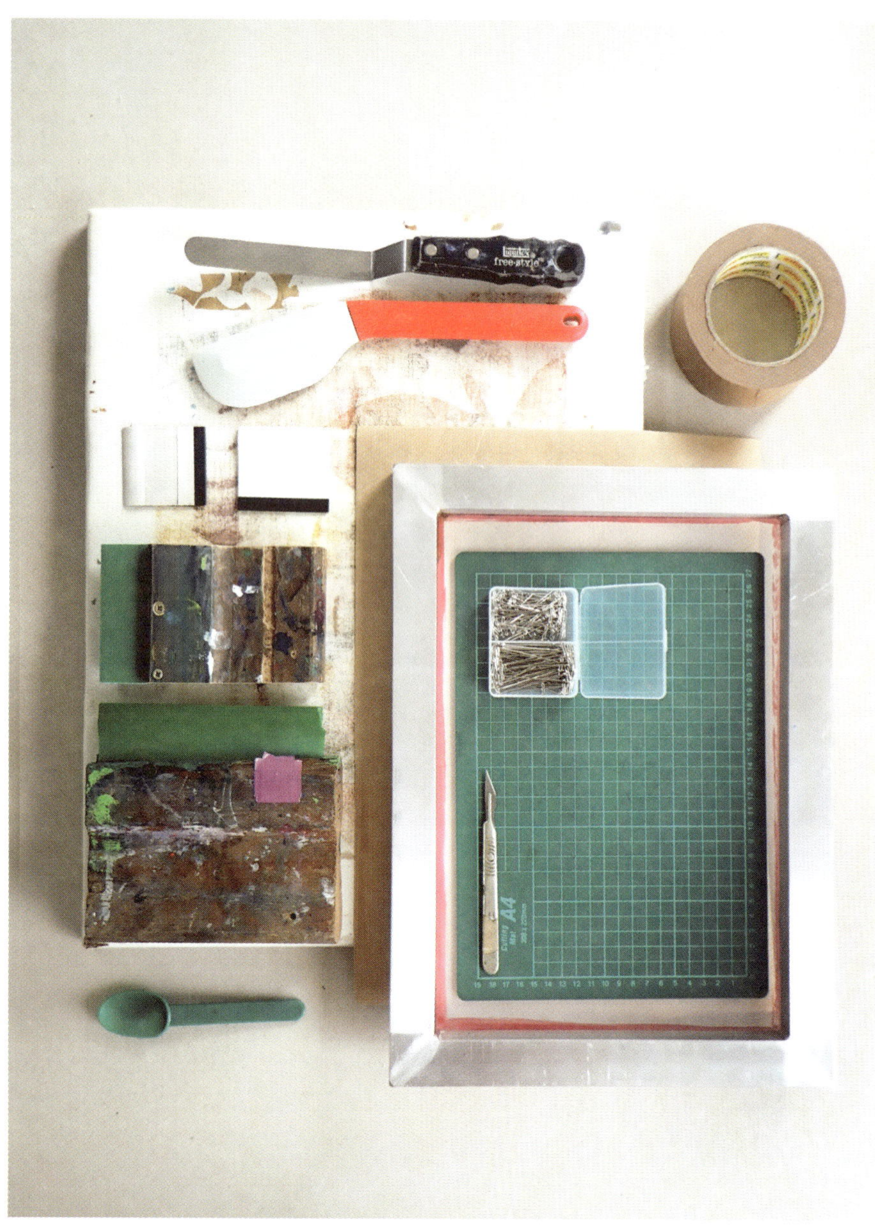

Other screenprinting-onto-textiles equipment and tools including spatulas, spoons, brown paper tape and T-pins.

INTAGLIO PROCESSES

Plates or Matrices

Plates for intaglio printmaking can be made from various materials, such as copper, zinc, other metals, acrylic sheets, plastics, shiny cardboard, Tetra Pak or juice cartons. Experienced printmakers will be practised in using specific plate materials but if new to intaglio techniques, the inside of a juice carton or some shiny thin cardboard is an ideal place to start for making plates using the simple drypoint method. Plates made from card won't be particularly long lasting but provide an ideal surface to try out the process with your own oil-based inks.

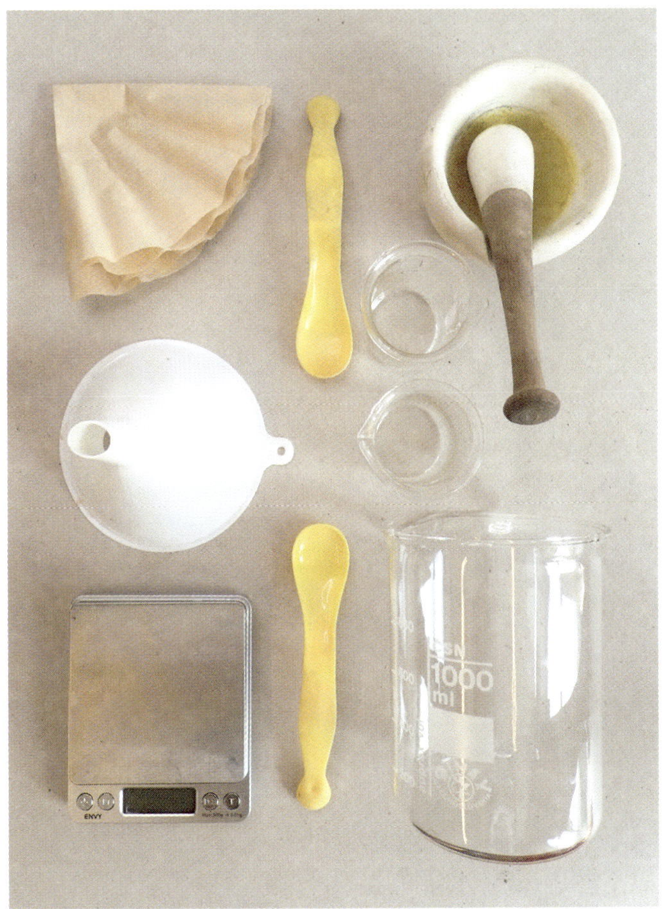

If you are going to make your own oil-based inks for relief and intaglio printmaking, at some point you will probably want to make a lake pigment. A simple kit for laking includes scales, a pestle and mortar, stirrers, a few beakers and some filter papers. A small saucepan (that is no longer used for food) is also useful.

Etching/Drypoint Needles

Drawing needles can be anything that will produce a scratch or a depressed line within your plate. Whilst specialist tools exist for different intaglio techniques, an inexpensive etching or drypoint needle can be purchased or something homemade will do the job. Avoid anything with an extra-sharp point, especially if planning to use cardboard as the plate. The role of the needle is to create a 'depression' within the plate, not to completely cut through the surface and create a hole. Experiment with different 'needles' such as a darning needle, a large blunt screw (stuck in a cork handle), an awl, or a 'pointy' tool of some sort from an old clay tool set.

Small Paint Knives/Straight Edge Spatulas

Useful for making and mixing oil-based inks, these are also good for manipulating and loosening ink before applying to the plate.

Intaglio Press

Printing an intaglio print without a press can be challenging but many people don't own intaglio presses, which can be large, expensive and require careful maintenance. Consider joining an open-access print workshop or look at the variety of press alternatives that people have tried. These range from a pasta maker, a home die-cut machine and a mangle – my first press was an adapted mangle. The Open Press Project have made presses much more accessible now with their tiny 3D-printed presses, which are easily transportable and affordable. It is also worth experimenting with different hand tools such as a metal spoon or a hand baren to see if an acceptable result can be achieved. Other useful intaglio printing stuff includes mountboard scraps, paper soaking tray, scrim, tissue, newsprint or scrap paper, blotting paper and weights for drying prints.

RELIEF PRINTING PROCESSES

Plates or Matrices

Plates for relief printmaking can be made from lino, lino substitutes, wood, plywood, self-adhesive foam or anything where negative space can be cut away from the design. Both the paper and the textile projects in this book use lino but experiment with some different options if you are not familiar with relief printing techniques. Lino substitutes may be easier to start with, especially if you do not own specialist cutting tools.

Cutting Tools

Cutting tools are a necessity if you wish to create detailed relief prints but the type and quality are often determined by the process or technique you plan to try. Inexpensive lino tools with interchangeable blades are okay for cutting softer lino substitutes and allow for experimentation, but are not particularly suitable for cutting harder materials such as wood. Remember that if you invest in more expensive tools, you'll also need to learn how to sharpen them. Simple relief plates for block printing can be made from self-adhesive foam attached to mountboard and don't require specialist cutting tools – this technique is used in Chapter 6 to demonstrate different block-printing patterns.

Rollers/Brayers

Different rollers exist for different printmaking processes from general-purpose budget rollers through to fine art rollers made for very specific print techniques. There are also sponge rollers available for textile printing methods. Try the entry-level products before investing in more expensive options. I find the softer rollers more to my liking, but this is specifically for nature printing.

Hand Baren

A hand baren is a tool that can be used for hand-printing and in place of a press. Many different types are available from simple plastic barens through to specialist ball-bearing barens. They were traditionally made of bamboo and braided cord. You can also make your own or use something like a metal or wooden spoon that is smooth, easy to hold and allows even pressure to be applied to the back of the print.

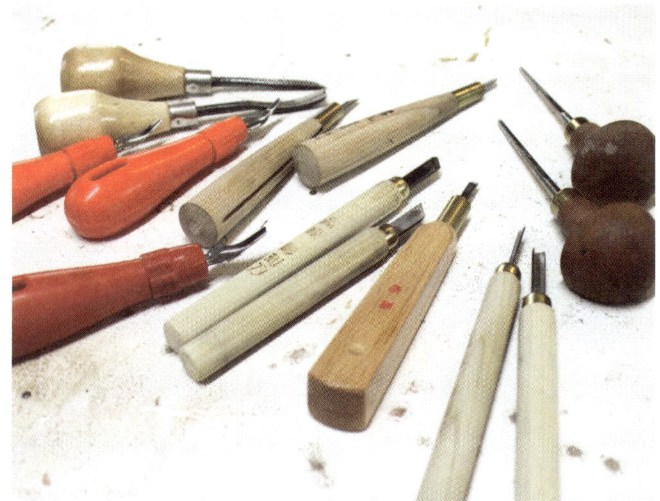

Cutting tools for creating relief plates.

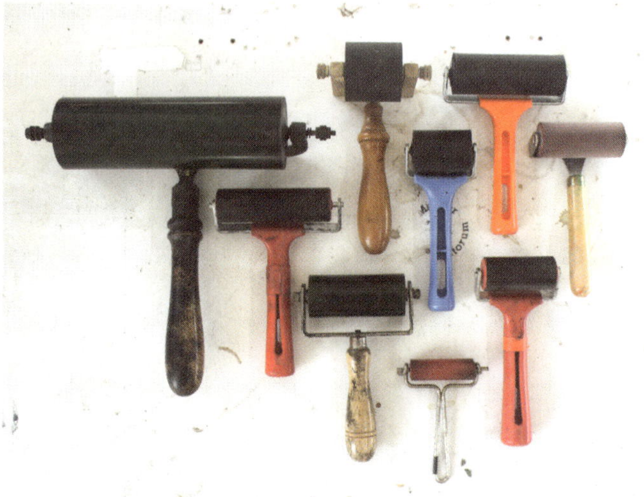

A variety of rollers and brayers are available. Experiment with the budget rollers before purchasing the more expensive makes. My favourites are the soft 'orange-handled' rollers for oil-based inks and the 'blue-handled' textile roller for fabrics.

SUBSTRATES

It is impossible to have tried and tested all the different papers and fabrics available with their varied weights, finishes, fibre types, sizing, weaves and colours, though I wish I could and that I had the time and the money to do so. However, there are a few things to be aware of when choosing a substrate (the thing you are going to be printing on) to work with, though nothing can beat trying it yourself before starting a big project.

Fabrics

When working with natural dyes and plant-based colour, it is recognised that the use of natural fibres for your textiles is preferable. This is because synthetic fibres are generally non-porous and can't absorb dye very easily, though some will take up natural dyes. I prefer to work with natural fibres primarily because of the environmental aspect but also because it feels right to be working with natural dyes and natural fibres in a symbiotic way. My experience with synthetic fibres is extremely limited – it may be worth referring to natural dye books and articles for a broader knowledge base, although there seems to be limited information available on the use of natural dyes on synthetic fibres.

It is a more complex process to print natural colour onto fabric rather than paper. This is dealt with more comprehensively in Chapter 5, but essentially this is because textiles usually need to be washfast, which is an unlikely requirement for work printed onto paper.

In all my tests and experiments, plant-based colour printed onto textiles performed better (became more washfast) when allowed to cure on the fabric. By curing, I mean leaving the fabric to air dry and hang exposed to the air for as long as possible. This should be at least 24 hours, although I would recommend a week or even better a month, if not longer. John Marshall, author of *Singing the Blues*, the well-known book about using indigo, cures his fabrics for at least three months.

Natural dyes will also need setting, and this should be done before the fabric is cured. Setting can be done in a number of ways with the most accepted successful method being to steam your fabric. You can also steam-iron your fabric, which isn't as effective as traditional steaming but does help and is a lot more accessible to most people. These techniques are described in Chapter 6.

WOOL

Wool is an expensive fabric to use for your textile printmaking projects, especially if you want to use the finely woven, lightweight versions. It can also be quite hard to find an undyed wool that suits your requirements. Second-hand white and light-coloured blankets are an option but keep in mind that they often have too rough a surface and lack the smooth texture needed for techniques such as screenprinting.

Wool is considered one of the best fibres to use with natural dyes because it takes the colour so well and is so receptive to the process. However, in my experience and when testing different fibres and textiles, I found it one of the hardest fabrics to produce a strong colour on when applying the colour locally. Steaming improves the colour and colour take-up but I've still achieved better results when using cellulose fibres. I suspect that fine-tuning the steaming method would improve the results.

Wool is considered a sustainable fibre as it is completely natural and fully biodegradable, though vegans usually prefer not to use it. Rising flock sizes and over-grazing are an issue, and the animals' welfare is an important consideration when using wool.

SILK

Silk is a beautiful fabric and fibre to work with although I have mixed feelings about using it. Silk is made from the cocoons of silk worms, most often from the domesticated *Bombyx mori* moth. The moth secretes a continuous filament to make the cocoon for the silk larvae and it is this that is used as the silk thread. The filaments are damaged by the larvae emerging from the cocoon, so they are killed either by heating or boiling the cocoons before this happens. Peace silk supposedly allows the moth larvae to emerge undamaged before the silk is used.

However, the smooth and lustrous surface lends itself beautifully to being printed on and the protein fibres take the dye extremely well. Silk can be an expensive fabric to use but I would recommend working with it or at least trying it, if you can accept the production methods used.

COTTON

Cotton (*Gossypium spp.*) is the fabric I use the most as it is an accessible, reasonably priced and ideal surface to print on. I use either second-hand textiles (such as tablecloths or duvet covers) or organic, unbleached and recycled cottons from specialist suppliers. Conventional cotton cultivation can be environmentally damaging requiring large amounts of water, chemical pest control and habitat loss so using a sustainable source is an important consideration. There is a huge amount of choice when using cotton but if the project doesn't depend on a certain type of material, choose a light- to mid-weight fabric with a smooth and tight weave (especially to start with), as this allows good detail and easy transfer of designs when printing.

LINEN

Linen is made from the flax plant (*Linum usitatissimum*) and is enjoying a resurgence in popularity, especially in the UK. Its environmental and sustainable capabilities make it a good choice for ecologically aware printmakers, although it can be an expensive product to purchase, especially if you limit yourself to responsibly grown linen.

However, if you can find a source of second-hand, vintage linens you are a lucky person. Because of their age, these linens are usually extremely good quality and have been washed many times meaning that they don't need much scouring and often take the dyes extremely well when compared to their newer counterparts. Linen production is a long and time-consuming process (hence its expense) but is much more sustainable than growing other cellulose fibres such as cotton and bamboo.

Other cellulose fibres such as ramie, hemp and bamboo should also be considered. Ramie (*Boehmeria nivea*) is made from a plant in the nettle family and the process of making it is very similar to how linen is produced. Ramie is considered a sustainable fabric, though not suitable for clothes due to its brittleness. Hemp is made from the *Cannabis sativa* plant, it grows quickly and doesn't require much water but is time-consuming to make and is relatively expensive compared to other cellulose fibres. Bamboo (*Phyllostachys spp.*) fabric covers a range of different types and how they are made determines their sustainability, so can be a complex choice for people interested in using the most sustainable textiles.

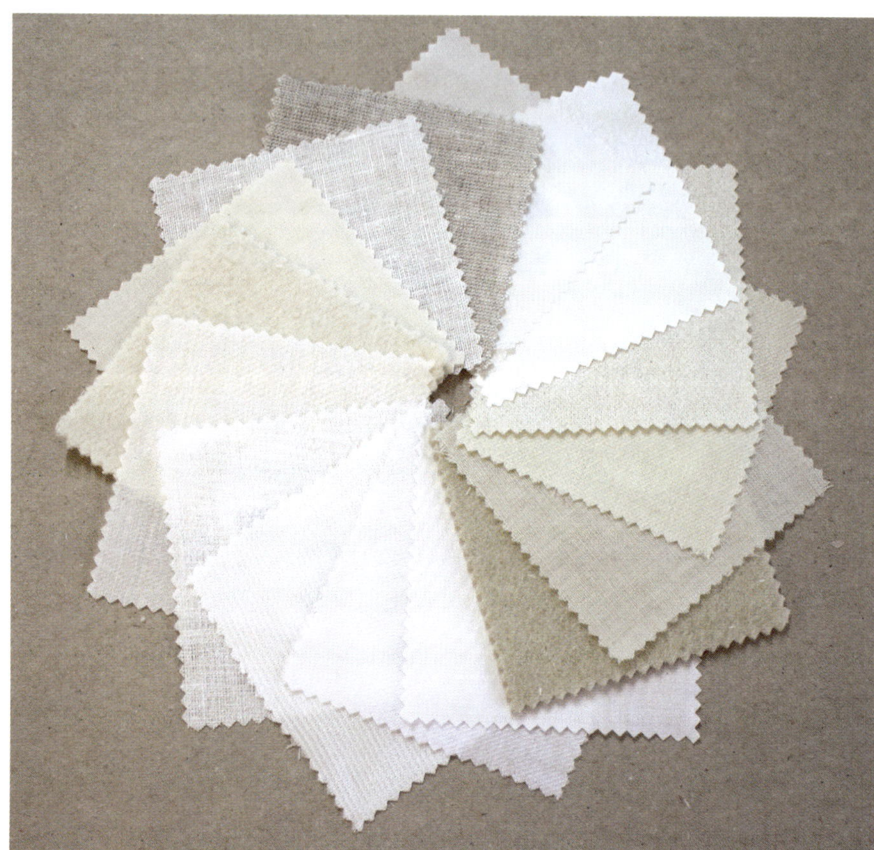

Fabrics: a seemingly endless variety of protein and cellulose fabrics are available. Find second-hand fabrics or source recycled, organic or sustainable fabrics from suppliers.

Papers

There are lots of different papers made specifically for different printmaking techniques and processes, although often a general printmaking paper or good-quality paper will suffice. Paper should be chosen to suit each particular project, the budget and the printmaking process.

There are extra considerations to be made when working with plant-based colour. These include:

PAPER PH

Most good-quality papers will have a neutral pH and be acid free. Paper manufacturers should either list this on their websites or be able to provide this information on request. Whilst a neutral pH isn't an absolute must for printmaking with plant-based colour, it is important to know the pH value of the paper. This is because many natural dyes are pH sensitive, so the pH of a paper can affect the final colour of the dye applied.

Both papers were immersion-dyed in a madder dye for the same amount of time but the redder paper at the back contains a calcium carbonate buffer and has a pH of 7–9. This has affected the final colour of the paper.

BUFFERS

Buffers are often added to papers to counter the effect of acids absorbed from the air. Acids can attack the paper and cause foxing, therefore the addition of a buffer, most often in the form of calcium carbonate, helps to prevent or at least slow this down. Calcium carbonate is mildly alkaline so can also affect the final colour of a natural dye once applied to the paper.

SIZING

Sizing is either applied during the making process to the pulp (called internal sizing), to the surface of the paper (called surface or tub sizing) or both. It is used to affect the absorption and spread of liquids applied to the surface of the paper. Heavily sized papers (also called hard-sized) will cause paints and water to bead on the surface with little spread, whilst papers with no sizing will readily absorb water which will spread outwards from where it was applied.

Most printmaking papers have little or no sizing especially on the surface, which allows ink to penetrate the paper more efficiently. For screenprinting with plant-based colour and plant-based mediums, sizing might be advantageous in that it allows less ink and water to be absorbed, reducing cockling. *See also* 'Heavyweight Papers'. For relief printing with thickened water-based inks, especially when printing finer lines and detail, this may not be an advantage as heavily sized paper may 'reject' the ink.

HEAVYWEIGHT PAPERS

Plant-based colour and mediums for screenprinting are often much 'wetter' than their synthetic counterparts. Remember that the paste you are using has no plastic content, it is purely water, starch, a little alum and colourant so will be absorbed into the paper much more readily. This can make the paper cockle more easily than you are used to. Use a heavyweight paper if the project allows. I use Saunders Waterford Hot Pressed 638gsm watercolour paper, which withstands the application of many layers of colour.

SURFACE TEXTURE

Surface texture will impact the final look of a print, though this doesn't particularly affect plant-based colour differently to synthetic colour. However, plant-based colour can be rather transparent and the rougher texture of some papers can be emphasised by the print, particularly in screenprinting where large areas of flat colour are often applied to the paper. This may be something you wish to exploit or to avoid.

Rhubarb root paste screenprinted onto hot pressed (HP) paper.

Rhubarb root paste screenprinted onto rough paper.

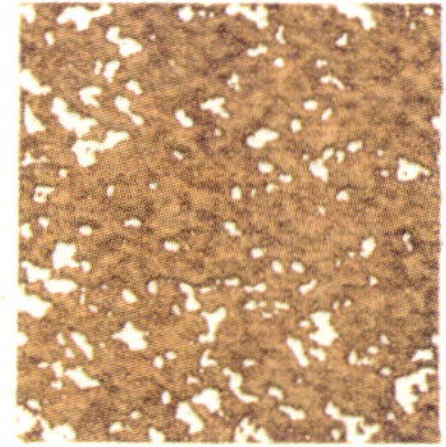

Rhubarb root paste screenprinted onto thick handmade paper.

HANDMADE PAPERS

I've also found handmade paper to be more forgiving for screenprinting. Handmade paper doesn't have a grain direction and though it will stretch, it does this evenly and has minimal cockling that also seems to reduce on drying. Khadi paper copes really well with getting wet and also receives the plant-based colour effectively. As it is made from recycled T-shirt off-cuts, it has a good environmental ethos with the company supporting their staff and workers in India where Khadi paper is made.

Washi is also a useful paper to experiment with, though be aware that some washi doesn't contain any sizing which can lead to bleeding and spread of colour. Washi is used for mokuhanga or Japanese woodblock printing where the whole sheet of paper is dampened. It has a very high wet strength but in my experience the paper doesn't particularly cope well with getting unevenly wet, where only some parts are dampened by applying heavy layers of water-based colour, such as in screenprinting. It is beautiful paper though and unbeatable for certain applications.

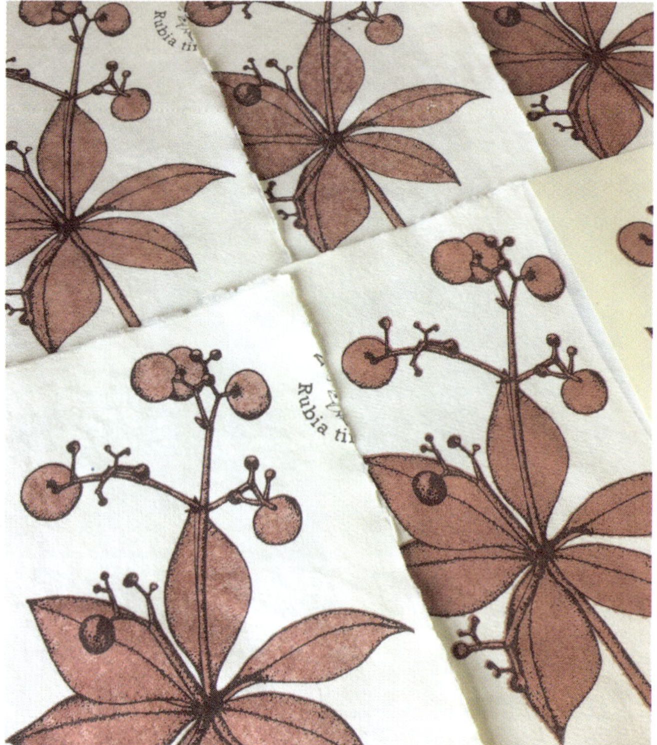

Madder screen print tests on handmade paper.

MORDANTS, TANNINS AND ASSISTS

Natural dyes and plant-based paints, inks and pigments are not inert colours. They will respond, adapt and modify their behaviours, which include colour changes, with the addition of different chemicals, substances and compounds.

Anyone who has tried natural dyeing will know of mordants, though they are often thought of as a tricky and complex area of the craft. This is likely due to the many options and variables available – there isn't one set answer and it is often recommended that you experiment to find the solution that suits you the best. Mordants are metallic salts that have an affinity with both the fibre and the natural dye, which allows a chemical bond to be created between the two. By applying a mordant to your fabric or your paper, you are creating an environment where the dye can attach more readily to your substrate.

Mordants are of prime importance when using natural dyes on fabric, although it is also worthwhile to use them on paper as they are considered helpful in improving lightfastness and they will improve colour uptake. They can also be added to your inks, paints and pastes, but remember that different mordants will affect the colour and how your solutions react to other additions or assists.

Tannins are naturally occurring substances found within many plants, although the ones most regularly used with natural dyes in the UK are oak galls and stag's horn sumac (*Rhus typhina*) leaves. This is because they are considered clear tannins and leave little colour on fibres, allowing the natural dye to be unaffected by the colour of the tannin. However, when tannins and iron are mixed, a strong reaction takes place that creates dark colours and blacks. Tannins also occur in brambles, alder cones and many tree barks.

Assists are so called because they are used in a supporting role or as a helper to the natural plant-based colour. These include chalk, soda ash and vinegar. Within the natural dyeing field some of these are often referred to as modifiers as they are most often used to change the tone of a natural dye. Iron is considered both a mordant and a modifier.

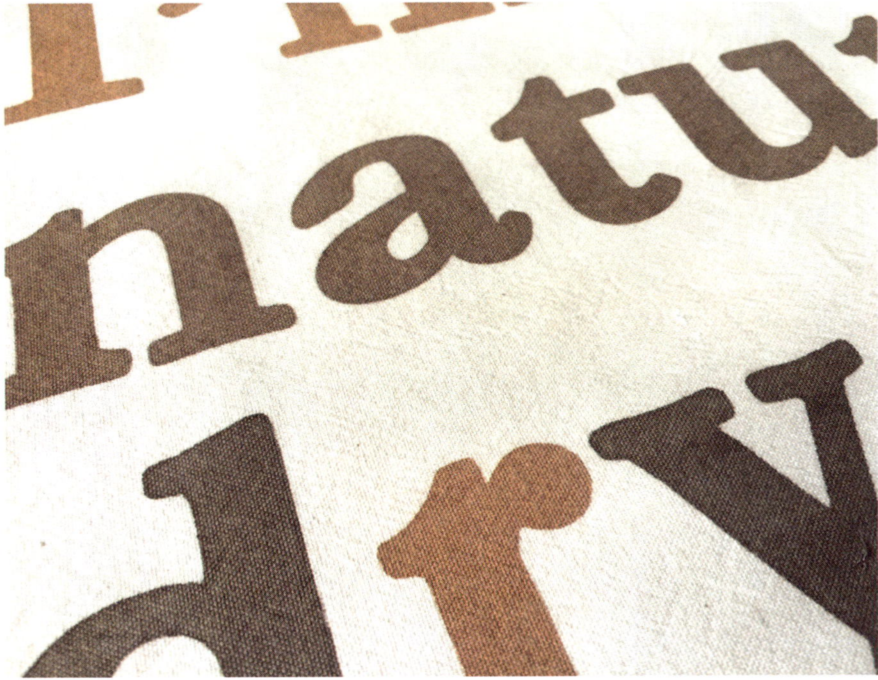

This mordant-printed fabric demonstrates the difference mordants can make to a dye and how much more of the colourant attaches to the fibres. The orange was printed with alum and the browns were printed with iron or an iron/alum mix before dyeing the whole piece with buckthorn bark.

Mordants

There are several aluminium mordants available to use, although the most common or perhaps the most well-known is potassium aluminium sulphate. In printmaking techniques mordants may be added to inks and paints, be applied pre- and post-printing on papers and fabrics or be added to pigments. Lake pigments are generally made with an aluminium-based mordant so it is considered unnecessary to add any more when using them to print with. Some dyes such as indigo don't require mordants, though for most natural dyes, mordants are considered a necessary addition.

It is normal to abbreviate the word aluminium to 'Al' but in this book it is shortened to alum, as natural dyers are familiar with this word. It was traditionally used to refer to potassium aluminium sulphate but is now frequently used more generally. In this book, where a specific alum is required, the term will also contain the second identifier, so alum acetate or alum sulphate. North American readers may be more used to the American English spelling of 'aluminum' rather than aluminium.

POTASSIUM ALUMINIUM SULPHATE $KAl(SO_4)_2$

Often referred to simply as alum, potassium aluminium sulphate is the most frequently used mordant in natural dyeing. It is usually supplied as a white granular powder that can easily be diluted in warm water. It is relatively non-toxic and is used widely in different industries including in food production, as a water purifier and as a flame retardant.

ALUMINIUM SULPHATE $Al_2(SO_4)_3$

Aluminium sulphate has a slightly different chemical make-up from potassium alum sulphate, though I have found them to be equally effective as a mordant. Alum sulphate has the one big advantage of usually being much cheaper. Always ensure alum sulphate is labelled iron-free before using it, as any iron present will affect the final colour of the dye. Alum sulphate can be used interchangeably with potassium alum sulphate, though the former is stronger – some recipes recommend a reduction in alum sulphate to allow for this.

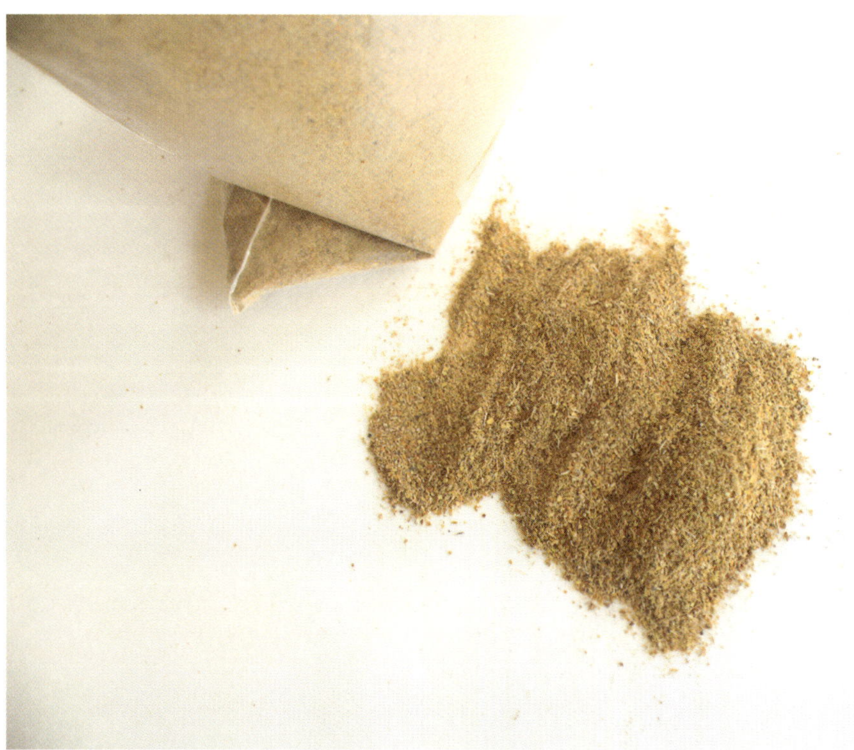

The symplocos (for example *Symplocos racemosa, Symplocos cochinchinensis*) plant is a bio-accumulator that absorbs aluminium from the ground. Its leaves can be used in place of a mordant.

Within natural dyeing, both potassium alum sulphate and alum sulphate are primarily used for mordanting protein fibres such as wool and silk, although when used in combination with tannin as a pre-mordant, they have also been used for mordanting cellulose fibres. Potassium alum sulphate is not used at all within this book as alum sulphate has been used. However, please just substitute one for the other rather than purchasing a new product.

ALUMINIUM ACETATE $Al(CH_3CO_2)_3$

Aluminium acetate is primarily used for mordanting cellulose yarns and fabrics as it has a greater affinity for the fibres than either potassium alum sulphate or alum sulphate. You can omit the tannin stage when mordanting with alum acetate, though in immersion dyeing I never get as good results compared to using tannin first either with potassium alum sulphate, alum sulphate or alum acetate. There are several forms of alum acetate – the formula above refers to aluminium triacetate but specific forms don't seem to be defined by suppliers when purchasing for use with plant-based colour.

Alum acetate, potassium alum sulphate and alum sulphate can be used within printing pastes for both fabric and paper to increase lightfastness, colourfastness and washfastness. Alum acetate is often used in mordant printing pastes, though I prefer to make an alum sulphate and sodium acetate mix for this process.

Other aluminium-based mordants include aluminium lactate and aluminium triformate, though I have little current experience with either, other than some brief immersion dyeing tests with alum lactate.

SYMPLOCOS (*SYMPLOCOS RACEMOSA, SYMPLOCOS COCHINCHINENSIS*)

Symplocos is not strictly a mordant, but the plant is a bio-accumulator and absorbs aluminium from the ground. The leaves contain aluminium and can therefore be harvested and used in place of a mordant. Artists who wish to keep their practice purely plant-based and eliminate any other substances are thus attracted to the use of symplocos. It grows in tropical climates and can be harvested without damaging the tree.

OTHER MORDANTS

Other mordants are available though they have generally fallen out of favour for contemporary use due to their toxicity. These include tin, chrome and, something I only use infrequently, copper. I do use iron within my work and you will see it appear regularly in the recipes throughout this book, though I tend not to use it as a mordant but as a colour modifier. Iron darkens natural colour, often called saddening, and is a useful addition to extend a colour range. When used in this way, it will still act as a mordant, it is just the order of application that differs slightly. As mentioned, I also use copper but only for creating samples to modify the colour post-dyeing. Weld is the only natural dye I might modify with copper as it produces the most glorious lime greens.

Iron can be purchased as ferrous sulphate, a light greeny-turquoise and granular powder. I use ferrous sulphate for convenience and when teaching, but homemade iron water is just as effective. Iron water can be made by immersing some rusty iron in water (or water and vinegar) for a number of weeks. The amount of iron present in your own iron water can be hard to determine but if using it as a modifier, just add gradually until you achieve the colour you desire.

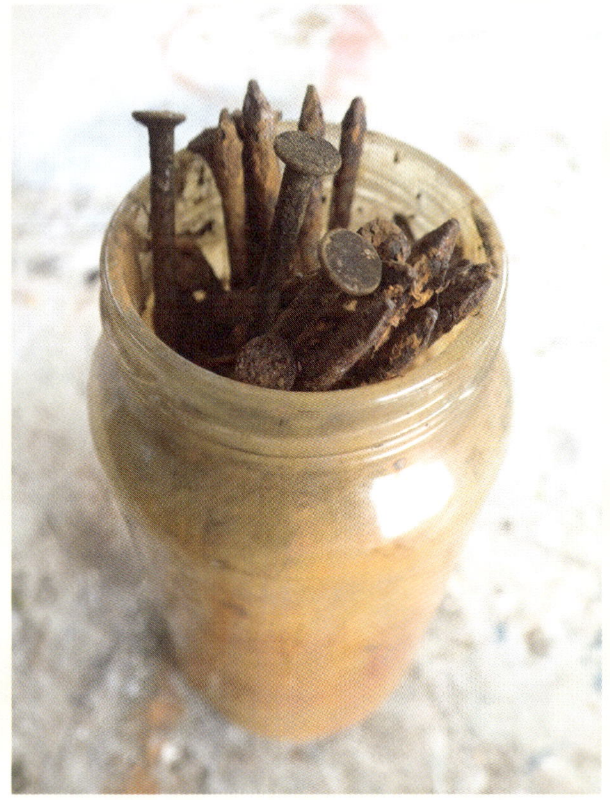

Rusty iron in water or a vinegar/water solution can be used in place of ferrous sulphate as a mordant and a modifier.

Tannins

Tannins are found within many trees and plants, often in the bark and leaves of trees but also in perennial and biennial plants. It is the compound found in black tea or red wine that can pucker and dry your mouth. Tannin helps aluminium salt to bond to cellulose fibres, which on its own does not bond particularly well to cottons, linens and other plant fibres.

The science behind tannins is extremely complex and has only relatively recently been studied in-depth for specific natural dye use. However, their usefulness when using plant-based colour is unquestionable, especially to improve the effectiveness of alum when dyeing cellulose fibres both in yarn and fabric form. There is also evidence that tannin application improves the lightfastness of dyes. For printmaking with plant-based colour, it can be a useful aid to producing blacks and greys when used in combination with iron.

Good sources of tannin include oak (*Quercus spp.*) galls, sumac (*Rhus spp.*) leaves and brambles (*Rubus fruticosus*). Other sources of tannin are available, such as cutch (*Acacia catechu*), but the use of some may result in a colour change before dyeing.

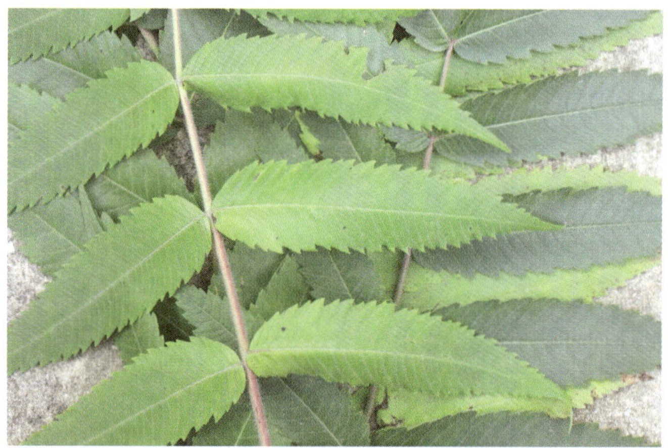

Staghorn sumac (*Rhus typhina*) leaves are a useful source of tannin.

Assists, Additives and Modifiers

Assists and modifiers are a group of chemicals and solutions defined by opinion, use and application. The ones mentioned below all have particular uses within printmaking processes; others that are often used exclusively for natural dyeing techniques have been omitted.

CHALK (CALCIUM CARBONATE)

Calcium carbonate, also known as chalk or whiting, is used within the mordant printing process and can be used as an ingredient in place of, or as well as, soda ash when making lake pigments. In natural dyeing it is most often used in soft water to brighten reds by raising the pH slightly.

IRON (FERROUS SULPHATE)

Use ferrous sulphate or make your own iron water using rusty iron. Iron is considered both a mordant and a modifier. Its presence will cause dye molecules to form a complex and to chemically bond with dye fibres, but it will also alter the colour. Useful in printmaking for creating blacks on tannin-dyed textiles, used extensively in mordant printing for creating darker colours and tones within a dye pot, it can also be used to alter colour in lake pigments and within water-based inks. Oak gall and iron is a classic combination and has been used throughout history as writing ink. Caution should be exercised when using iron as it can easily migrate to other surfaces, tools and equipment, creating black spots and smudges on work. It can also damage fibres and tools so as little as possible should be used, with only tiny increments being added at a time.

SODA ASH (SODIUM CARBONATE)

Sodium carbonate, also more commonly referred to as soda ash, is a highly alkaline compound that is used in lake pigment making to modify plant-based colour by changing the pH and as a scourer for cellulose fibres. Washing soda is a slightly weaker form of the same compound but is often more readily available if shopping locally.

VINEGAR

Used weak as a neutraliser for items that have been immersed in solutions with high alkalinity and also as a colour modifier. Clear vinegar is used in printmaking pastes for textiles as an anti-precipitant – a low pH helps prevent dye particles bonding to alum and then becoming an insoluble lake in print paste solutions. Check vinegar is a 5 per cent acetic acid solution and reduce amount used if the percentage is higher.

WHEAT BRAN

Used in the mordant printing process to help break down the gum of the thickened print paste. It is used in combination with calcium carbonate, which helps to neutralise the acids in the mordant paste.

RECORDING IDEAS, RESEARCH AND EXPERIMENTATION

Considered by many to be the most tedious part of working with natural colour, it is however vital to record and take notes of your processes and recipes. As a perfectionist, it can be hard to work with a messy 'working' journal. A book or something that is similar to an artist's sketchbook is something I have never successfully persevered with until I worked out a way around the 'messiness'. Initially, I separated out my daily dye notes and experiments from the 'official' records and sample cards I use as a reference and for front-facing work that is shown on social media, on my website and in workshops. This way, I could have a notebook full of thoughts and observations and random words but also have something separate to show others. In actual fact, the messy journal has now become something I often use as an example of what recording your research might look like.

BELOW
Keep a journal to record ideas, thoughts, notes, recipes, experiments and failures.

BOTTOM
Recipe book with reference numbers which allows for detailed notes that wouldn't fit on a label or lid of a small jar.

Different Methods of Documentation

There are various ways to track what you have done – the trick is to find what suits the individual. If you are unsure what works for you, try everything and see what sticks.

STUDIO JOURNAL
Informal notes, thoughts, scribbles, drawings, sketches, stuck-in experiments, collected items, pictures from magazines, used tapes and filter papers. My A4 journal is a treasure-trove of scribbled recipes, thoughts and notes, which I constantly refer back to and is an invaluable source of information.

RECIPE BOOK
A small notebook to record lake pigment recipes, ink recipes and methods, paint and ink mixes or colours. This can be useful as it can be impractical to record recipes on an ink label or a half pan of watercolour. Give each recipe or item a reference number that can easily be written on the jar or bottle and then correlate that to the same reference number in the book. Because I make so many lake pigments, I keep a separate book for the pigment recipes and give them a reference number that refers to date, dye source and how many were made that day. For example, 0103RTc refers to 1 March (0103), followed by *Rubia tinctorum* (RT) and it was the third (c) *Rubia tinctorum* lake pigment I had made that day. The year isn't required here as this is recorded individually.

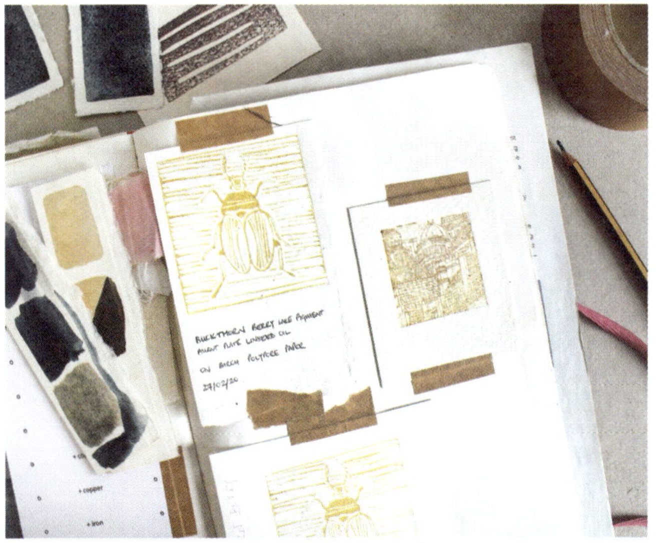

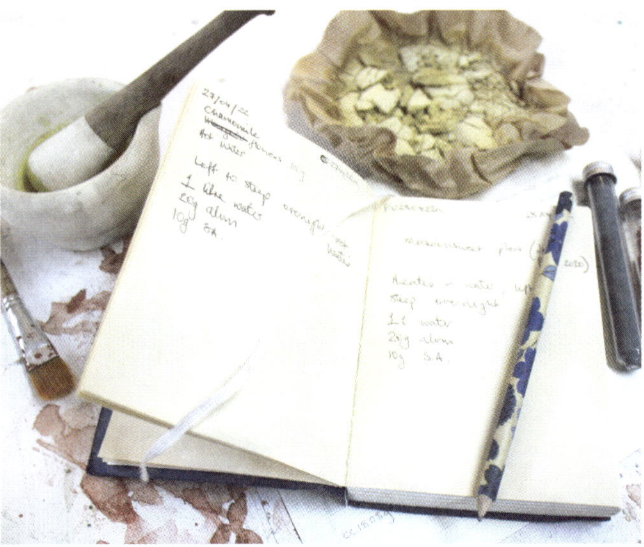

IMAGES (DIGITAL AND/OR PHYSICAL COPIES)

Take pictures of processes, plants used, locations, exact stages of approach. Whilst I don't habitually take pictures, social media has forced me to become better at it and in doing so, I have created a useful library of images.

SAMPLE CARDS

It can be useful to keep a book, individual cards or swatches with reference colours on. I recommend individual cards or elements as these allow colours to be swapped around, compared, taken out, referred to and lent to others without having to use your whole collection. As your library of natural colour swatches grows, it will become cumbersome to carry everything around. Having individual elements negates this. You may not want to make your library public and accessible online but I refer to mine regularly when I can't access the real thing and it has been incredibly useful to be able to do this on occasion. My library of natural colour has become an artwork in its own right – it contains A5 sample cards of dyed textiles, dyed papers, screenprinted colour on textiles, screenprinted colour on paper, water-based inks, oil-based inks – there are well over a thousand samples of plant-based colour in the collection.

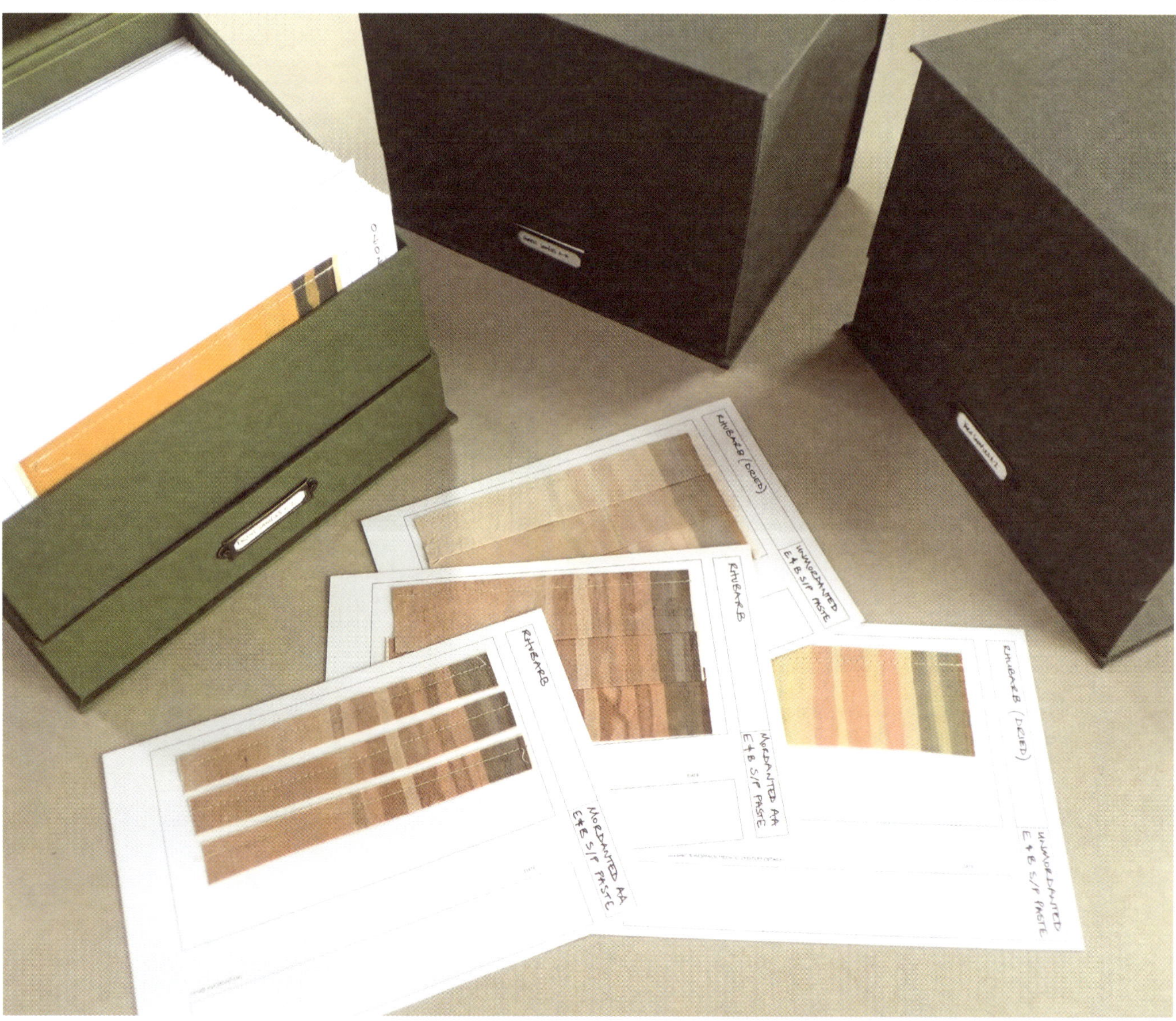

Clamshell boxes containing A5 sample cards. I have sets for screenprinted textile samples, dyed fabrics, dyed papers, mordant-printed colours, inks and individual commissions.

UNIDENTIFIED SWATCHES, DYES AND PIGMENTS

I can guarantee you will end up with pots of random liquids, printed colours, painted swatches and other unidentifiable items. Don't throw them away, they're still a record of what you have made and can still be used.

Information to Include

Dye plant details – include location, date and time picked, photograph of plant, parts used, weight when picked, weight when used, age of plant (if known), habitat, soil type. In reality, I record few of these points but they are all things I wished I had recorded at one point or another.

Bought dye supplies – supplier, weight, cost.

Weight of ingredients, methods, temperature, any observations whilst making.

Research and Experimentation

Approaching the use of plant-based colour within printmaking should not be considered a practice or an activity with a specific set of rules. It should be approached with an adventurer's spirit but with a healthy dose of science lurking in the background. Because many of the methods and processes used have either been superseded by synthetic materials or become irrelevant (due to toxic ingredients and recipes), I consider the use of plant-based colour in printmaking as an experimental activity. Try anything and everything – what works for me may not work for you and there is nothing wrong with questioning or disagreeing with my opinion if you have found a better method for your practice.

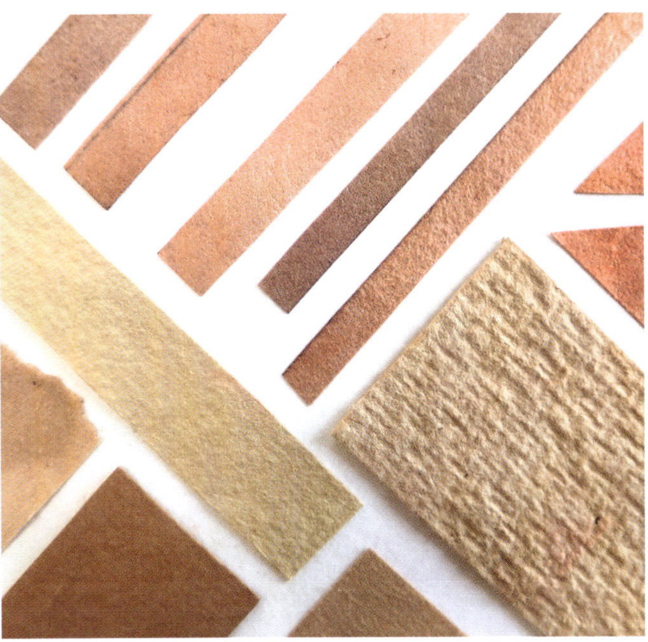

Offcuts are two handmade books containing unidentified papers and fabrics organised by colour. This is a page (detail) from *Offcuts (Paper)*.

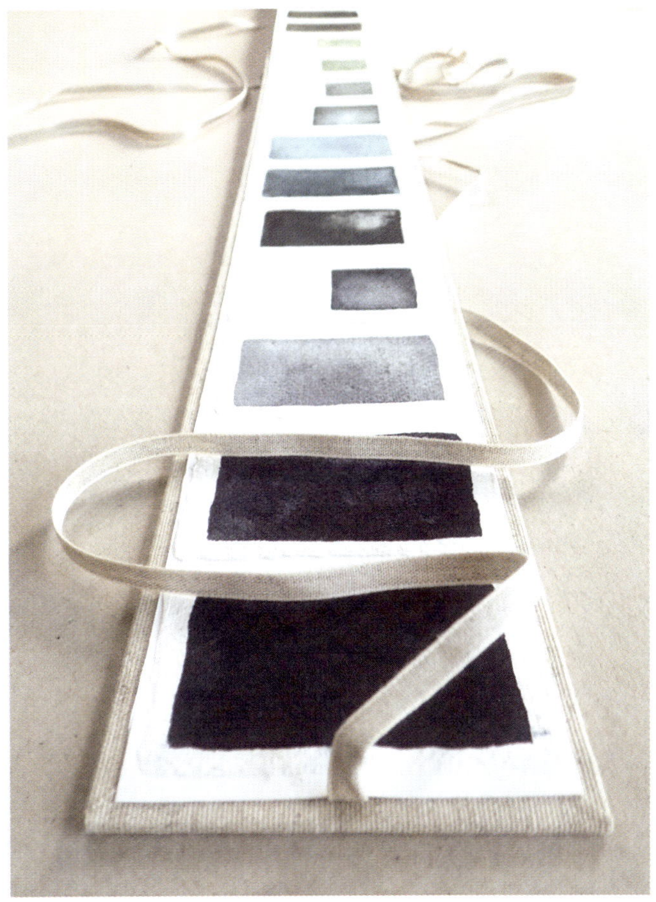

The Awkward Book Of Swatches is a concertina book of hand-painted swatches of plant-based colour, so-called because it is the most awkward-shaped book I have ever made.

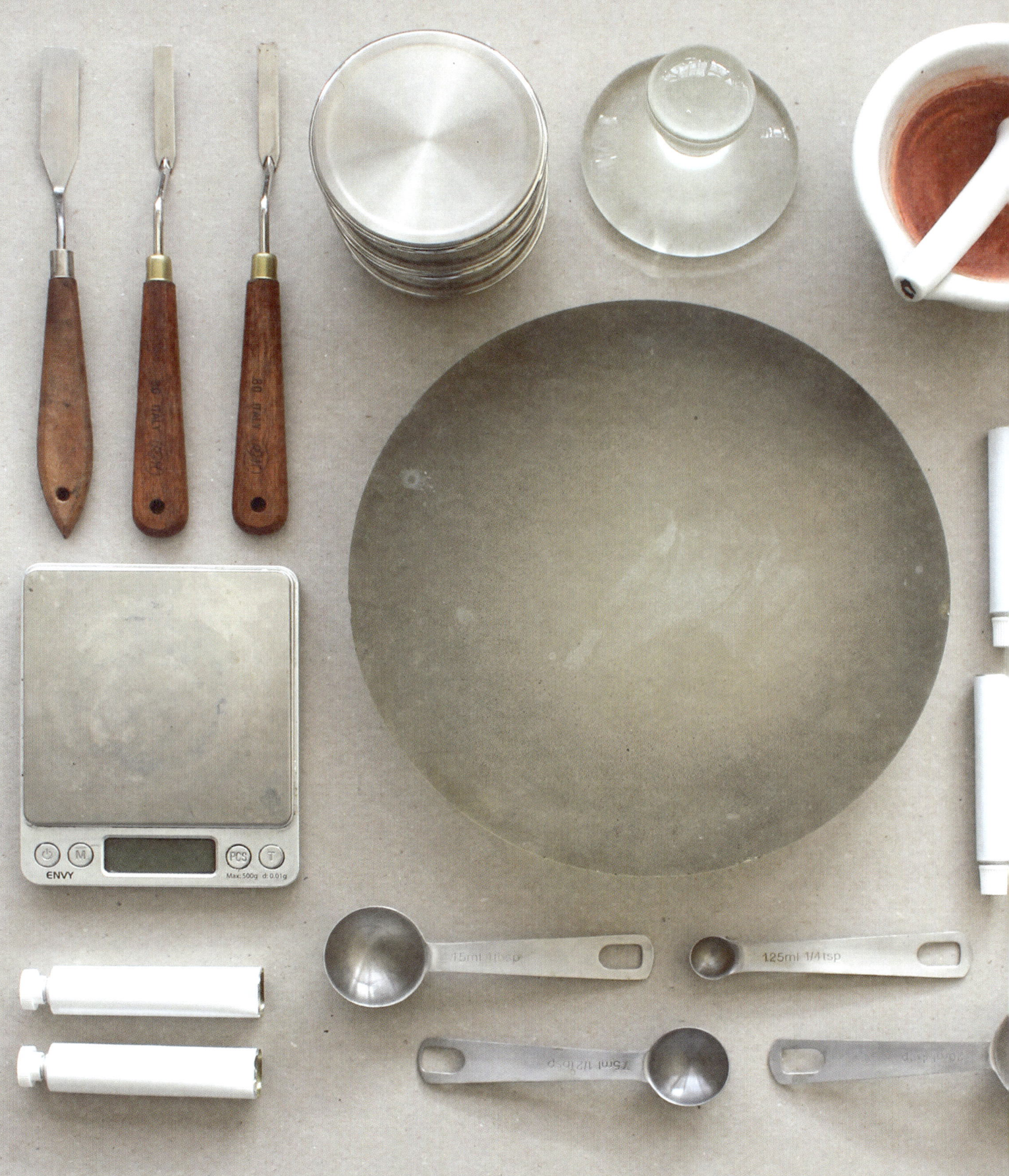
M
PCS
T
ENVY
Max: 500g d: 0.01g
1.25ml 1/4 tsp

Chapter Four

DYES, INKS, PAINTS AND PIGMENTS

FACING PAGE

Ink and paint-making equipment.

Learning to make inks, paints and pigments from plant-based sources plays a large part in working with natural colour. Most of the inks, pigments and colours you'll need or want can't be purchased off the shelf and many of the ones that are available can be expensive to buy because of the labour-intensive, small-scale and artisan methods of production. Additionally, part of the reasoning behind using plant sources for colour often means that site-specific plants and colour miles are important considerations within an artist's practice, therefore using home-grown or locally harvested materials can be a meaningful part of an artwork.

This chapter includes recipes for making water-based inks and lake pigments, both of which are fundamental to the foundations of using plant-based colour for printmaking. Not all methods and print processes require a lake pigment and not all require a concentrated water-based ink, but they do generally start with one or the other. The only technique that doesn't require either is mordant printing, which still requires the knowledge of how to make a dye bath (which is just a concentrated water-based ink prior to reduction).

Further definitions of dyes, inks, paints and pigments are given in an attempt to define their meanings both in relation to print and to natural colour, though I suspect providing definitive classifications might ultimately prove impossible.

THE SCIENCE AND THE CHEMISTRY

Jenny Dean has often said during teaching that she is not a chemist, and I have to admit to being in the same camp. Sometimes I wish I had studied chemistry, as it would be very useful now.

However, whilst printmaking with plant-based colour can be successfully accomplished without any knowledge of the science and the chemistry that affects natural dyes and other ingredients used in printmaking processes, it can be useful to understand some of the basics and have a little background knowledge of what is happening and why. This enables the printmaker to exploit the natural effects, outcomes and consequences of various chemical reactions with confidence and the ability to reproduce or avoid similar end results in future.

The classification of natural dyes can be a complex matter and there are various ways of categorising the different colourants contained within plants. These include chemical groups/classes of dyes, which look at the types of dye within the plant; method of application, which categorises dyes purely on how colour is best applied to fibres; and source of colour. Whilst further explanation about the difference between dyes and pigments is given later in the chapter, the subject is briefly discussed here to explain how natural dyes can be classified.

Chemical Groups and Classes

Plants contain many different colourants or colour sources and, whilst these colourants can be classified into dye classes or chemical groups, plants often contain several different dyes from different chemical groups. Even the category headings can be confusing, with some sources referring to dye classes and groups as the same thing and some sources defining them as separate.

The major chemical dye classes include anthraquinoids, flavonoids, indigoids and naphthoquinoids. Tannins and carotenoids are also sometimes included.

Anthraquinoids – mostly red dyes such as alizarin, emodin and purpurin.

Flavonoids – a large group that contains flavones (yellows such as luteolin, quercetin and fustin), chalcones and aurones (oranges such as coreopsis) but also anthocyanidins (often fugitive colours such as beetroot or blackberry fruits).

Indigoids – blues from indigo-containing plants. This group also contains the murex shellfish.

Naphthoquinoids – browns such as walnut and henna.

WHY IS THIS USEFUL?

It can be beneficial to know which dyes (and therefore also the dye classes they are from) are present in which plants, as it will often help determine potential lightfastness, method of application, how colours might react to other chemicals and what colours might be extracted both as a dye and as a pigment. In reality, becoming familiar with specific dye plants may be more useful and, with experience, a certain level of intuition can be applied to extracting specific colours.

WHY DOES FADING HAPPEN?

Fading occurs when the bonds in dye molecules are broken or affected (often by light) which means that the dye molecule can no longer absorb light at a particular wavelength and reflect other colours, which was providing the colour you could see. Fading is often defined as a 'lightening' of a colour but it actually means a colour change, of which weld is a good example. Weld has a high fade rating but this is because the yellow darkens with age rather than becoming lighter. It is still considered one of the best yellow dyes.

Different species of plants in the same genus can also contain different dyes or amounts of dye, or even contain no useful colourant at all. For this reason it is useful to learn the scientific name of a plant alongside the common name, to determine the exact species being used. However, whilst binomial names have been used since they were first introduced by Carl Linnaeus in the 1750s, some are now proving problematical both in a cultural sense and, since the onset of DNA testing, because of scientific classification. Thus, some scientific plant names may change as the plants are reclassified but they are still more accurate than the use of a common name that can change by country, region or even a specific local area. It is probably useful to include both the common name and the scientific name, but this can get a little long-winded on occasion.

Substantive, Adjective and Vat Dyes

Dyes are also often classed into substantive, adjective and vat dyes. The word substantive means to have a separate or independent existence and therefore it makes sense that substantive dyes are those that don't require a mordant to fix the colour. These include dyes such as walnut and buckthorn bark and are often high in tannins.

Adjective dyes (that need something adding) are those that require a mordant to fix the colour permanently to fibres. Most natural dyes fall into this category and dyes from the substantive category can often be improved by the use of a mordant.

Vat dyes are those that require a completely different process to extract the colour than most dyes, and the only natural plant dye that falls into this category is indigo. The indigo pigment is not soluble in water until it is reduced into its leuco-indigotin form. Tyrian purple is also considered a vat dye, but is extracted from shellfish and therefore not relevant to this book.

PIGMENTS AND DYES

Covered more thoroughly in Chapter 1, the terminology used in natural dyes and in printmaking can be counter-intuitive and contradictory. For example, what makes paint 'paint' and when is an ink a dye are questions that often have answers based on personal choice, where and when these terms were learnt and what the materials are ultimately being used for. This is stated merely to point out the potential confusion that can arise from these words.

Paint

'A coloured substance, which is spread over a surface and dries to leave a thin decorative or protective coating'.

We often think of the coloured solution used in printmaking as ink, when in fact it is often paint, with further additives – it is purely the process it is used for that makes it an 'ink'. Most screenprinters use a water-based system to print with, mixing acrylic paint with a screenprinting medium to apply the colour. They start off with paint, but it would never be referred to as paint whilst printing; it would be referred to as ink. Printmakers often mix different mediums into paints to turn them into a suitable consistency or thickness for printmaking.

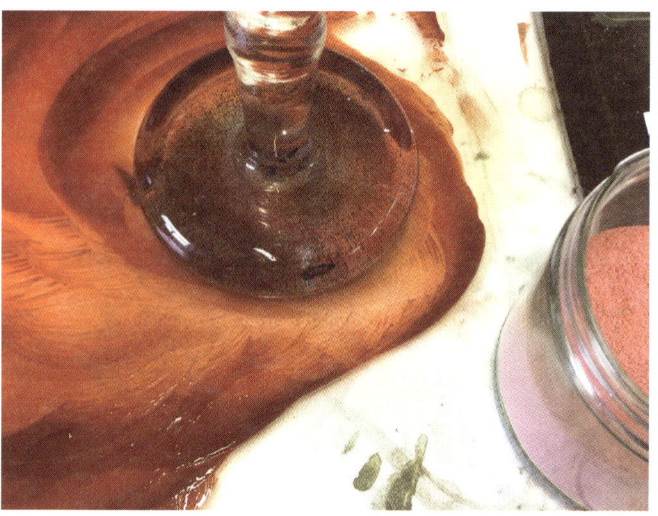

A water-based ink being mulled.

Ink

'A coloured fluid or paste used for writing, drawing, printing or duplicating'.

Ink covers a vast range of substances and mixes, which can cause mistakes, so it is always useful to define what is meant by the word being used. Oil-based inks are generally used within printmaking techniques such as intaglio and relief processes, and are usually a mix of a thickened linseed oil and pigment. Water-based inks are generally used for writing, drawing and painting, being much thinner and without the viscosity and saturated colour required for many paper-based printmaking techniques. These writing and drawing inks can be dye-based or pigment-based. Thickened water-based inks (or what are called 'pastes' in this book) are most often used for printing onto textiles.

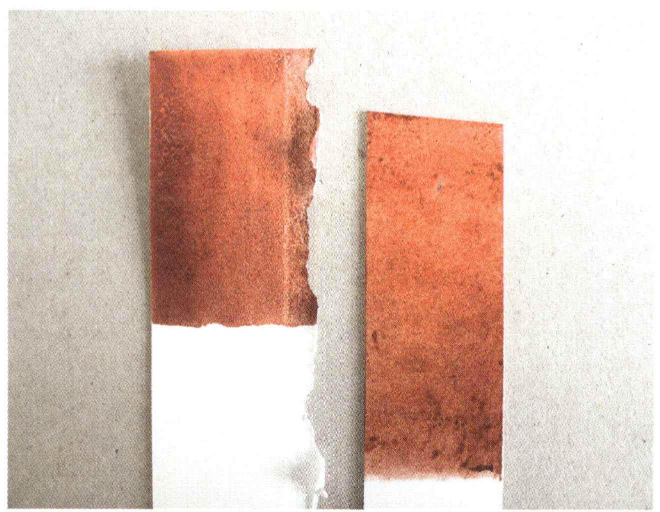

Madder ink – water-based (left) and oil-based (right).

Dye

'A natural or synthetic substance used to add colour to or change the colour of something'.

Dyes are used within this book most often in the form of printmaking pastes and mixes but also as a source of plant colour before it has been made into a pigment. Because most plants contain colourants that can be extracted in water, we usually start out with a dye before turning it into a pigment or a thickened dye. We might not be 'dyeing' cloth in the traditional meaning of immersion dyeing but by applying water-soluble colour to certain areas of a textile or paper, we are still dyeing the fibres.

Pigment

'A substance used for colouring or painting, especially a dry powder, which when mixed with oil, water, or another medium constitutes a paint or ink'.

Pigments cause further perplexity with their meaning easily misconstrued and misunderstood.

Pigment in art and creative industries most often means small particles of colourant that come in the form of a dry powder and are insoluble in liquid. However, the colour in organic substances is also called a pigment and is easily confused with the artistic meaning of the word.

Definitions from *Oxford Languages* (Oxford English Dictionary).

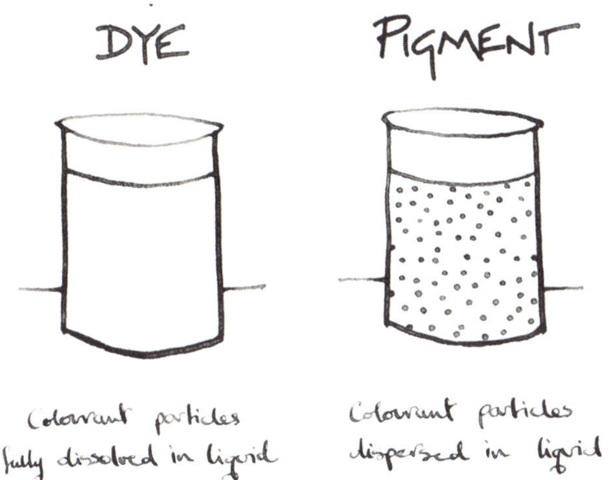

Dyes and pigments.

EXTRACTING COLOUR

Extracting colour from most plantstuffs can be delightfully easy – put plant and water in a container, heat (if impatient) and wait for colour to leach into the water. It is exactly like making a pot of tea; just don't drink it once brewed.

Most plants that are considered dye plants can be made into a serviceable dye bath by following the above steps. For the printmaker (and the natural dyer wanting to be a little more rigorous in their practice), it's not quite that simple. Depending on which dye plant is being used and the printmaking process or technique that the colour will be used for, there are different approaches and methods of extracting the colour to give the best results. Some useful dye plants to start using are described in detail in Chapter 2. They are some of the most well-known sources of plant-based colour and have been used for centuries to dye both fabrics and yarns, alongside many being used for paints and inks.

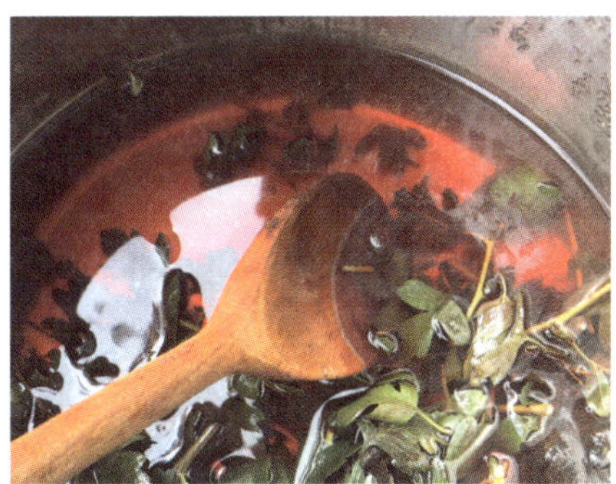

Extracting colour from hawthorn leaves and twigs.

This chapter provides different recipes to extract colour for making the dyes and pigments needed for most printmaking processes, although all plant-based colour (apart from vat dyes and dye extracts) originates from the same starting point: plantstuff + water = liquid natural dye.

Fresh and Dried Dyestuffs

Fresh and dried dyestuffs can be grown, foraged, purchased commercially or even saved from some food stuffs such as onion skins. The amounts needed are variable, as different plant types contain different amounts of dye or colourant. Some, like coreopsis, are highly pigmented and require only small amounts of plantstuff to provide a strong colour. Some require a lot more plantstuff to achieve a strong colour and it can be challenging to translate this through to printmaking inks and pastes. Even within the same plant type there will be different amounts of dye. This is affected by individual plant strains, habitat, climate, soil type, amount of sun, amount of rain, when the plant was harvested, how it was stored and many other factors. Any relevant tips or advice for specific plants are included with the dye plant descriptions in Chapter 2.

The amount of water in comparison to the amount of plantstuff needed for extracting the colour will change depending on what the dye will be used for. However, aiming for as strong a colour as possible is generally best for printmaking techniques. Keep in mind that whilst a highly concentrated liquid may be required for a recipe, the plantstuff still needs enough water to be completely submerged, allowing the colour to leach fully into the water. In traditional dyeing practices, the water-to-dye ratio is generally thought of as unimportant but for these processes it is a key consideration. Much like a sauce or gravy is reduced to intensify the flavour, a print paste made from 1 litre of dye reduced to 100ml will be much stronger in colour than a paste made from the same litre of dye which hasn't been reduced.

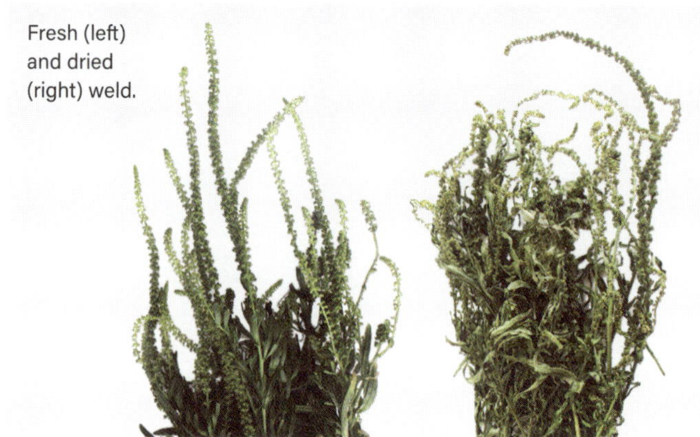
Fresh (left) and dried (right) weld.

THE WEIGHT OF FIBRE (WOF) RULE

It is useful to refer to a natural dye instruction book or recipes to decide how much dyestuff to use. Most dye baths for immersion dyeing are created using the WOF rule. WOF stands for Weight Of Fibre and it is a useful way of working out how much dye to use, depending on what the fibres weigh. Dye recipes will list dyestuff weight as 50 per cent WOF or 20 per cent WOF or, most often, 100 per cent WOF. For example, if 500g of cotton is being dyed with madder and the recipe says to use 50 per cent WOF, 250g of madder is needed. Of course, this is irrelevant when using the dye liquid as an ink or paint but what the WOF information provides is an indication of the strength of the dye. Anything that has a 50 per cent or less WOF requirement is considered a much stronger dye containing much more colourant than a dyestuff that requires 100 per cent WOF or more. I achieved some nice greens from ivy leaves (and iron) when dyeing small samples of fabric. However, because the samples needed 800 per cent WOF to achieve this colour, I had to gather a mass of leaves and then boil them (ivy leaves have an extremely unpleasant and pungent smell when heated and are also considered poisonous) and it was just not worth it.

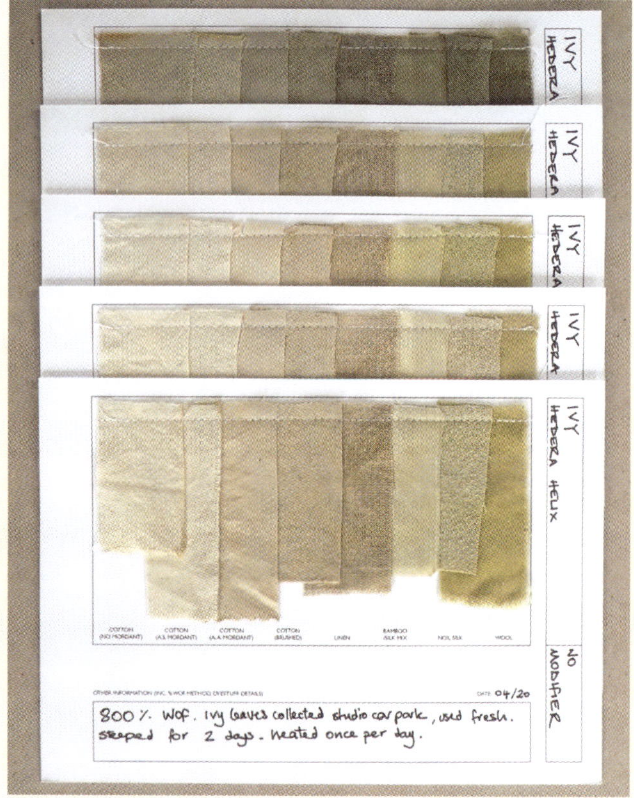

Ivy leaf fabric samples dyed with 800 per cent weight of fibre (WOF).

Vat Dyes

As discussed earlier, vat dyes require a different method of extraction to release the colour from the dyestuff as the colourants are not particularly soluble in water. This category is very small and the only plants included are indigo-bearing plants, such as woad (*Isatis tinctoria*) and Japanese indigo (*Persicaria tinctoria*). The different extraction method makes it a more difficult plant to work with when it comes to printmaking. This is because a water-based ink or solution made directly from a fresh or dried indigo plant just steeped in water will not be blue (apart from a teal made with extremely fresh indigo leaves). Obtaining a blue dye requires a particular process and fibres immersed in an indigo vat only become blue on removal from the liquid and as they oxidise. The blue is obtained by creating a highly alkaline liquid environment, then reducing the oxygen within the solution until the indigo-bearing pigment becomes available for dyeing – an approach incompatible with printing inks and pastes, which are processed and used with oxygen present.

However, insoluble indigo pigment can be extracted from indigo-bearing plants and then used very successfully within most printmaking inks and pastes, especially on paper, and has been used successfully as a surface application on textiles in Japan for centuries. I recommend researching the different methods and approaches to extracting indigo from plants if you are interested but, for most printmakers, it is more convenient and much easier to purchase indigo pigment that has already been extracted, especially to start with.

Indigo (*Persicaria tinctoria*) leaves ready for the pigment extraction process.

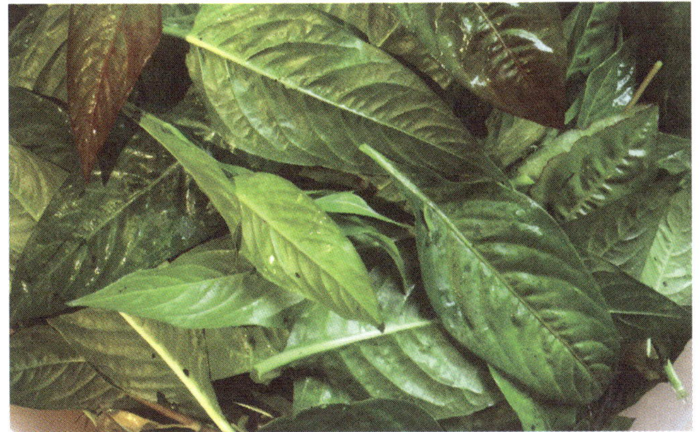

Dye Extracts

Dye extracts are highly concentrated powdered dyes that are soluble in water and can be used in place of dried or fresh dyestuffs. They are extremely suitable for printmaking as they provide strong colours that can be harder to achieve with just a concentrated dye bath made from raw dyestuffs. Extracts also come in a ready-made powdered format suitable for both water-based and oil-based inks. However, some of the processes and techniques used to produce dye extracts are not particularly sustainable and it can be hard to determine which method has been used for a particular extract. It can feel as though the procedures used by some companies are not always transparent, which may be just competitive secrecy or may be a form of greenwashing.

Briefly, these methods include aqueous extraction, solvent extraction, ultrasound-assisted extraction, supercritical fluid extraction, acid or alkali extraction and enzyme extraction. Supercritical fluid extraction is reported to have many advantages and is considered one of the most sustainable forms of extracting natural dyes, although it has high initial set-up and equipment costs.

Further studies into the sustainability of dye extracts and consequent publishing of information would be useful and would allow the end-user to make their own decision about whether to use dye extracts or not. Dye extracts are a seductive product for printmakers; an easy-to-use format, highly concentrated and extremely convenient. However, for artists that have concern for the environment and sustainability at the heart of their work, the questions around the production of dye extracts may be an issue.

I have also experienced some deterioration and colour breakdown in one or two older prints made with extracts. Additional tests and research into the use and longevity of dye extracts and how their various extraction methods affect results would provide further invaluable information for printmakers and other users. However, dye extracts and their use are a constantly developing and evolving part of the natural dye industry and it seems that every time I research the subject, new information and papers have been written about them.

WATER-BASED INKS

Starting with the creation of a water-based ink is a gentle introduction to producing your own plant-based colour. It is often simply a matter of immersing the dyestuff in water, as mentioned above, and reducing this solution down to concentrate the colour. Various binders and thickeners can then be added dependent on what the solution will ultimately be used for.

A basic recipe for making a water-based ink from a dye liquid is provided. This is preceded by a gum arabic recipe and can be added to the ink to act as a binder, aid the suspension of pigment in a pigmented ink (such as indigo) and it will also help to form surface tension, which is useful if using a dip pen and writing with the ink. Additionally, the gum arabic solution can change the appearance of ink by adding a slight sheen once dry. Gum arabic is available to buy as a pre-mixed liquid, if you prefer not to make your own.

RECIPE:

Gum Arabic Solution

Adding gum arabic to inks isn't an absolute must, they'll work perfectly adequately without but it is useful to try both approaches and see which you prefer. You may also want to omit the gum arabic if you plan to thicken the ink for screen or block printing, where a plant-based starch or guar gum is more suitable. Making the gum arabic solution first is recommended, as it is best to leave overnight before using. Whilst I don't usually bother using distilled water for ink making, I do use it when making a gum arabic solution. It will store for months in an airtight jar.

YOU WILL NEED:

- 50g gum arabic powder (or lumps)
- 250g distilled water
- 1–2 drops essential oil such as clove, tea tree or wintergreen oil
- Small non-reactive saucepan
- Scales
- Spoon/stirrer
- Lidded jar
- Heat source (portable hob, induction heater, buffet warmer or stove top)

METHOD:

1. Measure out 250g of cold distilled water into a saucepan. Add gum arabic powder, stir and gently warm. The gum arabic powder will clump but this will dissipate with time.
2. Once the solution is warm (not hot), turn off the heat and leave to cool. Occasionally stir.
3. Once cool, skim off any superfluous foam and pour the remaining solution into a clean jar. If you used gum arabic lumps, you'll need to carefully strain the solution, using muslin or other finely woven fabric. Add a few drops of essential oil to act as a preservative.
4. Leave overnight for any remaining gum arabic clumps to disappear, then use as needed. Store somewhere cool and out of the sun.

RECIPE:

Water-Based Ink

Whilst there are other ways to make water-based inks from plant-based colour including using an extract and a lake pigment, this recipe focuses on using a dye liquid as a base. The amount of dyestuff that is used is dependent on the amount of dye within the plant and will vary from dye plant to dye plant. Experimentation will be required to determine how much of a particular dye plant is needed, though 50g of dyestuff to 500g of water is a useful place to start with most well-known dye plants. Some dyestuffs, particularly barks, will soak up a lot of water so adding 1kg (1 litre) of water may be preferable to 500g of water. Purists may want to use distilled water though I use tap water, whilst understanding that this may give different results depending on location and water type.

ADDING ALUM

I do not usually add alum until I know exactly what I will be using ink for. If ink will be used for paper-based work, go ahead and add 5 per cent weight of the ink in alum, first dissolving in a little hot water. If planning to use in a textile print paste, keep your ink as it is for now. The alum can be added later.

YOU WILL NEED:

- 50g dyestuff
- 500g water
- Alum sulphate (optional)
- Essential oil (optional)
- 2 litre non-reactive saucepan
- Scales
- Spoon/stirrer
- Filter paper or fabric filter such as muslin
- Heat source (portable hob, induction heater, buffet warmer or stove top)

METHOD:

1. Add 50g dyestuff to 500g (or enough to cover your dyestuff) of water in a saucepan. Gently heat and allow to 'not quite' simmer for 30 minutes to one hour. Keep an eye on your liquid during this time and add more water if needed. The aim is to reduce the dye liquid to approximately 50g–100g, though it can be hard to gauge with the dyestuff still in. The exact amount is a personal choice subject to what it will be used for and how strong a colour has been achieved. The liquid can always be reduced further once the dyestuff has been removed. Once reduced, take off the heat and leave to cool.

2. You can strain the dye liquid now to remove the dyestuff or you can leave it in the liquid to steep for longer. Leaving it for longer will extract more of the colour – overnight or even a few days for some of the woody and fibrous dyestuffs is ideal. Strain, using a coffee filter or muslin with a micro-perforated colander, sieve or funnel. This may take some time but don't rush it – the aim is to remove all the plantstuff from the ink otherwise it is likely to go mouldy.

3. If not using immediately for a print paste, pour the filtered ink into a jar, and add between 5g–10g gum arabic solution, if required. Add one to two drops of essential oil.

Any dried or fresh dyestuff can be used in this recipe. Remember, you are making a dye liquid but then reducing it to concentrate the colour. If the colour isn't strong enough, more dyestuff can be added to the ink and the above steps repeated.

LAKE PIGMENTS

A dye is a colourant that is typically soluble in water whilst a pigment is a colourant that is insoluble in water or other liquid. Lake pigments are insoluble pigments that have been created from a dye liquid and are a compound of an organic colourant and an inert substance, usually a metallic salt such as alum sulphate. Making a lake pigment is therefore a way of extracting colour from a plant (first using the same method that you use to make a natural dye liquid) and turning it into a dry powder (or sometimes a wet paste) that can be mixed into different vehicles (such as linseed oil or gum arabic) to create paints and inks. This is especially useful when making inks with oil-based mediums that initially require dry colourants.

Surprisingly, the word 'lake' does not come from the fact the pigment has been made from liquid but is thought to have originated from the use of the pink dye lac (a resin secreted by the *Kerria lacca* insect) as a lake pigment.

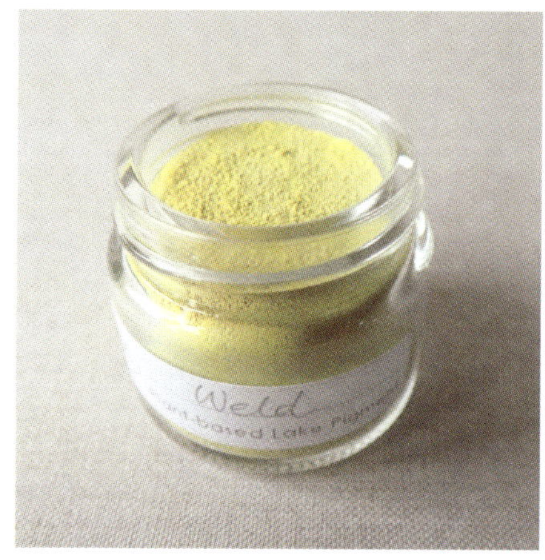

Weld (*Reseda luteola*) lake pigment, dried and ground ready for use.

The Lake Pigment Process

Lake pigments are made by precipitating a soluble dye onto a metallic salt to create an insoluble pigment. This makes it possible to create a dry powdered pigment from a liquid natural dye. Essentially the soluble colourant in the liquid is made insoluble by adding the metallic salt (most often potassium alum sulphate or alum sulphate), and an alkali (usually soda ash or sometimes calcium carbonate or a mixture of the two), which produces a chemical reaction and causes the pigment to precipitate to the bottom of the container. Alum sulphate or potassium alum sulphate are acidic and are soluble in water. After the alum has been added to the dye liquid and it bonds with the colourant, it is only once the alkali is added (and the liquid is no longer acidic) that the alum becomes insoluble, along with the dye molecules that have been adsorbed into the alum.

The excess liquid is siphoned or filtered off and the remaining coloured substance is washed, dried and then ground into particles to be used as a pigment. This pigment can be used for any process where a dry coloured powder is required such as watercolour paint, pastels, crayons, oil paint, oil-based printmaking ink and also for colouring or tinting other dry powders and mixes. It can be used to make a pigment-based drawing and writing ink and can be used to colour inks and pastes. In all cases, particle size will greatly affect the final outcome and this can be controlled through the use of scientific sieves to filter out larger particles.

For water-based paints and inks, it may be considered superfluous to completely extract the water content from the pigment. Using the pigment in its wet 'gloopy' form negates the need for grinding the powder once dry. This is especially useful for making screenprinting pastes, as they require an ink with small particles which will pass through a screen's mesh. However, drying the pigment provides an incredibly shelf-stable material that can be stored for many years before using.

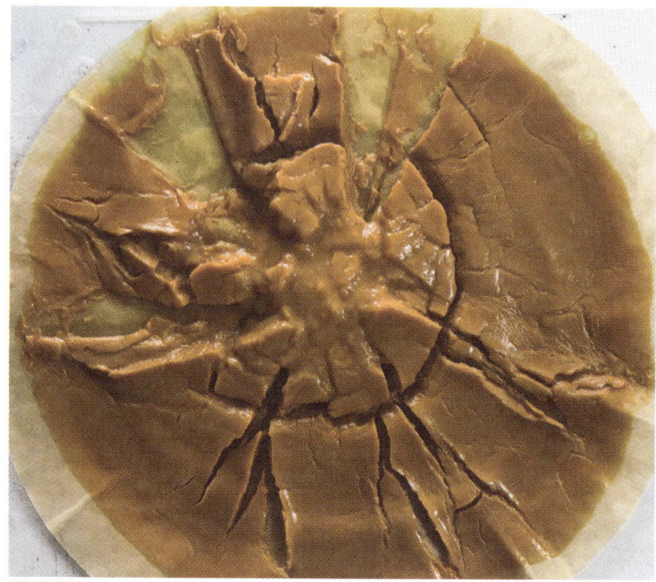

Buckthorn berry (*Rhamnus spp.*) lake pigment. Lake pigments can be made into a screenprinting paste whilst still wet.

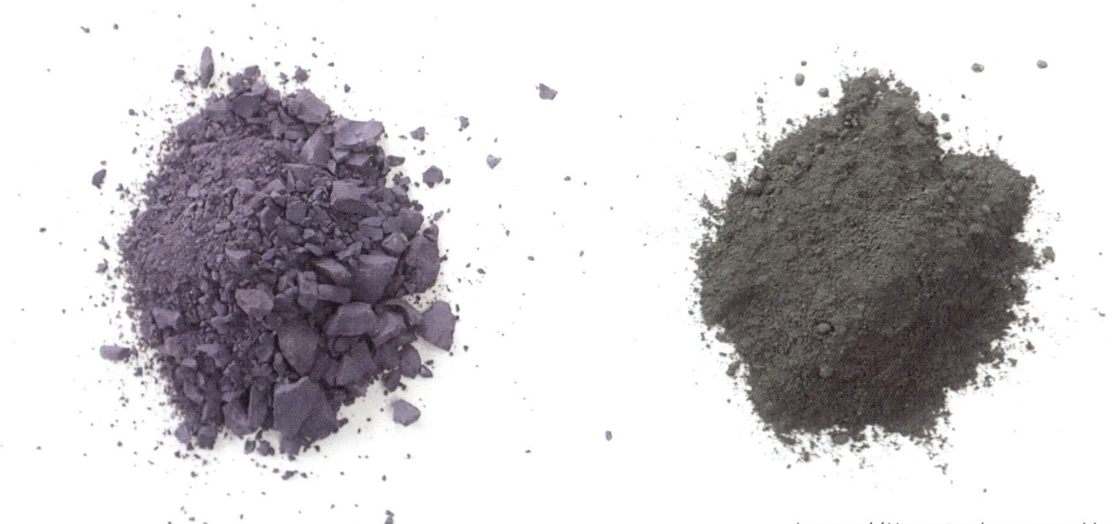

Logwood (*Haematoxylum campechianum*) lake pigment, freshly made (left) and two years old (right).

Using alum (which is also used as a mordant in dyeing) to make the pigment should also improve lightfastness. However, those dyes that are considered fugitive when used in immersion dyeing are not particularly improved in the lake-making process – for example, beautifully purple logwood pigments will soon turn to greys. Moreover, adding alum and soda ash to your dye liquid will also change the pH, which can drastically alter the colour of your pigment. Many an excitingly strong red or pink liquid has been reduced to an olive green in my lake-making experiments.

Many other factors will influence the resulting shade of pigment and no standard rules exist for every natural dye. Some lake pigments are affected by temperature during production and using different alkalis can alter the texture and colour of the final pigment.

Whilst a standard recipe has been provided overleaf, there are lots of recipes available for making lake pigments and changing the ratio of the metallic salt to the alkali will affect the final colour. Though historical recipes and formulas often contain toxic ingredients, they are a fascinating area to explore once the basic recipe below has been tried. However, don't focus on variables and modifications to start with. It will unnecessarily confuse and complicate the process.

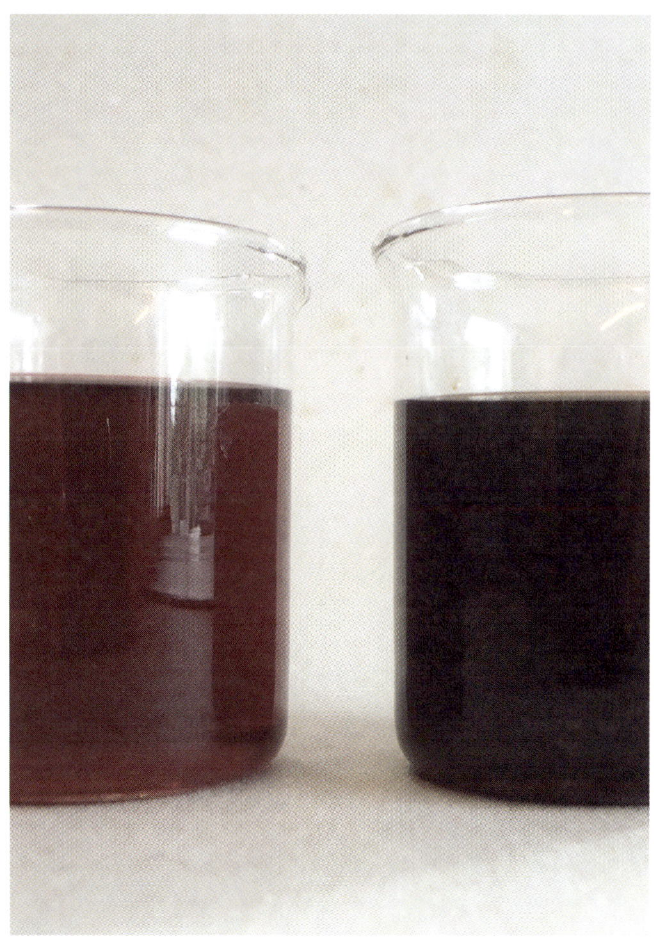

Red onion skin dye liquid (left) and after alum has been added (right).

RECIPE:

Making a Lake Pigment

(See page 84 for step-by-step sequence.)

YOU WILL NEED:

- 1.2kg (approx. 1.2 litres) of water
- 50g of dried or fresh dyestuff
- 10g alum (alum sulphate or potassium alum sulphate)
- 5g soda ash
- Extra hot water for dissolving alum and soda ash
- 2 litre (or bigger) saucepan
- Scales
- Kitchen sieve/funnel
- 2 × coffee filter papers (or squares of muslin)
- pH papers
- Large container (at least double the volume of dye liquid)
- Glass beakers or similar for dissolving alum and soda ash
- Stirrers
- Heat source (portable hob, induction heater or stove top)

METHOD:

1. To begin, make a dye liquid by gently simmering the dyestuff in the water for one hour. Don't let the liquid boil – this can affect the colour of some dyes (refer to the previous section for further information on how to extract colour from plantstuffs or consult other natural dyeing resources if required). If time allows, leave the dyestuff steeping in the water overnight to allow the colours to develop.

2. Strain out any solid plant matter from the solution using a kitchen sieve, a coffee filter or similar (the plant matter can be composted or used again to extract further colour). Ensure there are no bits of plant left in the liquid. You should have approximately 1kg (1 litre) of coloured liquid. Don't worry if you have too much or too little, although if you prefer to start with an exact amount, you can either reduce the liquid down by gently simmering or increase the liquid by adding more water. If you are going to do either, return the dyestuff to the pan to extract the maximum colour possible.

3. Put the dye liquid in a large container – one with high sides is best and the container should be no more than half full after you have added your dye liquid. Separate into two containers if you don't have one that is big enough. Glass containers are useful as they allow you to see the solution more easily but are not essential. It doesn't matter if the liquid is hot or not but adjusting the temperature of the dye can change both the final texture and tone of the pigment. Aim for a warm temperature to start with but similarly don't worry if it's hotter or colder – fine-tuning and experimentation can be done when you're more experienced.

4. In a separate beaker, add 10g alum to 50–100g of boiling water and stir to dissolve. You can use normal stainless-steel cutlery for stirring but make sure it is clearly marked and is no longer used for cooking. Once the alum has dissolved, add it to the dye solution and stir gently.

5. In a second separate container, add 5g soda ash to 50–100g of boiling water and stir to dissolve. Add to the dye solution and stir gently. The soda ash will react with the alum, which will make the solution bubble up and effervesce (this is why you need a large container). This doesn't always happen, especially if the liquid is cold, so don't worry too much if there isn't an immediate and obvious reaction. You should be able to see solids starting to form in the solution. If the solution doesn't react and you can't see these solids forming, you may need to add more alum and soda ash. Reduce the amount to 50 per cent of the original weight (5g alum/2.5g soda ash) and repeat the process, adding to your solution. You can also check whether you need to add more alum or soda ash by testing the pH, which should be a neutral pH 6–7.

6. Leave the solution to stand for at least one hour, though it can sometimes take up to 24 hours, until the liquid at the top becomes clearer and there is solid matter forming at the bottom of the container. Drain off as much of this clear liquid as possible (a big syringe is useful for this or use careful and slow pouring). At this stage you can 'wash' your pigment several times, which removes any remaining alum or soda ash not affixed to the pigment. To wash your pigment, add clean water to your remaining gloop after draining off the first amount of liquid. Stir and wait for the pigment to settle again. Do this twice more, removing as much of the clear liquid as you can. This process is recommended but is very time-consuming.

7. You can now strain the remaining solution through a double layer of paper coffee filters (or muslin) held in a funnel or large sieve. Once the liquid has strained through the paper filters (which can take a day or more), you can dispose of the liquid down the drain though I prefer to pour mine onto the ground rather than into the septic tank.
8. The remaining gloopy mixture is your wet lake pigment. The wet pigment can be stored at room temperature in a tightly covered jar. It can be used to make watercolour paint, a water-based printing paste (refer to Chapter 7) or be reconstituted back into a dye bath (which requires a further process, adding citric acid). However, if you want to use it in its dry powdered pigment form, follow the next steps.
9. Leave the mixture on the paper filter to dry. This will take a long time (a few days to a few weeks) and will become lighter and dramatically reduce in size as it dries. Open up the filter paper so it's as flat as possible and spread the gloopy pigment out so it is not in a clump. You can speed up the drying process by placing the damp filter onto a plaster bat (usually used in ceramics to dry clay out), putting it somewhere warm or in a dehydrator but it's not essential.
10. Once the pigment is completely dry, scrape it off the paper filter and grind the dried mixture in a pestle and mortar – you now have a pigment that can be used for paint and ink. Remember that once the pigment has dried, it can no longer be used as a dye. This is because the particles are now insoluble and whilst they might disperse throughout the liquid, they won't dissolve.
11. Whether or not you now sieve the pigment to separate the larger particles is up to you, though it is recommended for making oil-based ink. Sieving your pigment also removes any impurities, such as bits of filter paper, dirt or dried pieces of plant. You will need a sieve, a lid and a receiving pan. *See* 'Scientific Sieves' in Chapter 3 for further information.
12. Put the sieve on top of the receiving pan (all the elements should be stackable) then pour the pigment into the sieve, ensuring you brush all the pigment from the mortar. Put the lid on the sieve and start gently shaking the whole sieve stack. You may have to tap it against a hard surface, especially if you're using a sieve with a very fine mesh. In laboratories, they have a special machine called a 'sieve shaker' to carry this action out. You will quickly realise why – it is a tedious, messy and time-consuming job.

Safety First

Always wear a mask when working with dry powders. I wear a half-face respirator mask with changeable filters, of which I have both a gas and particulate filter attached. I also wear nitrile or rubber gloves. Whilst a well-ventilated area is useful and recommended, you are working with extremely fine powders that should not be inhaled so extra precautions should be taken.

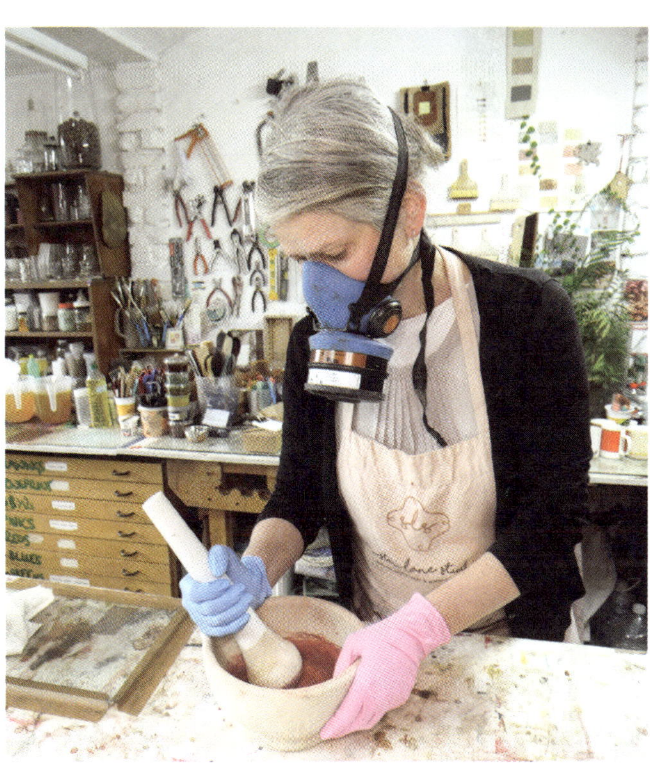

Wearing a half-face respirator and gloves to grind lake pigments.

Step-by-step guide to making a lake pigment

1

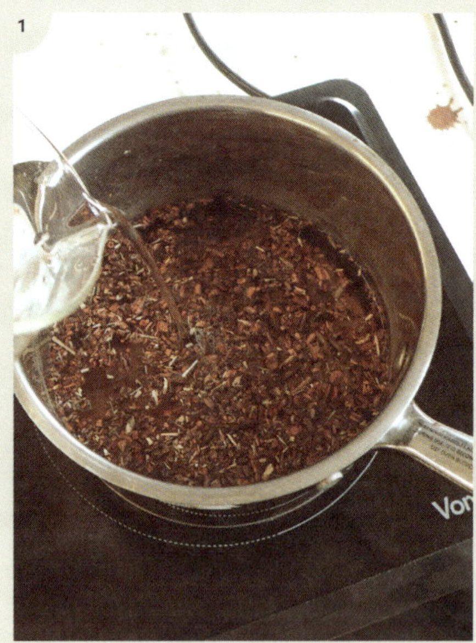

Measure out dyestuff and water then add to a saucepan and simmer for one hour.

2

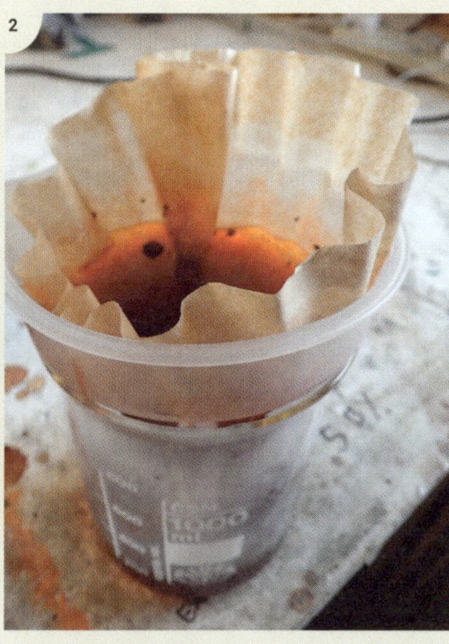

Leave dyestuff to steep for as long as possible, then strain to remove all plant matter.

3

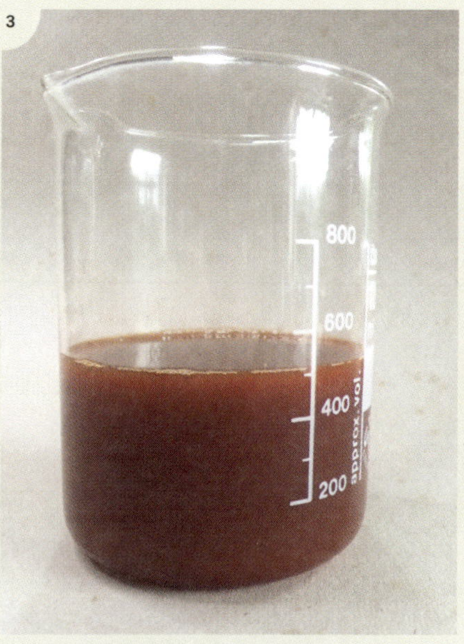

Add the strained dye to a large tall container, which should be less than half full once the liquid has been added.

4

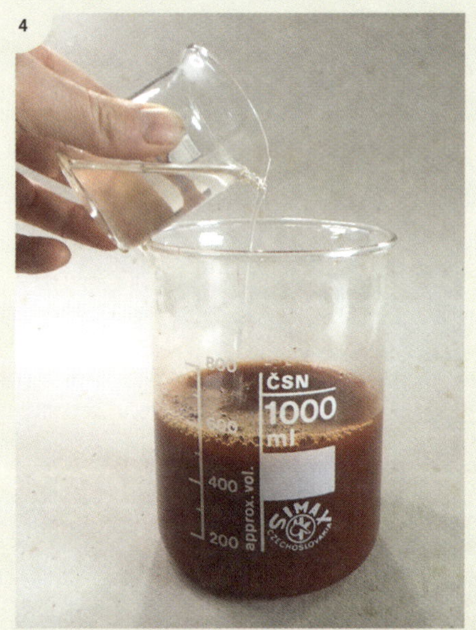

Dissolve alum in a little hot water and add to the dye liquid. Stir well, then do the same with the soda ash.

5

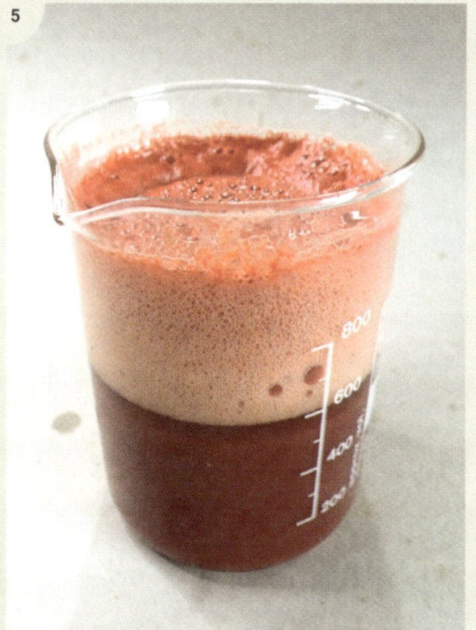

Adding the soda ash will probably cause an effervescent reaction and the solution will start to separate.

6

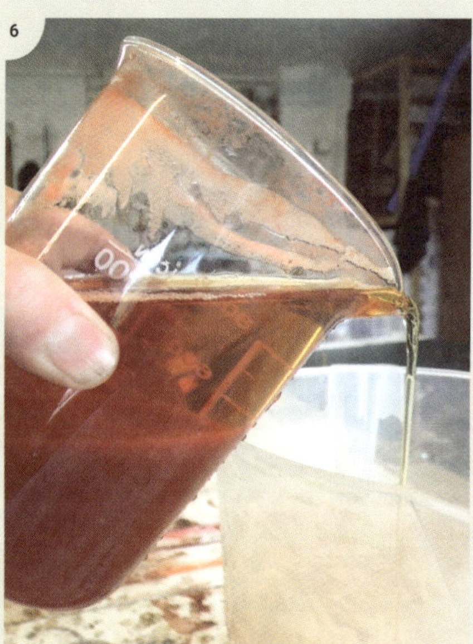

Wait for the pigment to separate, then carefully pour off the excess liquid. Add clean water and repeat this process to wash the pigment.

7

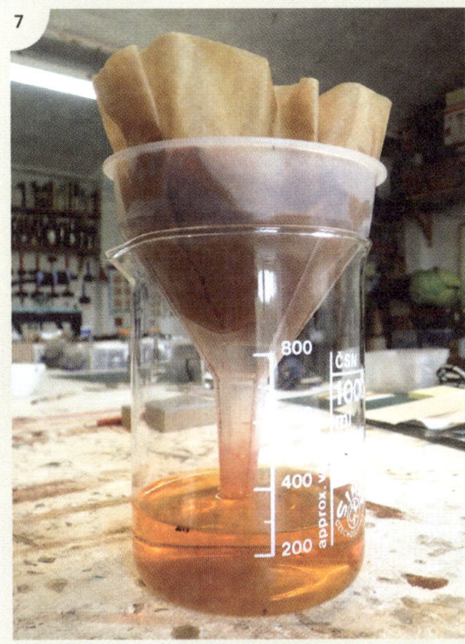

Pour the washed pigment into a filter and wait for the liquid to drain off.

8

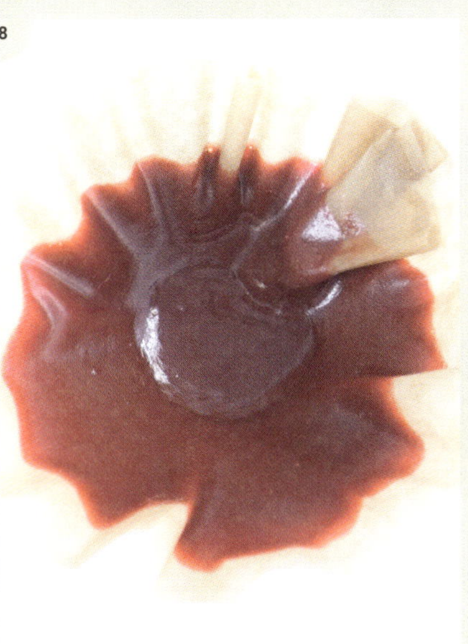

Once the liquid has completely drained from the pigment it can be discarded. This may take 24 hours or more.

9

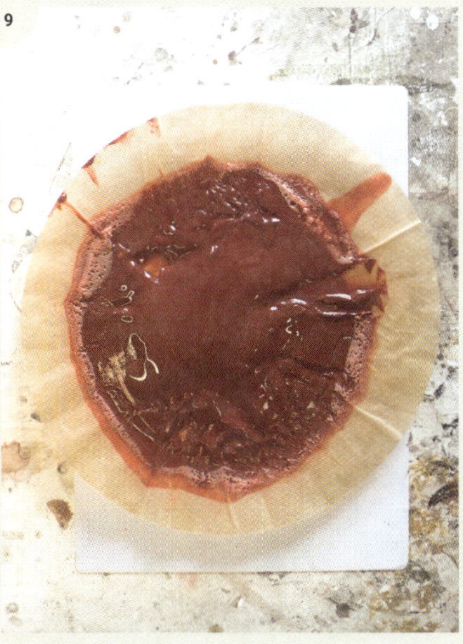

Open up the filter paper and place on an absorbent surface to dry. A dehydrator can be used to speed up the process.

10

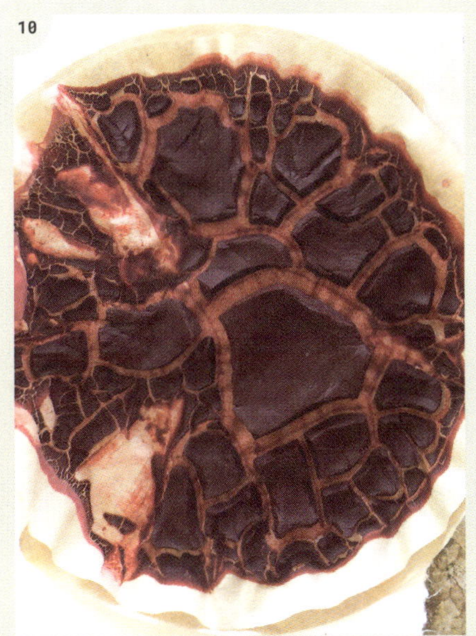

As the pigment dries, it will lighten and start to crack, whilst reducing considerably in size.

11

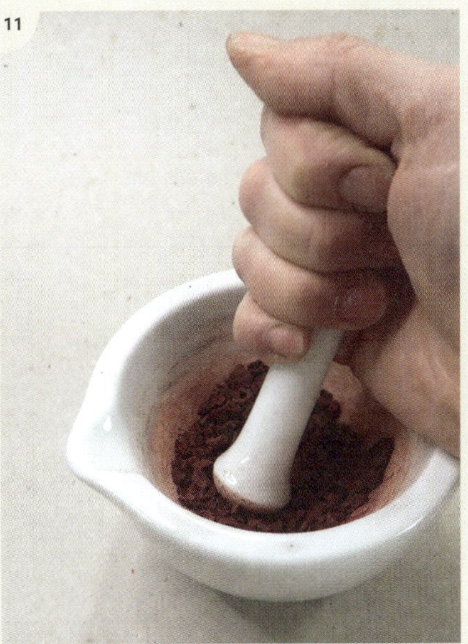

Once dry, the pigment can be added to a pestle and mortar and ground into smaller particles.

12

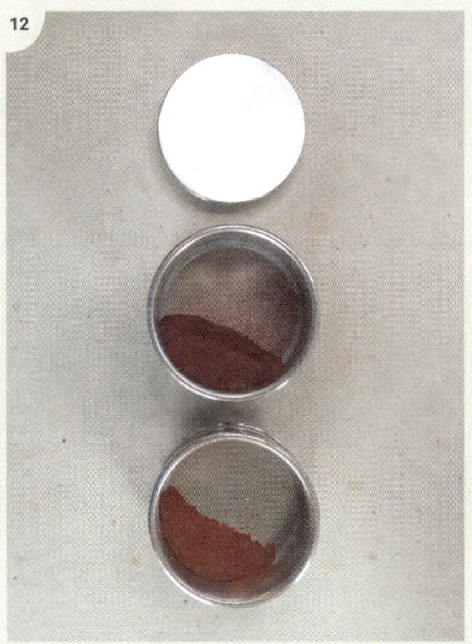

Dried and ground pigment being sieve sorted.

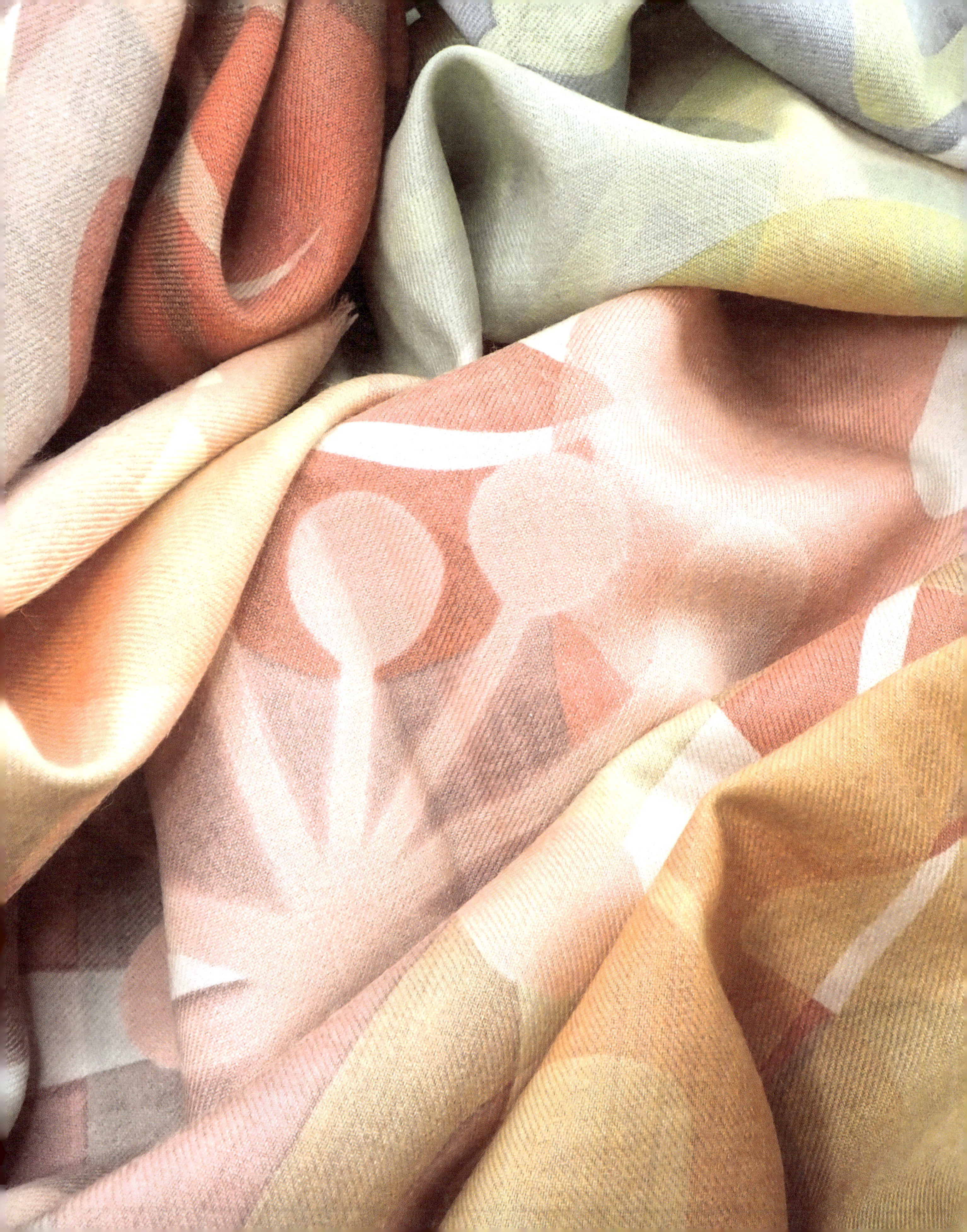

Chapter Five

PLANT-BASED COLOUR AND TEXTILES

FACING PAGE

Pure wool scarves screenprinted with plant-based colour.

Using plant-based colour to print onto textiles requires a slightly different approach to printing onto paper. This is because the colour must be washfast, which of course, isn't usually a requirement for paper. Rather than just printing the colour onto the surface of the substrate as one would with paper, the areas of the fabric where colour is applied ideally need to be 'dyed' rather than just have a surface application of the colourant. Printed fabrics can be divided into four distinct 'styles', which are not the different techniques of printing but the ways in which the pattern is achieved. These include the 'dyed' (mordanted) style, the 'resist' style, the 'discharge' style and the 'direct' style. They are all fairly self-explanatory, apart from the 'dyed' style, which could be considered misleading when using plant-based colour as all of these styles are achieved by dyeing the fabric (apart from the method of using insoluble pigments applied with a binder such as soy liquid). *See* 'Textile Printing Styles'.

The typical approach in contemporary printmaking with plant dyes is to combine the alum (or other mordant) and the dye into a print paste, which is thickened and then applied directly onto the textile, then cured and set by steaming. The paste includes a percentage of vinegar in the liquid, which helps to keep the solution strongly acidic and acts as an anti-precipitant. If the mixture becomes neutral and is no longer acidic, the alum and the dye form a lake and become insoluble before the paste can be applied to the textile. Pre-mordanting the fabric before printing rather than adding a mordant to the print paste is also a consideration. However, this is generally thought to be wasteful of the alum because the mordant is only needed where the colour/dye will be printed. If working on a small scale and covering a lot of fabric with colour, there is no reason not to mordant the cloth prior to applying a print paste. Care should be taken when washing the fabric for the first time as the presence of a mordant on parts of the fabric that have not been printed means that there is the potential for excess dye to attach to unwanted areas of the cloth.

Theoretically, any thickener can be used to make the print paste a suitable consistency though different print techniques might suit different thickeners. For my textile printing pastes, I prefer using guar gum but do try some other gums and thickeners to see what works best for you. Starch thickeners can change the handle of the fabric, leaving a somewhat stiff texture, so should primarily be used for printing onto paper rather than cloth.

For relief/block printing, a thinner paste will give you better results, especially as you want to avoid the paste striating or clumping on the block. In the past, blocks with large flat areas were flocked or felted so that a more consistent and even print could be achieved.

Local resources, common ingredients or items left over from a previous project might dictate what is ultimately chosen as the thickener. There is no need to purchase a different thickener if you already have some in stock.

TEXTILE PRINTING STYLES

Dyed (mordanted) style – different mordants are applied to textiles in different strengths and/or ratios, which are then dyed in a single dye pot.
Resist style – a resist (such as wheat paste, rice starch paste or wax) is applied to the textile before colour is added, for example by dyeing or brush application.
Discharge style – textiles are dyed and then colour is removed by the use of a discharge paste, such as citric acid.
Direct style – colour and pattern are applied directly to the textile. When using natural dyes, this ideally requires the mordant to be added to the paste before it is applied.
These styles can be mixed and combined to produce further effects and end results.

COLOUR TESTS AND RESEARCH

I have done a lot of tests of the best solutions and mixes to ensure good coverage, washfastness and strong colour. The results were surprising (and slightly frustrating) in that for different dyes, some methods worked better than others. Interestingly, this seems to be supported by textile printing books produced before (or around the time of) the invention of synthetic dyes, which describe vastly different approaches to dyeing dependent on which dye is being used, how the colour will be set, which fibre the material is made from and countless other variables.

Generally, the best results came from a dye, mordant and vinegar mix, applied using guar gum to thicken, before being steam set and left to cure for several weeks. However, acceptable results were also achieved using a dye liquid purely thickened with gum and/or steam ironing rather than steaming. All the samples shown overleaf have been hand-washed and then machine-washed once at 40°C using a pH-neutral liquid washing detergent. Whilst this isn't particular proof of the longevity of washfastness, it shows that the colour isn't going to be immediately washed out. More robust testing of fabrics and washfastness over a longer period would be a useful piece of research; this is touched upon later in the chapter.

Detail of the indigo print tests.

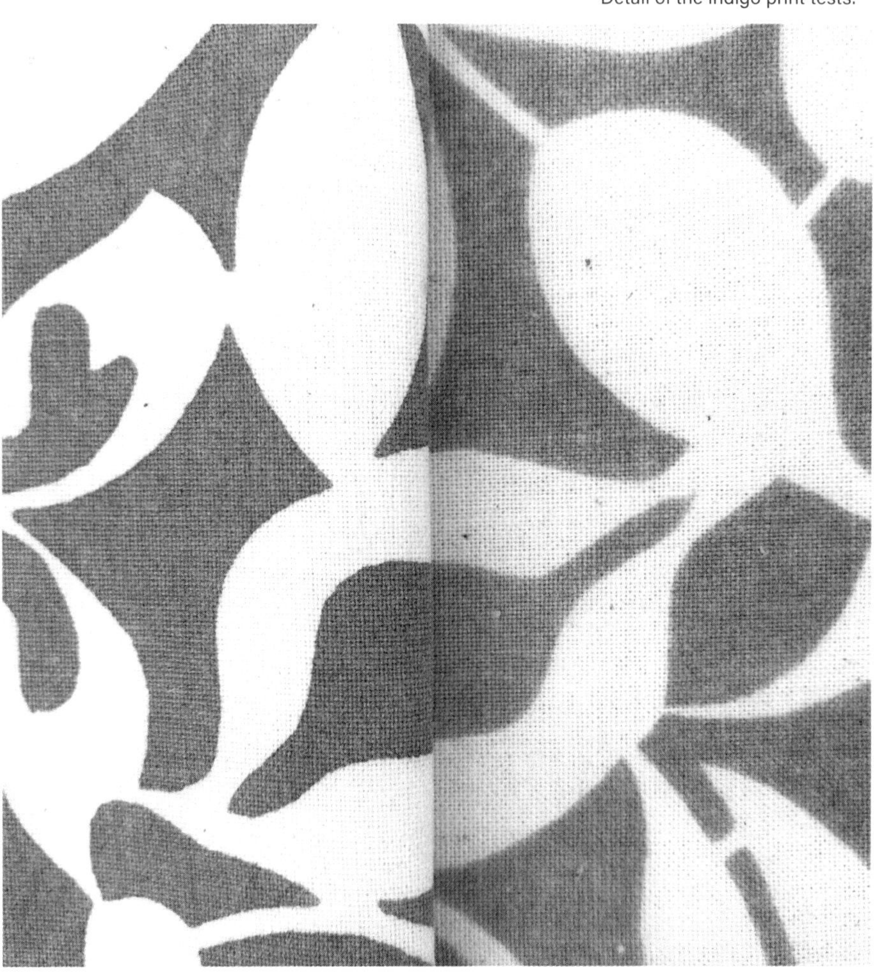

Screenprinted Plant-Based Colour Tests on Cotton

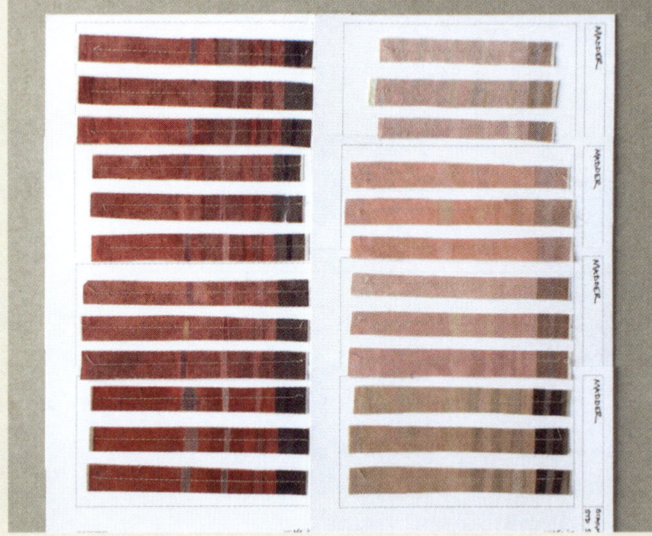

Madder extract.

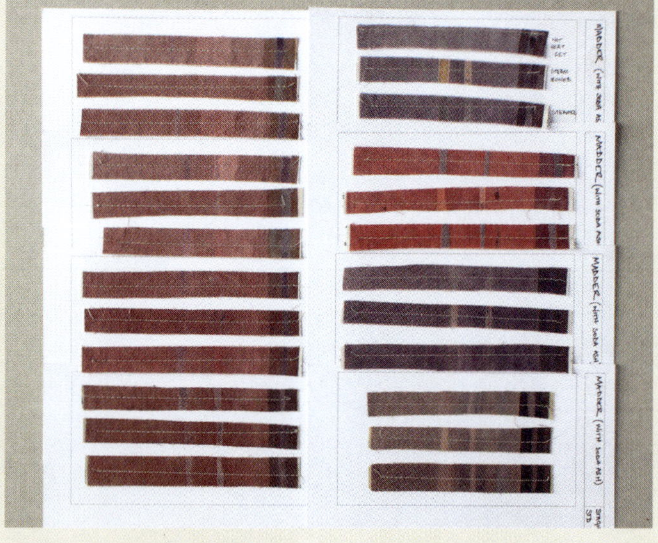

Madder extract and soda ash.

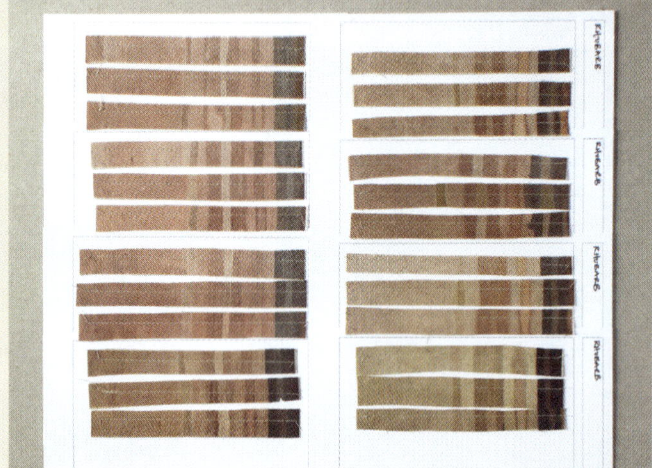

Rhubarb root extract.

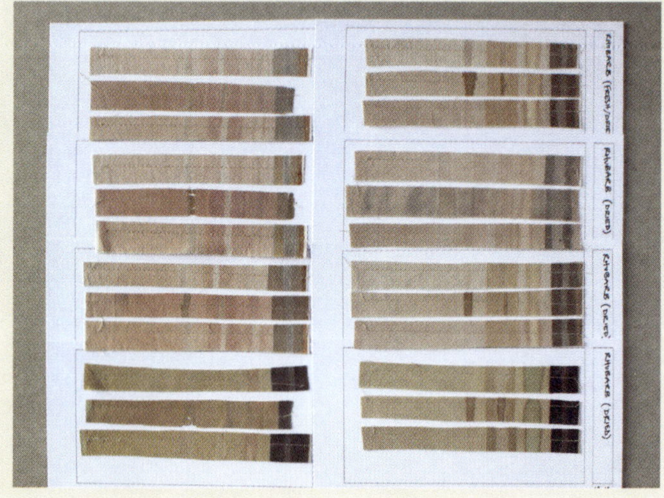

Dried rhubarb root.

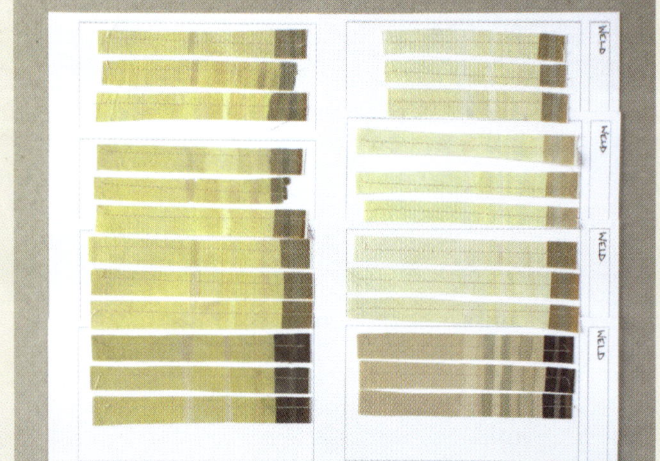

Weld extract.

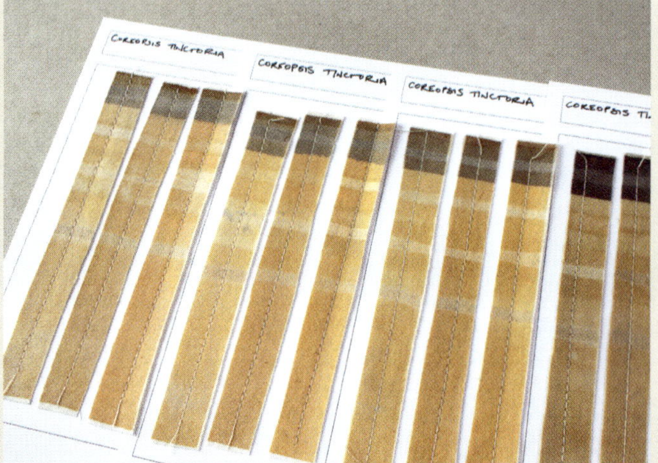

Coreopsis extract.

The colour experiments were printed onto a cotton fabric using a mordanted paste and a thickened dye paste for comparison. These pastes were mixed with 14 different dyes and dye combinations comprising predominantly dye extracts but also including two pastes made from raw dyestuffs. All were printed onto fabric which had been either just scoured, scoured and mordanted, scoured and immersed in a soy milk bath or scoured and then immersed in a sumac leaf tannin bath. Whilst I now largely discount the soy milk fabric tests as they were soaked in purchased soy milk rather than freshly made liquid, a difference can still be seen in the colour of these samples. Looking at further experiments done with freshly made soy milk shows an improvement in colour, though it should be remembered that soy milk is not a mordant. The soy is extremely high in protein and whilst soaking fabric in soy liquid before printing (or dyeing) allows more colour to bind to the fabric, it is not a chemical bond.

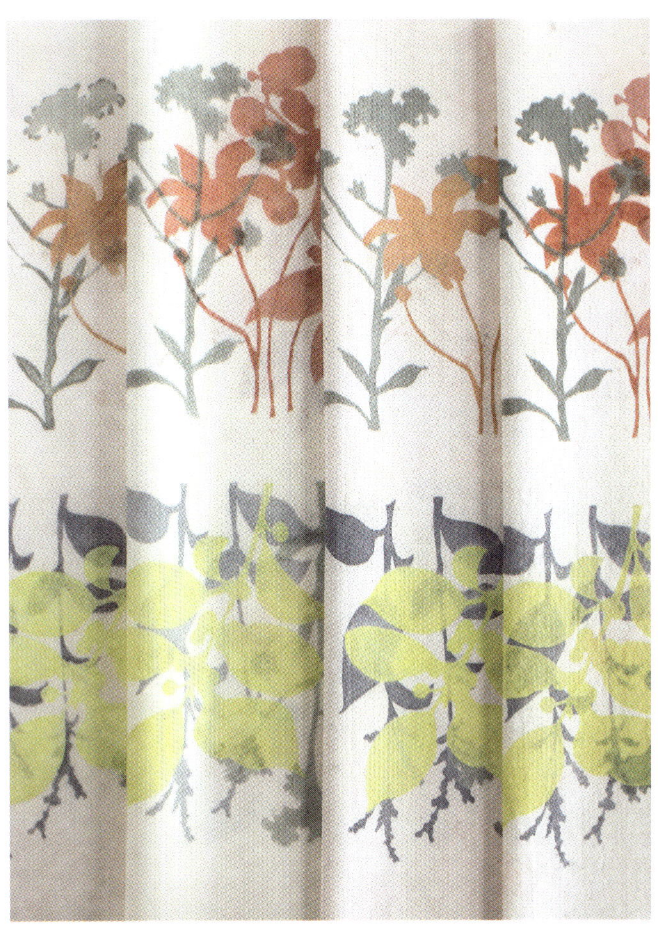

Soy liquid comparison tests on wool sized with soy (middle left) and cotton sized with soy (far right). The control fabrics (not sized with soy) show a difference in colour and a slight difference in colour retention. It would be useful to do further washfast tests on these samples.

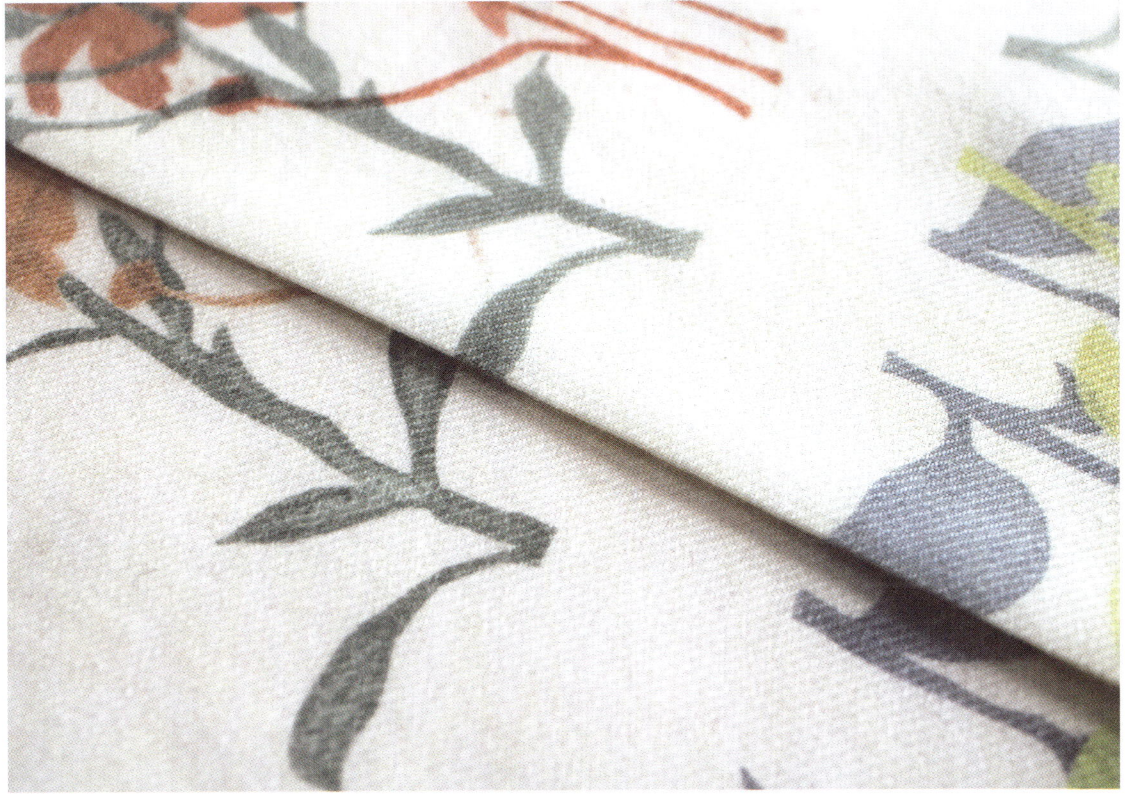

Detail of the soy liquid comparison test on wool showing a greater evenness of colour and colour retention on the soy-sized fabric (top).

The samples show areas of the printed dye where the colour has been modified by applying an acid, alkali or iron modifier. These were all done post application of the dye except for two sample colours, which were pre-modified before printing on to the fabric. Some modifiers were printed on and some were just painted on as a liquid and with no thickener added. Not all dyes will be susceptible to a colour change with modifiers – if unsure, it is useful to refer to a natural dye book or carry out tests before beginning a project. Where both an iron and an alkali modifier were applied or an iron and an acid modifier were applied, further colour changes were achieved.

The fabric that had received a tannin bath prior to printing proved especially effective when the iron modifiers were applied, with a dramatic change in colour due to the iron and tannin reaction. This was especially useful for dyes that have little reaction to modifiers as it created the appearance of a colour change when in reality it was the iron reacting with the tannin in the fabric, rather than the dye.

One thing to note was how the application of a citric acid modifier was extremely damaging to some of the screenprinted fabric that had received direct heat (with a steam iron). All dyes and modifiers were applied before being either just cured (with time), set with a steam iron and then cured, or set by steaming then cured before all samples were washed. On the first wash, many (but not all) of the fabrics that had been steam ironed literally disintegrated where the citric acid modifier had been applied. Avoid this issue by curing and setting fabrics, washing and only then applying a citric acid modifier (which doesn't need to be heat set) before washing again.

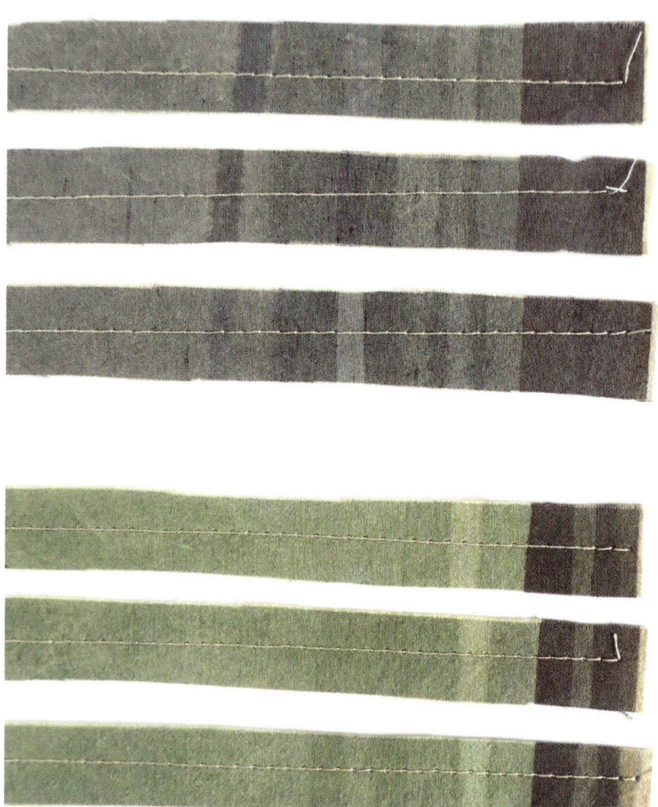

Immersing fabric in a tannin bath prior to dyeing or printing can affect the colour of the dyes and will allow for colour modification with iron, even on those dyes that don't react to modifiers. Here the iron is reacting with the tannin in the fabric rather than the dye.

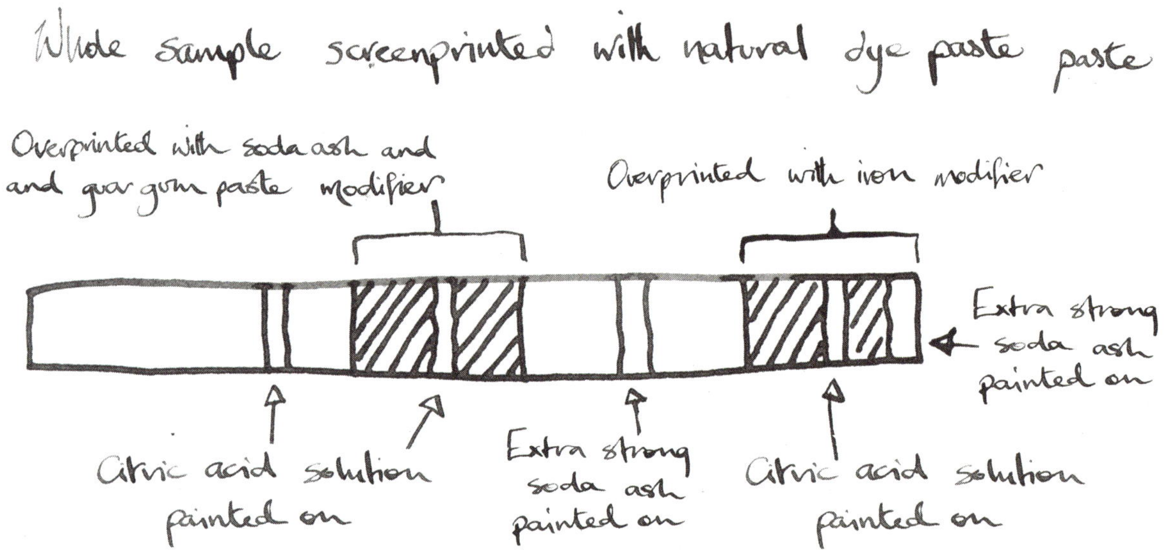

A key to the modifiers and method of application for the screenprinted textile sample tests. Where there are three samples on a card, the top sample wasn't heat set, the middle sample was 'steam iron' heat set and the bottom sample was steam set.

The Printing of Indigo

It should be remembered that whilst an indigo paste is included in the sample tests and is shown here for comparison, the paste was made with an indigo pigment and in this form, using a simple direct printing paste, is unable to 'dye' the fabric. It is purely a surface application. Whilst not particularly surprising that the indigo seemed to perform better with an unmordanted paste on unmordanted fabric (because indigo does not require a mordant), a stronger blue was produced on the areas modified with citric acid (chemists may be able to explain why!).

Traditional indigo printing paste recipes contain toxic chemicals to achieve the required reduction in oxygen and are not recommended, both in concern for your personal health and for the environment. Some research has been done using a sugar solution and an alkali to print indigo successfully and may be worth exploring further. There is also a method of immersing fabric printed with indigo into a fructose and alkaline bath (a fructose indigo vat without the indigo) but both are beyond the scope of this book. However, I have briefly experimented with a fructose/alkaline bath and the initial results look promising.

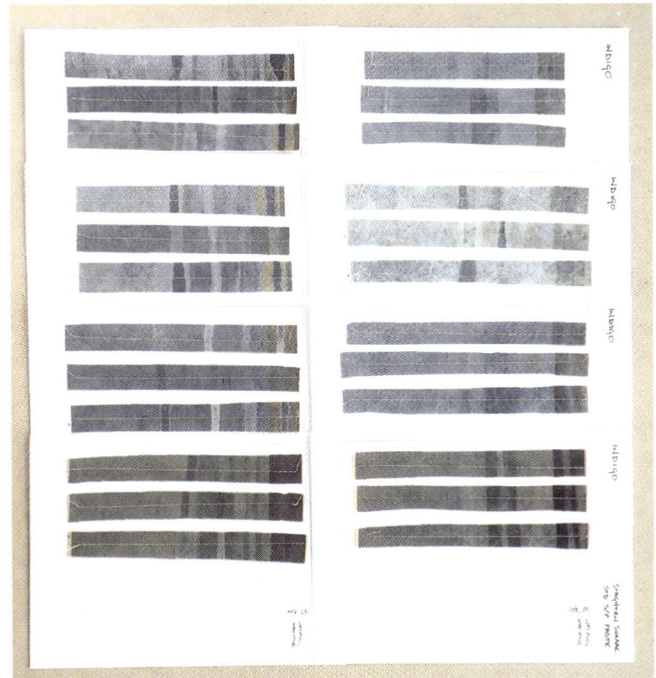

Screenprinted indigo on fabric samples. This paste contained indigo pigment dispersed through the mix rather than as a dye where the colourant is in solution.

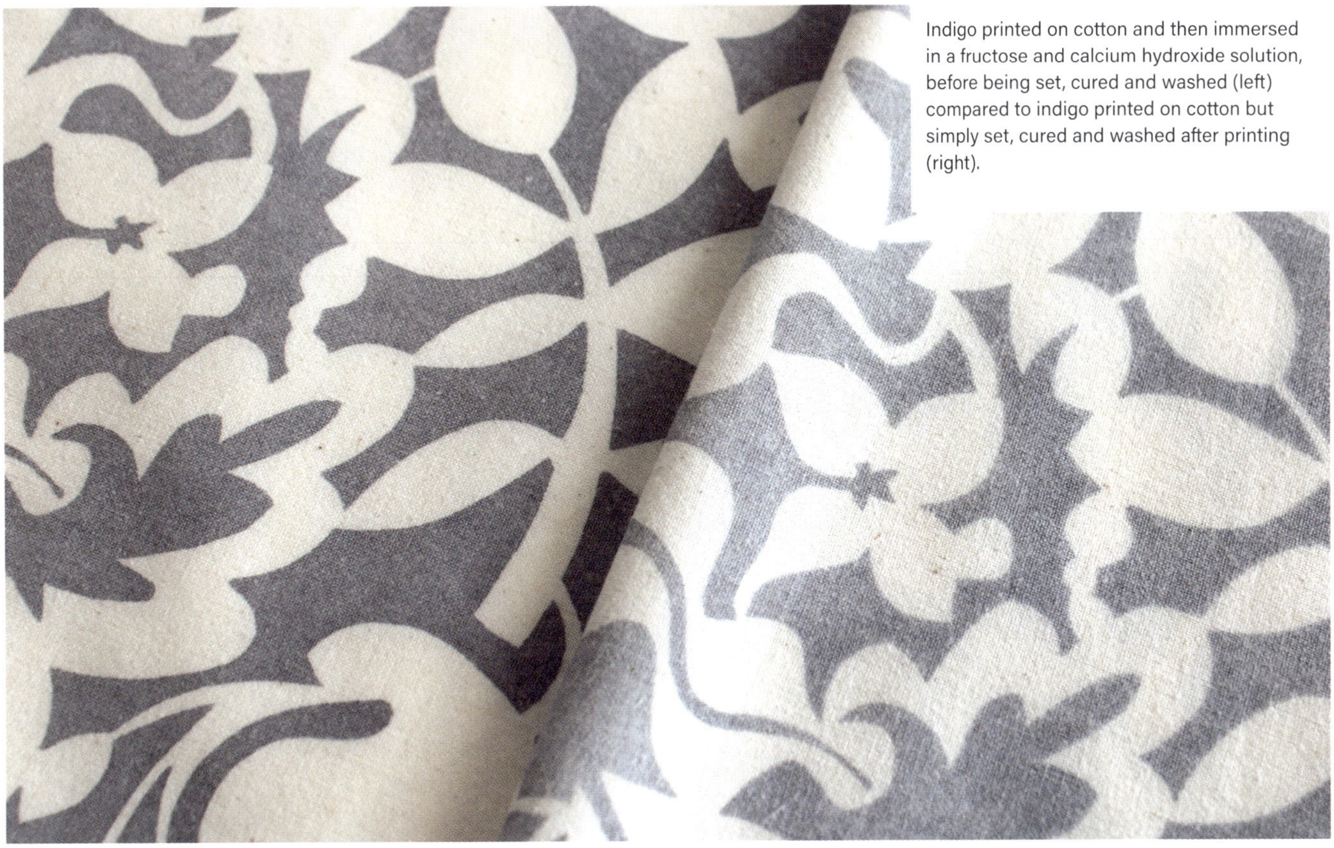

Indigo printed on cotton and then immersed in a fructose and calcium hydroxide solution, before being set, cured and washed (left) compared to indigo printed on cotton but simply set, cured and washed after printing (right).

Colour Mixing

Further colours can be achieved by over-printing dyes but also by pre-mixing dyes prior to printing. A vast array of colours can be created by using dyes in different percentages and by mixing dyes with each other. Different recipe mixes also have an effect on colour and the variations seem endless. Therefore, it is useful to create a colour chart of various mixes and percentages, as the results are sometimes surprising especially after washing. It is also a good idea to keep an unwashed comparison piece, which provides an understanding of final results and allows for more informed colour decisions to be made during printing. The type of fabric used to print on will also change how these colours appear.

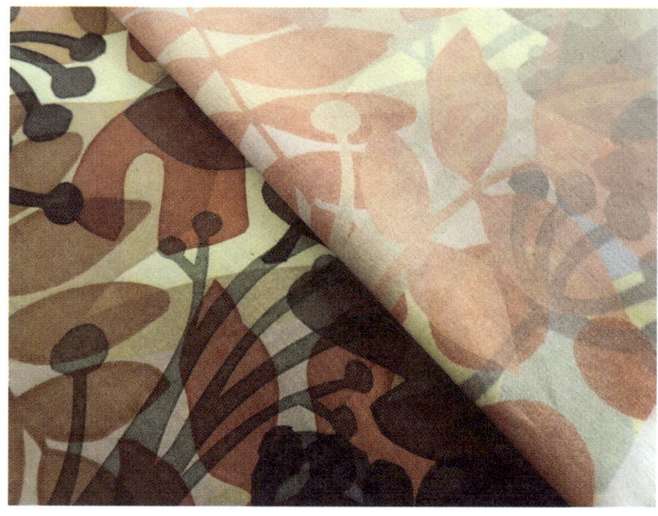

Think about keeping unwashed and washed samples as a colour reference aid when designing and printing textiles.

Colour mixing plant-based colour before it is printed and by over-printing layers.

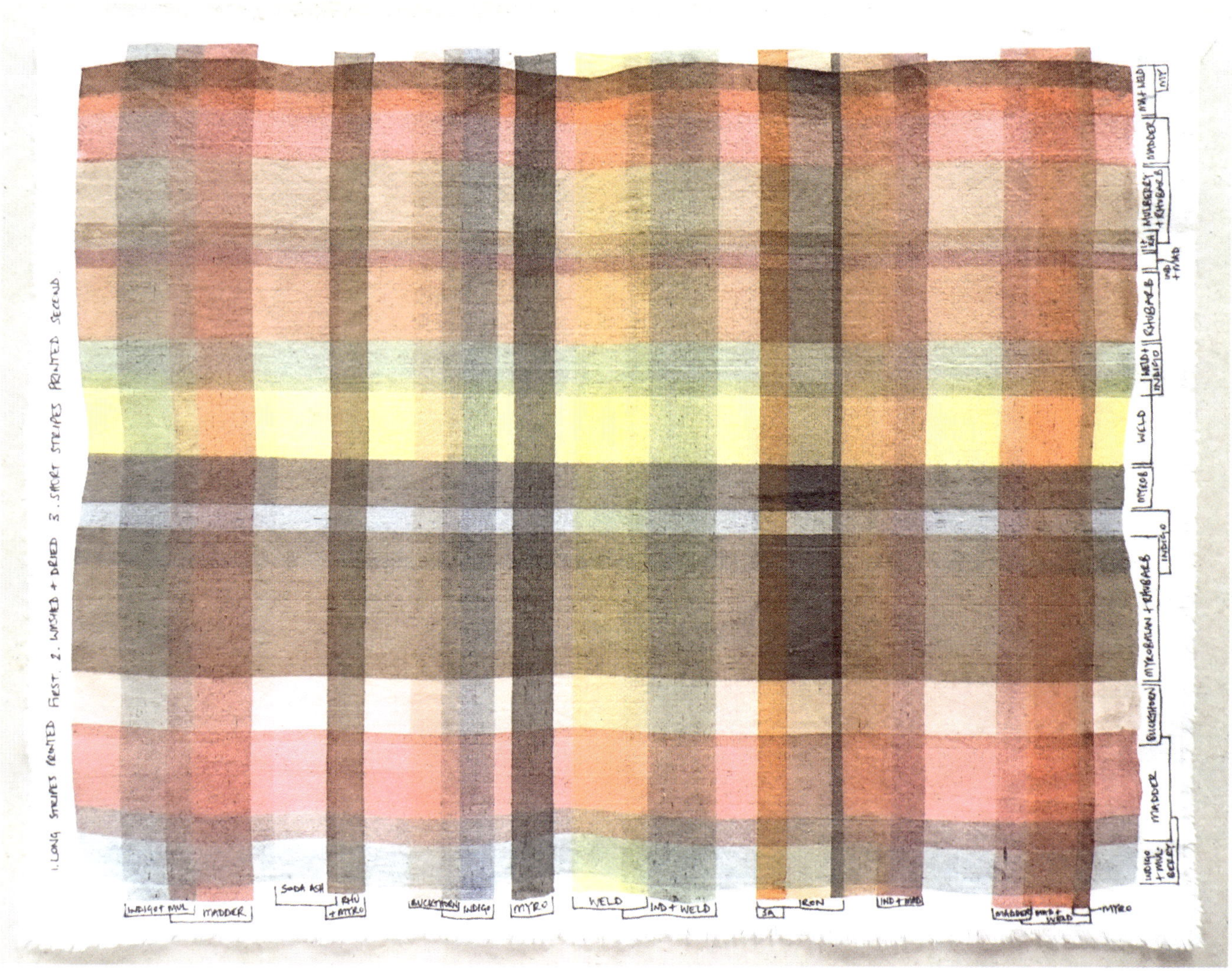

Different Techniques for Achieving Different Effects

Using different print techniques will give very diverse final results on fabrics. It is worth considering the final appearance required before deciding on the best process to use. The chosen method will largely depend on the preferred effect, the size of project, personal preference and access to equipment. Screenprinting will provide a very flat and even colour so is useful for printing large open areas in a design and, of course, it allows for highly detailed clean and crisp designs to be printed when using exposed screens. However, if executed seamlessly, it can lose that 'handmade' quality and appear machine produced.

Block printing retains a handmade quality and allows for easy repeat patterns to be made. It can be a very accessible method of printing as anything from a cut potato or clothes peg to a professional woodblock can be used. However, block printing with water-based inks and plastic-free mediums can be problematic if a flat, even colour is required. Different block 'materials', different print paste thicknesses and various methods of applying the paste to the block will all result in a different quality of print. By far the best result in terms of producing a flat, even colour when block printing was achieved using a water-based ink (or reduced dye liquid) with no thickener added. The fabric would benefit from a little sizing to inhibit the capillary action of the dye liquid around the edge of the block. A slightly thickened print paste is the most convenient to use for finer detail blocks, as thin liquids can easily clog a block and cause patches and blobs of dye to print rather than the design of the block. However, too thick a paste can cause exactly the same problem so testing and printing on spare fabric with blocks before starting a project is recommended. In commercially produced blocks, the deep recesses of the cut-away parts of the block help to prevent clogging from both too thin a liquid and too thick a paste. If producing your own blocks, it can be challenging to cut such deep recesses.

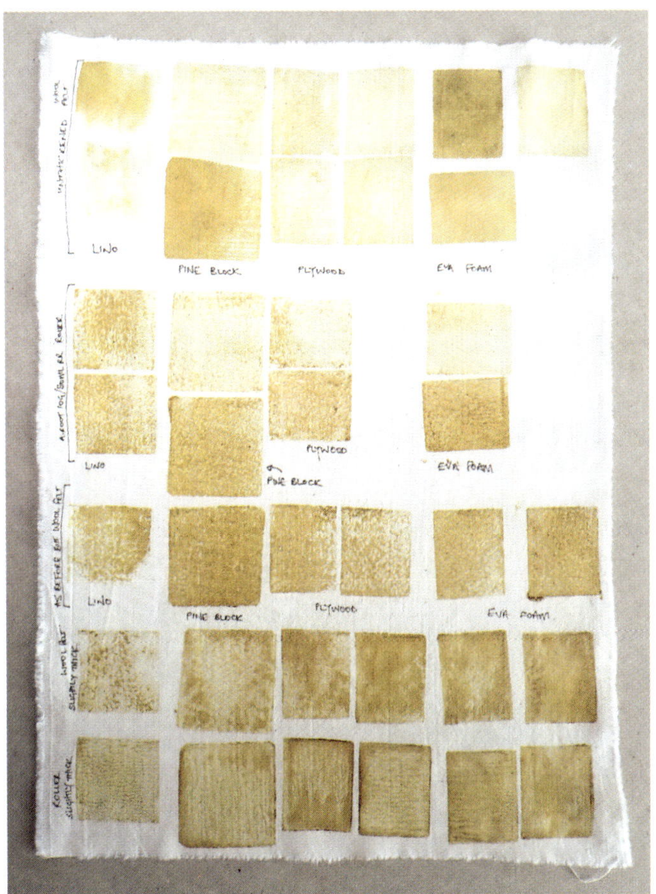

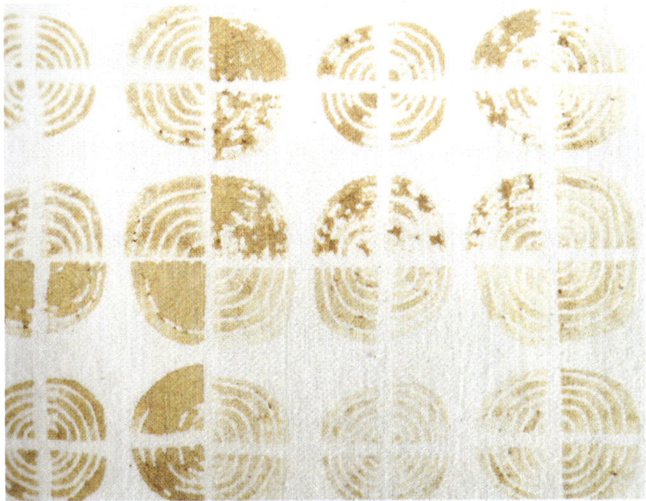

TOP
Using different materials and different paste mixes has an effect on the quality of the print when block printing. Lino, plywood, wood and EVA foam are all used here to show the variety in the marks made.

ABOVE
Issues caused by the use of too thin and too thick a paste when block printing.

DIRECT PRINTING PASTES

Recipes for both an extract paste and a fresh/dried dyestuff paste are included below. Use the recipes provided as a starting point but don't be afraid to adapt and modify ingredients and amounts. There are so many variables when using natural colour, it is best to experiment to find the methods and the mixes that you like the most. Experiment with different ratios of vinegar to water, dyestuff amount, dye extract percentages and type of mordant. As mentioned previously, substitute different thickeners depending on preference and what is available. *See* Chapter 4 for the recipe if experimenting with a thin water-based ink for block printing rather than a thickened paste.

RECIPE:

Water-Based Printing Paste for Fabric (using dye extracts)

This recipe uses dye extract, which gives a very concentrated colour. The recipe makes a little over 100g of paste. It's only a very small amount but the quantities can be increased once a satisfactory paste is made.

YOU WILL NEED:

- 5g dye extract
- 5g alum sulphate
- 50g hot water
- 50g vinegar (5% acetic acid)
- Guar gum to thicken
- Kettle
- Scales
- Heatproof glass beakers or similar for dissolving dye extract and alum sulphate
- Stirrers
- Lidded container for finished paste

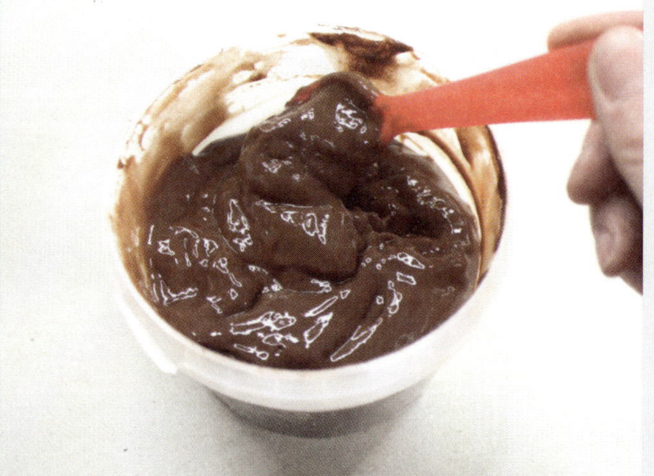

METHOD:

1. Dissolve the extract in approximately half (or more, if needed) of the hot water. Stir to ensure there are no lumps left in the solution. Dissolve the alum in the remaining hot water. Keep the extract solution and the alum solution separate.
2. Add the vinegar to the dye extract solution. Then add the alum solution to this and stir to combine.
3. Once the solution has cooled, the guar gum can be added to thicken the mix. Add the guar gum powder ¼ tsp at a time using a small sieve and tapping a little into the solution, stirring to combine and then adding more. The gum may cause lumps within the mixture. Combine as much as possible but don't worry – the paste will even out with time as the gum becomes absorbed. If the paste is lumpy, leave it a little thinner than required because as the lumps of gum are absorbed, the paste will continue to thicken. Alternatively, the guar gum can be added using a small whisk or electric hand blender to minimise lumps.
4. Store your paste in a sealable container in a cool, dark place. The vinegar should preserve the paste and act as a mould inhibitor.

Madder print paste made with dye extract. This is about the right consistency for screenprinting but should be thinner for block printing.

RECIPE:

Water-Based Printing Paste for Fabric (using fresh or dried dyestuffs)

The fresh or dried dyestuffs must be reduced down to achieve a concentrated colour. The recipe makes a little over 100g of paste, which is only a very small amount but the quantities can be increased once the right consistency and depth of colour have been achieved. You may find that different quantities of dyestuffs are required depending on the amount of colourant in the plant, and that more or less water is needed, depending on the type of plantstuff used (barks and roots absorb more water than other plant parts).

YOU WILL NEED:

- 50g dyestuff
- 500g water
- 5g alum sulphate
- 50g vinegar (5% acetic acid)
- Guar gum to thicken
- Kettle
- Scales
- Small stainless-steel saucepan
- Heatproof glass beakers or similar for dissolving alum sulphate
- Filter paper or fabric filter such as muslin
- Stirrers
- Heat source (portable hob, induction heater, buffet warmer or stove top)
- Lidded container for finished paste

METHOD:

1. Add the dyestuff to the water in a small saucepan and start to heat the liquid. Whilst the dyestuff is in the water, it can be left overnight either before or after heating to allow the colour to develop more fully.
2. Gently heat the dyestuff and the hot water together and, once the liquid has reduced by approximately two-thirds, remove the dyestuff by filtering with a tightly woven mesh or filter paper. Continue gently reducing the liquid until approximately 50g of liquid remains. Do not boil the liquid as this may damage the colour. A shallow stainless-steel tray on a buffet warmer is a handy way of gently reducing liquid without allowing it to get too hot.
3. Add the vinegar to the reduced dye liquid and stir to combine. In a separate beaker, dissolve the alum in a minimal amount of hot water and add to the dye solution. Remember that any liquid added to the solution at this point is diluting the colour.
4. Once the solution has cooled, the guar gum can be added to thicken the mix. Add the guar gum powder ¼ tsp at a time using a small sieve, tapping a little into the solution, stirring to combine then adding more. The gum may cause lumps within the mixture. The paste will even out with time as the gum becomes absorbed into the mixture but combine as much as possible first. Alternatively, the guar gum can be added using a small whisk or electric hand blender to minimise lumps.
5. Store your paste in a sealable container in a cool, dark place.

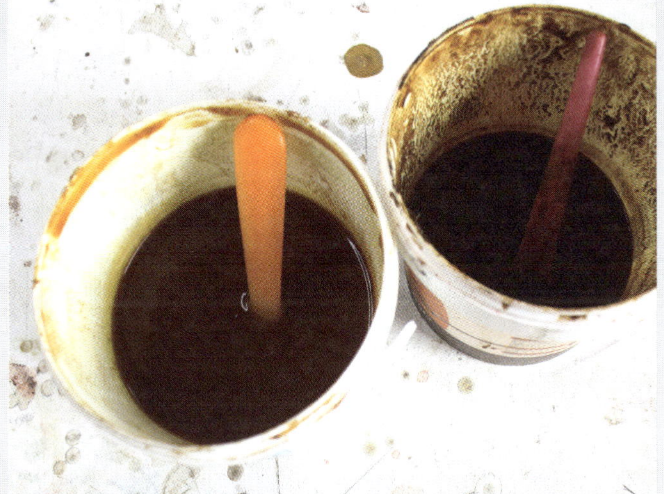

Rhubarb root paste made from dried dyestuff (left) and dye extract (right). This is about the right consistency for block printing.

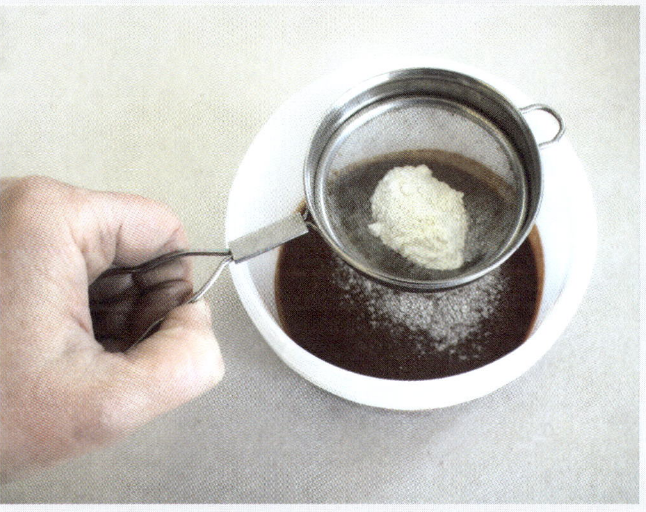

Use a tea strainer or small sieve to add guar gum if you don't have a stick blender.

Storing Plant-Based Printing Ink

Keep as cool as possible but do not store in the fridge when not using – the paste becomes thin and watery much more quickly. The vinegar in the mix helps inhibit mould and acts as a preservative, so mould growth should not be too much of a problem.

The paste will become thinner over time but more guar gum can be added to thicken. Bear in mind that additional ingredients will dilute the colour.

Substitutions and Recipe Modification

USING DIFFERENT ALUMINIUM MORDANTS

Try substituting alum acetate or alum lactate for alum sulphate. Tests show that an alum acetate-based print paste does make some difference to the colour achieved on textiles both for protein and cellulose fibres. This would be expected on cellulose fibres but was surprising on the wool and silk fibres. When using madder there was a minimal colour difference, with the alum acetate paste producing a slightly more brick-coloured red with slightly less pink but not on all fibres. As both the alum acetate and alum lactate mordants are much more costly than alum sulphate, it doesn't seem to be worth it, unless they appear to be substantially more washfast over repeated washing and exposure to light, which will require further testing. There also seems to be little or no degradation in colour as the paste ages, though adding extra guar gum or liquid may dilute the colour and make it appear to be less effective.

OMITTING THE MORDANT

If you prefer to mordant the fabric rather than the paste, just omit the mordant from the recipes above. If doing so, the vinegar can also be removed and more water added in its place. The vinegar is only required as an anti-precipitant for the dye and mordant solution and is not needed for unmordanted pastes, though it is a useful preservative.

INCREASING THE MORDANT AMOUNTS

Logic would dictate that the more mordant added to the paste, the better the bond between the dye and the fabric it is printed onto. Initial tests show that is not the case, with increased mordant percentages seeming to have an adverse effect on the strength of colour achieved. Too much mordant added to a print paste may cause a lake to start forming, which would render the colourant insoluble and unable to dye the fabric.

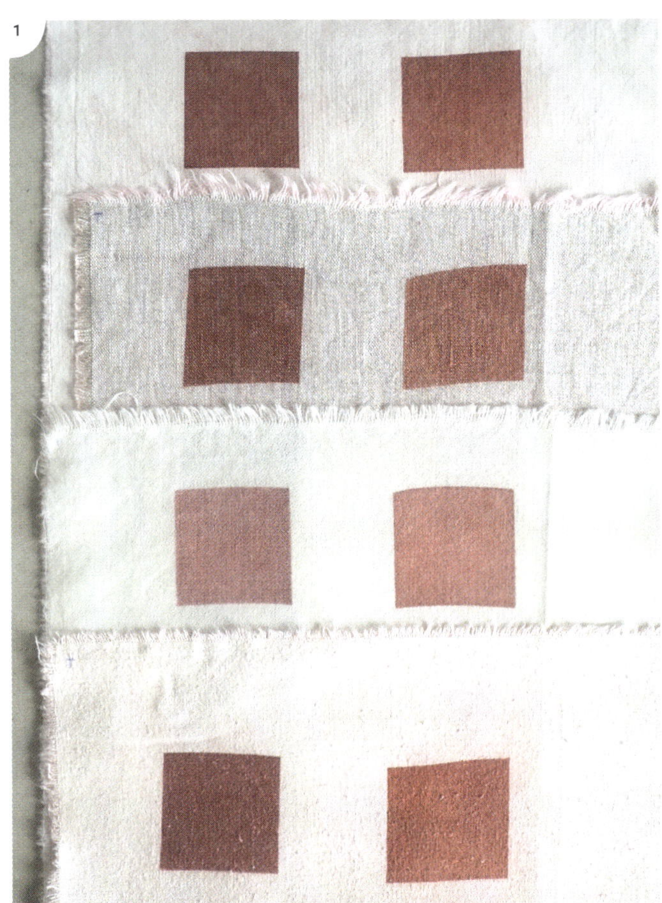

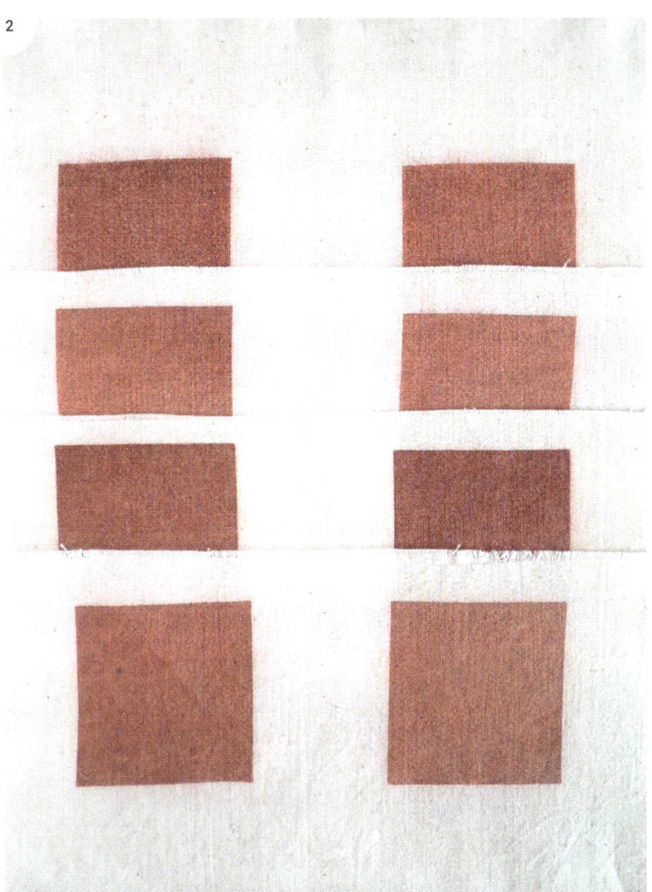

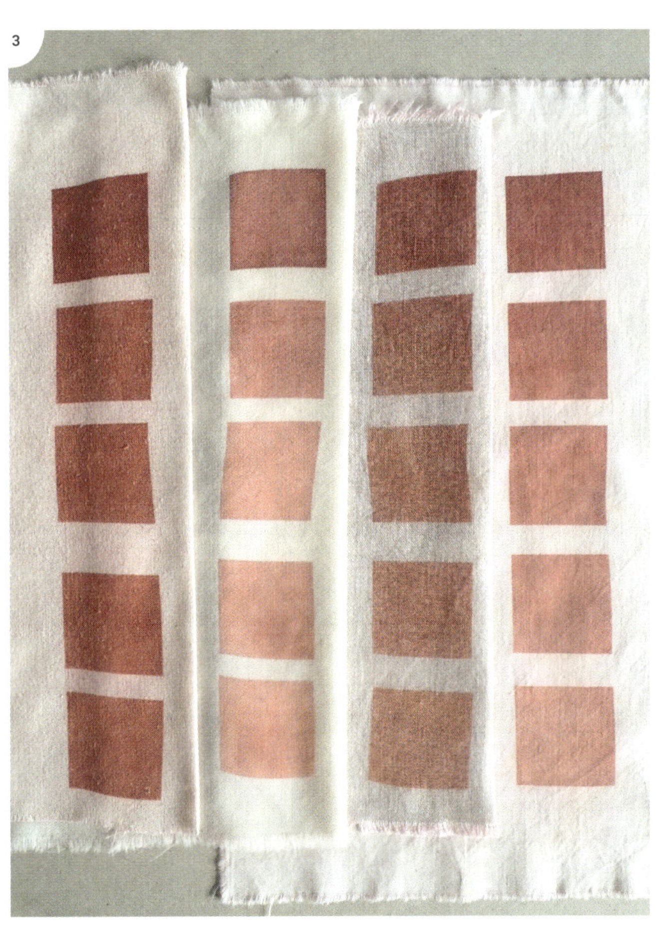

1) Madder printed with an alum acetate mordant paste (left column) and an alum sulphate mordant paste (right column) on cotton, linen, wool and silk (top to bottom).

2) Madder printed with an alum acetate mordant paste (left column) and an alum sulphate mordant paste (right column) on day one, day seven, day fourteen and day 28 (top to bottom) after the paste was made. All samples were set, cured and washed in the same way (allowing for human variation, which may explain the slightly darker colour on the third row).

3) Increasing the amount of mordant in the print paste seemed to have an adverse effect on the colour. These madder pastes had increasing amounts of alum sulphate added and the colours on silk, wool, linen and cotton (left to right) all seem to have reduced in strength.

Troubleshooting

Paste too thin – add more guar gum. Gently sprinkle on top of printing paste and mix in. It may take one to two hours or overnight for the gum to be incorporated fully.
Paste too thick – add more water and mix in. If the printing paste is very thick and requires a lot of liquid, consider adding a 50:50 ratio of water to vinegar.
Paste not thickening – I have found that some dye extracts can inhibit the guar gum's thickening action. If this happens, put a small amount of printing paste in a separate container and add guar gum to this, rather than the full amount. Make it overly thick and then start adding a little of the thin printing paste to the thickened amount, until enough printing paste is made. Vinegar can also inhibit the gum's thickening properties so make sure the vinegar is a 5 per cent acetic acid solution. If any higher, water down or add less vinegar to the printing paste.
Lumpy printing paste – usually solved by leaving paste overnight to allow the gum to be fully incorporated into the mix. Alternatively, use a small squeegee with a flat sieve or splashguard to force the paste through the mesh and remove any lumps.
Streaky or spotty printing paste – often caused by not mixing or dissolving a dye extract properly. Mix a few days before using to avoid this issue.

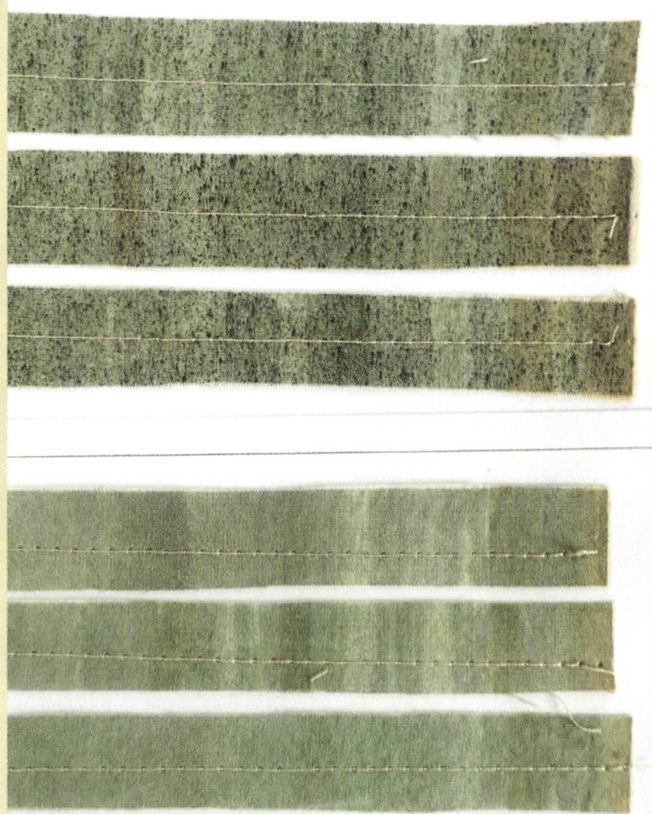

Streaky or spotty prints are the result of the dye not being dissolved properly or mixed thoroughly into the paste, especially when using dye extracts. The samples shown here were printed immediately after mixing the paste (top) and a week after mixing (bottom).

GUAR GUM

The amount of gum has not been specified in recipes as I have found guar gum can become less effective the older it gets. This means more gum is required to achieve the same consistency. However, between ½–1 teaspoon should be ample for 100g of paste to make a thick jam-like consistency. Add enough so that the paste has only a thin jam-like consistency, as it will continue to thicken overnight. Experiment and if the paste is too thick, add a little water. If the paste is too thin, add some more gum. Plant-based pastes generally perform best when thicker than standard acrylic screenprinting pastes, but this is very much personal preference.

Force paste through a splatter guard or flat sieve if the paste is lumpy.

MORDANT PRINTING PASTES

Mordant printing is an alternative to directly printing plant-based colour onto textiles. It has a long history of being used to create highly detailed and patterned cloth, especially in India. It then became popular in Europe during the seventeenth century when mordant-printed textiles began to be imported. Whilst it now isn't a particularly well-known or well-utilised technique in the West, it is becoming more popular once again, especially as people look to more sustainable ways of producing printed textiles.

Rather than printing with 'pre-coloured' printing pastes, different strengths of various mordants are applied to the cloth using various application techniques and with both thickened and unthickened mixes. After processing, the cloth is dyed in a single dye bath to achieve a range of tones and shades. The dye bonds with the mordant on the fabric but only in the areas that have been mordant printed, producing various colours from the dye according to the type of mordant and the strength of the mordant used.

The process is most effective when used with adjective dyes – those that best bond to the fabric when using a mordant. If mordant-printed textiles are dyed with substantive dyes (that don't generally require a mordant), the effect is less noticeable as the dye will also bond to the areas that haven't been printed, reducing the contrast between the printed areas and the non-printed areas. It is also best used on cellulose fibres, as the efficient take-up of colour by protein fibres such as wool and silk without a mordant prevents a strong design being achieved.

Whilst this is a fairly complex process and it can be quite difficult to realise good results (especially if using iron), the effort is worth it. The satisfaction of dyeing textiles in a single dye bath and achieving a range of colours is greatly pleasing. The colours achieved are also exceptionally washfast, withstanding regular washing by machine. Nevertheless, remember that any dyes susceptible to a pH colour change will still be affected by coming into contact with acids or alkalis so spilt lemon juice, human sweat or even aluminium-based deodorants can affect the colour.

When mixing and using mordant pastes, be prepared to work quickly and for a short, sustained period. The pastes should be used as soon as possible after making so it's best to have either a lot of projects prepared or only make a small amount of the paste. The pastes will last but may become less effective over time, although I have used them with good results a week or two after making. Using a small amount of paste can be problematic if screenprinting, as a certain amount is needed on the screen for the squeegee to run smoothly.

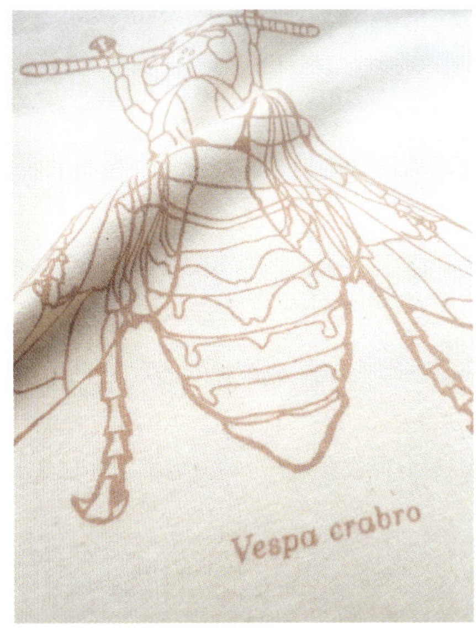

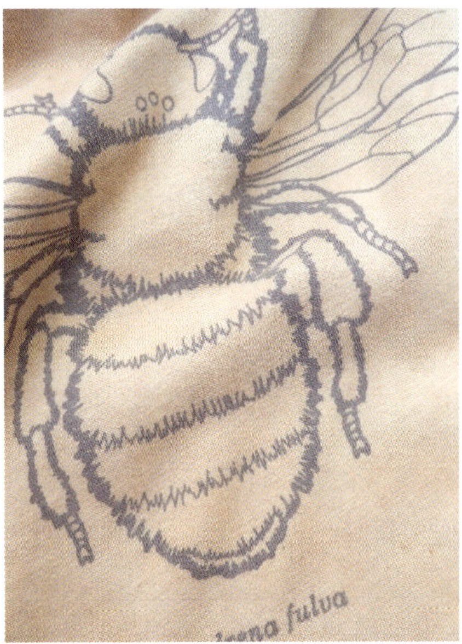

Mordant-printed with iron using exposed screen. TOP: before dyeing. ABOVE: after dyeing with rhubarb root.

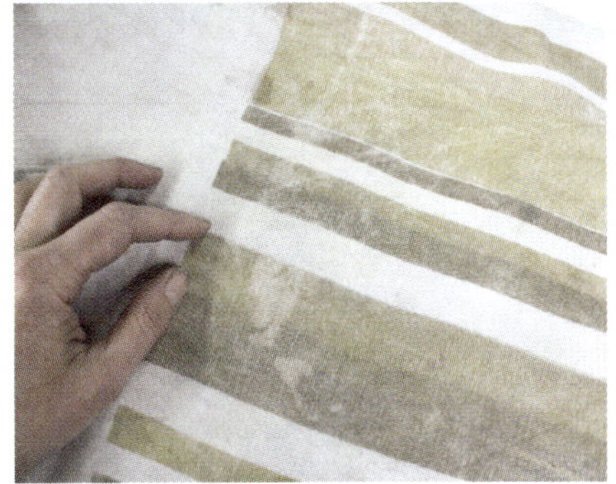

Mordant-printed textiles are exceptionally washfast but are still susceptible to pH changes and liquids. This tea towel has been used to wipe up spilt lemon juice.

Using Different Mordants and Application Methods

Using different mordants will alter the colour achieved after dyeing and this can be used to create a range of colours and tones on your fabric. Using an alum mordant will result in a strongly saturated area of colour, whilst an iron mordant will often darken the colour, depending on which natural dye is being used. These mordants can be mixed together in different percentages to create further colour results and can also be strengthened or weakened in increments to create additional shades of colour.

Mordant pastes can be applied to textiles in any way it is possible to transfer the paste to the fabric. Screenprinting, block printing, stencilling and painting are all effective ways of applying the mordant to the fabric, although each different method will produce different finishes and end results.

Combining Mordant Pastes

Alum and iron pastes can be mixed together to create further tones and shades. Try a 50:50 mix to start with and then adapt accordingly for designs. A 20 per cent neutral paste to 80 per cent mordant paste will create only a subtly lighter colour when dyed than the full-strength mordant paste whereas a 20 per cent mordant paste to 80 per cent neutral paste will create a significantly paler colour. Increments of 10 per cent create subtly different tones of colour. Twenty- nine different shades can be produced using 10 per cent increments of alum to neutral paste, iron to neutral paste and iron/alum mixtures. This large number of colours demonstrates the variability and control that can be exerted when using mordant pastes and mixes. Whilst it is not suggested that this level of complexity should be used in a first mordant printing project, it does serve to show how pastes can be manipulated to realise subtly different colours.

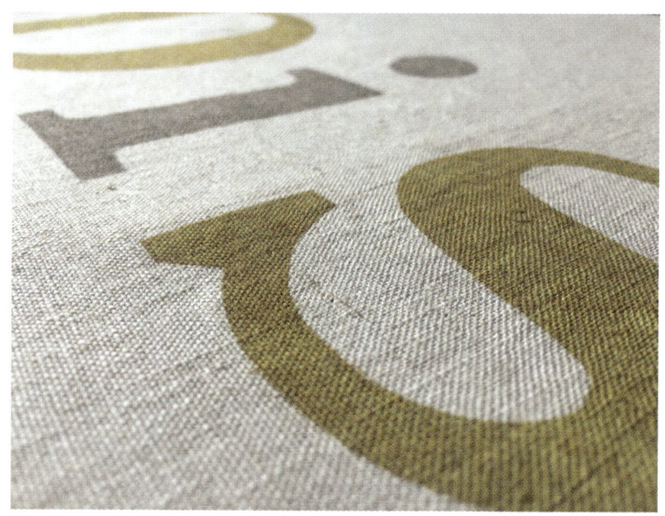

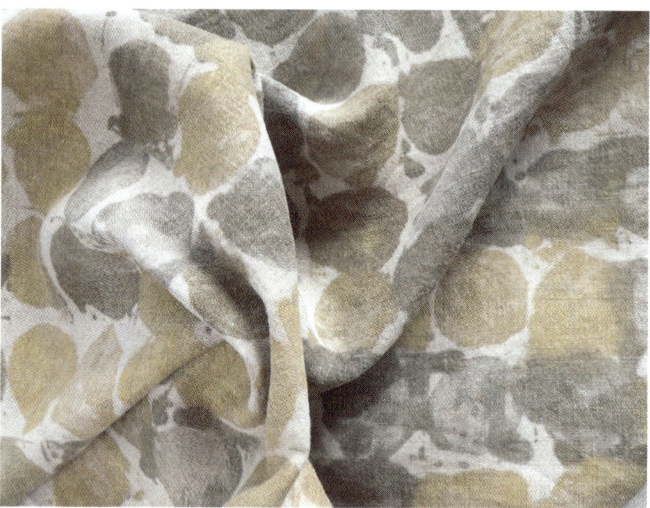

TOP Mordants screenprinted using paper stencils, then dyed with heather.

BOTTOM Mordants block printed then dyed with heather.

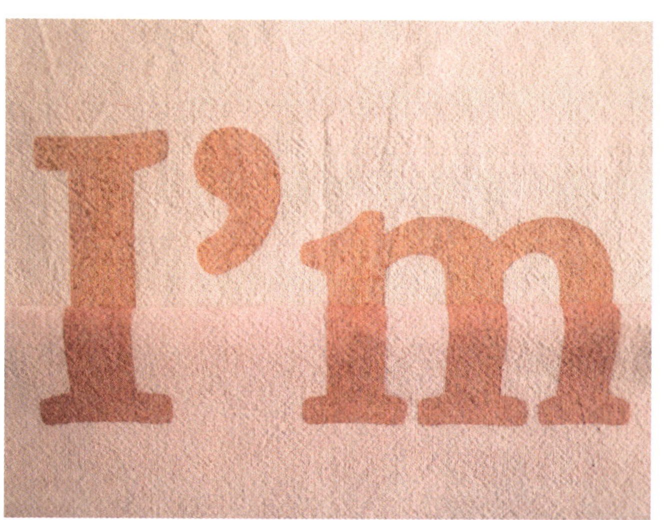

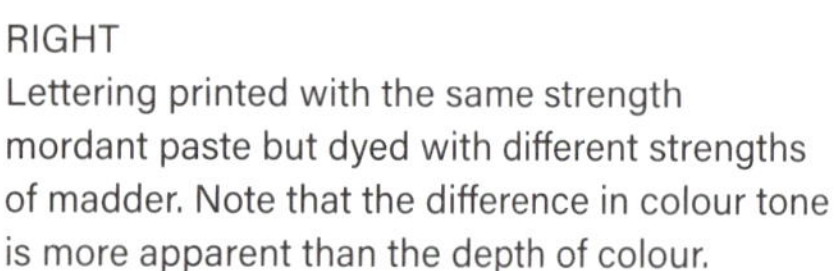

RIGHT
Lettering printed with the same strength mordant paste but dyed with different strengths of madder. Note that the difference in colour tone is more apparent than the depth of colour.

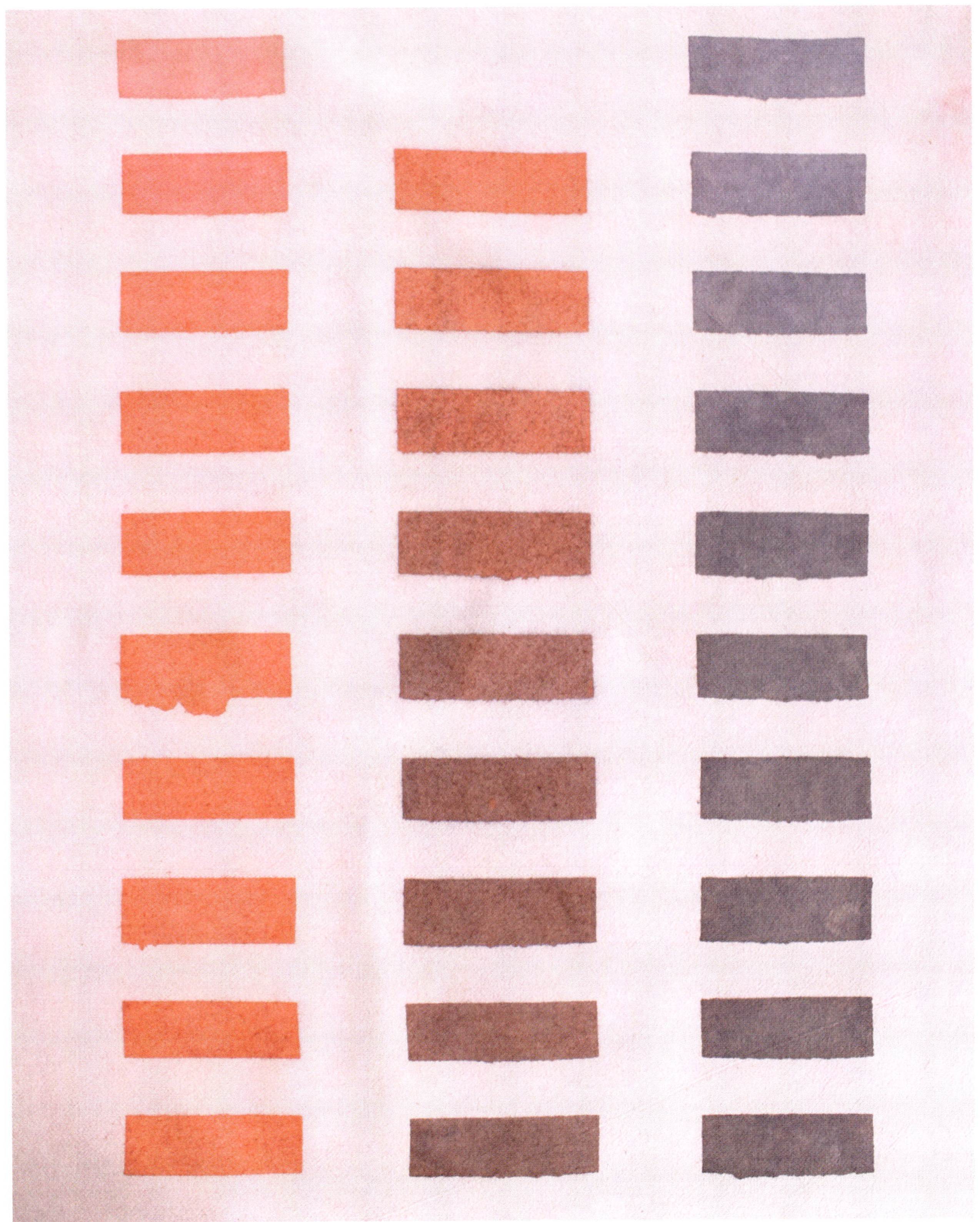

ABOVE
This madder-dyed sample shows 29 shades of colour made using 10 per cent increments of alum in a neutral paste, an alum to iron mix and an iron in a neutral paste (left to right columns).

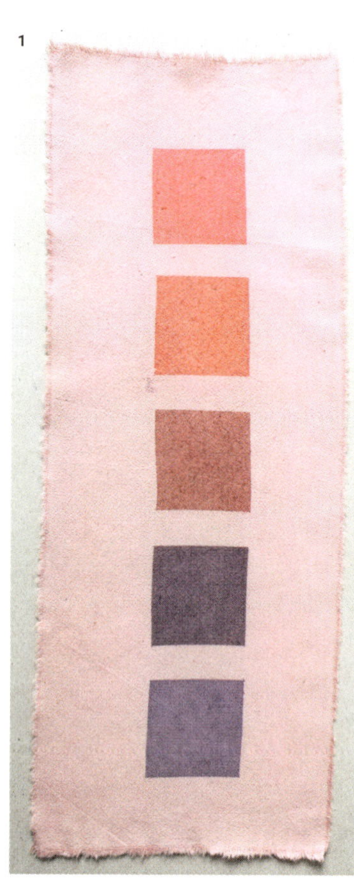

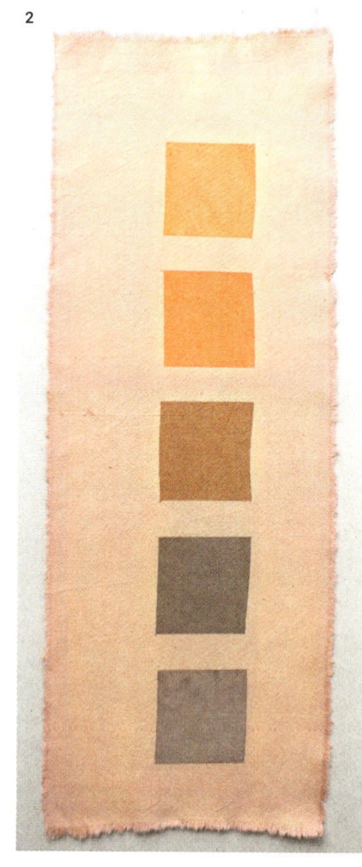

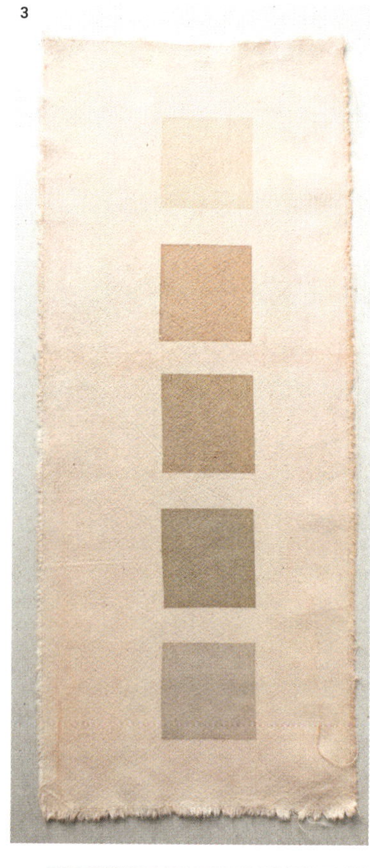

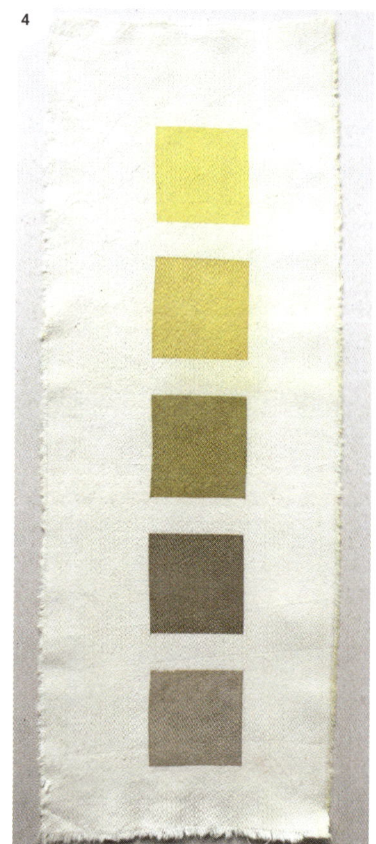

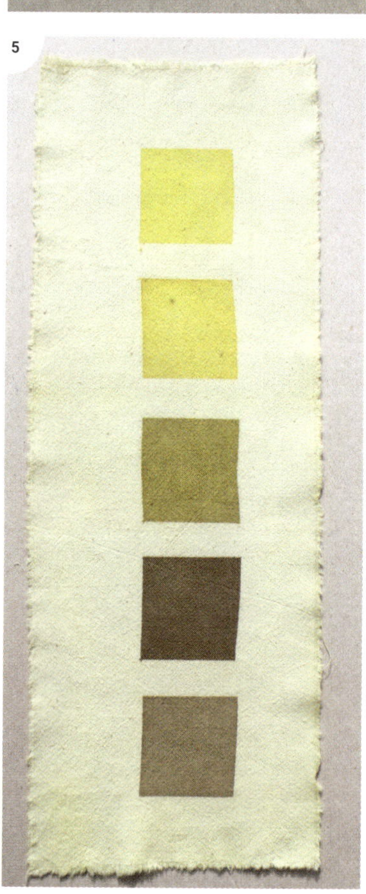

1) Mordant-printed sample, dyed with madder.

2) Mordant-printed sample, dyed with coreopsis.

3) Mordant-printed sample, dyed with rhubarb.

4) Mordant-printed sample, dyed with buckthorn berries.

5) Mordant-printed sample, dyed with weld.

RECIPE:

Alum Mordant Paste

This recipe uses alum sulphate and sodium acetate, which can both be substituted by alum acetate (remove the alum sulphate and the sodium acetate from the recipe and replace with just 5g of alum acetate). However, I often struggle to get alum acetate to dissolve efficiently when using in a mordant paste and it seems to 'sit' on top of the fabric, creating a patchy effect once dyed.

YOU WILL NEED:

- 10g alum sulphate
- 10g sodium acetate
- 100g hot water
- Guar gum to thicken
- Kettle
- Scales
- Stirrers
- Lidded container for finished paste

METHOD:

1. Dissolve the alum sulphate in the hot water, stirring to ensure it has completely dissolved. Add the sodium acetate and stir to dissolve.
2. Wait for the water to cool and then gradually add guar gum to thicken, stirring continuously.
3. If the mixture contains lumps, leave it a couple of hours or overnight to gradually absorb the gum into the mixture. A stick blender or whisk can be used to prevent lumps forming.

It is useful to add a small amount of dye or dye extract to your alum mordant paste to colour it slightly as the paste is completely colourless once dry. Whilst it is relatively easy to see where the paste has been applied when cloth is held up to the light or when a screen is removed, it is very hard to see how much coverage has been achieved, especially whilst screenprinting. If using dye extract, dissolve this first and add a little at a time until the paste is faintly tinted. If using a dye liquid (rather than an extract) either include this in your hot water weight at the start or add an amount afterwards and be prepared to add more gum to thicken. Sappanwood was traditionally used as it is not particularly lightfast and will not affect the final colour.

RECIPE:

Iron Mordant Paste

This recipe creates quite a weak iron paste, which will produce dark colours with some dyes but others may require a slightly stronger solution. Increase the ferrous sulphate and the sodium acetate for darker tones. I use a 4g ferrous sulphate and 4g sodium acetate mix for details and dramatic colour changes.

YOU WILL NEED:

- 1g ferrous sulphate
- 1g sodium acetate
- 100g hot water
- Guar gum to thicken
- Kettle
- Scales
- Stirrers
- Lidded container for finished paste

METHOD:

1. Dissolve the ferrous sulphate in the hot water, stirring to ensure it is completely dissolved. It is sometimes necessary to strain this liquid through a paper filter as little particles of iron can remain at the bottom of the container.
2. Add the sodium acetate and stir to dissolve.
3. Wait for the liquid to cool and slowly add the gum, stirring continuously to avoid lumps forming.

Remember to keep the stirrers and pots used for iron separate to other tools and containers. This paste doesn't need colouring as it is a strong rust or dark brown colour and is easily visible when printed.

RECIPE:

Neutral Paste

Make up enough neutral paste for your project. Start by making 100g if unsure how much is needed.

METHOD:

1. Weigh out 100g of cold water and slowly add gum until it's the thickness you want to print with. The neutral paste (just gum and water) is useful to weaken mordant pastes to create a tonal range. Make up the paste and then add it to the mordant pastes in increments.

COLOUR MODIFIERS

The colour of the printing paste can be modified in a similar way to how a natural dye colour might be modified on fibres either during or after dyeing. The colour of the print paste can be changed either before applying to the textile by adding a little alkaline, acid or iron solution to the mix or after printing by application directly onto the fabric on top of the printed dye colour.

Look at the printed samples earlier in this chapter to see how modifiers might affect a colour or refer to a natural dyeing instruction book, which should offer guidance on how colours will change. Broadly, iron tends to darken or 'sadden' colours, acids tend to lighten colours and alkalis either concentrate or quite often bring out pinky tones, especially in dyes that contain a red pigment. Modifiers will have little or no effect on some dyes such as indigo.

It is advisable to be careful with the amounts of modifier when making the paste and only add a little at a time. This is because modifiers can have an adverse effect on the textiles if added in too great a quantity. Additionally, a large amount of soda ash (or other alkali) can change the pH enough to allow the dye and alum to react, bonding to become a lake pigment. Remember that iron migrates easily to surfaces, utensils and clothing so be careful to keep any tools and equipment used for iron modifiers separate to avoid black and dark spots across work.

Modification recipes are provided here, although the process is very adaptable to experimentation by adding a little of the modifier to a print paste, checking the colour, then adding more if a greater adjustment is required. More modifiers can always be added but they can't be taken away. If modifying the dye paste rather than creating a separate modifier paste, try decanting a small amount of the paste and modifying that first. An easy way to test potential colour change is to paint or dab some print paste onto some spare fabric, and then quickly apply a drop of modifier on top or a couple of grains if in granular form. Very quickly the dye will react with the modifier and you'll get an indication of the colour reaction.

Once washed, the appearance of modifiers can be greatly reduced and it can be disappointing to see the different colours achieved revert back to a tone similar to the unmodified areas. These effects and colour changes after washing also depend on the dye and modifier used. This primarily happens with the application of a soda ash modifier, which raises the pH levels. On weld, it can be particularly disappointing where the strong yellow evens out to the unmodified colour, and on rhubarb root where the lovely pink almost disappears. Try applying modifiers after the first wash or at least leaving the textile to cure for a number of weeks before washing for a greater effect.

RECIPE:

Alkali Modifier Paste

YOU WILL NEED:

- 5–10g soda ash
- 100g hot water
- Guar gum

METHOD:

1. Add the soda ash to the hot water and stir to dissolve.
2. Allow to cool and then add guar gum to thicken.

Once thickened, this can be used just as you would the direct printing pastes. It is fairly colourless but will change the tone of many natural dyes it comes into contact with, regardless of whether they have been printed on or the fabric has been dyed.

If you want to change the colour of the direct printing paste before printing, add a little soda ash to hot water to dissolve and then stir into the paste. Add slowly and only a little at a time, stirring in between each addition to avoid a strong effervescent reaction between the alum and the soda ash.

RECIPE:

Iron Modifier Paste

YOU WILL NEED:

- 1–5g ferrous sulphate
- 100g hot water
- Guar gum

METHOD:

1. Add the ferrous sulphate to the hot water and stir to dissolve.
2. Allow to cool and then add guar gum to thicken.

Use this paste just as you would a direct printing paste but be very careful to properly clean any utensils and equipment after using.

It is good practice to apply iron paste at the end of a printing session, which helps reduce cross-contamination. Iron modifier paste can also change the colour of undyed fabric so be careful where the paste is applied.

The printing pastes that already contain colour can be modified by directly adding ferrous sulphate dissolved in a little hot water. Add extra guar gum if required.

RECIPE:

Acid Modifier (discharge) Paste

YOU WILL NEED:

- 5–10g citric acid
- 100g hot water
- Guar gum

METHOD:

1. Add the citric acid to the hot water and stir to dissolve.
2. Allow to cool and then add guar gum to thicken. Add more guar gum if needed to get the desired consistency.

The amount of citric acid can be amended to make the paste a colour 'lightener' or a colour 'remover', acting as a discharge paste. Experiment with different dyes and amounts to get the preferred effect. For a more gentle paste, try other acids such as lemon juice or vinegar.

Do not apply direct heat (such as an iron) to citric acid paste before washing as it can damage the fibres and cause them to disintegrate. If printed colour requires setting, do this before applying an acid paste. On washing, the citric acid paste can easily bleed into the surrounding colour and create patches. Don't allow the fabric to sit and soak in the water – wash it quickly and fairly vigorously to remove the paste as quickly as possible.

WASHFASTNESS TESTS: WELD, MADDER AND INDIGO

These images show the results of cotton, linen, silk and wool screenprinted with plant-based colour and then subjected to a series of washes. The first wash was a gentle hand-wash to remove any excess dye and mordant, with all subsequent washes done in a machine on a 40°C standard cycle and washed alongside other fabrics and clothes but in mesh bags to contain the samples. The detergent was a standard laundry sheet. Normally wool fabrics would be washed by hand or on a wool cycle, but I wanted to treat the fabrics in exactly the same way. This has caused the wool to felt so further tests with appropriate washing techniques are required.

Whilst there is an initial loss of colour from the first wash, this test does show that subsequent washes cause only a minimal loss of colour on the weld and madder dyes. This would probably have been improved by only hand-washing. The indigo has suffered a greater loss of colour as it was applied as a pigment without an insoluble binder. Indigo on cotton was missed out and forgotten during the testing stage. *See* earlier in the chapter for further information on printing with indigo on fabric.

Cotton

WELD

MADDER

FACING PAGE
INDIGO

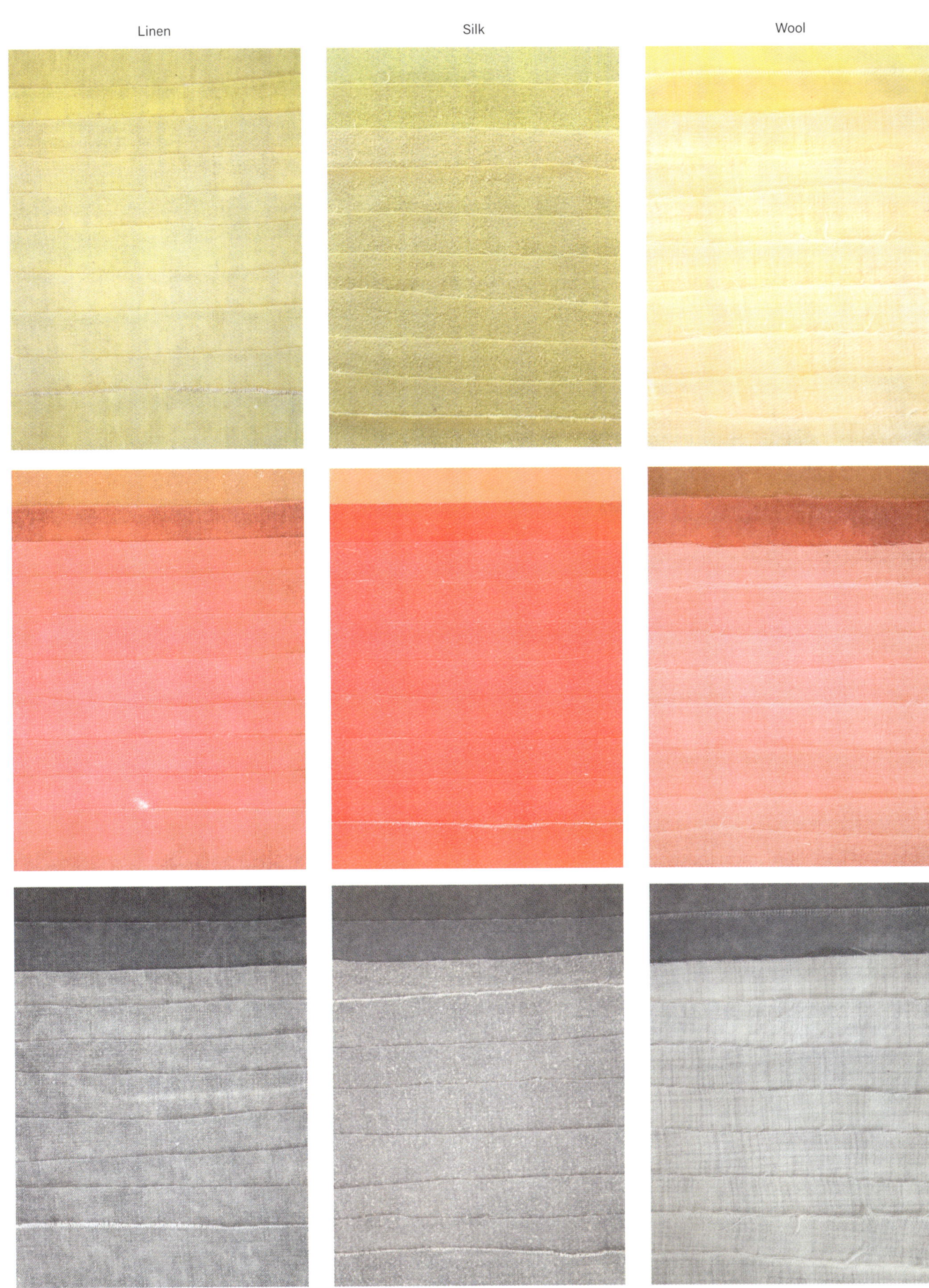
Linen
Silk
Wool

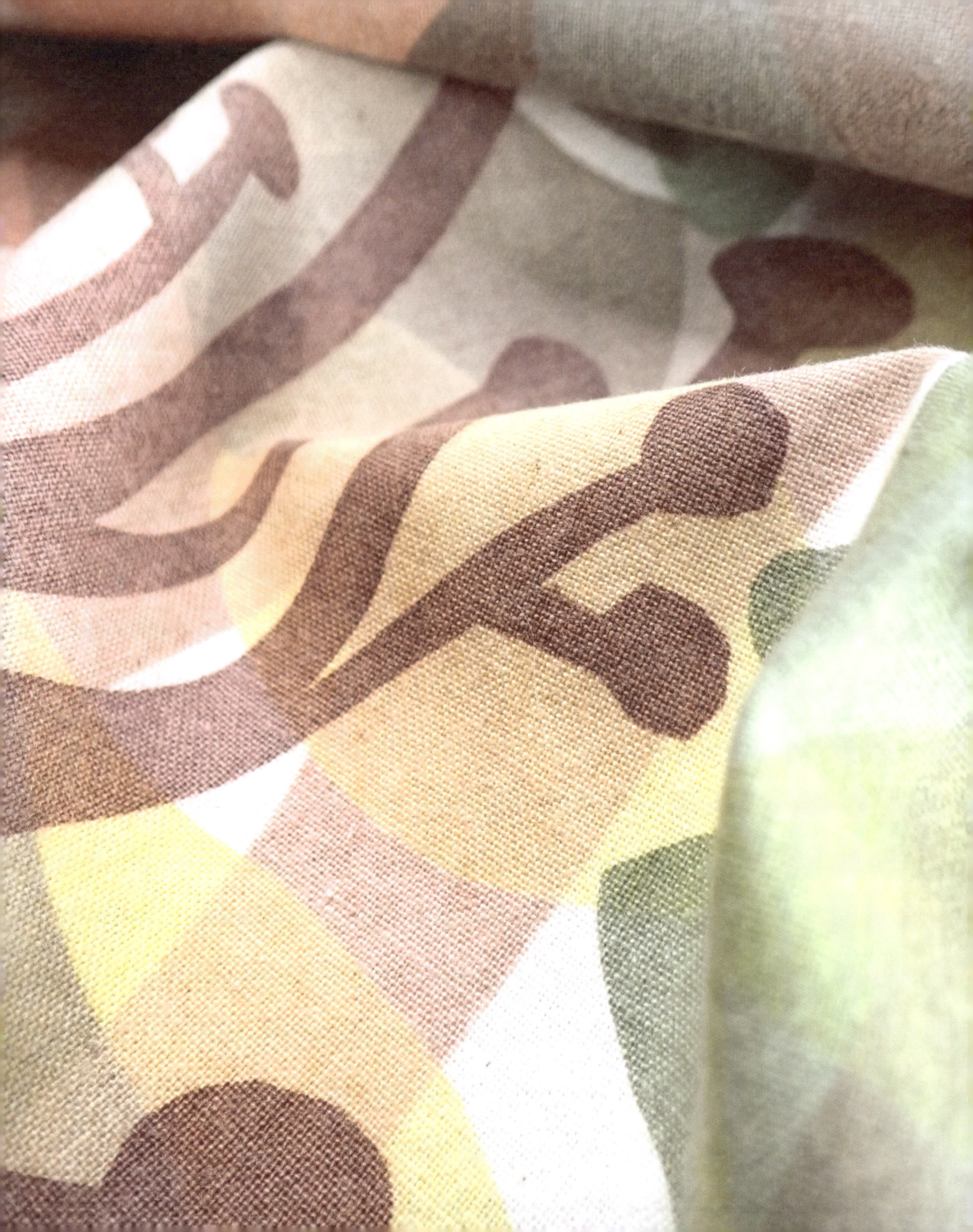

Chapter Six

PRINTMAKING PROCESSES FOR TEXTILES

FACING PAGE

Plant-based colour screenprinted onto cotton fabric using hand-cut stencils.

These projects can be followed step-by-step as an introduction to different printing techniques or can be adapted to incorporate your own designs. However, they are not meant to be directive and shouldn't dictate exactly what to produce – they are merely an aid to either starting out with some new techniques or incorporating plant-based colours and dyes into your work. Templates and stencils have not been provided. If stuck for inspiration or ideas, just use simple shapes such as freehand drawn and cut circles, rectangles, natural form silhouettes or random marks and lines. These projects are about learning a technique using new and unfamiliar materials, not about producing a finished piece of work.

FABRIC PREPARATION

There is a certain amount of preparation that must be carried out before printing with natural dyes onto fabric. Scouring is essential and whilst it might seem time-consuming and pointless, it is one of the most important stages of the process. The task is made less onerous by scouring a lot of fabric at once and then storing. Whether the fabric is mordanted or not depends on the project and personal choice, but it is worth trying out the assorted recipes to see what suits your practice and what results can be achieved from the different approaches.

If smaller pieces of fabric are needed to be cut from a larger piece (and the fabric is relatively lightweight), each piece does not need to be laboriously cut by hand. Fabric can be torn quite easily by making a small cut at the edge and then decisively pulling apart each side to rip the fabric. This has the advantage of dividing along the fibres and giving you straight lines, which can be hard to achieve with more slippery textiles. It should also cause much less shedding and fraying at the edges. Beware doing this with thicker or more heavyweight fabrics as it can stretch and distort them – test on a spare piece first.

Choosing Fabric

Fabric should ideally be as smooth as possible with a tight, rather than loose, weave. Cotton sheeting or similar is ideal to start with. However, experimenting with other fabrics and weaves is worth exploring and may give pleasing results. See Chapter 3 for further information on fabrics.

1) Plant-based colour screenprinted onto a smooth, tightly woven cotton fabric.

2) Plant-based colour screenprinted onto a rough, loose-weave linen fabric.

3) Plant-based colour screenprinted onto a twill weave wool fabric.

1

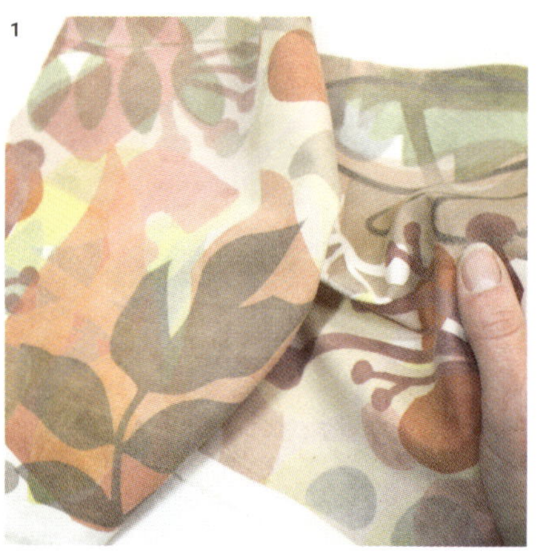

2

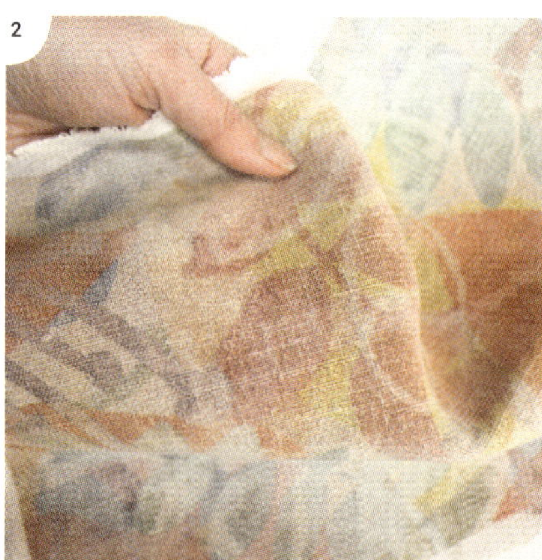

3

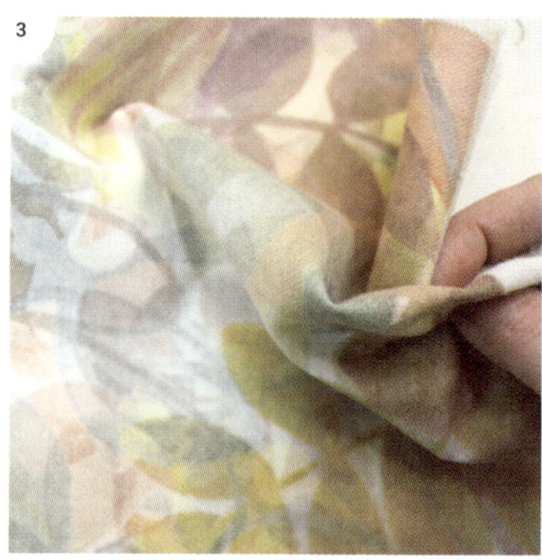

Scouring Fabric

Before printing, fabric must be scoured to remove any oils, pectins or waxes that are in the fibres, which would prevent colour take-up. Scouring essentially means to wash something, though there are specific techniques for doing so before dyeing. Even if fabric is sold as 'Prepared for Dyeing' or 'Ready for Dyeing', it should still be scoured. Printed work can be ruined by not properly scouring fabric so it is best not to take the chance. Secondhand fabric is great to use as it will often have been washed so much that most of the waxes and oils will have long since disappeared. It should still be washed at least once, especially if the fabric's prior treatment or use is unknown. Don't use fabric conditioner on fabrics as this leaves a coating, which will undo all the hard work of scouring the fabric in the first place.

COTTON AND LINEN

Cotton and linen should be scoured in a large vessel that provides enough room for the fabric to move freely when inside. Weigh the fabrics and make a note. Add 1 per cent WOF washing-up liquid and 2 per cent WOF soda ash to the vessel with water and stir well before adding the fabric. Bring to the boil and simmer for at least one hour, before leaving to cool and then rinsing. If the water is particularly dirty and yellowish, repeat the process. Linen often requires two washes to get clean. If fabric is secondhand, it has likely been washed enough to remove any fabrication residue – a wash in the washing machine should be adequate.

SILK AND WOOL

Silk and wool need to be heated gently in a pot with 1 per cent WOF washing-up liquid. Keep the water under a simmer for one hour, then leave to cool before rinsing. Remember that protein fibres can be shocked when changing them from hot to cold water or vice versa, so a gradual temperature change is always preferable.

Mordanting

Mordanting fabric is a personal choice. If using print pastes that already contain a mordant, it isn't necessary to also mordant the fabric. However, you may decide that it is easier to mordant the fabric than it is to mordant the pastes. Do not mordant fabric that is going to be mordant printed – this is explained further in Chapter 5.

To mordant cellulose fabrics such as cotton and linen, use alum acetate or alum lactate at 5 per cent WOF. To mordant protein fibres such as wool or silk, use alum sulphate or potassium alum sulphate at 10 per cent WOF.

Step 1: Weigh the dry but previously scoured fabric and make a note of the weight, then calculate how much mordant is needed.

Step 2: Before mordanting, immerse the fabric in water to ensure it is completely wet – this may take one to two hours if it is a heavyweight fabric.

Step 3: While the fabric is wetting out, dissolve the chosen mordant in a little hot water and add it to a large vessel. Add enough water to this vessel for the fabric to move about freely.

Step 4: Add the fabric and bring the solution to a simmer, stirring occasionally. Keep at this heat for one hour and then turn off the heat, allowing the fabric to cool in the pot.

Step 5: Once cool, rinse lightly, dry and label as 'scoured and mordanted'. Make sure this step is completed – it is hugely frustrating to have a piece of fabric and not know whether it has been mordanted or not.

Fabric can also be mordanted using a cool method, allowing it to be done in a large plastic container or trug. Prepare the mordant bath as above but don't heat, add the fabric and leave in for 24 hours, rather than heating for one hour. Occasionally stir the fabric and ensure it is completely submerged under the water.

SCREENPRINTING

This screenprinting project uses hand-cut stencils but exposed screens can also be used if preferred. The designs are based on previous drawings of dye plants that were ultimately printed on paper as fine art prints, using exposed screens for both the background colour and the key layer. The colours used were extracted from the dye plant depicted in the work. A few examples of the finished pieces can be seen throughout this book. The background colour 'shape' has now been simplified and hand cut into a stencil made from Tyvek 55gsm paper, although brown paper is also a good material to use for stencils.

Repeat pattern printing, designing repeat patterns and dealing with large scale projects are covered extensively in other textile printing books, so it is not necessary to cover these techniques here.

Stencils

For a first project, use simplified patterns and freehand shapes cut directly into the stencil paper. Keeping a first attempt simple and embracing mistakes is important. Alternatively, existing designs or artwork can be translated into stencils and a key layer if required.

When cutting stencils, separate the colour elements of the design and cut these individual elements onto individual sheets of stencil paper. Ensure the stencil has a margin of at least 50mm. This reduces the need to add extra tape to the screen to mask off open areas. Tape needs to be very carefully removed from screens when they are being washed, as it can leave glue residue on the screen.

The finished design was printed with madder, a weld/madder mix, weld, indigo and a weld/indigo mix before being set, cured and washed.

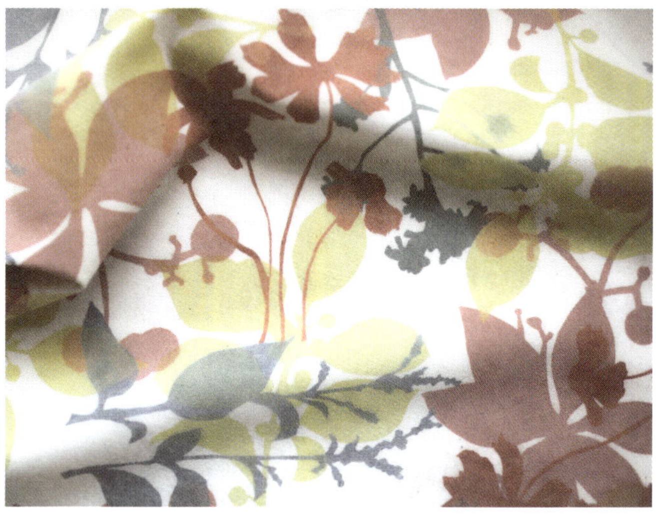

Stencils with only a small margin require extra tape to be added on top of the screen, which prevents excess paste from spilling over the side.

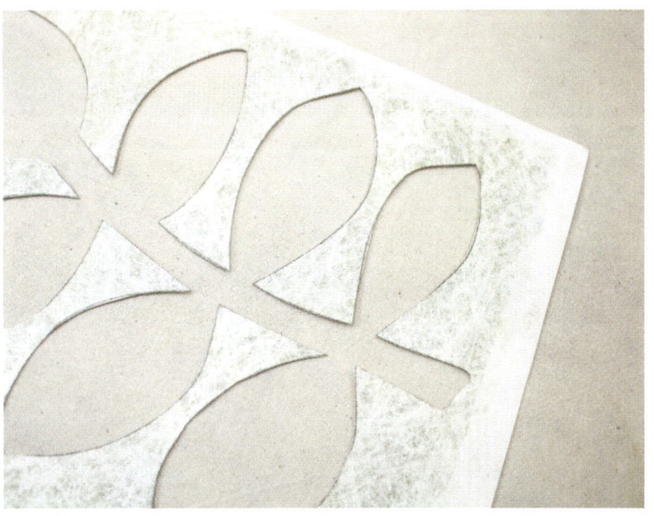

Ensure you leave a good margin of at least 50mm on your stencil, which saves having to use extra brown paper tape.

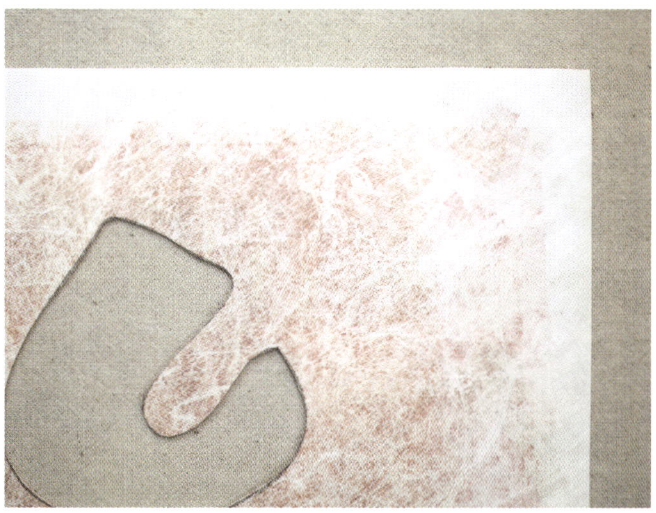

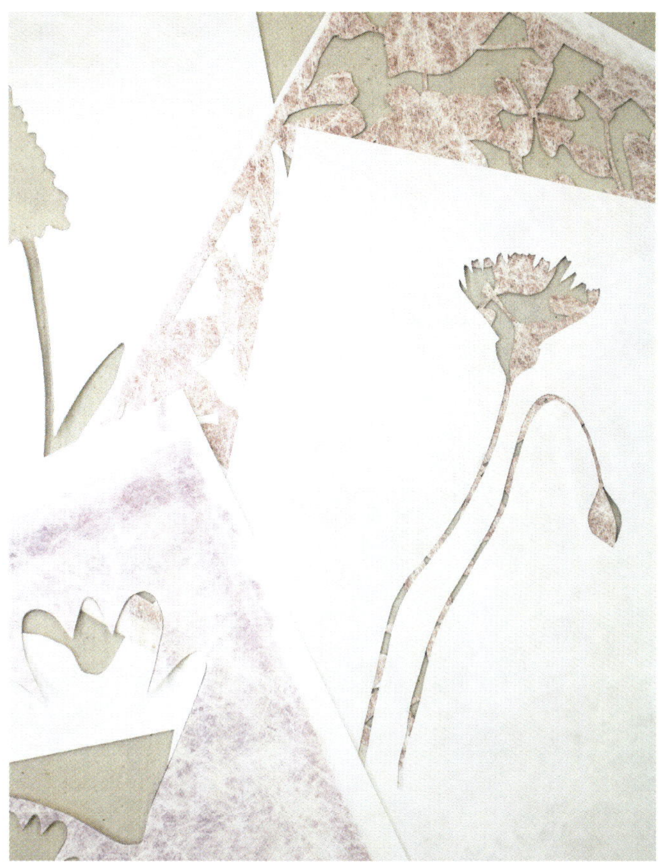

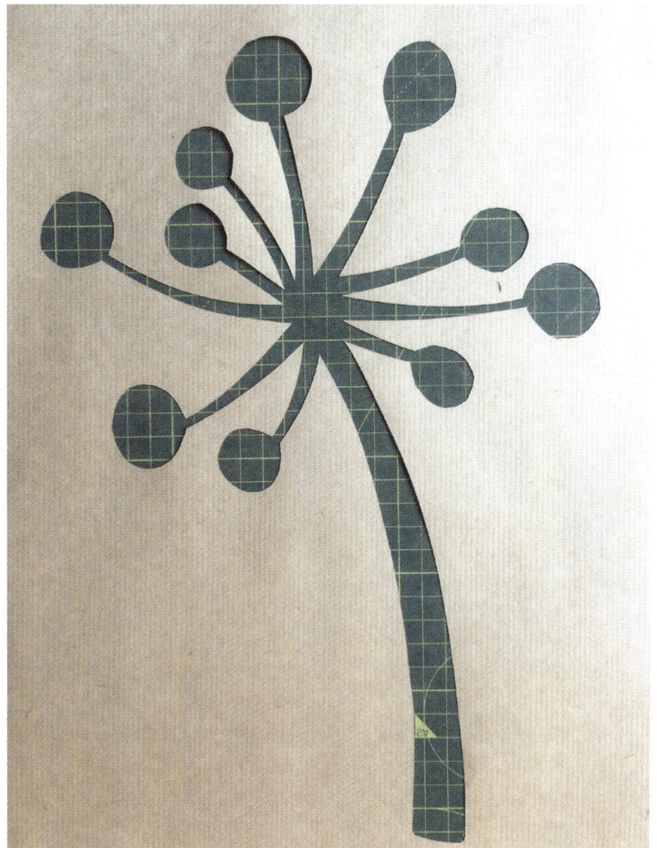

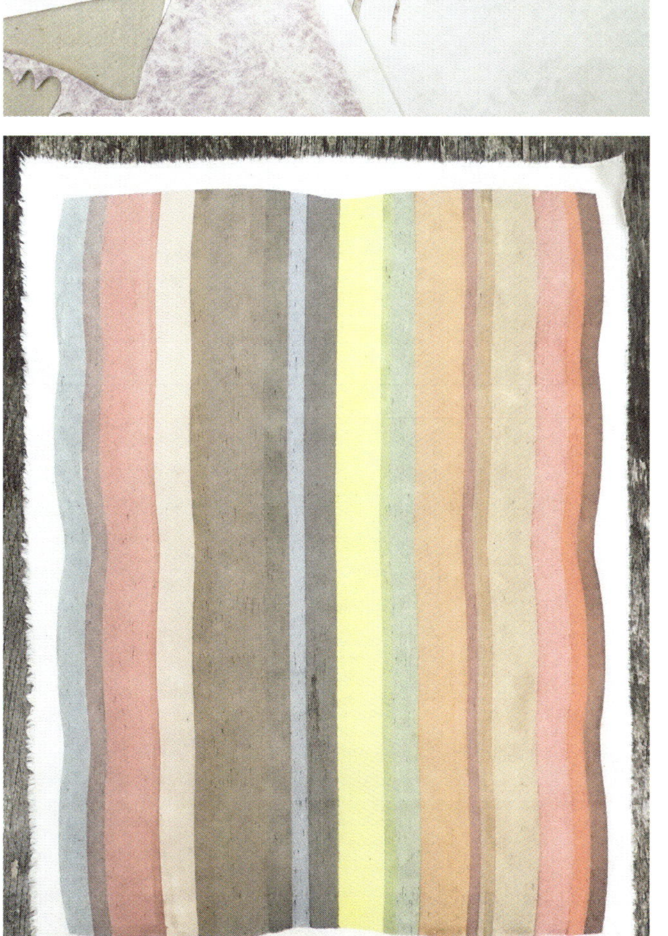

TOP LEFT
Tyvek paper is a good option for stencils that will be re-used as it can be washed and dried.

TOP RIGHT
Brown paper is also a good choice for stencils: use the laid paper that has a slightly shiny side, as it's less absorbent than the slightly pulpy-looking equivalent.

LEFT
If fabric is pinned or taped too tightly or irregularly, it will cause straight lines to become wavy once washed.

REGISTRATION

There are different ways of registering designs onto fabric, depending on which technique is being used and the design that is being printed. Repeat patterns on a long length of fabric will require much stricter control than smaller pieces and is normally done on a print table with fixed points to slot the screen into along the edge of the table. Refer to 'printing on textiles' books for detailed information about registration, although doing this by eye is often good enough for a lot of projects.

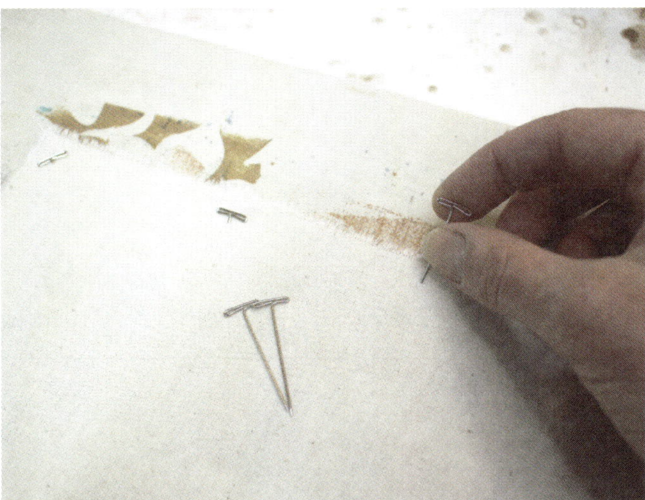

T-pins used to secure edges of fabric on printing pad.

Brown paper tape used to secure edges of fabric on printing pad.

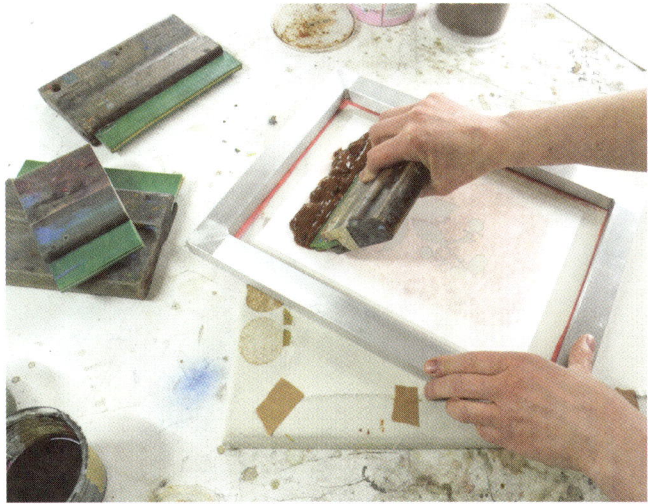

Ready to print the first colour using a Tyvek stencil.

The Screenprinting Process

Before printing, fabric should be completely dry and preferably ironed flat. Ironing fabric prior to printing has a minor disadvantage – it flattens and compresses fibres, reducing places where the dye can attach to the fabric, but better an ironed fabric than completely creased. Creases can cause paste to be applied unevenly and can negatively affect the design.

Step 1: Attach fabric to a print pad or print table using T-pins or paper tape. The fabric should be as flat and as taut as possible. This is achieved by placing pins (or tape) at the centre of the shortest edge, then the centre of the longest edge then working around the fabric gradually moving out towards the corners. Beware pulling too tightly at each point as this will affect the line of the weave and may impact the design.

Step 2: Position the paper stencil on top of the fabric, where the design will be printed and place the screen gently on top – the stencil does not need to be stuck to the screen. Additional tape can be added to the top surface of the screen mesh if required because the stencil margin is too small. This will guard against excess paste reaching the edge of the stencil and marking the fabric underneath.

In this project, the piece being printed is unique and only needs positioning by eye but if an accurate repeat pattern is required, careful registration will be needed.

Step 3: Add print paste to the reserve space at the top of the screen, on top of the stencil or tape and spread out in a line ready to be pulled across the screen with the squeegee. There are several options for holding the screen in place whilst the squeegee is being used. If printing a relatively small area, the screen can be held in place with one hand and the squeegee pulled with the other hand. If the screen and print area is bigger, it is worth enlisting an assistant to hold the screen whilst printing. Alternatively, heavy weights can be used to weigh down the screen – old scale weights or pattern weights are ideal. Textile screens were traditionally made of a heavy steel to help counter movement during printing, although it is harder to source these nowadays.

Step 4: Pull the paste across the screen with the squeegee held at a 45-degree angle. This first pull also makes the stencil adhere to the screen. Depending on the fabric, the screen mesh size, the size of the stencil, the type and size of squeegee and the thickness of the paste, this may need to be done twice or more to force enough paste through the screen onto the fabric and ensure a thick enough layer of paste is applied. Pull the squeegee in the same direction each time as it helps prevent screen movement and a potential blurring of the design. Add more paste as needed or use a crank-handled spatula to move the paste from the bottom of the screen to the top.

Step 5: Lift the screen carefully away from the fabric and prop one end onto a small object (such as an old roll of tape) before flooding the screen with paste ready for the next print.

Step 6: If printing just once, remove as much paste as possible before peeling the stencil away from the screen and then washing the screen, ensuring all bits of paste have been removed. Any tape added to the screen should also be carefully removed at this point. The Tyvek stencil is also washed and then retained so it can be used again. Brown paper stencils can sometimes be saved, dried and used a second time though they are often a little warped after the first use.

Step 7: If printing another layer of the same stencil, position the screen in the required position before pulling the squeegee across to force ink through the screen and stencil. The screen may overlap where the previous layers were printed and the wet paste is likely to transfer to the back of the screen. This can be avoided by either masking off the just-printed layer with newsprint or scrap paper or superficially drying the first layer with a blast from a hairdryer. It doesn't need to be bone dry, just not obviously wet.

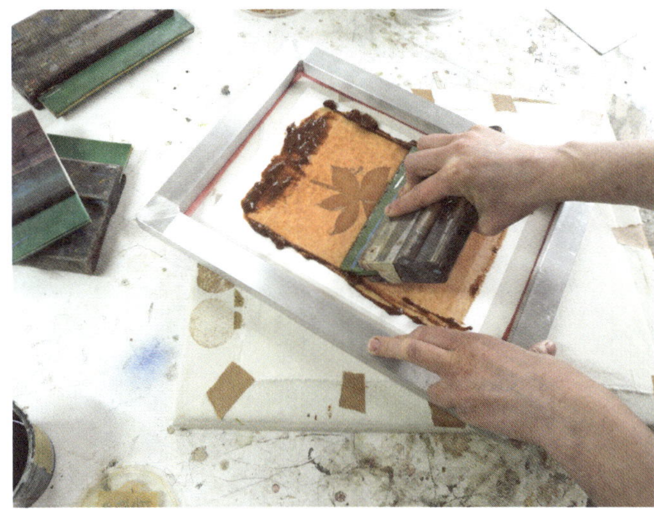

Pulling ink across the screen and stencil using a squeegee – this should be done several times to ensure good coverage.

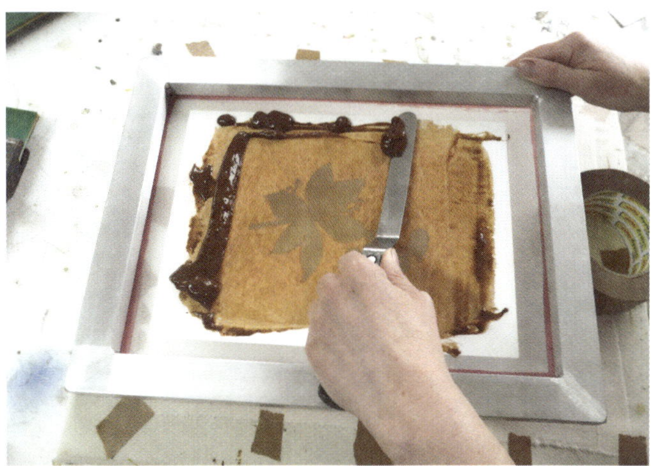

Move excess paste carefully to the top of the screen using a spatula.

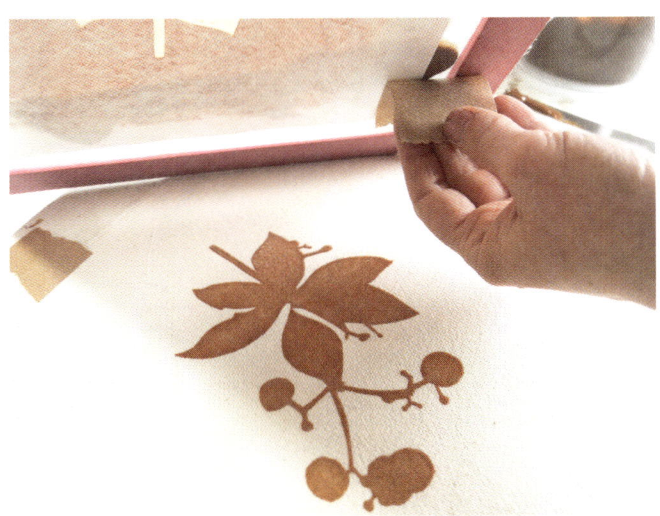

If paste overflows the edge of the stencil, lift the screen and mask off the area underneath using brown paper tape.

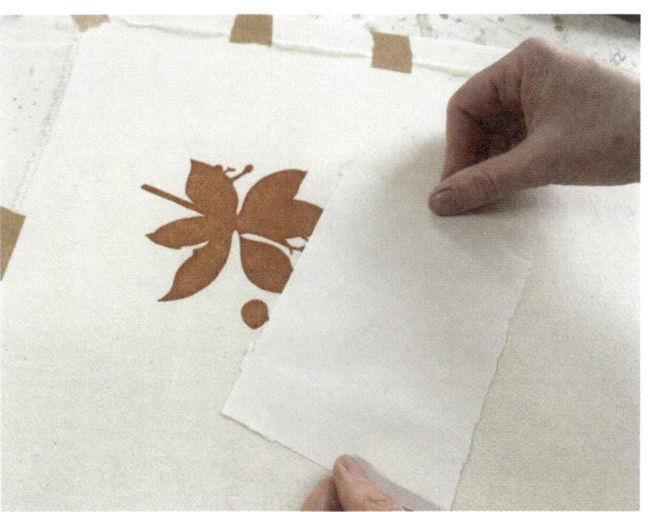

Mask off wet areas with a scrap of newsprint paper or half-dry it using a hair dryer.

The Resist Effect

Once a layer of print paste has been applied to fabric and dried, it will create a barrier for the next layer, preventing the new colour from fully reaching the fabric wherever there is print paste. This creates a resist effect, which can be exploited in the original design or avoided by setting and washing in between each layer. Another way to avoid this issue is to create a design that doesn't have overlapping layers – a tricky prospect if cutting stencils by hand and it also doesn't utilise the beauty of overlaid colours created when printing multiple layers.

Using plant-based mediums mixed with natural colourants means that prints are not going to be 100 per cent washfast immediately upon drying – they must be set using steam and then cured, and finally washed to remove excess dye and the gum/thickener. This is discussed later in this chapter.

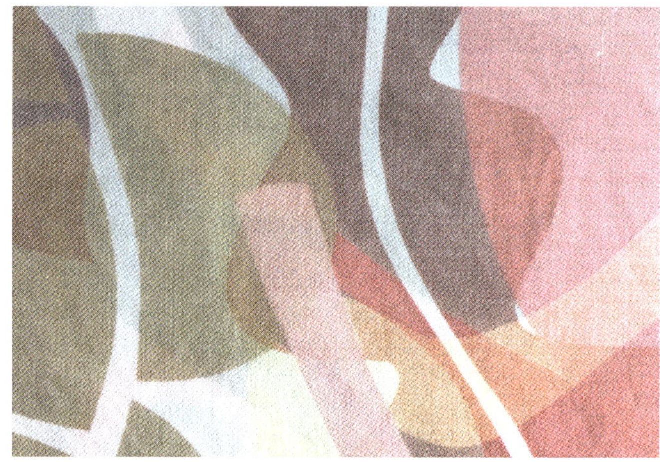

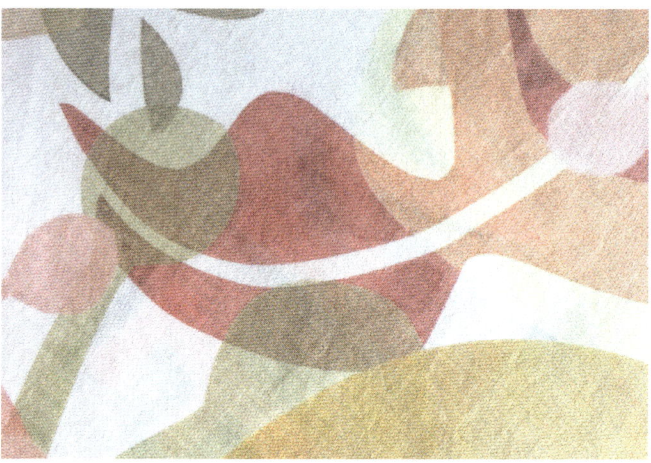

TOP
Printing with guar gum pastes creates a resist effect with some colours.

BOTTOM
The resist effect is less obvious when printing with stronger, more intense colours but some successful layering can still be seen.

Using Modifiers

Modifier pastes can be used to create further colours and tones within the design. Whilst they can have little effect on some dyes, they are a useful tool for expanding the range of colour, so are worth exploring. Modifier pastes can be applied in the same way as standard print paste. Recipes and further information is supplied in Chapter 5.

BOTTOM LEFT
Modifier pastes lose some of their effectiveness once washed. Keep both an unwashed sample and a washed sample to aid in design and printing decisions.

BOTTOM RIGHT
Modifier pastes have been used here to create a four-colour design (including the base fabric colour) with just madder paste and an iron paste. An alkali paste could have been added to create further colour.

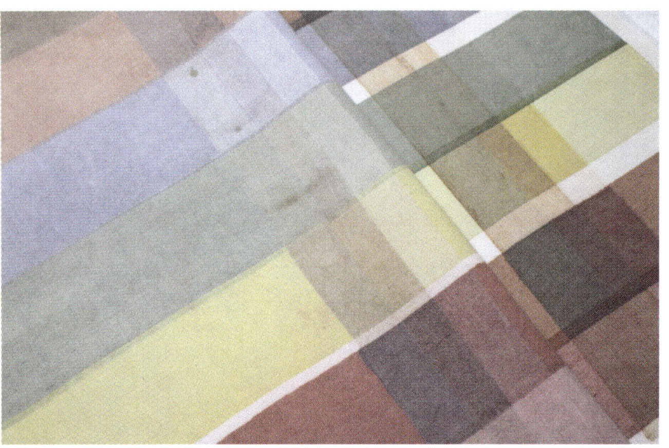

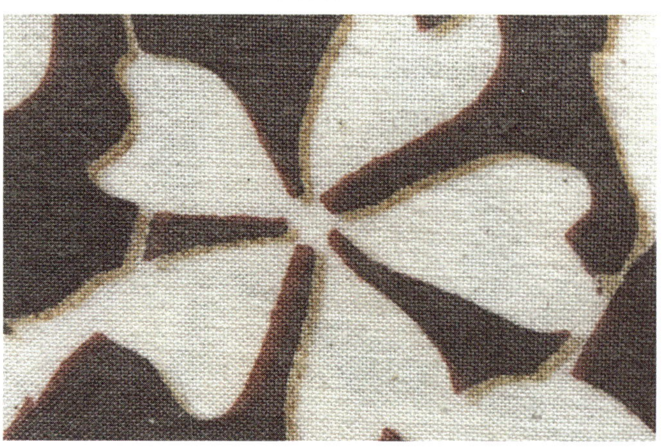

BLOCK PRINTING

This project uses one of the same drawings as the screenprinting process above, but the design is cut into a lino block. Block designs can be cut from a variety of materials including mount board and EVA foam, plywood, solid wood, MDF and lino. It can be hard to get an even colour across blocky shapes or large areas as the water-based dye struggles to cover the surface of the block evenly. In the past blocks were flocked to give a more absorbent surface. To start with it is best to use this imperfection as part of a design or concentrate on more linear designs that don't show these irregularities so much.

The design was printed onto the fabric with the mounted lino block, using three different ways of applying the thickened print paste. These show the difference each application method makes to the print quality. All use the same paste, which is a madder dye extract with mordant and vinegar, thickened with guar gum.

Designs can be printed as a repeat pattern, random placement or overlaid again and again. Refer to textile design books for ways to produce patterns but try the different options on spare fabric first. Try blocks made of different materials to achieve a variety of effects and finishes.

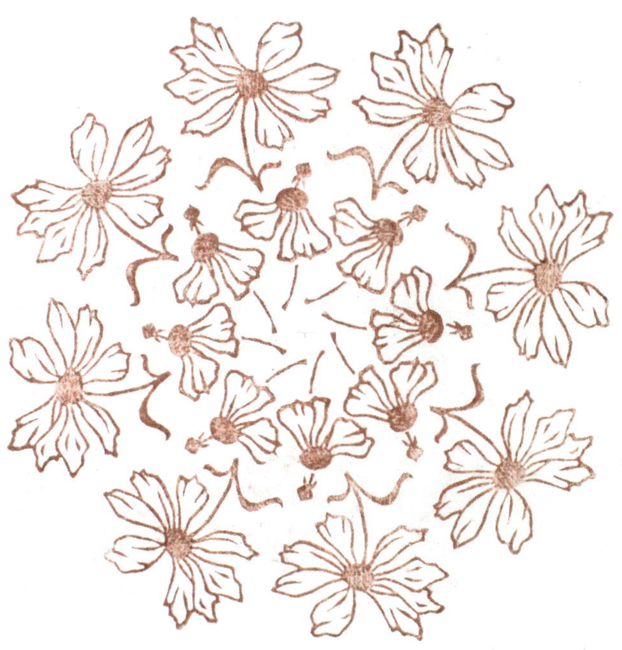

LEFT
The block-printed textile, cured and washed.

BELOW
Different methods of applying paste will result in different qualities of line. Block pressed into wool felt covered with a thin piece of cotton fabric (left), paste applied with roller (middle) and block pressed into wool felt (right).

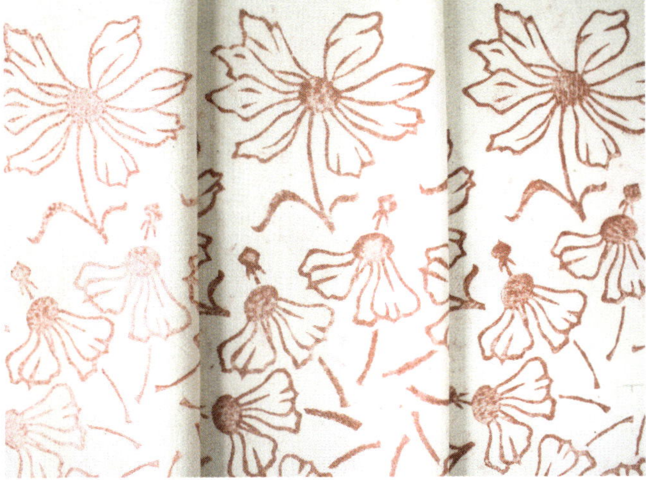

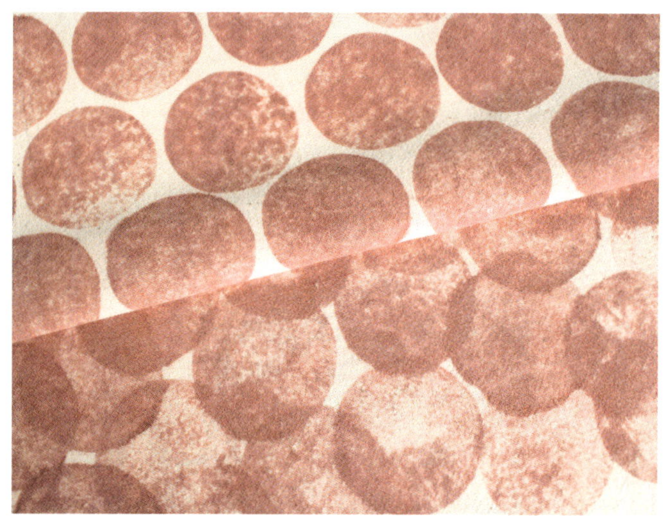

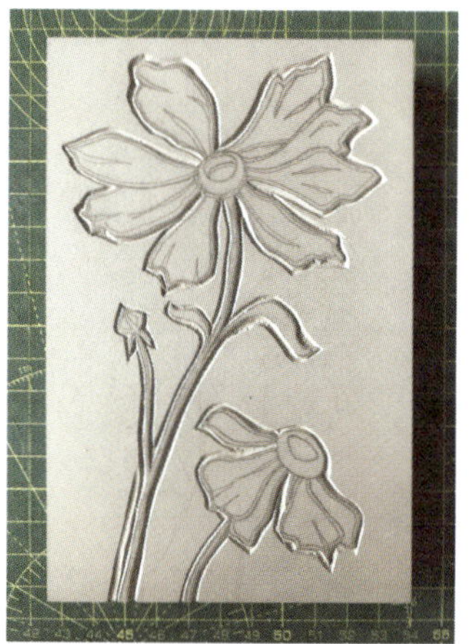

Mounted lino block with the edges of the design cut away.

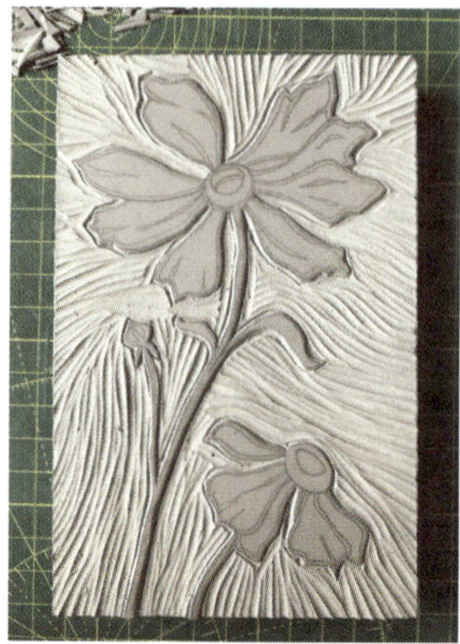

The lino block with the background partly removed.

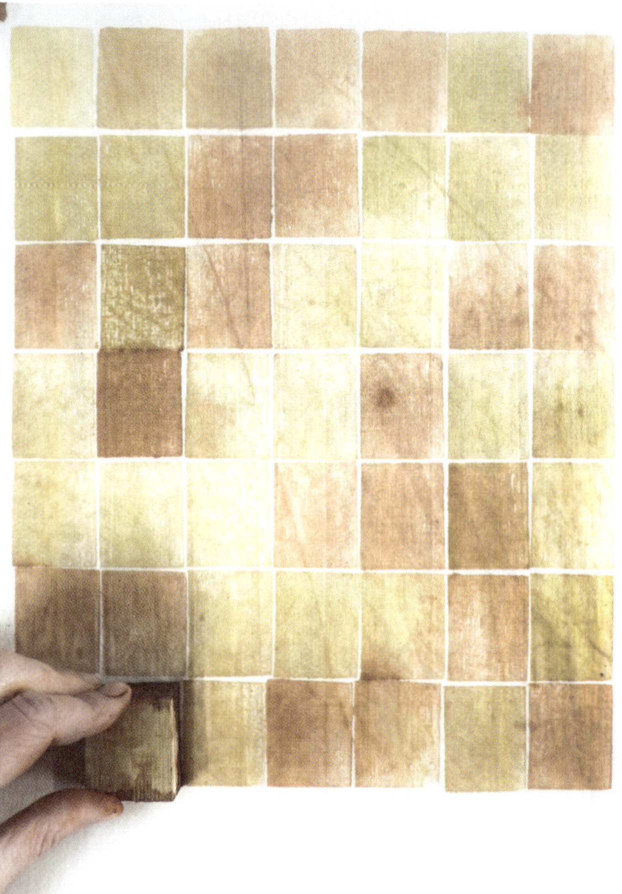

Applying Paste to Printing Blocks

Various techniques can be used to apply colour to the print block. Traditionally, something called a printer's sieve was used, which consists of a well of thickened colour with a floating tray (or sieve) on top, that allows colour to seep through taut layers of fabric onto which the block is pressed. A much simpler version of this is used here, though a roller, paintbrush or sponge can also be used. It is important not to apply too much paste, which will fill the cut away areas of the block and negatively impact the design.

Place a square of felt into an ink tray (or something equally flat and waterproof) and add enough print paste to saturate the felt. Force the paste into the felt with the use of a spatula or plastic squeegee. The felt should be saturated with ink but not have pools or lumps of it on top.

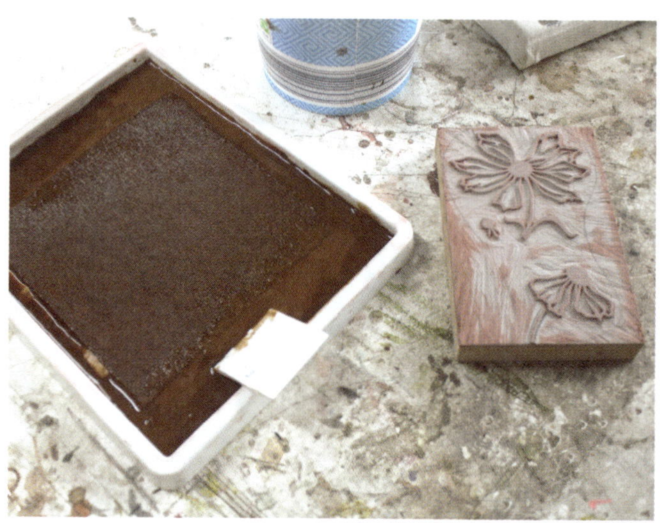

TOP
A repeat pattern design and a random overlaid design printed using self-adhesive EVA foam stuck to a wooden block.

ABOVE
Printing a block design with unthickened paste and a rectangle of plywood.

RIGHT
My version of a printer's sieve: an ink tray with a thick piece of wool felt, saturated with print paste.

The Block-Printing Process

Before printing, ensure the fabric is completely dry and ironed flat. Creases can cause paste to be applied unevenly and can negatively affect the design.

Step 1: Attach the fabric to a print pad or print table using T-pins or brown paper tape. If printing onto a tote bag or t-shirt, ensure the print paste will not soak through to the other side by placing something flat and absorbent inside. A small print pad is ideal but newspaper or newsprint will also be fine.

The fabric should be as flat and as taut as possible. Achieve this by placing pins (or tape) at the centre of the shortest edge, then the centre of the longest edge then working around the fabric gradually moving out towards the corners. Beware pulling too tightly at each point as this will affect the straightness of the weave and may impact the design.

Step 2: Press the block into the saturated felt. It shouldn't be pressed too hard or the paste will seep up into the cut away areas of the block. Alternatively, the paste can be rolled on using a fabric roller.

Step 3: Print a couple of tests onto practice fabric first to assess how much paste and pressure are needed to ensure a good print.

Step 4: Print the design onto the prepared fabric, applying paste between each print. Check the block periodically for any blockages or build-up of paste in the cut away areas of the design.

Step 5: Leave the fabric to dry before setting and curing.

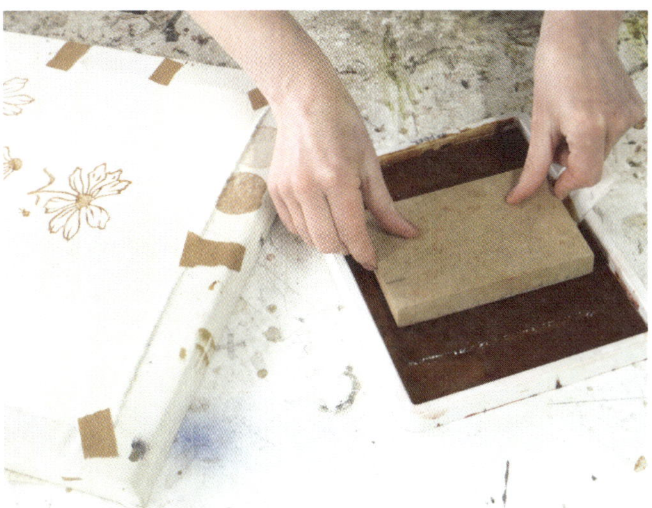

Applying paste to the block by pressing into the saturated felt.

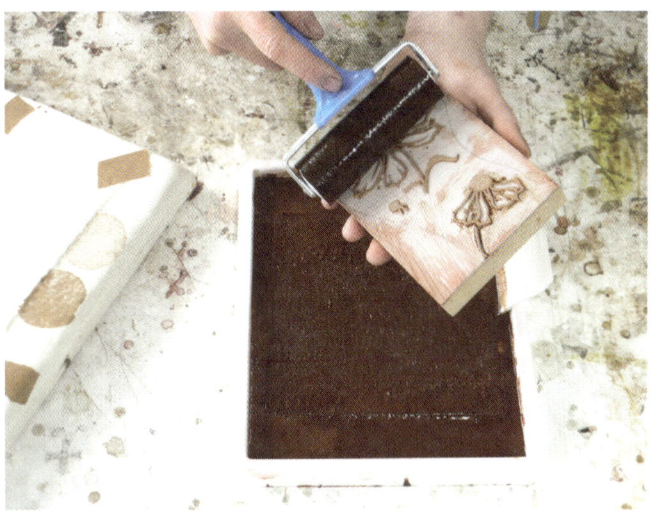

Applying paste to the block with a fabric roller.

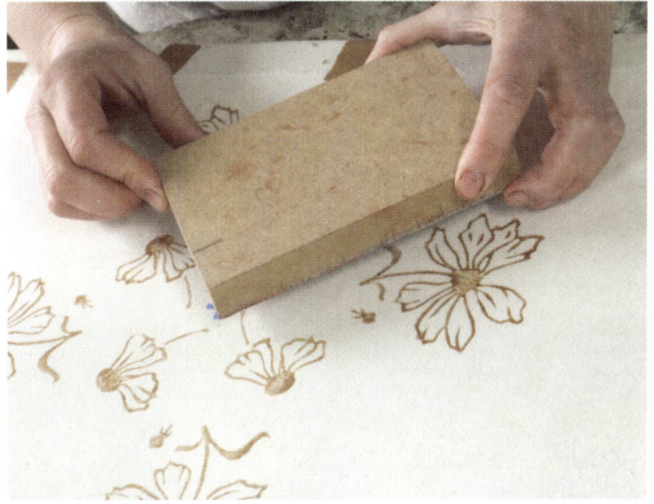

Printing the fabric with the lino block: press firmly and decisively. Some printers use a mallet to apply pressure.

MORDANT PRINTING

This project uses an exposed screen for printing to demonstrate the process but any method of applying mordant pastes and mixes to fabric can be used. In Chapter 5, you can see the subtle graduation of colour that can be achieved by using varying strengths of mordants but a useful place to start is to print a full strength alum paste, a full strength iron paste and a 50:50 mix of the two. Another option is to use a neutral paste to weaken the mordant pastes to achieve different, lighter colours.

The Mordant Printing Process

Before the pastes are mixed the fabric should be prepared and made ready to print on. Fabric needs to be scoured but not mordanted – remember that it will be mordanted with the mordant printing paste. Make sure fabric is ironed with no creases, which can cause irregularities when printing. The fabric also needs to be extremely dry unless a softer, blurred edge to the print is required. The paste (and therefore, the mordant) can wick along the fibres of the fabric if it is wet. (See the start of this chapter for further information about preparing fabric for printing.)

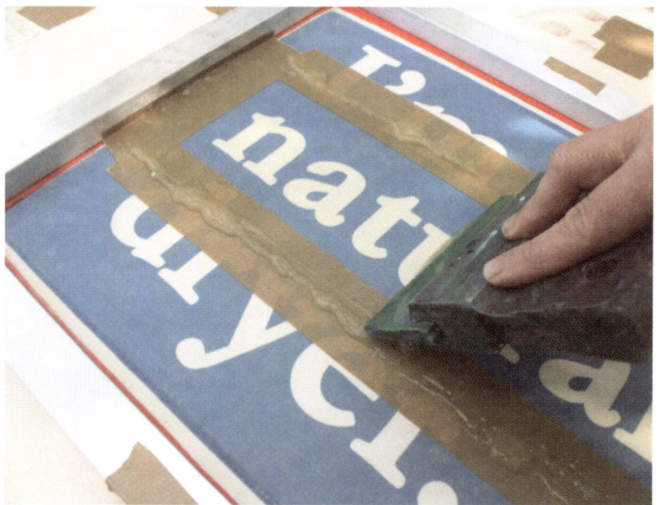

Screenprinting mordants onto fabric using an exposed screen.

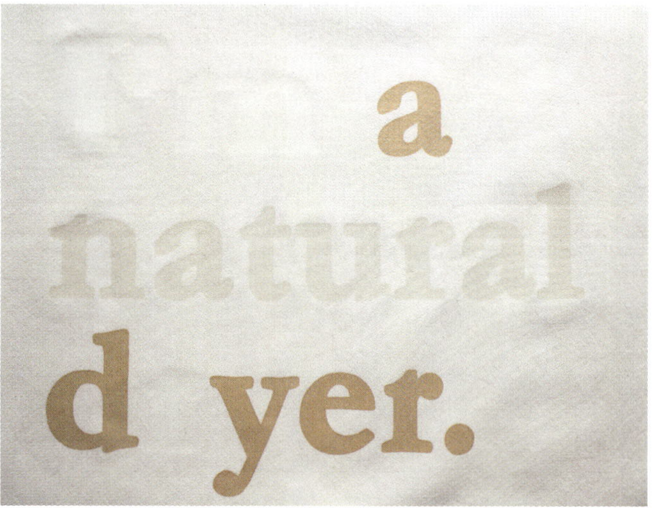

The dried mordant, before dunging and dyeing. Even though the mordant pastes haven't had any colour added, they are clearly visible on the cloth, especially the iron mordant.

Step 1: Apply the mordant paste to the fabric using the chosen method of printing (screenprinting, block printing, stencil brushing, painting, etc.). Each layer must be allowed to dry before printing the next mordant paste layer. I recommend using the iron mordant paste last to limit the likelihood of iron transference from one area of the fabric to another. Ensure any tools such as screens or blocks are well washed after using the iron paste.

Step 2: Leave the fabric to dry for at least 24 hours after printing, or longer in a damp climate. This allows the mordant to fix onto the fibres, helping to ensure a clearer, more defined print after dyeing. The fabric must be completely dry before moving on to the next stage and whilst air-drying is advised, the process can be speeded up by using a hair dryer or other source of dry heat. An alum mordant paste that emits a slight vinegar smell requires a longer drying time.

Dunging

After curing, the mordant printed textile should be 'dunged' to remove any unattached mordant and the gum, which was used to thicken the paste. This procedure used to be done using cow dung, which is why it's called 'dunging' and is an important step in the process. Excess mordant can create patchiness and blur designs whilst any remaining gum on the textile can act as a resist during the dyeing stage, preventing the dye from accessing the fibres.

Step 1: Make up a dunging bath using a mix of calcium carbonate (chalk) and wheat bran in hot water. The calcium carbonate helps to neutralise the pastes and the wheat bran helps to dissolve the gum.

Place 5–10g of calcium carbonate and a small handful of wheat bran per litre of hot water into a large vessel. For a ten litre vessel, 50–100g of calcium carbonate and ten small handfuls of wheat bran is required. Place the wheat bran in a mesh bag to stop it sticking to the cloth. There should be enough water to allow the mordant printed textiles to move freely in the bath.

Step 2: The textiles are immediately added and allowed to soak for ten minutes. At this stage, it can be very easy for the iron mordant to migrate to other areas of the cloth, especially if the textile sits still in the bath. It is advisable to gently agitate the cloth whilst it is in the dunging solution.

Step 3: After ten minutes in the dunging liquid, test whether the gum has dissolved by lightly touching an alum mordanted area. If it feels slimy, this is the gum still attached to the textile. Leave it in the bath and check again in five minutes. The cloth can be gently rubbed to remove any remaining gum. The iron mordanted sections will turn either a light brown or a rust colour but the alum mordanted section will be clear (unless an extract was added to lightly colour the paste).

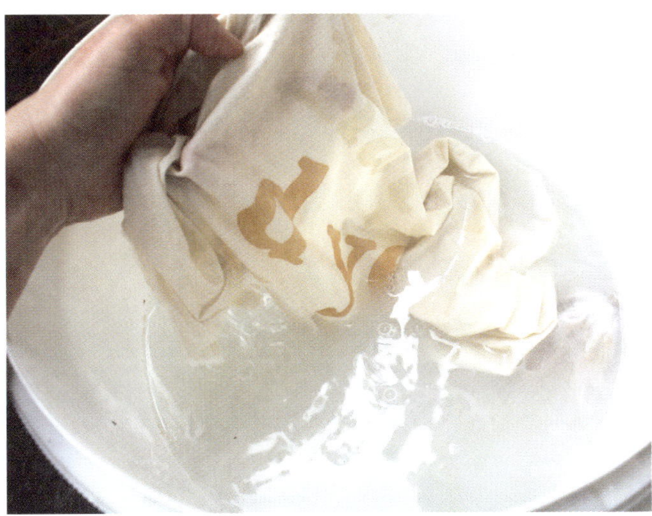

Dunging mordant-printed fabric in a deep vessel.

Step 4: Lightly rinse the fabric and either hang to dry ready for dyeing at another time or immediately dye in a dye bath.

Creating a Dye Bath

Refer to a natural dyeing book for detailed advice on how to make up a dye bath if needed. However, most dyes just need to be steeped in warm to simmering water to release the colourant but remember, this process will work best with adjective (those that require a mordant) dyes.

The amount of dyestuff required is usually based on the WOF (Weight of Fibre) rule, whereby fibres are weighed and then a percentage of that weight is used for the dyestuff. In dyeing mordanted fabrics, only enough dyestuff is required to dye the mordanted areas rather than the whole piece of fabric. The easiest way to do this is to roughly calculate how much mordant coverage is on the fabric. If there is approximately 50 per cent coverage and the cloth weighs 500g, a weight of 250g is a close enough calculation. Then if the dye being used requires 100 per cent WOF, 250g of dyestuff will be needed to colour the fabric effectively. If it requires 50 per cent WOF, just 125g is needed. This is a very basic approach to working out how much dyestuff is required – after all, areas with a strong alum mordant applied will take more colourant than areas with only a weak alum mordant applied, but is sufficient for most uses of this process. If multiple copies of the same print design will be created over a number of dyeing sessions, the amount of dyestuff can be adapted accordingly as more experience and knowledge of a particular colourant is gained. For example, I have found that a higher percentage of madder than I estimate is usually required to get good strong colours on mordant-printed pieces. Using a little more madder than calculated is a better choice than not using enough and getting disappointingly pale results after lots of hard work and preparation.

Step 1: Place the dyestuff in a mesh bag and add it to a vessel (a stainless steel stockpot is ideal) large enough to allow fabrics to move freely around in it. Then add water – the amount is unimportant; again the most important factor is the ability of fabrics to move in the liquid. The dye bath is heated gently and, once it is 'not quite' simmering, kept at this heat for one hour. Some recipes will advise to heat at simmering for one hour, and some will advise a cooler extraction. Higher temperatures can be damaging to some dyestuffs, affecting the colour, so a temperature just below a simmer is ideal. Some dyestuffs, for instance coreopsis, will provide brighter and cleaner colours if extracted in a cool or just warm solution.

Step 2: Once the colour has been extracted from the dyestuff, it is safest to remove the mesh bag of dyestuff from the dye bath before adding the fabric. Close contact between the dyestuff and the textile can cause patchiness in the final result. However, the dyestuff can be left in overnight to extract the maximum colour before dyeing the fabric – it is up to the dyer to decide when this might be as so many factors can affect it.

Step 3: Add the damp or pre-wetted mordant printed fabric to the dye bath, ensuring there are no air bubbles or hard creases in the fabric, and stir gently. The mordanted sections of fabric will begin to take up colour very quickly and can be a satisfying sight after so much preparatory work. The dyeing process can be done with a warm or cold dye bath, it is just a slower process with cold liquid.

Step 4: Leave the fabric in the dye bath for at least one hour, occasionally stirring to rotate the fabric (for important pieces, I admit to stirring continuously for the first 10 to 20 minutes). During this time the dye bath can be heated if preferred or left to cool naturally. Heating the dye bath results in a quicker process but patches of colour can occur if the fabric comes into contact with the bottom of the pan and a direct heat source.

Step 5: Once the fabric has been dyed a satisfactory colour, remove it from the dye bath and rinse well. At this stage the cloth can be boil washed to remove unwanted background colour, but this is a personal choice. On occasion I have experienced an unwanted change of colour after boiling mordanted fabrics so I prefer not to do so.

Step 6: Hang to dry. The mordant printed and dyed fabric is ready to be used.

When caring for the fabric, handwashing is recommended, although textiles dyed using this process are remarkably colourfast and will withstand machine-washing.

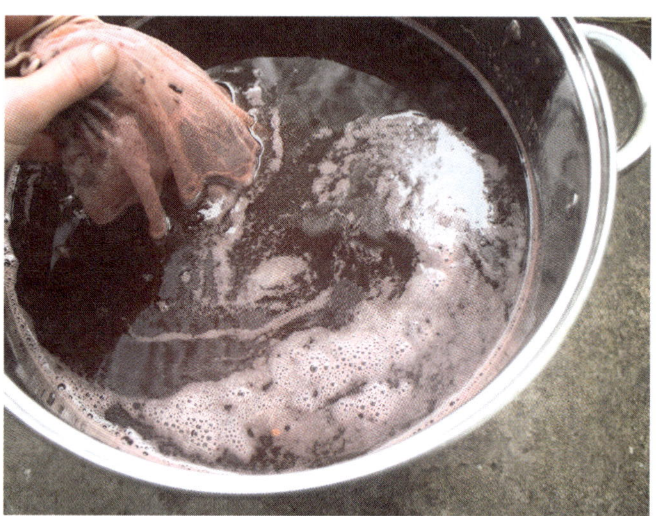

Making a dye bath by adding dyestuff contained in a mesh bag to hot water.

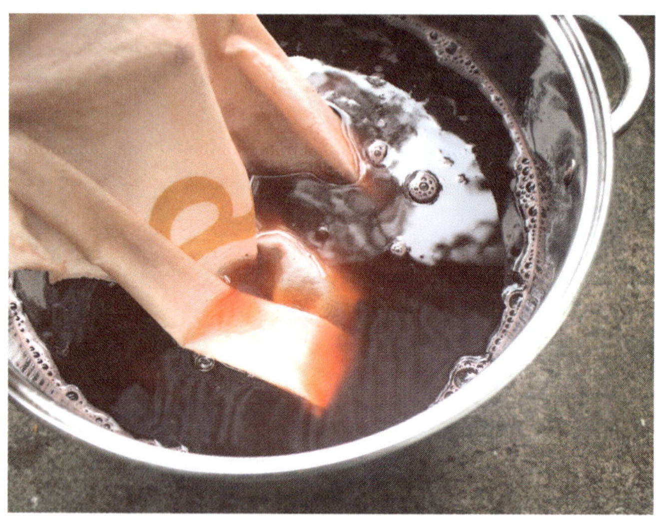

Adding the wet mordant-printed fabric to the dye bath.

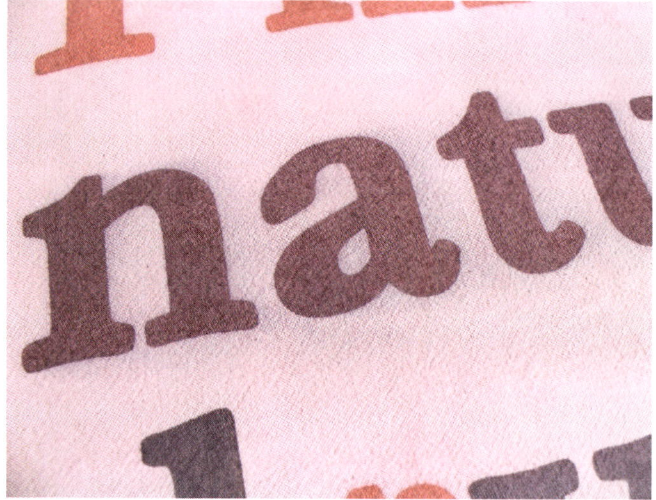

If excess mordant is not properly rinsed away during the dunging process, it can spread across the fabric and cause colour contamination.

I'm a natural dryer. Tea towel mordant printed and dyed with madder. The pink was printed with alum mordant, the burgundy with a 50:50 mix of alum to iron and the purple was printed with an iron mordant.

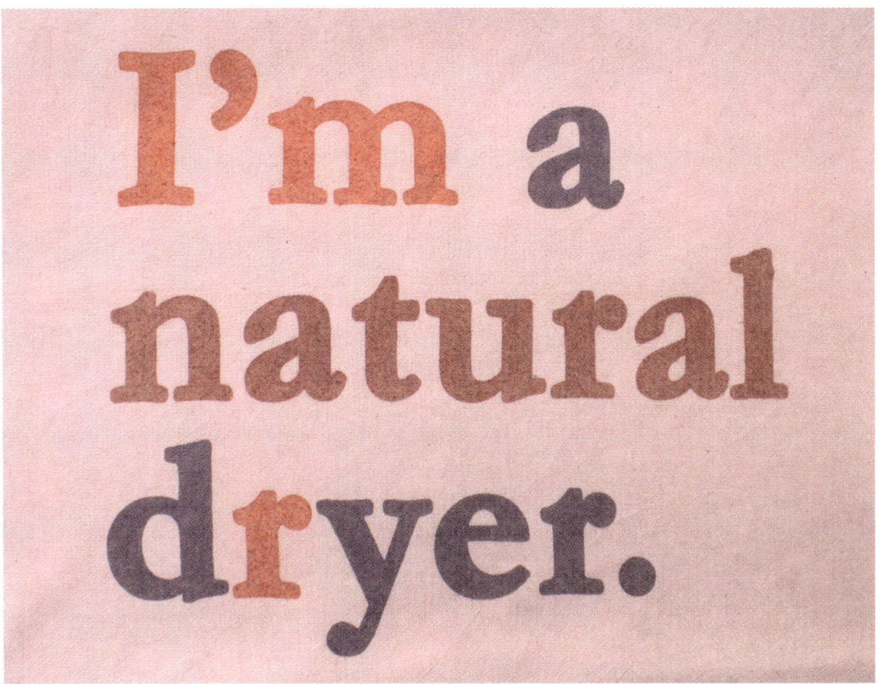

I'm a natural dryer. Tea towel mordant printed and dyed with buckthorn bark.

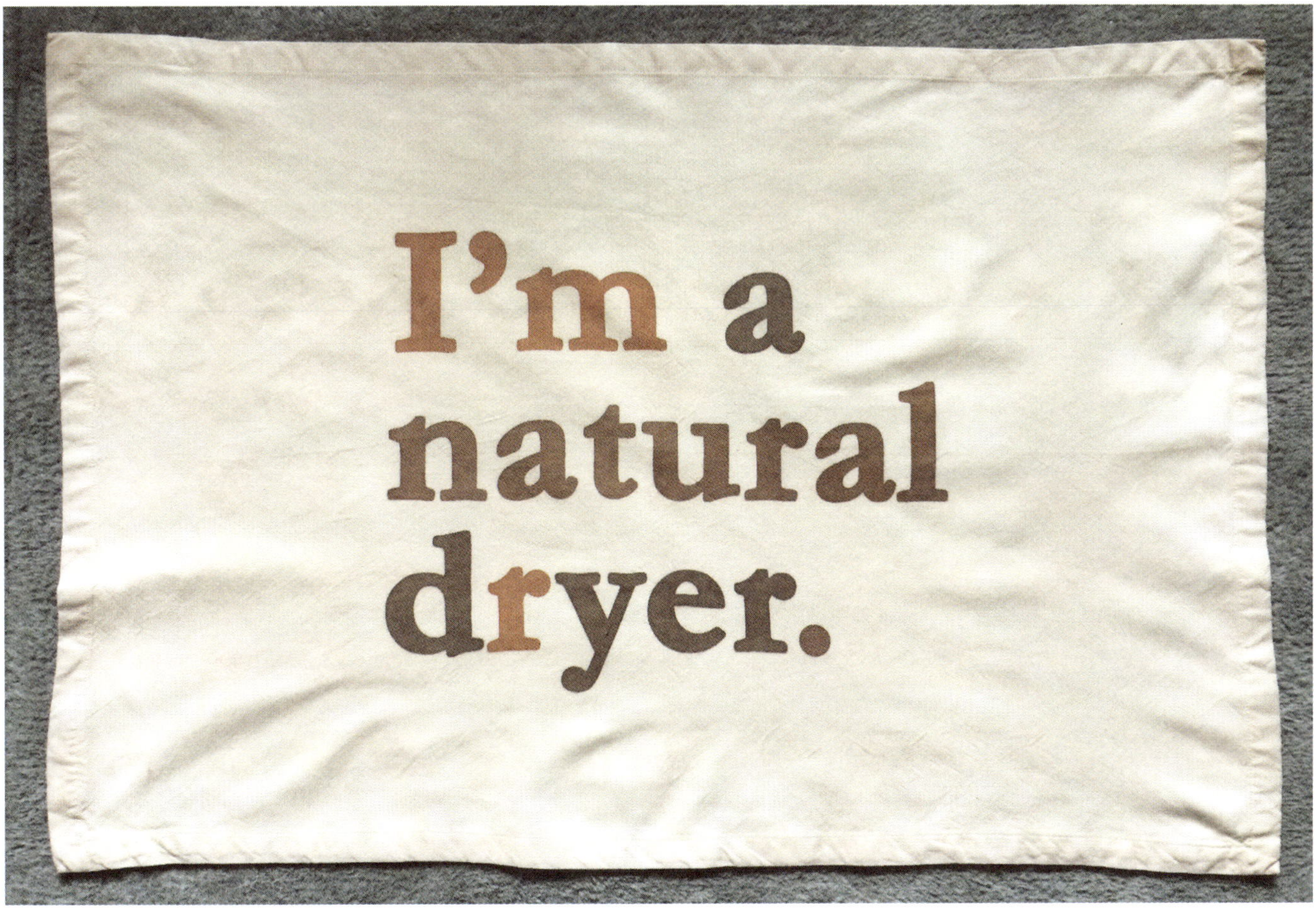

AFTER-TREATMENT

The post-printing stage is an important step after applying directly printed plant-based colour on to textiles. Whilst acceptable results will be achieved by leaving the print to dry and then gently hand-washing to remove the paste thickener, colour fastness and the depth of colour achieved on the fabric is vastly improved by both steaming and/or curing before washing. These processes both help to fix the colour onto the cloth by allowing the mordants and dyes to chemically bond within the fibres. Washing will then remove any unfixed dye and mordant along with the gums and thickeners used to print the paste. This is irrelevant for mordant printed textiles, which require a different process.

The stages of after-treatment I recommend are:

1. Following printing, hang textiles to dry for 24 hours or longer depending on climate, fabric type and amount of print paste applied.
2. Steam (five minutes to an hour depending on process and patience).
3. Cure by hanging and allowing fabric to air for one week or longer.
4. Gently hand wash using a pH neutral detergent.
5. Iron if needed.

Fabric should be thoroughly scoured before applying colour to remove dirt, oils and waxes. These wool scarves were scoured before being screenprinted with a direct printing paste.

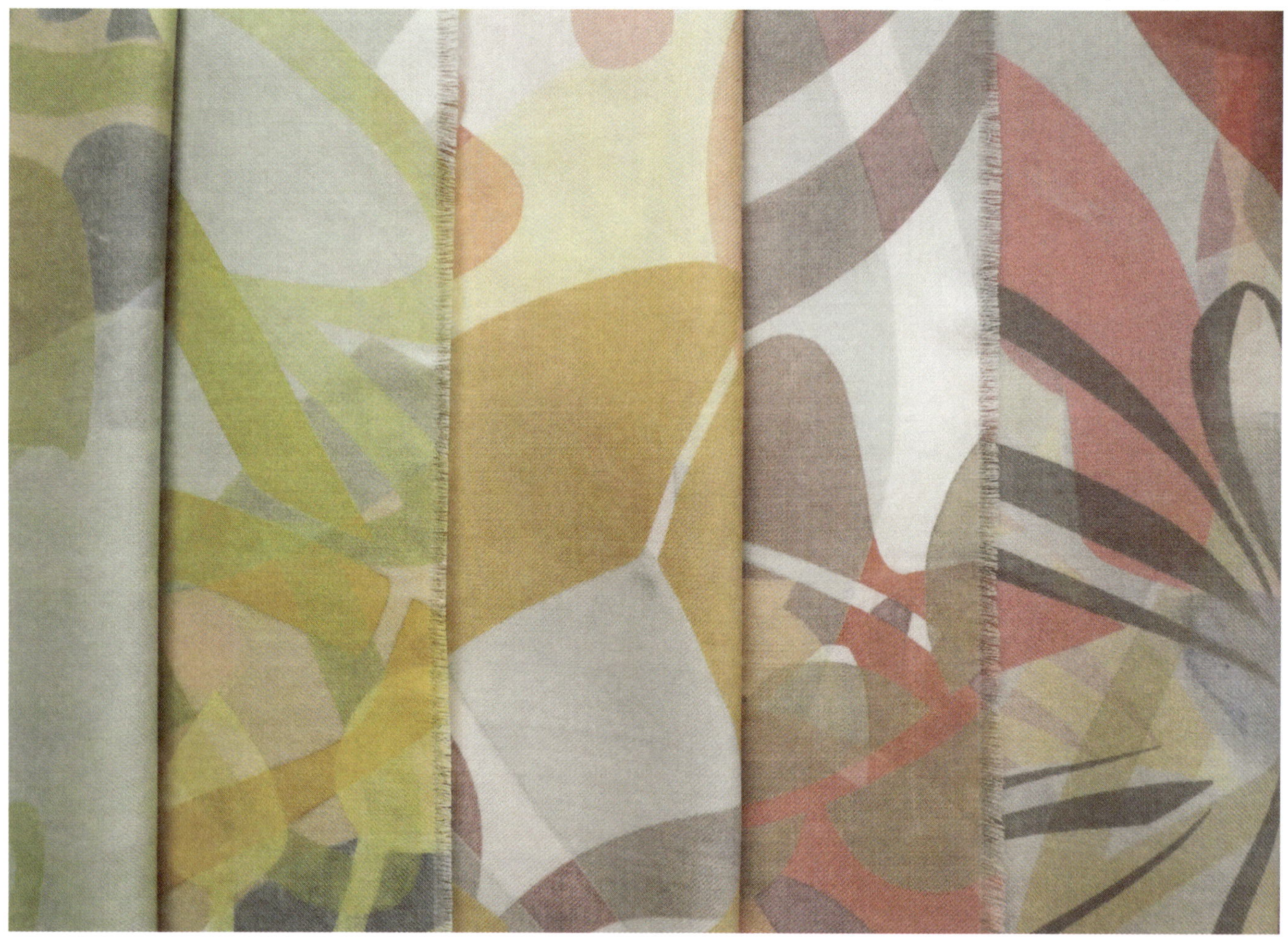

Steaming

Steaming (or fixing) the dye is an important step in the after-treatment of printed textiles. The process helps the dye to fix more successfully into the fibres, although requires a careful balance of heat and moisture, especially when not using a professional steamer or steaming machine. Professional steamers will regulate the amount of steam, the 'wetness' of the steam and the pressure within the steaming chamber to provide the perfect combination for fixing the colour upon the cloth. I use two techniques for steaming, neither of them perfect but they suit my current practice and allow relatively fast in-house processing.

The first method, generally used for small pieces, samples and in workshops is simply to use a steam iron. The printed textile is placed between two old tea towels (or old, clean fabric) and 'ironed' on each side with the steam setting on maximum. After an initial blast with the iron pressing down hard on top of the fabric, I usually remove the top tea towel and then carry on ironing but with the iron held just above the surface of the printed textile and moving it backwards and forwards over the whole design. With most steam irons, this causes more steam to be released, which can then directly reach the dye printed onto the fabric. The piece is then turned over and the whole process repeated. On a piece the size of a tea towel, I would generally iron for about three minutes on either side.

The second method, used for larger pieces when a steam iron would be impractical, is to use a home-made vertical steamer. Vertical steamers (also called bullet steamers) can be purchased but it is relatively easy to make a homemade version of one. I made mine using a wallpaper steamer attached to a large piece of galvanised ducting in which I hang my rolled-up printed textiles. The fabric should be loosely rolled between either newsprint or a large piece of clean cloth (which can be washed and used again and again) and then hung vertically above the source of steam inside the ducting or pipe. The pipe should be wide enough so that the rolled fabric doesn't touch the sides and high enough so the fabric is well above the source of the steam and doesn't get wet. Any drips or condensation from above should be prevented from dripping onto the rolled fabric. Aim for the fabric to be steamed, not to get dripping wet, which can cause the dye to run and ruin the design. The piece is steamed for one hour before being removed and immediately unrolled, removing the extra fabric or paper and hung to dry and cure before washing. If using a wallpaper steamer or any system that doesn't automatically refill with water, care should be taken to keep the water topped up and not allowed to boil dry.

Many people use a stove-top or small electrical food steamer for smaller pieces and find these easy and practical to use. I often find my textiles get too wet using this method though this shouldn't prevent you from trying it out to see if it suits you.

Curing

If hanging fabrics to air dry, make sure they are not folded or too closely packed together. If space is an issue, use a sock hanger or similar to air larger pieces by attaching in an open zig-zag formation. Try to avoid any part of the printed design touching the hanging system or airer which can cause unwanted lines in the colour.

Washing

Hand washing textiles will give you the best results though I have machine washed many pieces without the colour drastically decreasing or being washed away. The main advantage of hand-washing is that the agitation of the fabric can be controlled and done gently. I have found that the machine can abrade the fabric and cause white lines to appear where colour has been applied. This can be somewhat offset by placing textiles in a wash-bag and using a gentle cycle.

Mordant printed pieces are much more robust and can be machine-washed in a normal cycle and with other washing. The background colour may fade but the mordant printed areas should remain a strong colour.

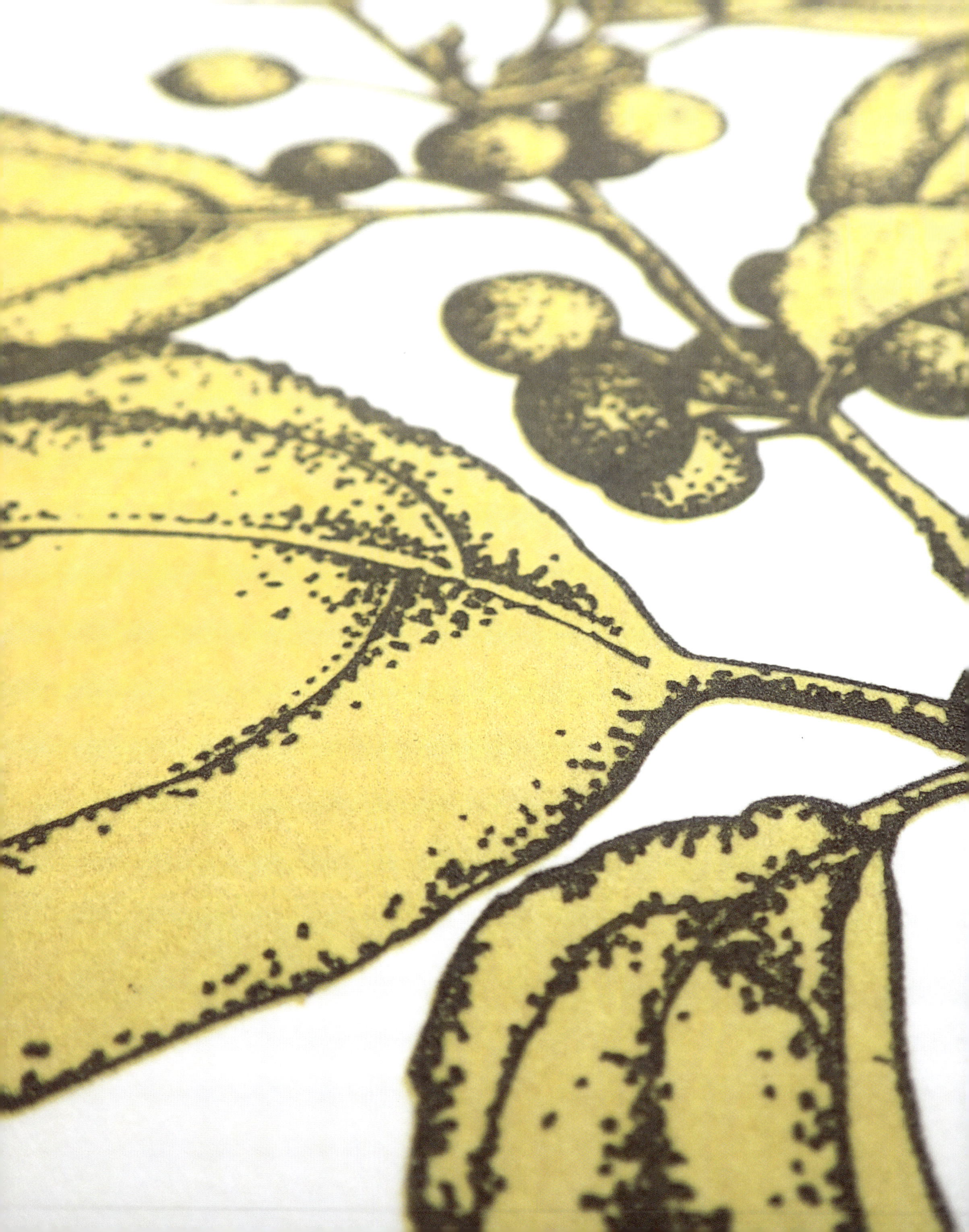

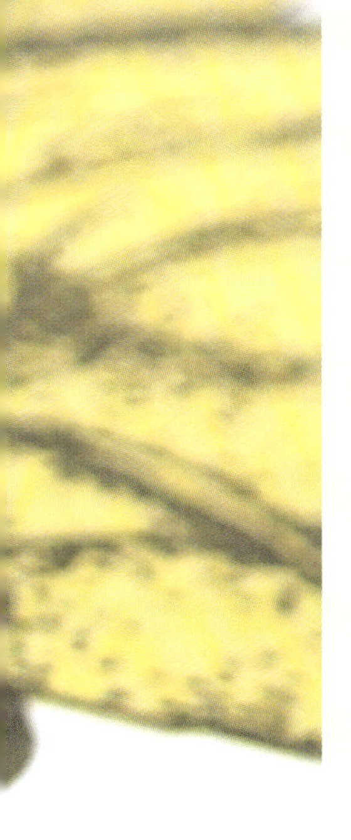

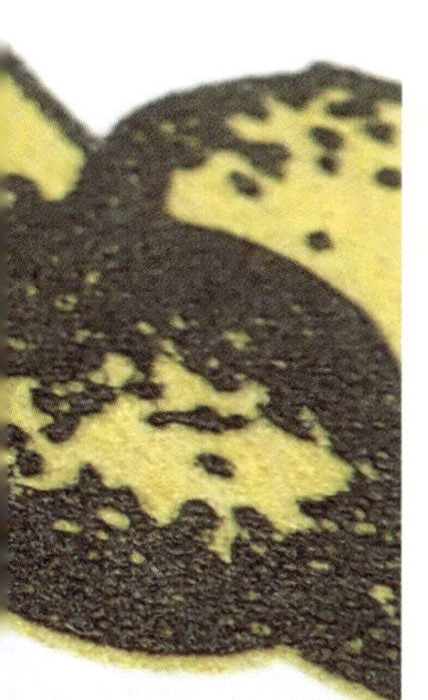

Chapter Seven

PLANT-BASED COLOUR AND PAPER

FACING PAGE

Rhamnus cathartica. Two-colour screenprint using buckthorn berry print paste and willow charcoal print paste.

Printmaking with plant-based colour is, on the whole, the same as printmaking with synthetic colour. There are difficulties and challenges in using plant-based colour but this is primarily to do with making the inks and pastes rather than the materials being used. The main difference is, for the most part, you can't purchase the plant-based inks, mediums and pastes you may need directly off the shelf. This means that printmakers wanting to create fine art prints, be they etchings, relief prints, screenprints or any other type of print must learn how to make their own art materials from the raw plantstuffs or purchased extracts and lake pigments.

Learning to make a lake pigment is an essential part of the process for printmaking, especially for those wanting to make oil-based inks for relief and intaglio processes. Here I must confess to a lack of knowledge of some print processes, lithography being one of them. This technique is not included within this book, primarily due to my inexperience in this process and I felt it would be a superficial and not entirely honest addition. However, I see no reason why lithographers shouldn't be able to use these recipes and inks for their processes – it is purely a matter of understanding what type of ink is needed, what the ink's qualities should be and how to adapt the provided recipes to achieve a good ink.

Whilst making a print washfast is not a requirement of paper-based prints, other potential challenges exist such as prolonged exposure to daylight, how to mordant a substrate that is usually kept dry and using modifiers that will possibly damage paper fibres. A lot of paper-based artwork will be exhibited on walls, galleries and in constant daylight, therefore making something as lightfast as possible may be an important consideration for some artists. Special UV glass can be used when framing and advising purchasers to keep work out of direct sunlight is prudent, whilst a certain acceptance of colour change is the compromise made for using sustainable colour. As both mordants and tannins can help with lightfastness, the addition of these into printing pastes and mixes, and being applied to the paper (before and after printing) should also be explored.

Water-based inks and pastes made from plant-based colour for screenprinting work particularly well. However, using these pastes or similar mixes for relief printing (not including mokuhanga techniques) raise the same issues that water-based synthetic inks have (obviously excluding the water-safe ranges that mimic oil-based inks). Striations and patches on the surface of plates resulting from the texture of the paste can be hard to avoid. Using designs with fine lines rather than large areas of colour can make this patchiness less apparent. In some instances, it is usually better to make an oil-based ink (or accept the limitations).

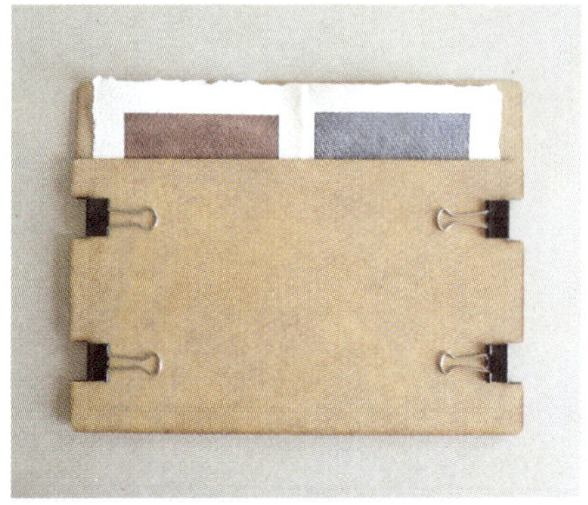

Testing screenprinted colour for lightfastness. Part of the print is covered up and then placed on a wall that doesn't get direct sunlight.

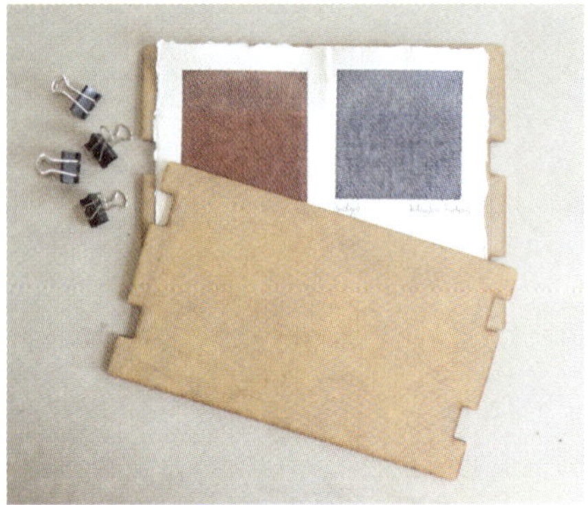

Lightfastness tests can be checked periodically for fading and colour change. This was after two years.

WATER-BASED PRINTING INKS AND PASTES (for paper)

Printing with plant-based colour onto paper is a rewarding experience: the colours achieved with plant dyes, extracts and pigments can have both a subtlety and surprising richness to them once applied to paper. The inks differ from a standard acrylic paint with acrylic medium mix in that they are much more transparent and the colours much more forgiving. Colours won't clash or fight each other on the paper – they will get along quite happily. The recipes provided are generally suitable for screenprinting techniques, though they can be used for other methods by adapting them as required.

The easiest place to start is by using plant dye extracts, which can be purchased from natural dye suppliers. Plant dye extracts are highly concentrated powders made from natural dyes and they provide a simple solution to achieving 'screenprintable' plant-based colour – strong colours, easy to mix and quick to use. Refer to Chapter 4 for more information about natural dye extracts.

As you become more confident in the use of plant-based colour within your printmaking work, you'll probably want to experiment with using your own plant dyes and pigments. There are usually a number of methods or approaches to achieving a particular colour. For example, a pink can be created from madder but also from quebracho (*Schinopsis spp.*) wood or rhubarb root and an alkali. Whilst each method will have its own advantages and disadvantages, bear in mind that once the different techniques have been learnt, you won't be restrained by which plant extracts are available to purchase commercially; you'll be able to grow, forage and create your own colour formulas and recipes.

A comparison of dye extracts and dried dyestuffs made into screenprinting pastes for paper shows the colour differences and variables between the two. In each case, dye extracts were mixed at 1 per cent, 5 per cent and 10 per cent

LEFT
Jelly Bean Monday (detail) shows how layering up transparent plant-based print pastes creates further colours.

RIGHT
Wim's Whim (detail) uses weld, indigo and madder to create secondary colours of green, orange and purple. Here you can see the purple created by overprinting indigo with madder.

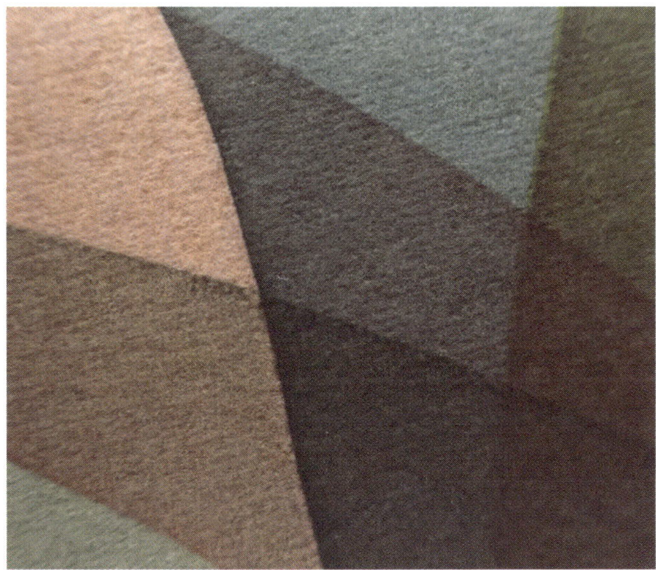

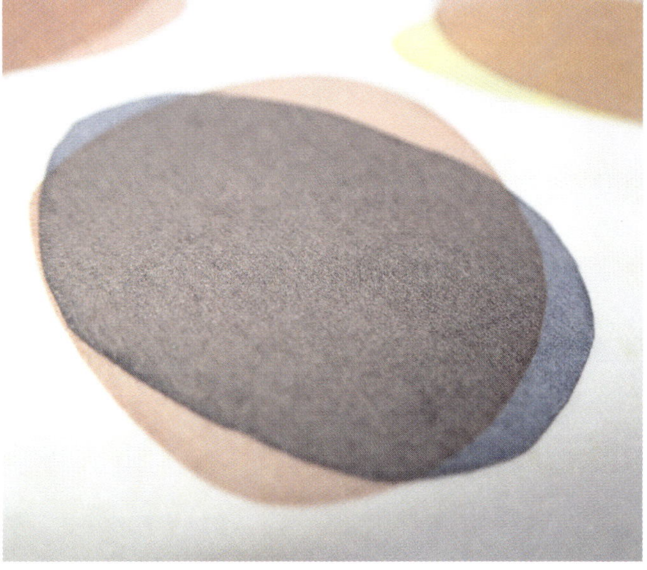

of total paste weight and applied using two pulls of the squeegee, followed by a four-pull test with the 10 per cent solution. The dye liquids for the dried dyestuff pastes were made from 50g of dyestuff heated in 500g of water, reduced down to 100g. These were then printed with two pulls and four pulls of the squeegee. The significantly different colour comes from the mature buckthorn berry paste, which is a strong green compared to the dye extract. I would expect a more yellow colour if immature berries were used, although it can be hard to purchase these. However, the green is likely to become yellowish quite quickly because the colour can be fugitive. Weld, buckthorn, rhubarb, coreopsis, madder and indigo are some of the dye plants that can be grown in the UK climate and ones I use regularly. As discussed in Chapter 2, a more complete colour wheel could be achieved by adding sappanwood, logwood and others, but it is a personal choice as to whether these are included in your practice.

Remember that lake pigments are not soluble in water-based solutions so if they are being used as the colourant in a screenprinting paste, they must be ground small enough to go through a screen's mesh. Alternatively, a lake pigment can be stored as a wet gloopy solution, rather than drying the pigment and then storing it as a dry powder. This means it can easily be added to an existing screenprinting paste or simply thickened and used as a paste. Whilst a wet solution might not be quite as shelf stable, it is a good option if it will be used in the near future.

I have experimented with various natural thickeners and gums to make screenprinting pastes and have found that plant starches are a good and low-cost substitute for acrylic mediums when printing onto paper. They aren't perfect and each type of starch comes with its own set of idiosyncrasies but they are plant-based and require only water and heat to create a usable thick paste.

A reduced dye liquid can be used in place of water when making up screenprinting paste. This will add colour from the start and remove the need to add colour afterwards. Bear in mind that a strongly coloured liquid is required to get a good colour paste – so make a dye bath as usual but with as little water as possible – the aim here is to get a super-concentrated colour. Make sure that any plant material has been filtered out to prevent it getting into the paste. Then just add the alum sulphate and starch to make up the mixture. You'll need to be careful not to overheat the paste if the dye is one that reacts to high temperatures.

These recipes are for printing onto paper and surfaces that will be kept dry. If printing colour onto textiles that will be washed, a different approach must be taken to make the colour washfast. Refer to Chapters 5 and 6 for further information.

MIXING NATURAL COLOUR WITH ACRYLIC MEDIUM

Plant dye extracts and lake pigments can simply be mixed with screenprinting acrylic medium which has been developed to create a colourless paste that is easy to print with, won't quickly clog or dry in the screen and acts as a perfect carrier for the added colour. However, acrylic mediums, like acrylic paint, contain plastic polymers, which if disposed of incorrectly, are adding micro-plastics to water and damaging the environment and wildlife. Personally, it feels contradictory to be using a renewable plant-based resource as colour and then adding it to a plastic-based medium. A sump installed under sinks and wash-out booths might be something to consider and is good practice.

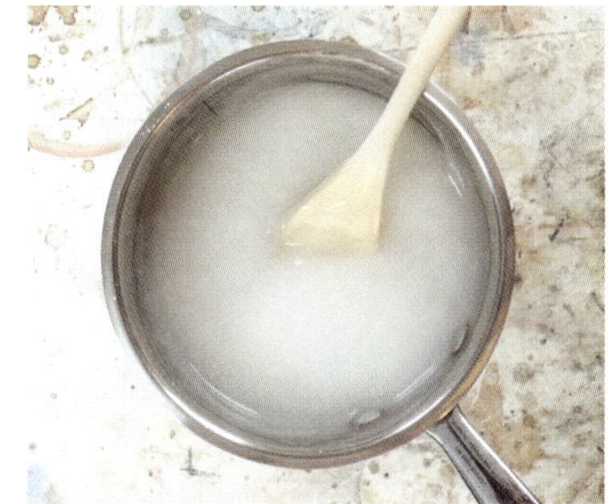

Plant starch paste is a good way to thicken a dye liquid for printing on to paper. Either add starch directly to a reduced dye liquid and heat to thicken or add dissolved dye extract to a ready-made paste.

Screenprinted colour using dye extracts and dried dyestuff

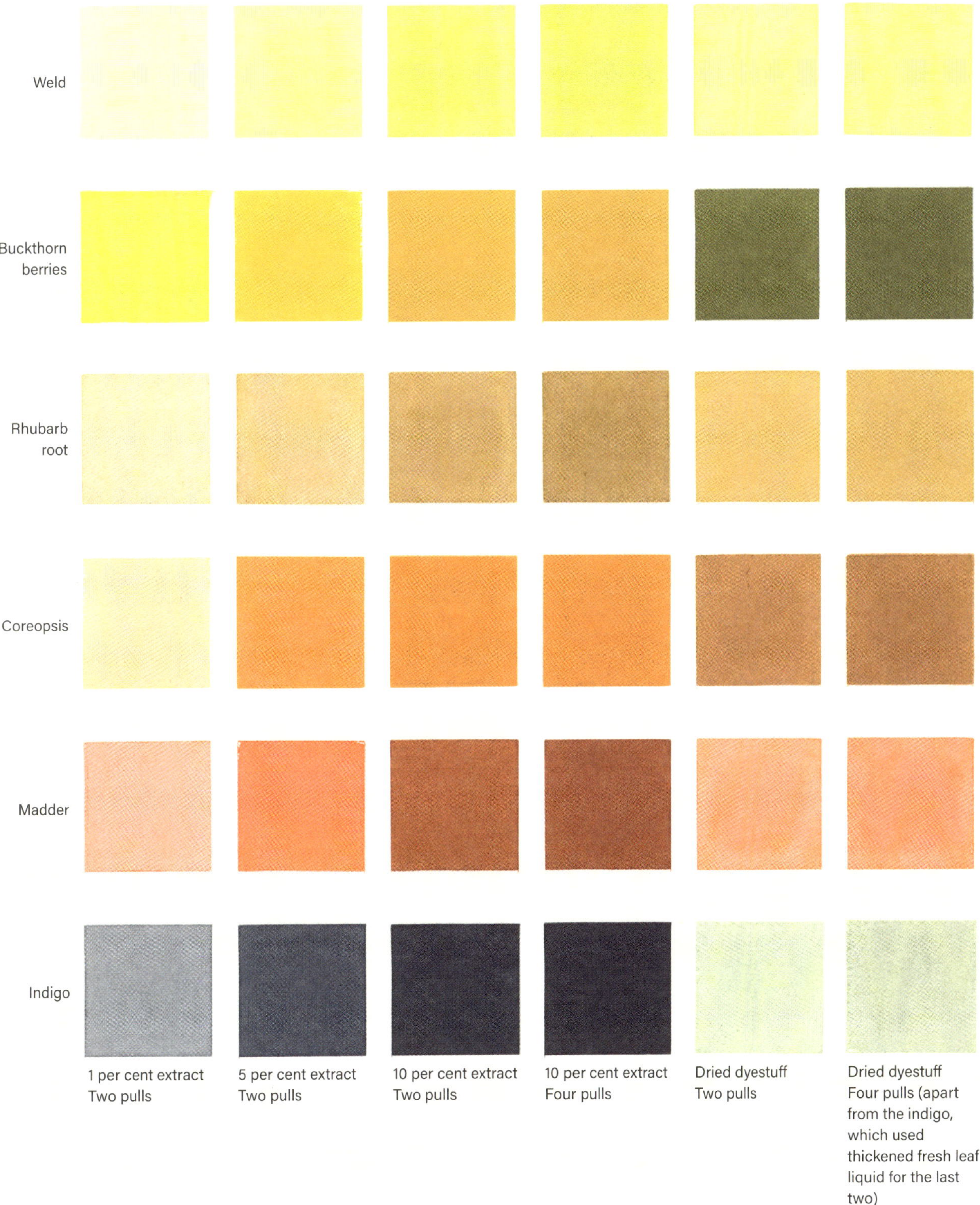

RECIPE:

Water-Based Printing Paste for Paper (using dye extracts)

This recipe uses dye extract, which gives a very concentrated colour. The recipe makes a little over 100g of paste. It is only a small amount, but the quantities can be easily increased. If increasing the amount of dye extract, keep all the other ingredients the same. When working with such small amounts of paste this makes little difference, although if you were scaling up amounts, further tests would be required.

YOU WILL NEED:

- 5g dye extract
- 5g alum sulphate
- 100g hot water
- 10g wheat (or other) starch
- Kettle
- Scales
- Small stainless-steel saucepan
- Heatproof glass beakers or similar for dissolving dye extract and alum sulphate
- Stirrers
- Heat source (portable hob, induction heater or stove top)

METHOD:

1. Dissolve the extract in a heatproof beaker using approximately half of the hot water. Stir to ensure there are no lumps in the solution – this may take some time and a lot of stirring. The liquid can be heated gently to help the extract dissolve if the initial hot water didn't completely dissolve it.
2. Dissolve the alum in the remaining hot water and then add it to the dye liquid. Allow to cool.
3. Add starch to the cool dye liquid and stir to combine fully. Heat gently in a saucepan, stirring continuously. The paste will suddenly start to thicken so keep a close eye on it. Alternatively, you can heat the solution in a glass beaker in a water bath. This will take much longer but is a useful way of thickening very small amounts of dye paste. I often do this when I have several small amounts of different dye pastes to thicken.
4. Heat until the mixture starts to bubble and then keep stirring until the paste reaches the desired consistency. Make it a bit thicker than traditional screenprinting paste. With practice, you'll get to know the thickness you like – keep in mind that the paste will become slightly thicker as it cools.
5. Once the desired thickness is achieved, take the paste off the heat and allow it to cool. The mixture will thicken as it cools and may develop a slight skin, which can be stirred into the mix. The thickness of the paste can be adjusted at a later stage, if required.
6. Store your paste in a sealable container in a cool, dark place.

RECIPE:

Water-Based Printing Paste for Paper (using fresh or dried dyestuffs)

This recipe uses fresh or dried dyestuffs, which must be reduced down to achieve a concentrated colour. The recipe makes a little over 100g of paste. It's only a very small amount but the quantities can be increased once the right consistency and depth of colour have been achieved. With different dyestuffs, more water is sometimes required as the solution heats. Dyestuffs such as roots and barks will absorb a lot more liquid than dyestuffs such as flowers and leaves, so adapt the recipe accordingly. Remember that different plants also contain different concentrations of dye so if you want to make a colour stronger, add more dyestuff and/or consider leaving it to steep for longer. I recommend beginning with the same amount of dyestuff to water – 50g dyestuff to 500g is a good place to start and this provides a baseline from which to expand your knowledge. You are strongly encouraged to change the recipe to suit your own requirements.

YOU WILL NEED:

- 50g dyestuff
- 500g water
- 5g alum sulphate
- 10–15g wheat (or other) starch
- Kettle
- Scales
- Small stainless-steel saucepan
- Filter paper or fabric filter such as muslin
- Heatproof glass beaker or similar for dissolving alum sulphate
- Stirrers
- Heat source (portable hob, induction heater, buffet warmer or stove top)

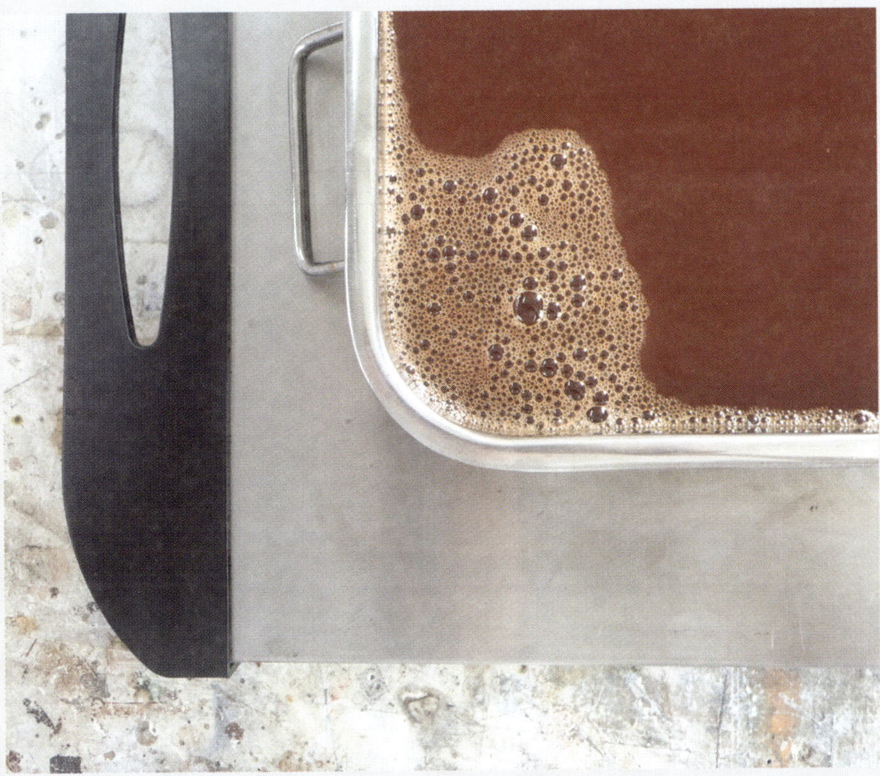

Reduce dye liquids over a gentle heat so the colours aren't affected. Portable induction hobs and stove-top hobs can be hard to keep at a low temperature so a buffet warmer or hot plate is a helpful piece of kit.

METHOD:

1. Add the dyestuff and enough of the water to cover the dyestuff to a saucepan and start to heat the mixture. Whilst the dyestuff is in the water, it can be left overnight either before or after heating to allow the colour to develop more fully. Add more water if required to ensure the dyestuff is completely covered.
2. Continue heating the dyestuff and water without boiling until the liquid has reduced by at least two-thirds. At this point, remove the dyestuff by filtering the liquid through a tightly woven mesh or a filter paper. Ensure all plant particles are removed.
3. Continue gently reducing the liquid until approximately 100g remains. Do not boil the liquid, which may damage or alter the colour. A shallow stainless-steel tray on a buffet warmer is a handy way of gently reducing liquid without allowing it to get too hot.
4. Dissolve the alum in a little hot water and add it to the reduced dye liquid, then allow it to cool.
5. Add starch to the cool dye liquid and stir to combine fully. Heat gently in a saucepan, stirring continuously. The paste will suddenly start to thicken so keep a close eye on it. Alternatively, you can heat the solution in a glass beaker in a water bath. This will take much longer but is a useful way of thickening very small amounts of dye paste. I often do this when I have several small amounts of different dye pastes to thicken.
6. Heat until the mixture starts to bubble and then keep stirring until the paste reaches the desired consistency. Make it a little thicker than traditional screenprinting paste. With practice, you'll get to know the thickness you like – keep in mind that the paste will become a little thicker as it cools.
7. Once the desired thickness is achieved, take the paste off the heat and allow it to cool. The mixture will thicken and may develop a slight skin which can be stirred into the mix.
8. Store your paste in a cool, dark place.

RECIPE:

Plant-Based Screenprinting Medium

This recipe can be useful when making up a number of screenprinting paste colours. Make a large batch of this colourless medium, divide up and then add the colour. The medium works best with dye extracts due to their concentrated form. If using fresh or dried dyestuffs, it is best to use the dye liquid in place of the water, rather than this recipe, which is more suitable for adding concentrated colour at the end of the process.

The measurements below make approximately one small pot of paste. If dividing to use with multiple colours, double or quadruple the amounts.

YOU WILL NEED:

- 15g wheat (or other) starch
- 100g cold water

METHOD:

1. Add the water and wheat starch to a stainless-steel saucepan and stir until combined. Heat gently, stirring continuously. The paste will suddenly start to thicken so keep a close eye on it.
2. Heat until the mixture starts to bubble and then keep stirring for a few minutes. Take off the heat and leave to cool. The mixture will thicken and, once completely cool, will look quite solid. It needs to be thicker than pastes already containing colour as further liquid will be added if using a liquid or dissolved dye extract.
3. Once cool, colour can be added to the paste. Lake pigments, liquid plant dyes or dissolved dye extracts can be used – add in small amounts until the required colour is achieved. Test the colour and consistency by smearing a little across paper. If the paste seems thin, you can add wheat starch and reheat. However, with small amounts of paste it is often more convenient to add a little guar gum powder. This has the benefit of thickening the paste quickly and without the need for heating. I prefer to use wheat starch on pastes for paper as guar gum paste can become thin fairly quickly, but the gum is a very quick and convenient thickener when added in small amounts.

Using Lake Pigments

Lake pigments can be used to make pastes for screenprinting onto paper. The lake making process precipitates the dye molecules onto a metallic salt (usually potassium alum sulphate or alum sulphate) and the excess liquid is filtered off. The remaining pigment is used as the colourant in the screenprinting paste.

If the original dye liquid has a lot of colourant in it (and hasn't been previously used to dye anything), the pigment will be a strong, concentrated colour but if the dye liquid was weak with little colourant, the precipitated lake pigment will be a paler colour. The concentration of colour in the pigment is also determined by the amount of alum and soda ash added to the dye liquid to make the lake. Whilst a standard recipe is given in Chapter 4, there are a lot of elements to consider and determining how much alum and soda ash to add to the dye liquid only comes with experience and after trial and error. Ratios and percentages of dyestuff, liquid, alum and soda ash can all be adapted and tailored to determine the best recipe for each particular dye and the specific requirements of use.

At this stage don't get caught up in details. I recommend starting with the recipe provided in Chapter 4 for every dyestuff you plan to use. This will provide a baseline from which to explore further. But remember, if you want a more concentrated pigment, just use more of the original dyestuff.

If using a lake pigment in its dry, powdered form for screenprinting, the most important thing to consider is the particle size. Pigments must be ground small enough that, once dispersed into the medium, they can still pass through the screen mesh and onto the paper. If the particles are too big for the mesh, the pigment gets caught, clogging the screen and preventing the colour from passing through the mesh and onto the paper, which results in a very pale layer of colour on the print.

Lake pigments can also be made into a screenprinting paste when in their 'gloopy' form and before they dry out completely. Refer to Chapter 4 and the lake pigment recipe for further information but stop at the 'strained pigment' stage. Once the lake pigment has had most of the liquid removed by filtering through a coffee filter or tightly woven cloth, the remaining gloop can be thickened by adding wheat starch and then heating to make it into a useable screenprinting paste. Don't be tempted to print with just the gloop, however suitable it seems. This gloop is made of pigment particles and water. Therefore, once the water evaporates, the pigment will become powdery and won't stick to the page particularly well – a binder must be added.

As the colourant is now an insoluble pigment rather than a dye, it is not going to 'dye' the paper, it will merely sit on top of the paper. The wheat starch now acts as a binder as well as a thickener – I like to add a little guar gum to this mix to help bind the pigment to the paper, although wheat starch on its own works perfectly well.

Screenprinted colour using 'wet' lake pigment paste. These have been printed with (left to right) madder, coreopsis, weld, buckthorn berry, rhubarb root and fresh leaf indigo lake pigments. The top row shows two pulls and the bottom row shows four pulls of the squeegee. Note the strength of colour but also the pureness of the madder red and the weld yellow.

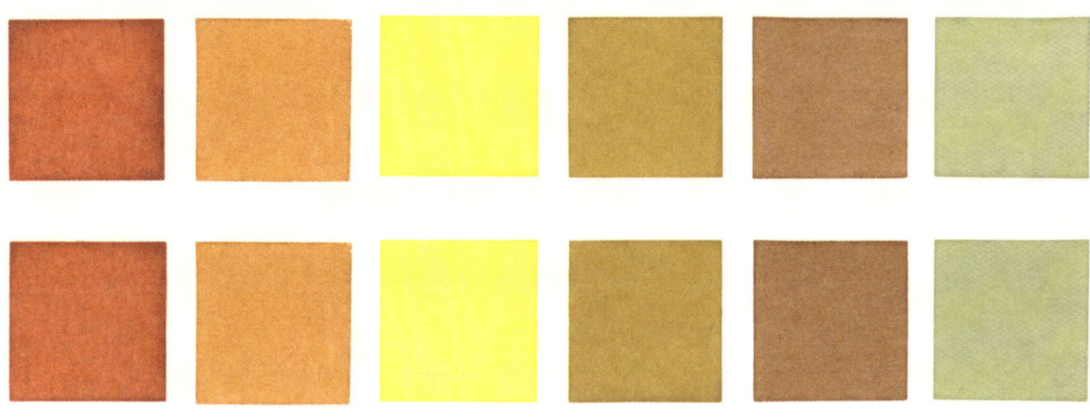

RECIPE:

Water-based Printing Paste for Paper (using 'wet' lake pigments)

The amounts given below make just over 100g of paste. The lake pigment is made from 1 litre of dye liquid with 10g of alum sulphate (or potassium alum sulphate) and 5g of soda ash added. The lake pigment 'gloop' you use might be more or less watery, depending on how long it was strained. More or less wheat starch may be required to get the right consistency for printing.

YOU WILL NEED:

- 50g of 'wet' lake pigment
- 50g water
- 10g wheat starch
- A little guar gum (optional)
- Scales
- Small stainless-steel saucepan
- Filter paper or fabric filter such as muslin
- Stirrers
- Small container for mixing wheat starch
- Heat source (portable hob, induction heater or stove top)
- Lidded pot for storing paste

METHOD:

1. Strain the freshly made lake pigment through a coffee filter or tightly woven fabric to remove any excess water (follow the recipe in Chapter 4 to make a lake pigment).
2. Leave the pigment in a cool, dry place for 24 hours or more to allow the water to drain fully. The aim is to have a gloopy mixture without any remaining 'puddle' of water sitting in the middle and it shouldn't have any lighter patches appearing where the gloop is starting to dry out.
3. Scrape this gloop off the filter paper or fabric into a small saucepan. There will probably be about 2–3 tablespoons but if less, just reduce the amount of wheat starch and water added in the next step. The aim is to add approximately the same amount of water as there is gloop.
4. In a separate pot, mix 10g of wheat starch with 50g of cold water (use a 1:5 ratio if using more or less than 50g of water) to combine fully and add this to the saucepan. Stir well and heat gently to thicken the paste.
5. Once thickened, allow the paste to cool before adding an optional sprinkle of guar gum. Stir to combine and wait 30 minutes before using. If the paste is too thick, add a little water and if too thin, add a little more guar gum. Sometimes the paste can feel a little jelly-like and doesn't print particularly well – add more guar gum to offset this problem.
6. Store in a lidded pot and use as needed.

Modifying the Colour

The colour of the printing pastes can be modified before printing by adding a little alkaline, acid or iron solution. Calculate the amount needed by first weighing the paste and then adding 1 per cent or 2 per cent of this weight of the modifier. For example, if the paste weighs 150g, add 3g of soda ash for a 2 per cent quantity. Dissolve the modifier in a little hot water and add to the paste, adding only a little at a time. The process is very adaptable to experimentation by adding a little of the modifier, checking the colour, then adding more if a greater adjustment is required. The effect is less noticeable with lake pigments.

Screenprinted colour modified with an alkali (soda ash) paste and an iron paste.

Indigo doesn't react to modifiers so has not been included.

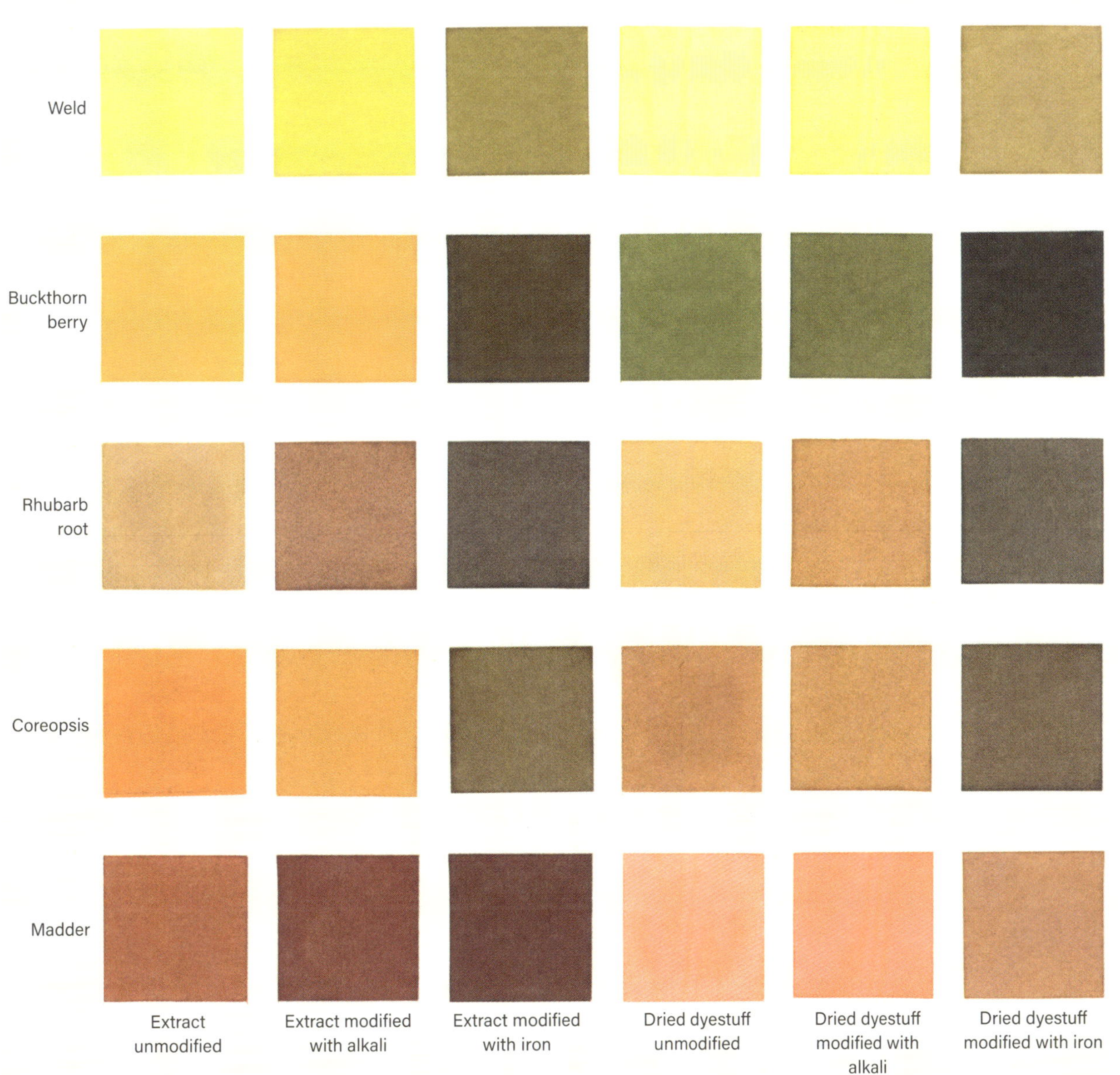

Paste Thickener Substitutions

Rice starch, arrowroot powder or cornflour (corn starch) can be substituted for the wheat starch. However, rice starch is relatively hard to get hold of in the UK and cornflour, whilst readily available and cheap, doesn't give as good a result as it tends to bleed under the screen. Arrowroot powder is my second choice after wheat starch. Other thickeners include alginates, carrageenan gums, guar gum, tapioca starch and agar agar. However, tapioca starch, agar agar and carrageenan gum are my least favourite thickeners for paper printing pastes and were eliminated from further tests after an initial test print, as the results were unsatisfactory.

Storing Plant-Based Printing Paste

Don't mix more paste than is needed as it will eventually go off. Keep in the fridge or as cool as possible when not using. The mixture may be stored like a normal paint but keep an eye on it – it will probably start to ferment and potentially make the container explode if it is glass or at the very least the lid might pop open – periodically let the gas out.

The paste will become thinner and probably go mouldy but keep using it – just scrape the mould off and reheat to thicken. More starch can be added to achieve the desired consistency. Pastes made with lake pigments seem to have fewer tendencies to go mouldy.

Other Techniques

Try eliminating the thickener completely or changing the consistency of the paste for other techniques and printmaking processes. For example, a stamp or a block made of absorbent material will print successfully onto some papers with just a liquid dye but a linocut plate requires a thicker solution or ideally an oil-based ink. The paper thickness, surface and sizing will also affect results. Experiment with what works for you.

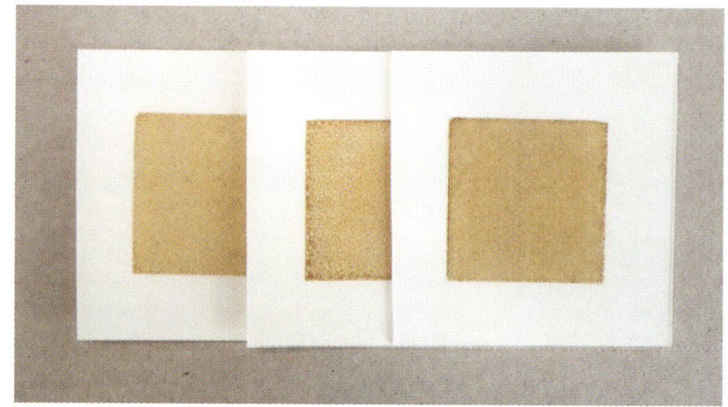

Unsatisfactory results from (left to right) guar gum, tapioca starch and carrageenan gum.

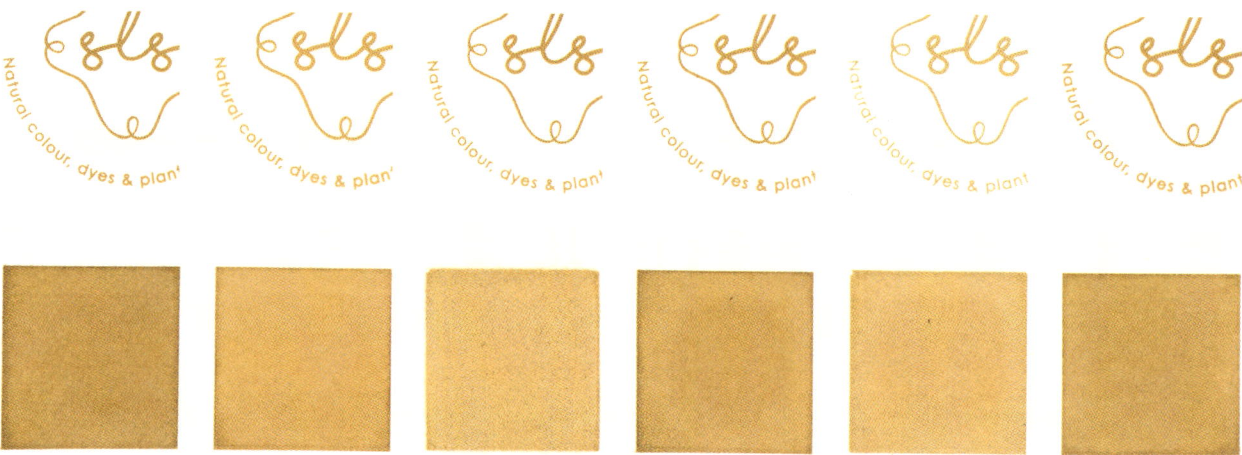

Different paste thickeners from left to right: arrowroot powder, cornflour (corn starch), guar gum, rice starch, sodium alginate and wheat starch. All were made from the same reduced dye liquid.

Troubleshooting

Paste too thin (causing seepage under screen, creating bubbles in print, paper stencil quickly becomes saturated) – add more thickener. If using a starch-based thickener, mix the starch in a little water, add to the printing paste and heat to thicken. A little guar gum can also be added to thicken paste quickly and without needing to reheat.
Paste too thick (quickly clogging screen, smearing in patches across the paper, not fully printing or sticking to squeegee) – add more water a little at a time and mix in. Before doing so, stir the paste well as it may loosen up when stirred.
Lumpy printing paste (clogging the screen, patchy results) – use a small squeegee with a flat sieve or splashguard to force the paste through the mesh to remove the lumps. Lumps in the printing paste can cause smears of starch to be printed, causing uncoloured patches or an uneven colour.
Mouldy printing paste (causing lumpy paste, discolouration and general unpleasantness) – mould can be scraped off and the paste used as normal. To prevent mould, ensure storage pots have well-fitting lids and have been cleaned thoroughly before adding paste. Paste can also be heated which may destroy the mould and stop it returning.

BLOCKED SCREENS

When screenprinting with plant starches and natural gums, don't let them dry in the screen – ensure screens are washed well and regularly. If a screen does become blocked with dried starch or gum, soak the screen in water to soften the dried areas before washing with a strong jet of water – a hose with a spray head or a showerhead is ideal. Alternatively, use a pressure washer if you have access to one.

Don't soak wooden screens in water as they will become warped and unusable. If wooden screens become blocked and won't clear with a strong jet of water, place a soaked cloth or tea towel over the screen and leave for one hour, ensuring the cloth remains wet. This should loosen the dried paste enough to wash it out of the screen.

Scrape the mould away from any paste that starts to go off and use to print.

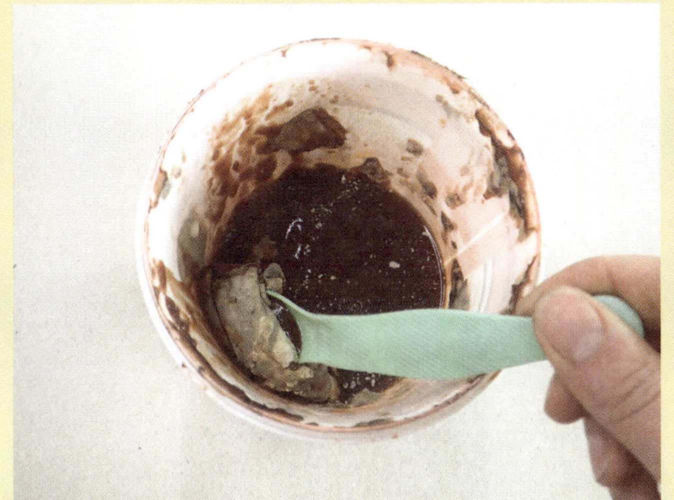

Lumps of wheat starch in the print paste can cause white patches on your print.

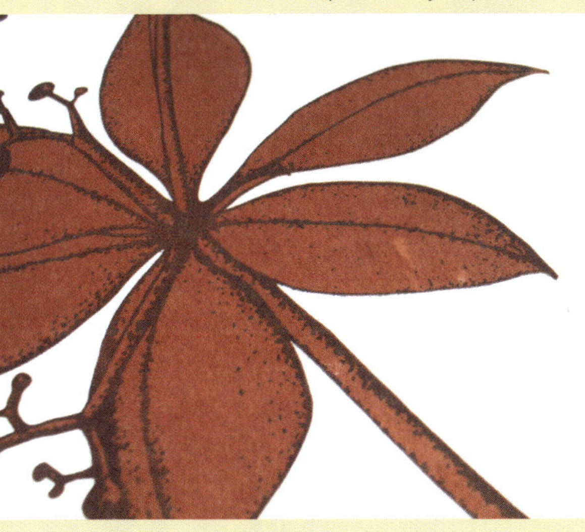

OIL-BASED PRINTMAKING INKS (for paper)

Oil-based printmaking ink is similar to any paint or ink – it consists of a pigment and a 'vehicle'. The vehicle is used to coat the pigment particles and 'stick' them to the paper. The vehicle is made of a binder and, most often in commercial paints and inks, other additives such as fillers, driers and preservatives.

Whereas watercolour paint most often uses gum arabic as the binder and acrylic paints use a plastic-based medium, in oil paint and oil-based inks, the binder (also called varnish in this case) is usually linseed oil. Other drying oils such as walnut oil or poppy seed oil are sometimes used. In oil-based printmaking ink, the binder is called copperplate, stand or burnt plate oil. These are all generally linseed oils but they have been treated to make them thicker and more viscous – an important characteristic of oil-based printmaking ink. Linseed oil is extracted from the seeds of the flax plant (*Linum usitatissimum*) which is also the plant that linen fabric and yarn are made from.

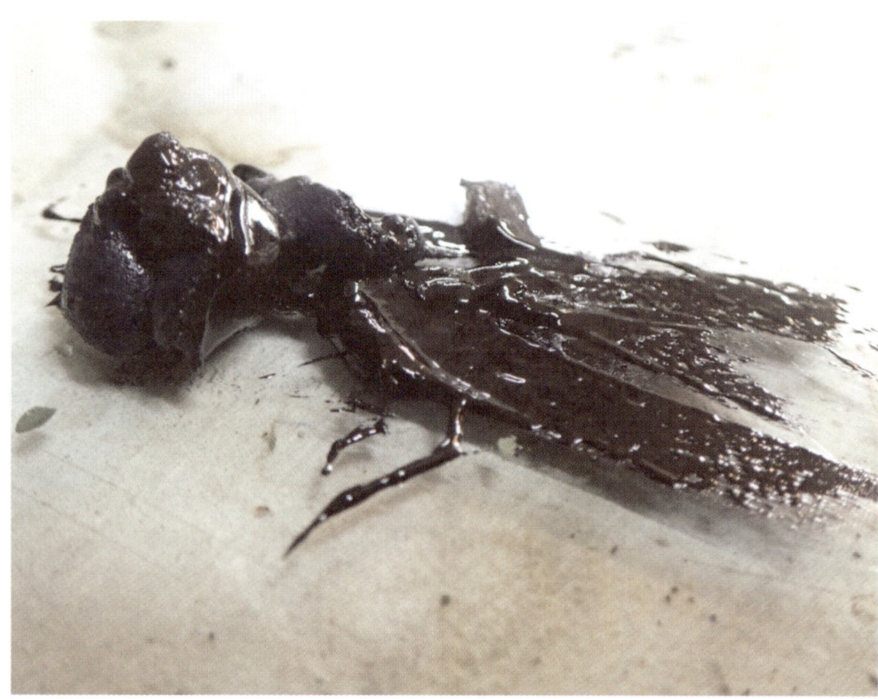

Oil-based ink made with madder lake pigment and indigo.

Ink Characteristics

Relief and intaglio inks differ in their characteristics and are dictated by the different requirements each technique demands. Relief inks should be short, tacky, fairly viscous, highly pigmented and with a very small pigment particle size. Further requirements of different types of relief printing processes are catered for in commercially-produced inks – for example, there is often a difference between the ink manufactured for a linocut compared to the ink made for metal type.

Intaglio inks should be more fluid and less tacky, which allows for easier wiping when inking up a plate. Whilst the particle size must still be small, it need not be as fine as for relief inks. If too small, it can be challenging to keep the colour from being wiped away completely from the plate's indentations. However, all processes that fall within the broad category of intaglio printing have further particular requirements of the ink being used.

Printmaking ink terminology can be confusing and perplex the beginner, particularly as there are differing opinions, definitions and information available. Therefore, the best way to learn about oil-based ink is to make some and use it to print with. As you get more familiar with making ink, you'll find you can adapt it to suit your individual requirements and for the specific technique employed. Learning to make ink gives the printmaker an opportunity to adapt and modify the ink's characteristics and to develop a practical understanding of the ink's properties.

It should be stressed that the same ink can be used for both relief and intaglio techniques, with only small adaptations but it is useful to understand the properties of ink when mixing it.

Ink Colourants

The pigments used in commercial printing inks are usually synthetic, although earth and mineral-based pigments such as ochres and umbers are also available and can be purchased from specialist art supply shops. For the artist committed to using plant-based colour and those wishing to go beyond the use of black ink, it becomes necessary to learn how to make your own plant-based pigments, also known for the most part as lake pigments. To make a dry, powdered pigment from plant matter can feel complicated on the first few attempts but is a useful method of obtaining waterless colour from plants – refer to Chapter 4 for a detailed recipe and further information about lake pigments.

Other options are to purchase lake pigments or plant dye extracts from suppliers, both of which can be used to make oil-based ink – essentially anything that is a dry coloured powder can be used. Indigo is a good example of this and is highly pigmented, producing a strong and deep colour. For black ink, consider different types of carbon – soot from inside a chimney makes a good pigment, especially as the particles are already extremely small (you should wear a mask and gloves if collecting soot). It may be easier to grind up some charcoal and sieve it to a small particle size (though still wear a mask that filters particulates). This approach allows specific woods and plants to be used, which will all have different tones and qualities. Particle size can be visually assessed by smearing some of the pigment across paper – finely particled pigments will colour the paper easily.

The size of the particles in the pigment will greatly affect the quality of the ink and as mentioned above, printmaking ink requires incredibly small particles of pigment. Scientific sieves of different grades can be purchased to filter out bigger particles if oil-based ink making becomes more than a hobby. I use a 45-micron sieve for printmaking pigments. However, to begin with, don't worry too much – it is just something to be aware of.

Smear dry pigment across paper to check its particle size. Fine particles will colour the paper whilst bigger particles will feel rough and gritty under your finger.

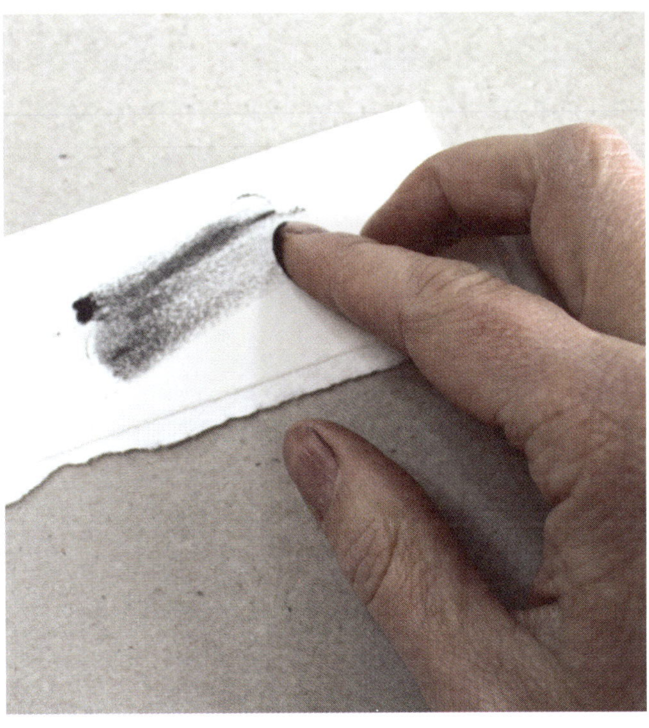

Ink Vehicles

The other main ingredient of printmaking ink is the binder – use a thickened linseed oil, called burnt plate oil, stand oil or copperplate oil, depending on the brand and how it is made. It is also sometimes referred to as varnish. Burnt plate oil was traditionally set on fire to thicken it, hence the name but nowadays most thickened linseed oils are stand oils, made by heating the oil in the absence of oxygen. These oils come in different viscosities from a light, fluid (weak) variety to a thicker, more viscous (strong) form. Confusingly, there are different classifications of measuring the viscosity of oils depending on the manufacturer, where the oil was made (there are European and American standards) and what the oil is intended for. Each has slightly different properties though a strong (also called high or heavy) oil and a light (also called weak or thin) oil should suit the beginner. You may see oils classified as poise (1 to 500 poise or more) and given numbers (#0000 to #8). In these cases, use lower numbers for light oils and higher numbers for strong oils.

Most experienced ink makers use a combination of different strengths of oil to give the ink specific properties and allow greater control over the end result. You might also consider making your own thickened linseed oil, but it requires specialist equipment and can be very dangerous, requiring oils to be heated above boiling points and thus beyond the scope of this book and the author's experience.

Theoretically, a thickened linseed oil can be made by allowing linseed oil to gradually dry and thicken in the sun, though keeping this oil clean and free from dust or debris would be challenging.

Ink Additives

Magnesium carbonate or calcium carbonate is sometimes used to thicken inks, though these will affect the colour of the ink. If the ink is too runny or thin, a good option is to add more pigment in the first instance. Driers such as cobalt drier, which speed up an ink's drying time, are toxic and something I avoid using.

Making Oil-Based Ink

Ideally a muller and a glass slab are required to successfully mix the pigment, the oil and any other additives. The most easily available mullers are made of glass but they are an investment and not particularly ideal for mixing oil-based printmaking ink. Glass mullers often have to be used on their edge when making oil-based ink as the ink is too tacky and stiff to allow for the flat base to be moved or rotated across the surface of the slab. The most useful mullers for this type of ink making are made from stone and are more rounded, without the sharp, hard edge of a glass muller but are much trickier, if not impossible, to source. It might be worth trying to borrow a muller, either glass or stone, before purchasing one to see if making your own paints and inks is something you'd like to do more of.

Both the muller and the glass slab can be purchased though it is relatively easy to make your own – *see* Chapter 3 for step-by-step instructions. The aim of using the muller and glass slab is to fully coat each tiny particle of pigment with your binder, not to grind your pigment into smaller particles – this should have been done prior to mixing your ink. Whilst a certain amount of grinding may take place, it is not the primary consideration here. Commercially produced printmaking ink is processed through a three-roll mill, where the rollers can be set to get gradually closer together, ensuring a well-mixed ink with little effort – something to wish for when your arms and shoulders are aching from mulling.

The ink can be stored in small containers or submerged in water to stop it drying out in the air. I find that making just enough for each printing session is ideal to prevent waste, though I often leave it overnight before using and it is always fine the next day, even sometimes improved. If ink does start to dry out, you can often reconstitute it with the addition of a little oil and some hardcore mulling, but make sure any harder bits are removed before using.

It can be challenging to create good oil-based printmaking ink using plant-based colour – this is in part due to the transparent nature of most lake pigments but is also affected by pigment particle size and the lack of specialist milling equipment. However, it is also incredibly satisfying, adds meaning to your practice and allows truly bespoke colours to be used within your work.

Remember – you should always wear a mask when working with powders and dusty materials.

RECIPE:

Oil-Based Printmaking Ink

It is recommended that you begin by using bought pigments from specialist paint and pigment suppliers, as they will have a small particle size and will provide a comparison for your own pigments. This will allow the beginner in ink-making to develop the skills required to make printmaking ink and understand how to change its composition for individual requirements before using what can feel like your priceless handmade lake pigments. However, any dry powdered pigment can be used. Remember that once you move on to making your own pigments, each one will be different (though this is often the case for commercially produced pigments too). Your pigments have not been made in a factory with exacting recipes so each pigment will require different amounts of oil and other ingredients every time. Part of the skill is in understanding your pigment and adapting recipes to create exactly what you want for the process you are using.

YOU WILL NEED:

- 10g finely ground pigment
- 10g stand oil (or burnt plate or copperplate oil) – use a combination of mostly strong oil and a little light (weak) oil but don't mix them at this stage
- Muller and glass or stone slab
- Paper tape
- Two small crank-handled (offset) spatulas or straight-edge painting knives
- Scales (ideally to 0.1g)
- Measuring spoons
- Vegetable oil and rags for cleaning

LEFT
One of the first oil-based inks I made was using purchased madder lake pigment. This page is from my *Dyeing (not Dying)* research in 2019.

RIGHT
Testing layering of oil-based inks including madder, logwood, weld and alder cone.

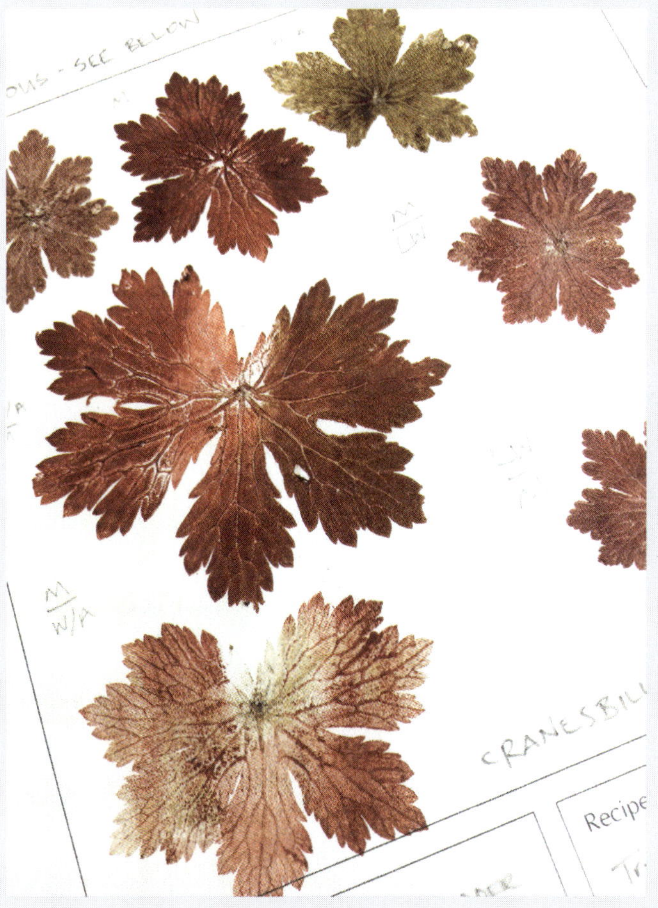

METHOD:

1. Before beginning, ensure the glass slab is securely fixed to the bench or table. Use paper tape to fix it down or a damp cloth underneath to keep it in place.
2. Start off small. Begin with 3g of pigment (a level teaspoon-ish) and place it onto the glass slab. Make a well in the centre of the pigment and add 1.5g of strong stand oil – the oil doesn't have to be weighed – use ½ tsp measuring spoon if easier. Different pigments need different amounts of oil – for example, indigo generally requires equal amounts of oil and pigment whereas weld extract requires much less oil and a madder lake pigment, much more oil. The amounts of pigment and oil included in the recipe allow for experimentation with ratios – you may not need all the pigment or oil for your first attempt.
3. Use a spatula to start gently mixing the pigment and oil together until there is no dry powder left. Add a little more strong stand oil if needed and work the ink backwards and forwards to fully combine the oil and pigment. Ink is thixotropic, which means it will get looser and runnier as it is worked. Don't get impatient and add more oil immediately – the ink needs time and effort to reveal its true nature. If it really is too thick and clumpy, add a drop or two of light stand oil to loosen the ink.
4. Use the spatula to gather the mixture to one side of the glass slab, leaving a small amount to start mulling. It's easier to use the edge of the muller by holding at an angle and pulling in a backwards and forwards motion rather than in a circular motion with the muller held flat. This is just because the ink will be very viscous and hard to mull. Go backwards and forwards several times and in different directions before using a spatula to gather the mulled ink and put to one side. Start on the next amount of ink and repeat until all the mixture has been processed. Repeat several times to make sure the pigment is dispersed properly throughout the binder.
5. The ink will gradually get more shiny and smoother – observe the ink closely to check its progress. Remember – the pigment is not being ground into smaller particles here, the pigment is simply being dispersed throughout the binder and the mulling ensures every particle is coated in oil.

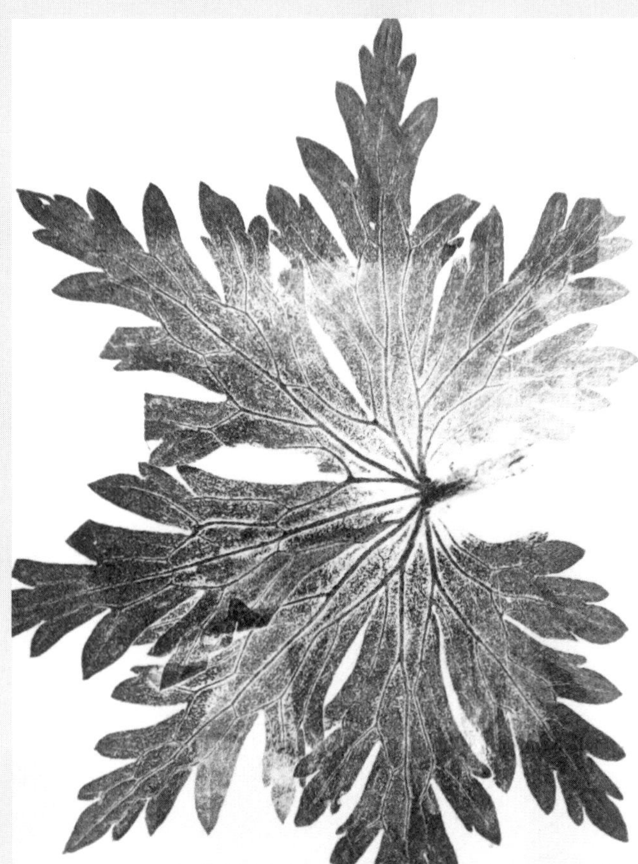

A hardy cranesbill (*Geranium spp.*) leaf printed with oil-based ink made using purchased *Indigofera tinctoria* powder, which is highly pigmented and usually very finely ground.

6. At this stage assess the ink. It may be ready to use immediately or you may need to add some further light stand oil to loosen it up. Mull the ink again after any extra ingredients are added.

   Intaglio ink needs to be thick enough to stay in the indentations of the plate but wipeable from the surface. If it's too thin, the ink will be completely removed when the plate is wiped. Relief ink needs to be thick but must roll out to an even layer. Initially, the best way to assess ink is to create a small test print and then adapt the recipe. Keep small offcuts of plate material to allow for quick testing.
7. Once mixed, either place in a small container and cover with water or use immediately. Clean up the glass slab, muller and tools with vegetable oil or a preferred petroleum-free cleaner.

Making Oil-Based Ink

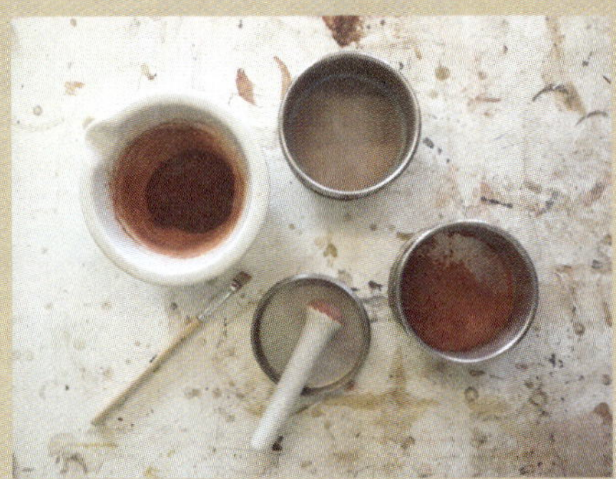

Madder lake pigment sieved and ready to make ink with.

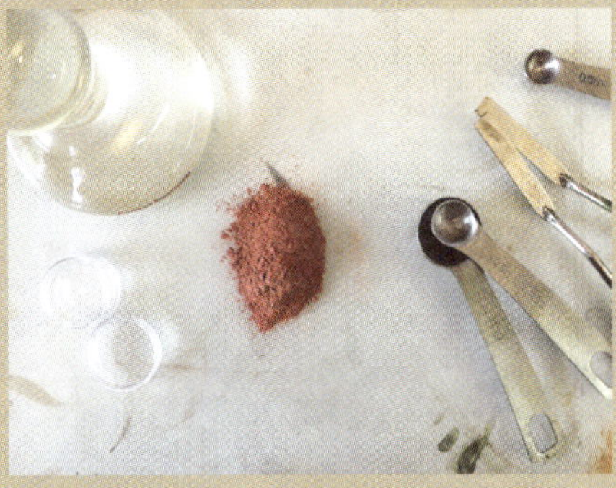

Place 3g of pigment in the centre of the glass slab. Alternatively, you can measure by amount (such as 1 tsp) but use the same measurement for the oil.

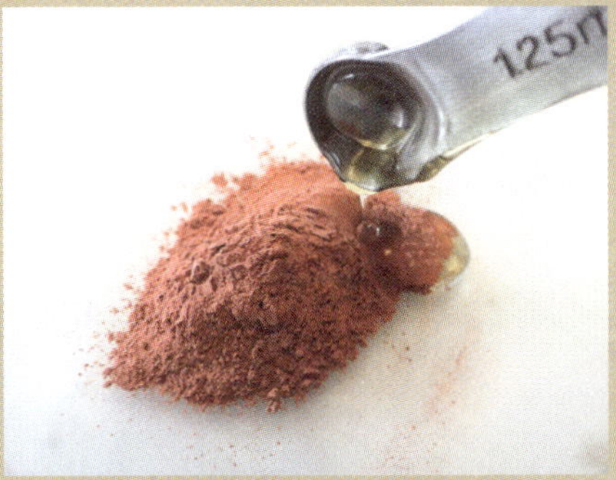

Add 1.5g of strong oil to the pigment. Start to combine and add a little more strong oil if needed, but use sparingly.

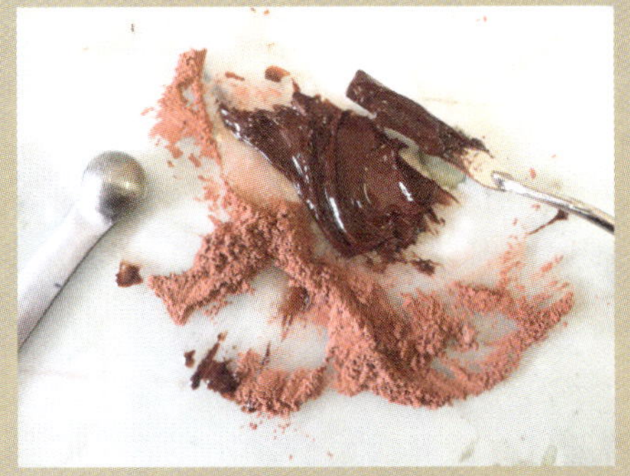

Combine the oil and the pigment using a spatula or painting knife. Add approximately 0.5g of light (weak) oil.

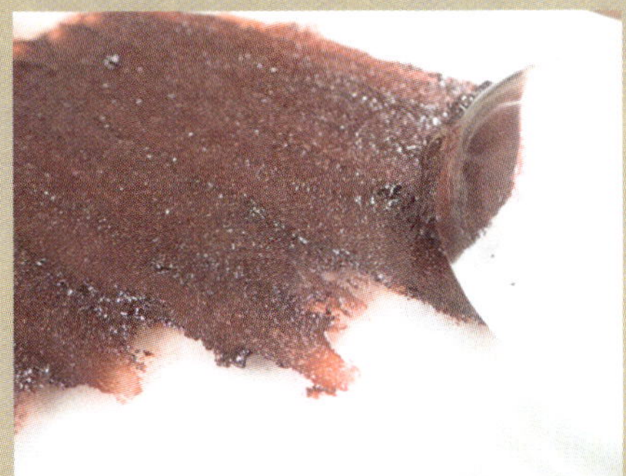

The ink will appear coarse before mulling because the pigment particles are still stuck together.

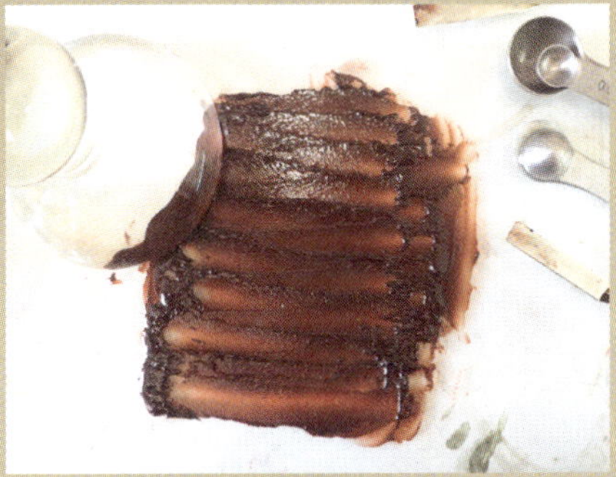

Using the edge of the muller, mull the ink in one direction. The ink is too thick to mull using a normal circular motion.

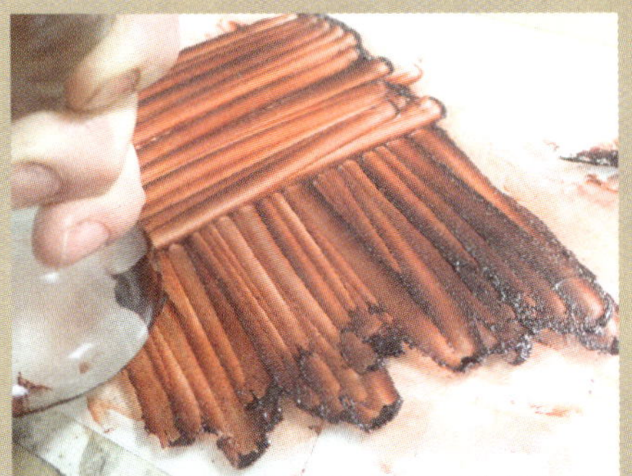

Mull in the other direction. Just mull a little ink at a time and repeat as necessary.

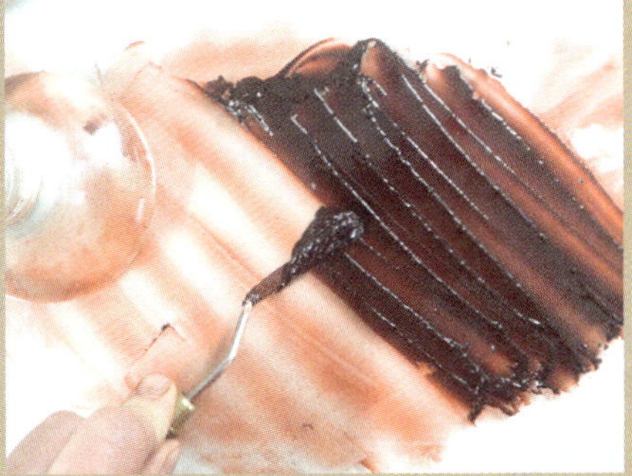

Scrape the mulled oil from the glass slab and test its consistency and tackiness.

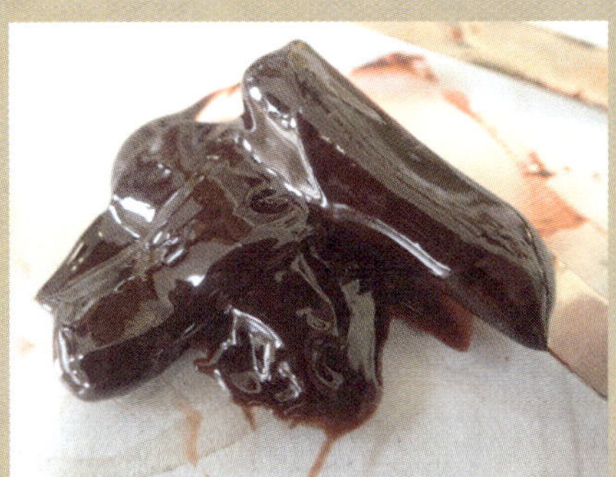

Once ready the ink should appear smooth and glossy, with no lumps or obvious changes in uniformity when manipulated.

WATERCOLOUR PAINTS FOR PRINTMAKING

Whilst watercolours may not immediately spring to mind for printmaking techniques, they are useful for many applications such as hand-tinting prints, sketches and monoprints (or monotypes).

However, one of their primary uses within the field of printmaking is for mokuhanga or Japanese woodblock printmaking. Mokuhanga uses water-based paints or watercolours to print layers of colour from cut woodblocks and there is a long tradition of using natural colour within this technique. A similar style and print technique inspired by mokuhanga evolved in North America called Provincetown Printmaking and used comparable materials, including watercolour paint, to produce prints.

There don't seem to be many contemporary mokuhanga artists who use natural colour within their work and whilst I have dabbled in the technique, I am certainly not an expert. However, I felt that the inclusion of how to make watercolours within this book was an important addition and perhaps might inspire mokuhanga artists to explore plant-based colour further.

Watercolours can be made and stored in a number of ways. This includes a pigmented liquid that acts in a similar way to a water-based ink; a semi-solid paint stored in a tube; or a solid, dry block of paint kept in a pan or half-pan (or any container that is open and allows the paint to dry out). The most useful for the mokuhanga technique is ideally paint kept in tubes but it is difficult to source small empty paint tubes and get the paint into the tubes without a lot of wastage. Small glass jars with lids are ideal containers for watercolours and the dry paint can be made wet with the addition of distilled water. Each different type of watercolour requires slightly different properties but all need two basic ingredients: the colourant (pigment) and the vehicle.

Watercolour paint is the same as any paint or ink – it consists of pigment and a vehicle, which is used to coat the pigment particles and 'stick' them to the paper. The vehicle is made up of a binder and, in paints and inks bought off the shelf, other additives such as fillers and preservatives. In watercolour paint, the binder is most often gum arabic, which is obtained from two species of the Acacia tree, *Acacia senegal* and *Acacia seyal*. Gum arabic is widely available and comes in lumps, powdered form and in a pre-mixed, liquid form. Other gums can be harvested and used – many of the *Prunus* species (including domestic cherry trees) will exude a sticky residue that can be used instead of a purchased gum arabic.

In watercolour paint, the vehicle also contains water with the addition of honey and/or glycerin, which acts as a humectant and, certainly in the case of watercolour pans and small containers, allows the paint to be re-wetted easily. I've also found it helps stop the paint crumbling as it ages.

When using plant-based colour as the pigment, it is most likely to be a lake pigment, a carbon pigment or indigo pigment. Inorganic pigments such as ochres or other earth colours or minerals may be used but are outside the scope of this book.

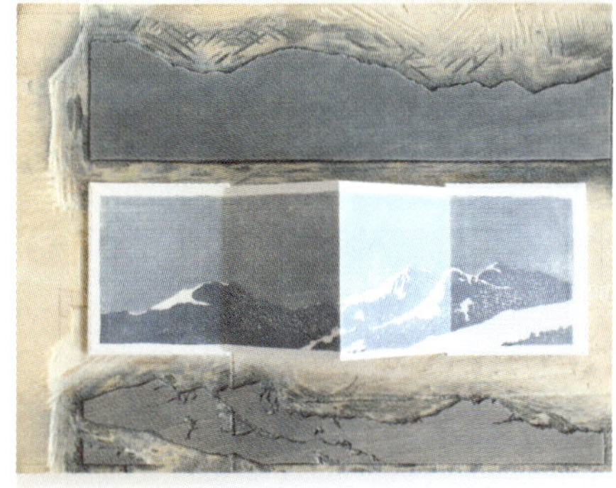

Yr Wyddfa. One of my first woodblocks and mokuhanga print made into a little concertina book. The print was created using my own indigo watercolour paint.

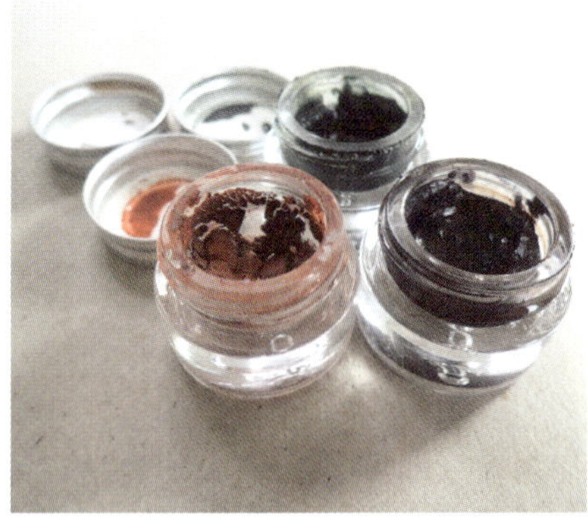

Storing paint in tubes can be problematic as it dries out, leaks and sometimes ferments so I keep some watercolour paints in small glass jars. This makes it easier to turn them into wet paint for mokuhanga printing.

Pigment Characteristics

Due to the diverse qualities of different lake pigments and other plant-based colours, it can be challenging to provide an exact and accurate recipe for making plant-based watercolours, although this provides a good starting point. Even synthetic pigments produced under strict controls in a factory and to exacting recipes require differing levels of binder, humectant and water. Be prepared to adapt amounts slightly to find the best mix for the pigment being used.

To make a dry, powdered pigment from plant matter can initially seem complicated but is a useful method of obtaining colour from plants – please see the section on 'Lake Pigments' in Chapter 4 for instructions on how to do this. As mentioned previously, other options include purchasing commercially produced lake pigments or plant dye extracts from suppliers, both of which can be used to make watercolour paint – essentially anything that is a dry coloured powder can be used. Indigo is a great pigment to use for your first attempt and is usually very finely ground, making it a good option for beginners. However, as watercolour paints are water-based, it isn't necessary to start with a dry powder – a concentrated liquid colour is also fine but the binder recipe would need to be adapted accordingly.

Plant-based watercolours can be easily mixed, in exactly the same way as commercial paints containing synthetic pigments. However, it is also useful to mix pigments prior to making paint, which gives you ready-made colour and removes the need for mixing.

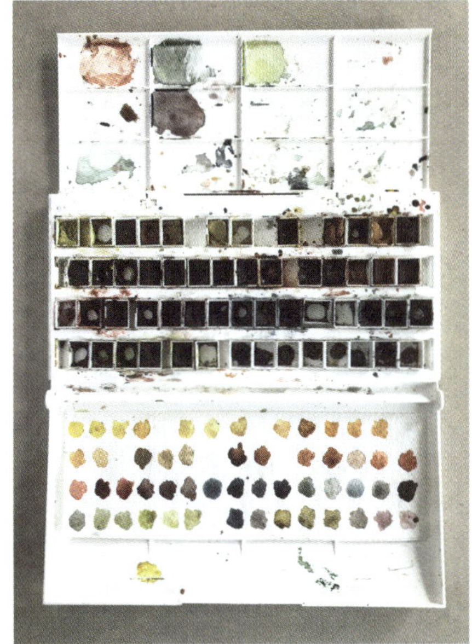

A full palette of plant-based watercolours.

RECIPE:

Watercolour Binder

YOU WILL NEED:

- 6g gum arabic
- 20g cold water
- 5g glycerin
- 1–2 drops of essential oil
- Scales and/or measuring spoons
- Small lidded jar

METHOD:

1. Mix two teaspoons (approximately 6g) of gum arabic powder with four teaspoons (approximately 20g) of cold water.
2. Add one teaspoon (approximately 5g) of glycerin and stir well. Leave in the fridge overnight to allow the gum arabic to completely dissolve in the water.
3. Add one or two drops of essential oil to inhibit mould growth. This will make enough binder to make at least six half pans of watercolour.

RECIPE:

Watercolour Paint

Combine equal amounts of watercolour binder with your dry, powdered pigment using a small spatula. The ratio of binder to pigment needed will change depending on each specific pigment but 1:1 is a good place to start. You can add more pigment or binder as needed – I generally find the paint requires approximately one part pigment to one to two parts binder. I also like to add a drop or two of runny honey to my watercolour paint which helps to re-wet it once dry.

Once the pigment and binder are roughly combined, use your muller in a circular motion to fully disperse the pigment into the binder. This ensures each particle is properly coated with binder and that no clumps of dry pigment are left in the paint. Add to your container and wait for the paint to dry.

If keeping in small glass jars, half fill the jar with paint and put the lid on. The paint will dry out but it is very easy to re-wet the whole jar of paint by adding a small amount of distilled water and leaving for one to two hours.

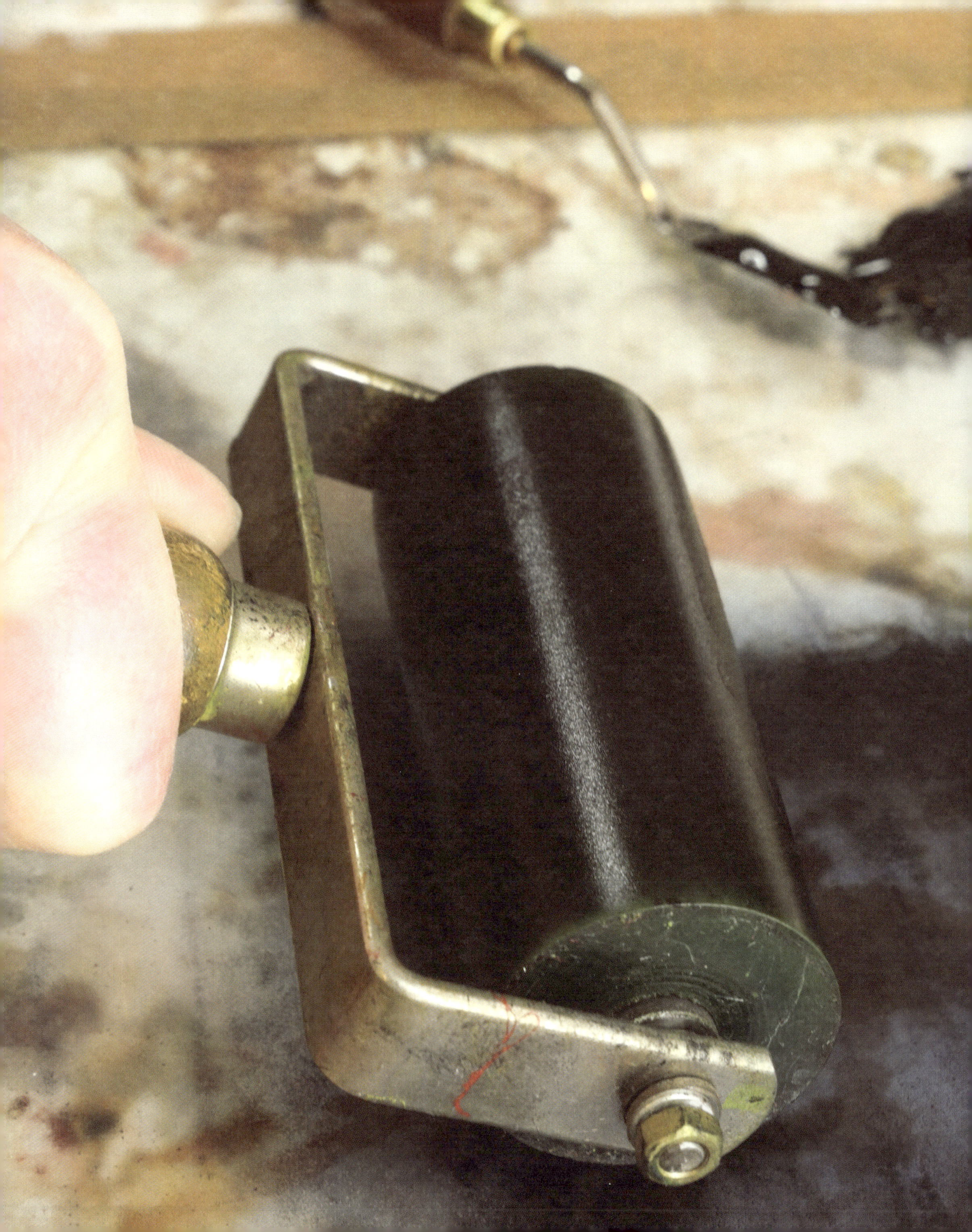

Chapter Eight

PRINTMAKING PROCESSES FOR PAPER

FACING PAGE

Rolling out an indigo and madder oil-based ink.

These projects have been included to show how printmaking with plant-based colour looks and functions across various printmaking processes for paper. It is possible to work through a project step by step but they have not been designed to be followed exactly – they are meant to be an aid to your own work and offer guidance on how to incorporate plant-based colour into your practice. If the inspiration for subject matter is lacking, think about using basic shapes and simple lines until a familiarity with the materials is reached. This is a useful technique even if you are an experienced printmaker, as there is a difference between printing with commercial inks and your own inks. It is therefore worth practising before starting an important project.

A composite of the *Graduation Colour* screenprints showing the layering of indigo and madder, indigo and indigo, indigo and weld.

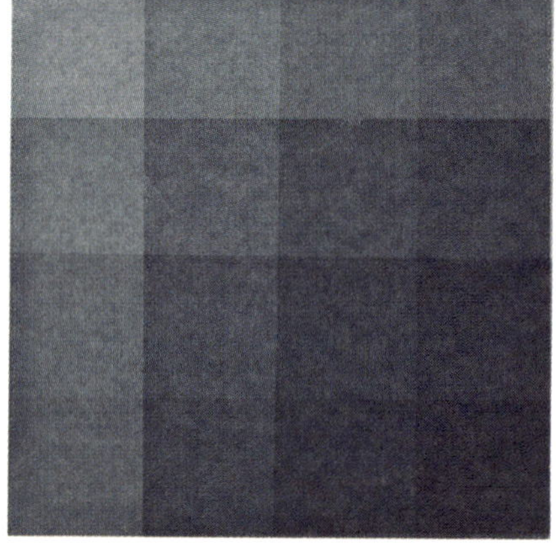

SCREENPRINTING

Keep your designs fairly simple to start with. Think about the shape of the stencils, the complexity of them and how hard it might be to print even and flat colour. It is best to start off with something very easy to cut and create, especially if cutting stencils by hand. Exact circles or shapes with lots of curves can be challenging. If cutting shapes by hand, try layering up two sheets of paper and cutting two at the same time. This works well for simple shapes but can be harder with more complex stencils, especially when using thick brown paper. If cutting thin or narrow stencils, don't make them too narrow. The thickness of the brown paper stencil between the screen and the paper can make it harder to print very fine shapes with a clear and well-defined edge. Experiment and see what can be achieved. A laser cutter, Cricut or a similar piece of equipment can be used to cut your stencils, which saves a lot of time and effort.

Stencils generally require the middle sections to remain attached to the outer sections or they fall away from the design. Think about the letter 'o' and how the middle would drop out if completely cut from a piece of paper. These loose sections are called 'islands'. This problem is usually offset by using 'bridges', which are little joins of paper between the main part of the stencil and the island. However, in screenprinting when you are ready to print, you can attach any loose pieces to your screen with a dab of water. This holds the loose islands in place until you run the first layer of print paste over the screen with the squeegee.

The centre of the letter 'O' has been kept attached to the stencil using 'bridges' cut into the paper.

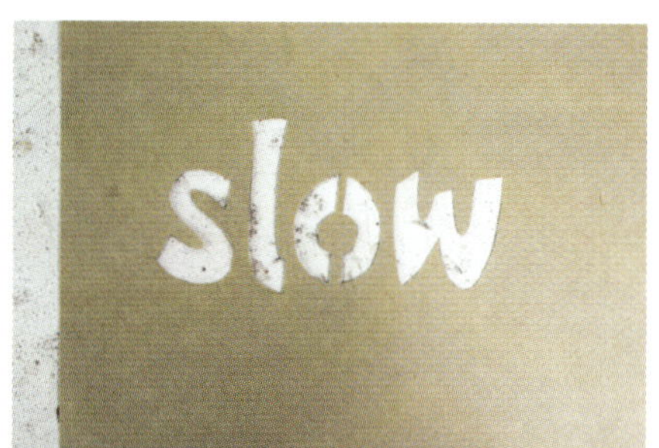

Whilst the centre of the 'O' has been cut out completely, it can be fixed in place on the underneath of the screen with a little dab of water when ready to print.

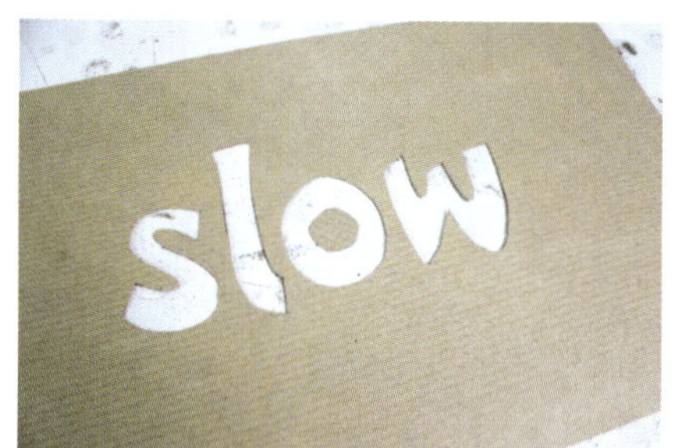

Edition and Size

Don't attempt a full edition to start with – keep editions small and the size of the work small. There is time enough to try printing at scale and to create a large number of prints. Refer to Chapter 3 for advice about choosing the right paper.

The Screenprinting Process

Step 1: Create a design and transfer it to the stencil paper. A small USB lightbox is ideal for this, or you could use carbon copy paper or print directly onto the stencil paper from a digital file.

Step 2: Cut out the stencils. Remember that any little nicks or cuts will show on the print, but this can be part of the design and shows it has been handmade. Make sure that the stencil has at least 50mm of uncut paper on each edge.

Step 3: If using hinge clamps, attach the screen to the clamps and place the paper beneath in approximately the correct position. The exact placement will be determined using the registration sheet at a later stage. If using a screenprint table/bed, attach the screen to the weighted hinged frame as usual.

Step 4: Set up a registration sheet with a strip of paper tape down the side to act as a hinge so the sheet can be flipped backwards and forwards. This will also act as protection for the paper when the first pull of the ink with the squeegee is carried out. Position the stencil on top of the registration sheet but underneath the screen. It doesn't need to be attached to the screen – the paste will do that on the first pull. Ideally the stencil should be in the middle of the screen, which allows for ease of printing and an even snap (the snap is the action of the mesh lifting away from the print after printing).

Step 5: Whilst it's not absolutely necessary, brown paper tape can also be applied to the top surface of the screen to help mask the open sections of the mesh. If the stencil has been cut a little small, the paste can occasionally go over the edge of it and transfer to the paper.

Step 6: Apply a line of print paste to the top of the screen, making sure it's on top of the tape and/or stencil and avoiding open areas of mesh. Put more paste on than you think is needed.

Step 7: Use the squeegee to pull the ink across the screen. Remember, this first pull is to make the stencil stick to

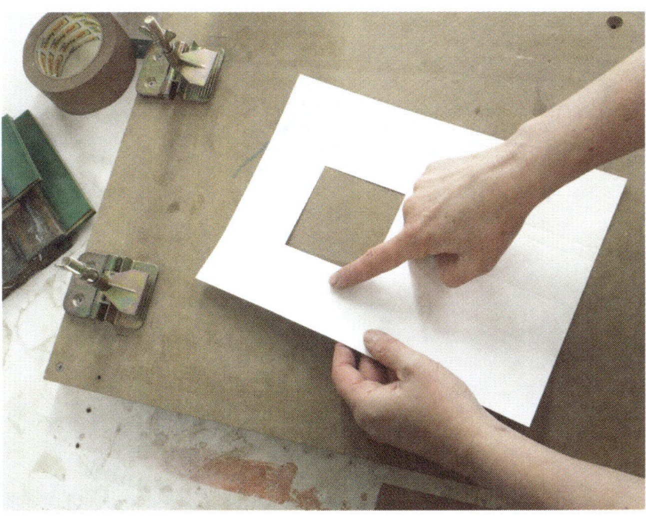

This stencil has a nice wide edge so won't need extra tape adding onto the sides of the screen to mask off any open areas.

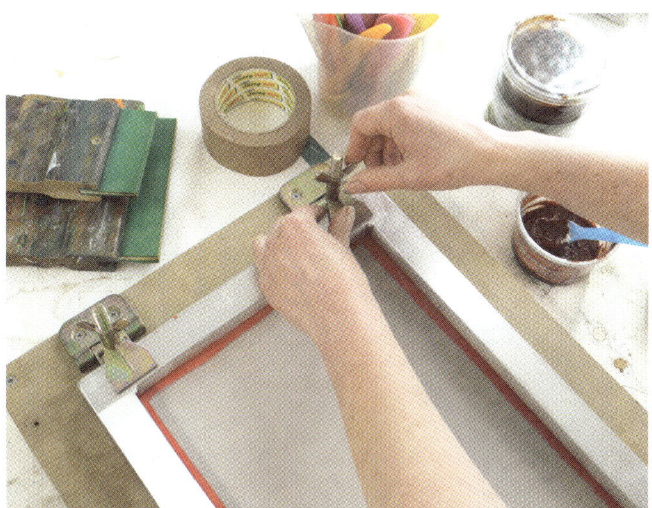

Attach the screen to hinge clamps or to the screen bed as normal.

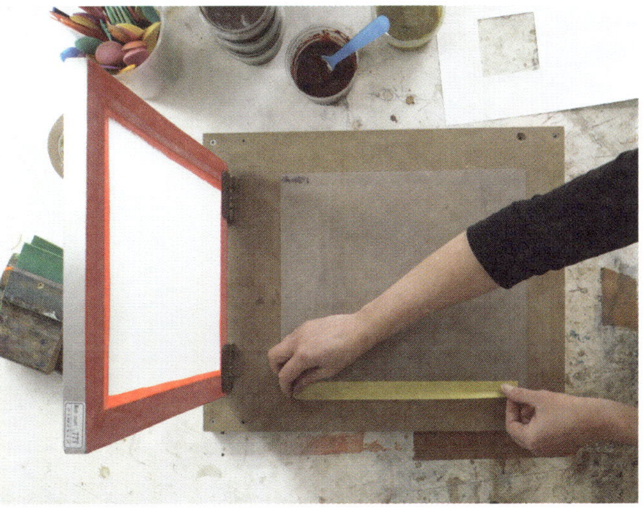

Use some clear plastic such as an acetate sheet for registration.

the screen and also to apply colour to the registration sheet. Use both hands and keep the squeegee at a 45-degree angle.

Step 8: Lift the screen away from the board, ensuring that the registration sheet doesn't stick to the screen. Also make sure the paper stencil has adhered adequately to the underneath of the screen. At this stage small strips of paper tape can be applied to the back of the screen to hold the stencil in place if required (but this shouldn't be necessary).

Step 9: Prop the bottom edge of the screen onto something to keep it from touching the paper beneath. I like to use an old roll of tape. Push the remaining ink on the screen back up to the top, ready for the next pull. This is called filling the screen or flooding the screen (though flooding can sometimes refer to putting too much ink into the mesh). It is important this is done as soon as possible, which also helps prevent the screen drying out or clogging with dried paste. A good discipline is to do this before looking at the print.

Step 10: Lift the registration sheet away, place the paper in position on the board, and then use the registration sheet to get an exact position for the paper. This stage matters less on the first colour but consideration of where the stencil will print and the relation of this layer to the rest of the layers should be taken into account. Once the position of the paper is determined, move the registration sheet out of the way and mark the exact position with three guides made from tape and/or thin card (this will allow each copy of the print to be placed in exactly the same position each time).

Step 11: Lower the screen and use the squeegee to pull ink towards the bottom of the screen. Aim for a firm, even pressure and for the squeegee to remain at the same speed – don't slow down as the bottom edge of the screen is reached.

Step 12: Lift and prop up the screen, flood it with ink and repeat this process for as many prints as are being made.

Step 13: Once the first colour is printed, scrape all the ink from the screen back into its pot. Remove the paper stencil and wash the screen well. At this point also carefully remove any paper tape – it is best to do this once it is wet. If access to a wash-out booth isn't available, use a sink or the bath. It's useful to have a showerhead attachment for washing the screen. Check it is completely clean by holding it up to the light and looking for spots of paste and colour.

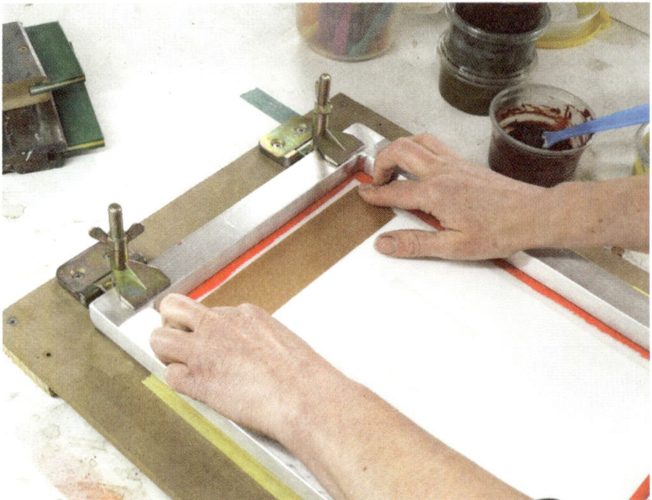

Extra tape can be added to the top surface of the screen to mask off open areas.

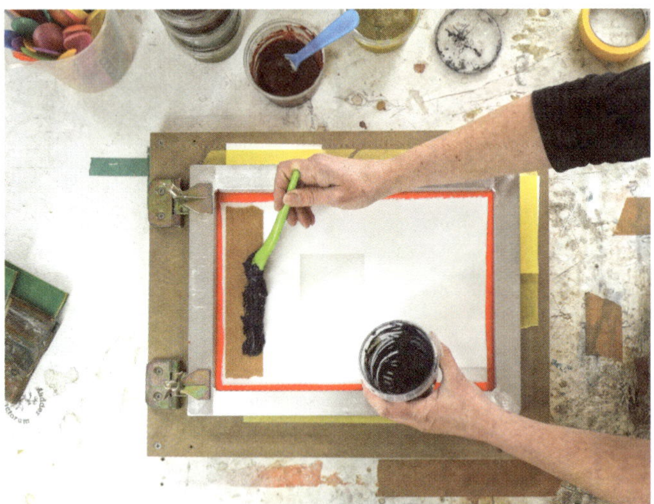

Put a thick line of paste on the screen. Make sure the paste doesn't spill onto open areas of the screen.

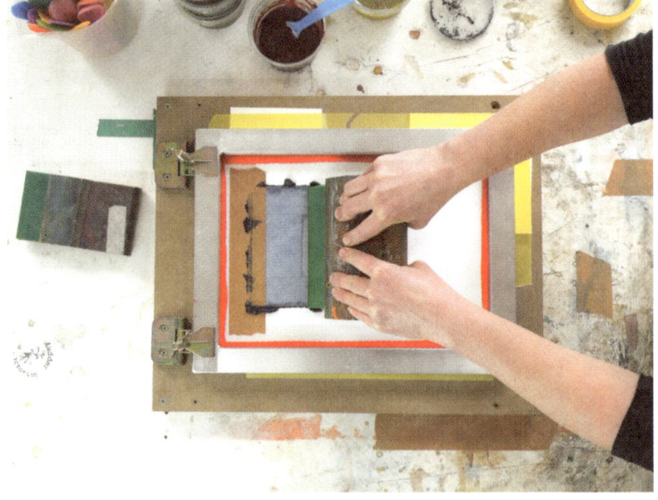

Pull ink across the screen in a firm and decisive manner, keeping the squeegee at a 45-degree angle.

Step 14: The screen can be dried by initially wiping it with a clean tea towel, using a hairdryer on its lowest setting (don't get too close to the mesh), putting it outside in the sun or just leaving it to air dry. Once completely dry, the next layer of the print can be started, or use a different screen.

Step 15: To register the next layer, move the registration sheet back into position and attach the screen to the hinge clamps. Place the next stencil on top of the registration sheet and beneath the screen – aim for placement in the centre area of the screen again but bear in mind that the print with the first layer will need to be positioned in relation to this second stencil.

Step 16: Repeat steps 7–15 for as many layers as are being printed. The registration sheet is vital for the second layer onwards as it allows careful positioning of the paper to get the correct placement.

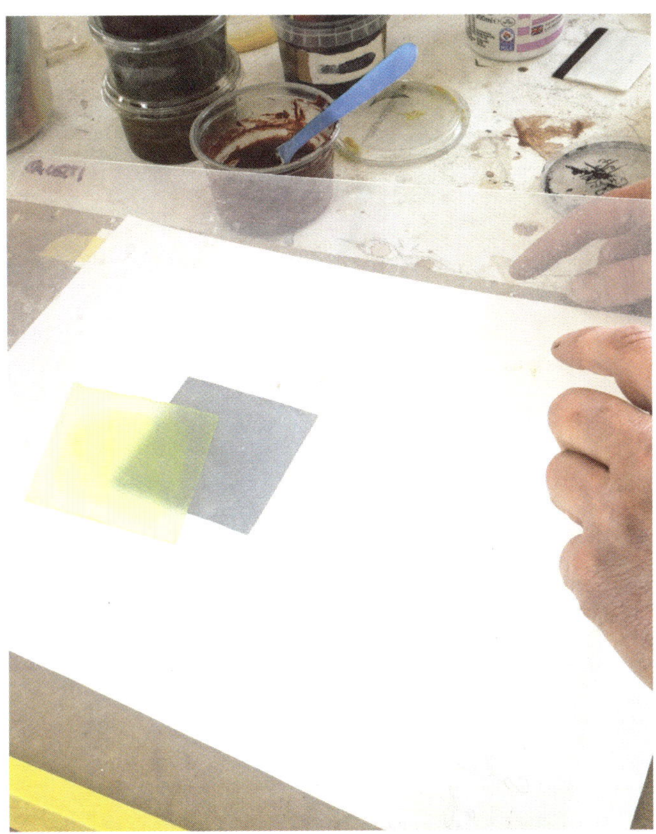

The registration sheet is useful for registering the paper's exact position to ensure each layer is placed where required. Whilst *Graduation Colour – Indigo* was created with repeat layers of blue, here I'm using weld print paste on the registration sheet so you can easily see the printed indigo layer underneath. You can see some of the finished *Graduation Colour* screenprints earlier in the chapter.

REGISTRATION TABS

Using a thin piece of card allows the paper to be butted up against the guides each time, which allows every print in the edition to be placed in the same position. I find it helpful to print onto a copy of my design first, which acts as a map and means I can ensure I've got the paper in the right place to start with. If using hinge clamps without a vacuum, it is also useful to attach small paper tabs to the printing table/surface to hold your paper in place, pulling the paper away from the screen as it is lifted – otherwise the paper can stick to the bottom of the screen, which necessitates peeling it off each time. This is time-consuming, annoying and can smudge the print.

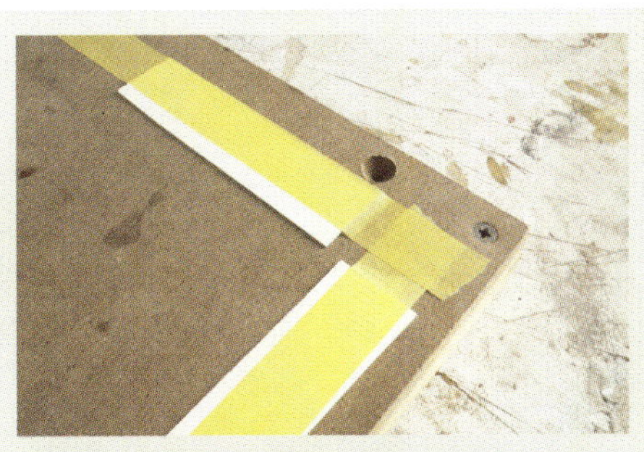

The yellow tape acts as a registration mark for the paper placement, whilst the card tabs hold the paper in place when the screen is lifted. These are unnecessary for beds with a vacuum.

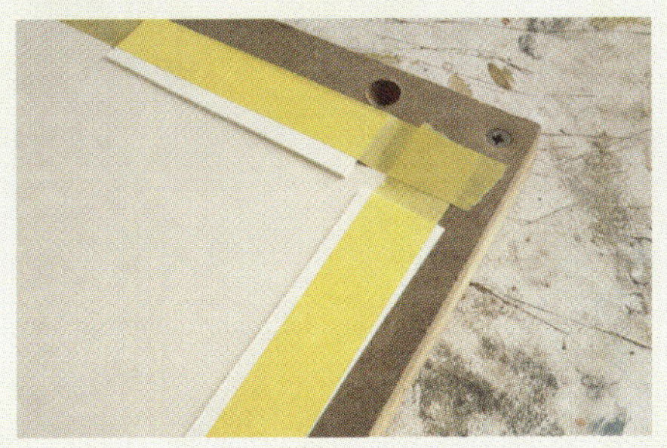

The registration tabs with paper in place.

Modifications

Ink colour can be modified before application with the addition of an acid, an alkali or iron straight into the paste. Care should be taken with all three due to the likelihood of these adversely affecting the paper fibres. Colour can also be modified once applied to the paper by making the modifier into a paste and printing as an overlay colour. This has the advantage of modifying multiple colours at once if required, though it may be tricky to judge exact colour before printing. *See* Chapter 7 for modification recipes.

Using Exposed Screens

I try to avoid using exposed screens because of the chemicals contained within both the photosensitive emulsion and the cleaning agents, but sometimes it is very useful to be able to create highly intricate and detailed designs on a screen. The level of detail that can be achieved with plant-based pastes is just the same as using commercial screen-printing pastes and mediums. Remember that if dried lake pigments are used to create the paste, the pigment must be ground small enough to allow the particles to pass through the screen mesh.

Colour

You may want to limit yourself to one or two colours to begin with. Plant-based pastes can be relatively transparent compared to commercial pastes, which makes them ideal for layering to create further colours and shapes. Using paper stencils (especially thicker brown paper stencils) also creates a slight 'step' or barrier to the ink when it is being pulled across the screen and creates a 'halo' effect around the edge of the stencil shape, where the ink is marginally thicker giving a slightly darker appearance. This is an attractive quality, creating an illusion of depth and is an easy way to recognise something that has been screenprinted with stencils.

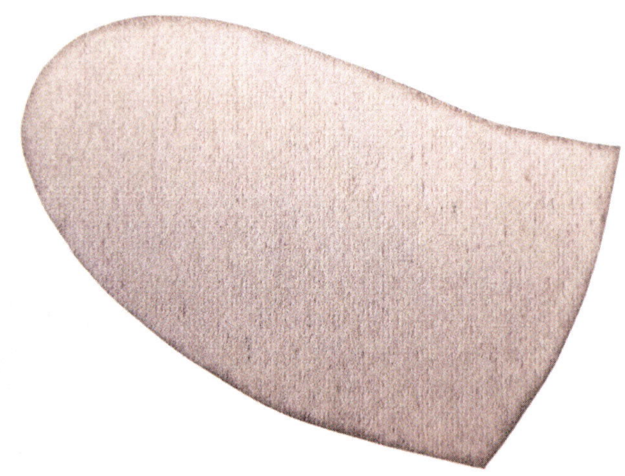

The first layer of *Jelly Bean Monday* showing the halo effect (a darkening at the edge of the stencil) created when using paper stencils.

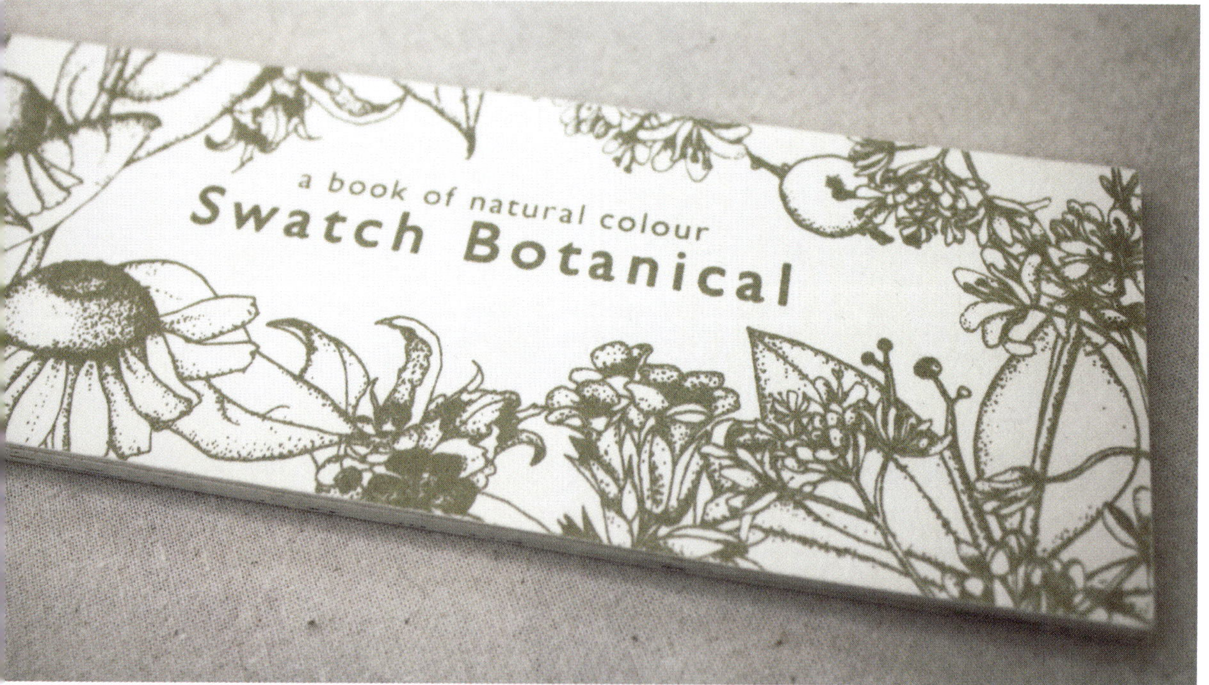

Swatch Botanical. Handmade book made using 100 per cent plant-based materials and colour. Sometimes it is necessary to use exposed screens to achieve a high level of detail.

TRACE MONOTYPES (AND MONOPRINTS)

Many printmakers will be familiar with this simple yet highly effective way of creating prints. A useful technique that is often used when teaching young people and inexperienced printmakers, the method usually produces just a single print and can incorporate pre-drawn images, the artist's own work or be drawn freehand directly onto the paper. The terms monoprint and monotype are often used interchangeably and/or incorrectly and some of the confusion likely arises from the fact that 'monoprint' seems to be a much more accurate description of producing a one-off print from a plate than the term 'monotype'. In this technique the prints can technically be either, depending on how the image is created. A freehand drawing is likely to produce a completely unique 'monotype', whereas tracing an image that can be repeated and only show small variations is likely to produce a 'monoprint'.

The ink needed for creating monotypes is one that can be rolled thinly and evenly without too much tack. Too much tackiness will cause the paper to stick to the ink and tear. Too low a viscosity will prevent an even layer from being rolled out. Aim for something in between a relief and intaglio ink. Refer to Chapter 7 for the ink recipe.

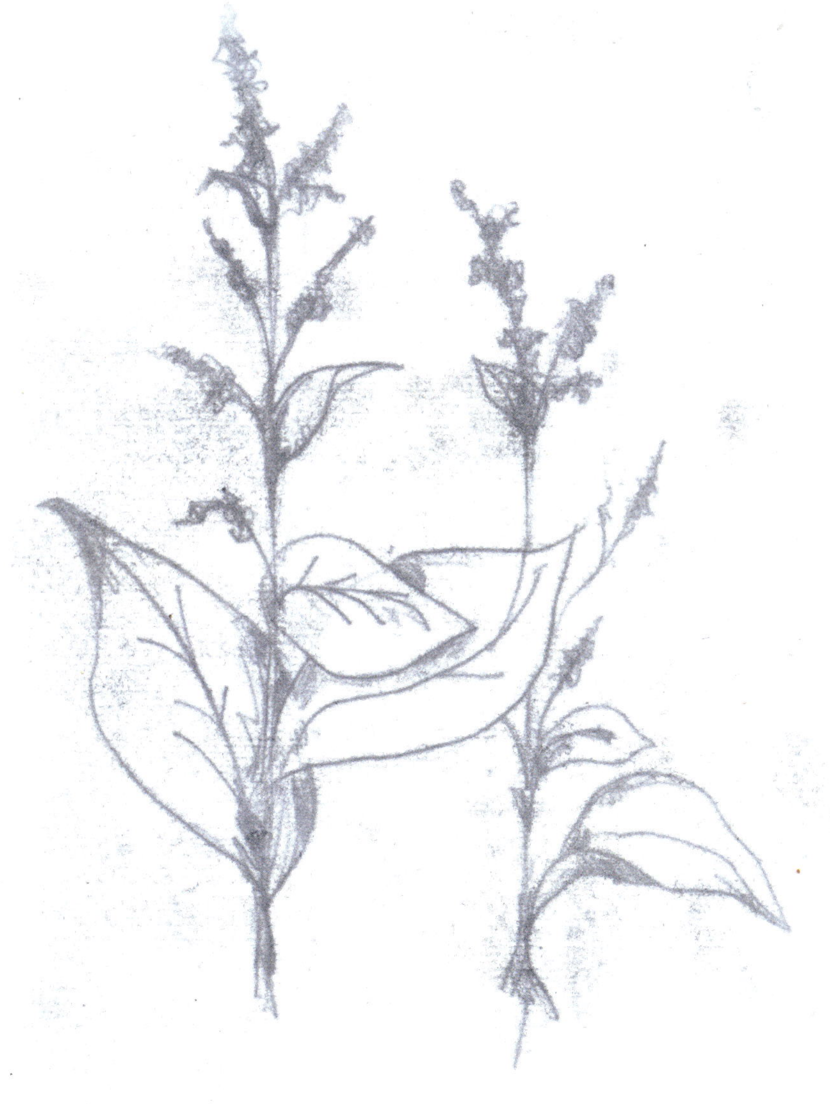

A quick monotype sketch of *Persicaria tinctoria* using indigo ink.

YOU WILL NEED:

- Oil-based ink
- Ink tray or toughened glass sheet
- Roller (or brayer)
- Spatula
- Plastic board (an A4 plastic whiteboard or a sheet of sturdy acetate is ideal)
- Masking tape
- Lightweight printmaking paper (less than 100gsm)
- Thin scrap or copier paper
- Pencil and other drawing implements

METHOD:

1. Apply a line of ink to the top of the inking glass and start rolling it out to achieve a thin and even layer. Once the ink is smooth, start applying it to the whiteboard or plastic sheet with the roller, in as thin a layer as possible. This is the key requirement – it must be almost non-existent. Ensure there are no bits of debris in the ink. If there are, pick these out and roll the ink again to get a flat layer.

2. Once the sheet is covered in ink (with a small un-inked area around the edge), place the lightweight paper on top and secure to the whiteboard using masking tape to make a hinge. Try not to press on the inked area.

3. Place a sheet of A4 copier paper on top and secure this to the whiteboard. This sheet of A4 paper may have the design printed or drawn on it already or just draw freehand – remember that the print will be a mirror image of the drawing. Make sure the whiteboard is on a strong, flat surface before starting to trace over or draw the design using a pencil. The print line will change in appearance depending on how hard and sharp the pencil (or drawing tool) is and how firmly pressure is applied.

4. Occasionally check the progress of the monotype by carefully lifting the paper and looking at the underneath. Lines should be appearing where the drawing has been made. If using a pre-drawn design, make sure it is printed or drawn in a lighter colour than the pencil you will be using to trace over it. This helps to show where the lines have been followed. Experiment with different pencil grades and other drawing implements to see what different results can be achieved.

5. Once finished, carefully peel the masking tape off and turn the paper over to reveal the monotype. The transfer of ink where the pressure of a hand and fingers has been applied whilst drawing is part of the charm of this technique.

6. The whiteboard can be re-inked with the roller and used for a fresh print, or wiped using a rag and vegetable oil to clean the ink off the board. Do the same with the roller and any tools used, making sure they are also wiped after cleaning with the oil.

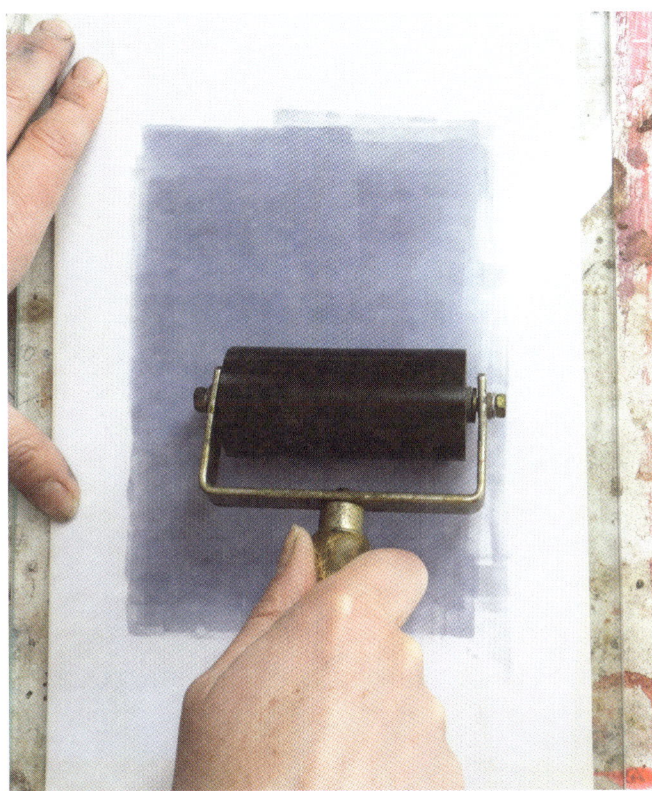

Rolling out a very thin layer of ink on a plastic whiteboard.

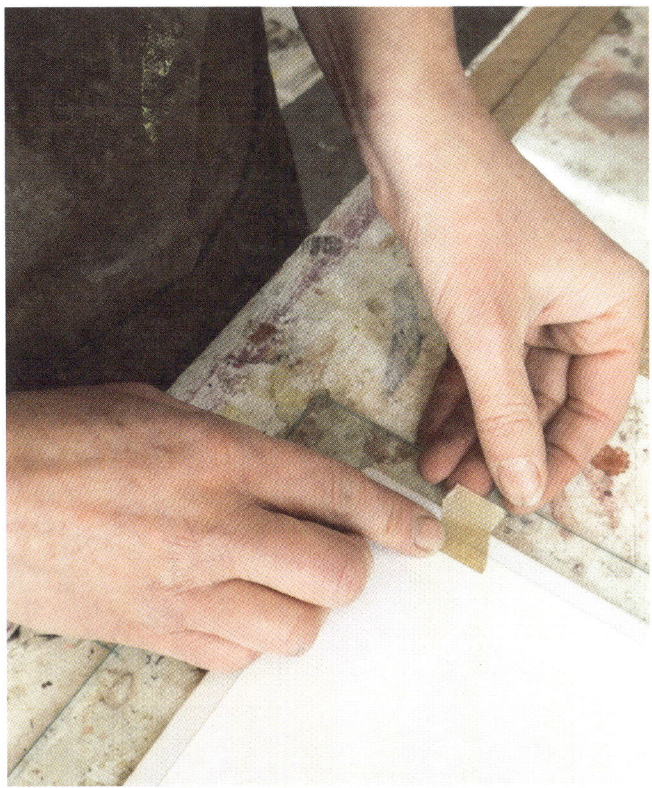

Attach the print paper and protective paper layer (which will be drawn on) to the whiteboard with tape.

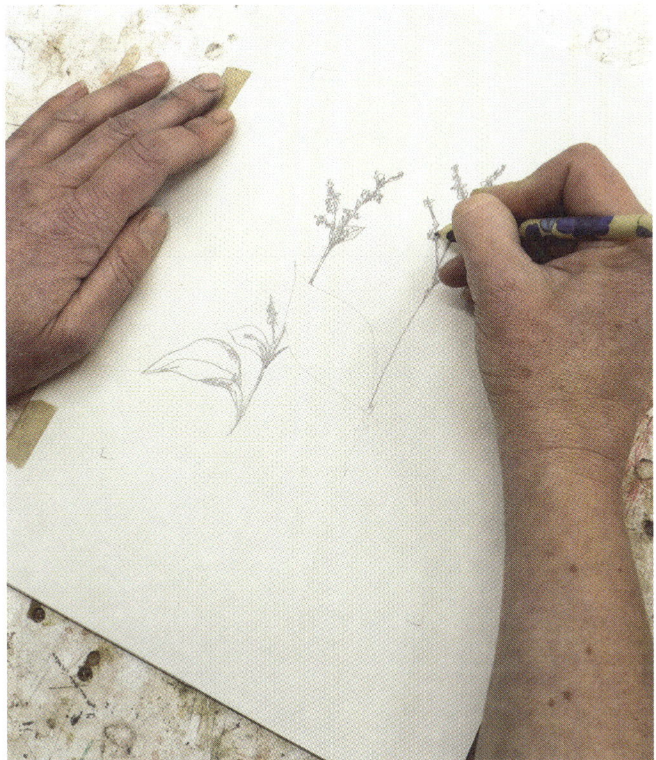

Draw the design on top of the paper. You can use a variety of pencil thicknesses, drawing implements and other tools to make a diverse range of marks.

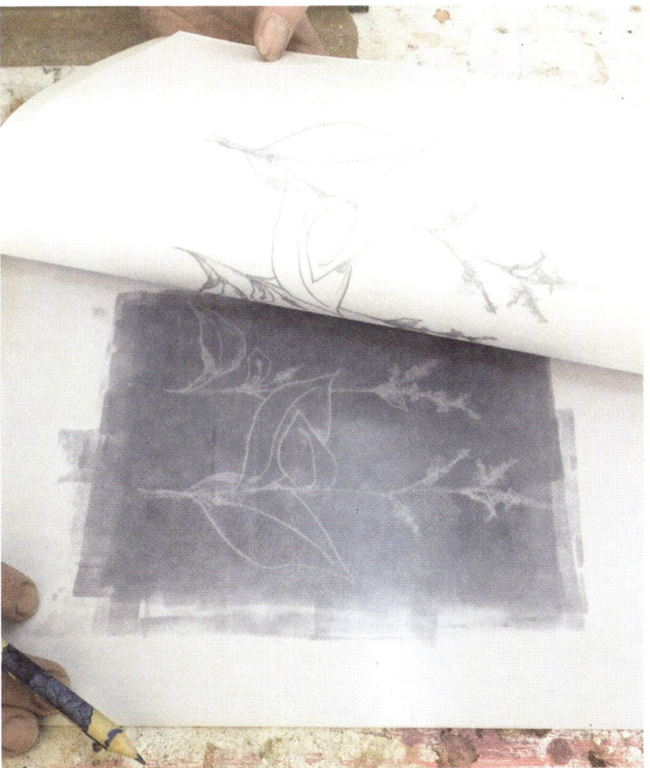

Lifting the drawing and print paper to check progress.

RELIEF PRINTING

Relief printing is so called because the parts of the plate or matrix that are printed are the sections that are in relief, the raised areas remaining after the rest has been cut away or removed. Ink is applied to these raised areas rather than being pushed into the cuts or incisions, and then the plate is printed onto paper with a vertical pressure. Relief printing techniques include wood engraving, linocuts, woodcuts and mokuhanga with plates made from any substance where sections can be removed and raised areas left for inking. The type of plate used tends to depict what the process is called. Most relief printing for paper is done with oil-based inks apart from mokuhanga, which is traditionally done using water-based colour. Chapter 7 provides a basic recipe for making watercolour paint for mokuhanga.

The project below uses traditional lino but there are many substitutes available that have different characteristics. These include Easicut, Japanese vinyl, Speedy-Carve and Softcut, all of which are different though most are designed to be easier to cut than standard lino. More experienced printmakers often find them a little spongey to work with, but they are easy materials to begin with.

Relief plates are much easier to print without a press than intaglio prints, by using a hand baren or burnishing tool to apply pressure from the back of the paper. An intaglio press can also be used in place of a platen or lever press with the aid of runners to lift the press rollers to the height of the lino.

Troubleshooting

Ink clumping when rolled – the ink either requires more mulling to distribute the pigment particles more fully or the particles were too big to start with. Counter this by using a softer roller or return the ink to the glass slab for further mulling. Consider saving this ink for intaglio plates (that generally require ink made with bigger particles) and starting again.

Ink is too runny and the roller is slipping or leaving lines in the ink – the ink probably has too much light oil in it. Add more pigment and re-mull it, aiming for a thicker ink. If it becomes hard to mull, add a little heavy oil, not light oil. Magnesium carbonate or calcium carbonate can also be added to stiffen the ink but do this cautiously and only add a tiny amount at a time.

Ink is too transparent – transparency is a characteristic of ink made with lake pigments and is hard to avoid. A little calcium carbonate can be added but this will lighten the colour. Try making ink with smaller pigment particles and making the lake pigment more concentrated (add more dyestuff to the recipe without increasing the alum and the soda ash) to saturate the colour.

YOU WILL NEED:

- Piece of lino
- Transfer paper
- Cutting tools
- Oil-based inks
- Spatulas × 2
- Newsprint
- Paper to print on
- Roller
- Glass (or similar) to roll ink in
- Hand baren (or press)
- Vegetable oil and rags for cleaning

METHOD:

1. Transfer the design to the lino remembering that it needs to be a mirror image of the original. If the design is complicated, it is worthwhile marking the areas that should be cut away and those that should be kept.
2. Cut the design into the block.
3. On the glass-inking surface, start working a small amount of ink with a spatula to loosen it. Do this for several minutes.
4. Spread some of the ink into a line and start rolling it out with the roller. The ink should be in a thin layer, with no striations or clumps.
5. Apply ink to the lino. It will need several layers but try to do these evenly and in one direction, especially for the last layer. Ink made with lake pigments is often quite transparent and can require a heavier deposit than inks made with other natural or synthetic pigments.
6. Print using a hand baren or press. Relief prints can be printed with both dry and pre-dampened paper – try both and see which is preferred. It will take a few prints to get the correct amount of ink needed so don't expect the first print to work perfectly.

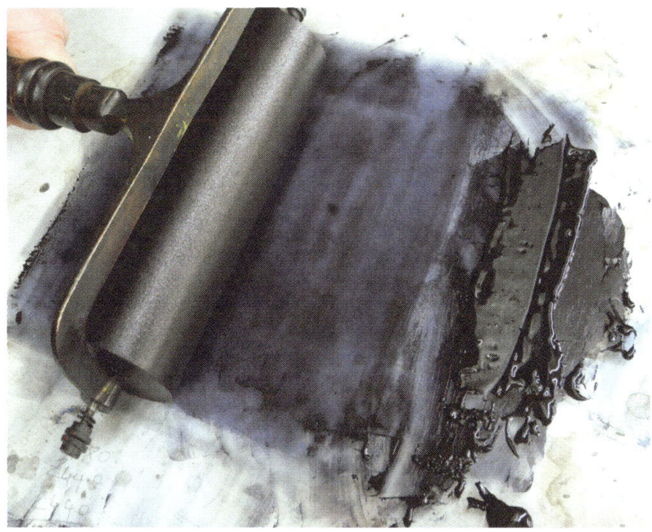

Ink should be rolled out in a thin, even layer before applying to a relief plate.

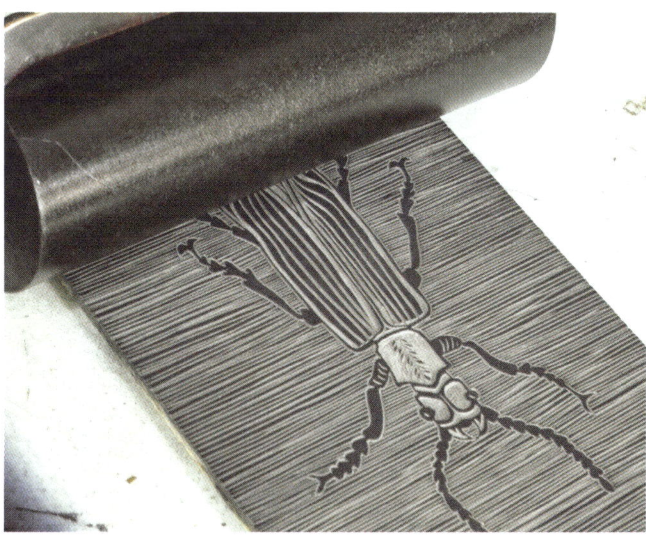

Ink is applied to the lino with a roller.

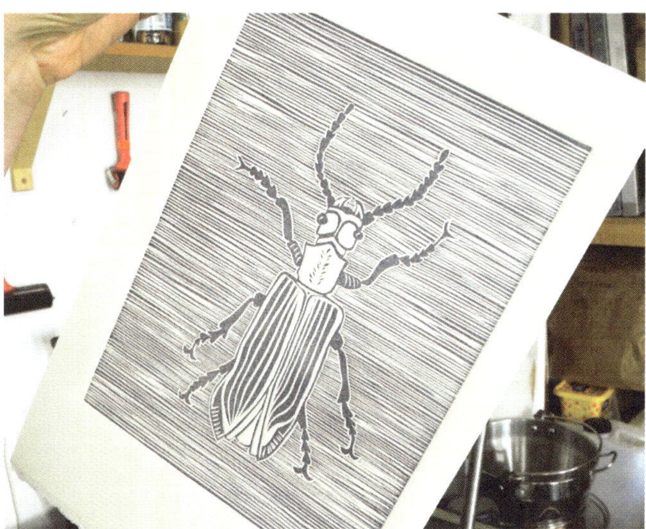

The finished one-colour lino print.

INTAGLIO PRINTING

Intaglio printing covers many individual processes such as etching, engraving, mezzotint and drypoint but all use the principle of ink remaining in the incisions or depressions of the plate with the higher parts of the plate being cleaned or wiped free of ink. Oil-based ink made using plant colour will work with any of these processes, although the one shown in the method below uses a shiny cardboard as the plate for a form of drypoint printmaking. The line is created by drawing or scratching directly into the plate using an etching needle or anything that will leave a mark. The plate can be an acrylic sheet, zinc, copper or anything that can be scratched into and then wiped clean after inking. Print suppliers have a range of different plate materials for intaglio processes.

Paper is traditionally dampened before printing with an intaglio plate. Fill a large tray or clean container with water and add sheets of paper one at a time to the water. Leave until thoroughly wet, which may take an hour or more depending on the thickness and weight of the paper. Remove the paper from the water and place between sheets of blotting paper for approximately 30 minutes before using to print. The paper must be damp but not shiny with water. Any excess can be removed by carefully blotting with a clean tea towel, which can be used in place of blotting paper if you don't have any.

Experienced printmakers will be aware of the equipment required and the environmental implications of the processes they want to use, although those less experienced or without access to a print workshop's facilities might choose the simpler intaglio methods to start with. The print can be made without the use of an intaglio press by using a spoon or hand baren to apply pressure (called burnishing), though it is much harder to get a good and full impression this way.

Paper should be soaked for intaglio processes but can also be soaked for relief processes that use oil-based ink. Remove excess water from paper by placing between sheets of blotting paper.

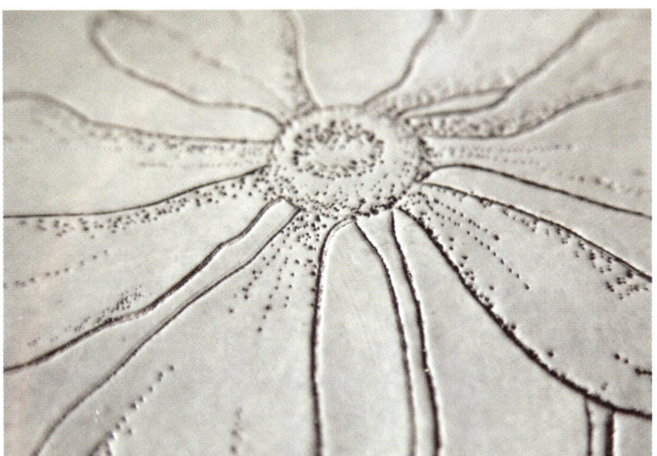

Shiny card can be used for drypoint plates in place of metal or acrylic plastic. Whilst it won't be a true drypoint (which relies on ink in the burr of the scratched line for its particular line quality), it does provide an easy and accessible material to use.

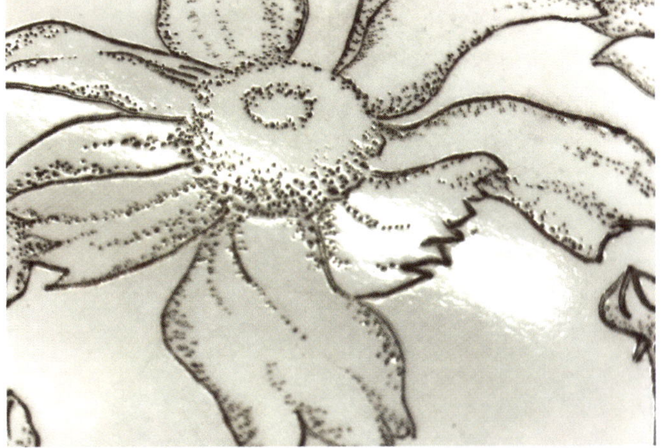

Once ink has been applied to the plate, it is easier to see the design. This can be done periodically to check progress.

YOU WILL NEED:

- Tetra Pak, Enviromount, shiny or mirror card
- Transfer paper
- Etching needle
- Oil-based inks
- Spatulas × 2
- Newsprint
- Tissue
- Scrim (or similar fabric)
- Old piece of squeegee blade (or some mountboard)
- Blotting paper or clean tea towel
- Paper for printing
- Intaglio press

METHOD:

1. Cut the card (or plate) to the desired size using a scalpel or scissors. Because the plate is made from cardboard it is very easy to make it a specific or bespoke shape rather than just a rectangle.
2. Transfer the image to the plate using carbon paper, tracing paper or drawn freehand. It is important not to press too hard and make indentations at this stage. A soft pencil is ideal. Remember that the image and any writing or detail that has a left/right side must be reversed on the plate.
3. Using the etching needle, start scratching the design into the plate. The needle must be pressed hard enough to make an impression but not so hard that it goes right through the cardboard.
4. If using cardboard or Tetra Pak, parts of the surface can be removed to create areas that will print as a solid colour rather than as a line. Carefully score around the edge of the shape required with a scalpel and use the edge of the blade to lift the shiny surface of the cut area. Pull it away from the card, leaving an absorbent papery section underneath. This part will absorb ink and isn't wipeable, so will print as a block of colour.
5. Put some oil-based ink onto a glass inking plate or similar and work it backwards and forwards to loosen it. This is optional but is a good idea, especially when using handmade inks. The process allows an assessment to be made of the ink's viscosity, its condition and whether any dried bits or debris need removing. The more the ink is worked, the looser it becomes (a property called thixotropy) which makes it easier to both apply to the plate and wipe sections away.
6. Place the plate onto a clean surface (a section of the glass inking plate is ideal) and apply ink using a dabber, some scrim, a soft toothbrush, a piece of squeegee blade or mount board.
7. Work the ink into all parts of the plate using a circular motion and ensure the whole plate is covered. Wipe any excess away to remove the majority of the ink.
8. Using some scrim (or stiff cloth), start rubbing the plate in a circular motion and clearing away any excess ink. The plate must be wiped hard enough to remove surface ink but not wiped so hard that all ink is removed from the drawn or scratched areas. This requires some skill and is made more challenging by the use of handmade ink. Each ink will have slightly different properties and characteristics but knowledge

The cardboard plate ready to be inked and then printed. The design was created from the original drawing of the Coreopsis tinctoria screenprint.

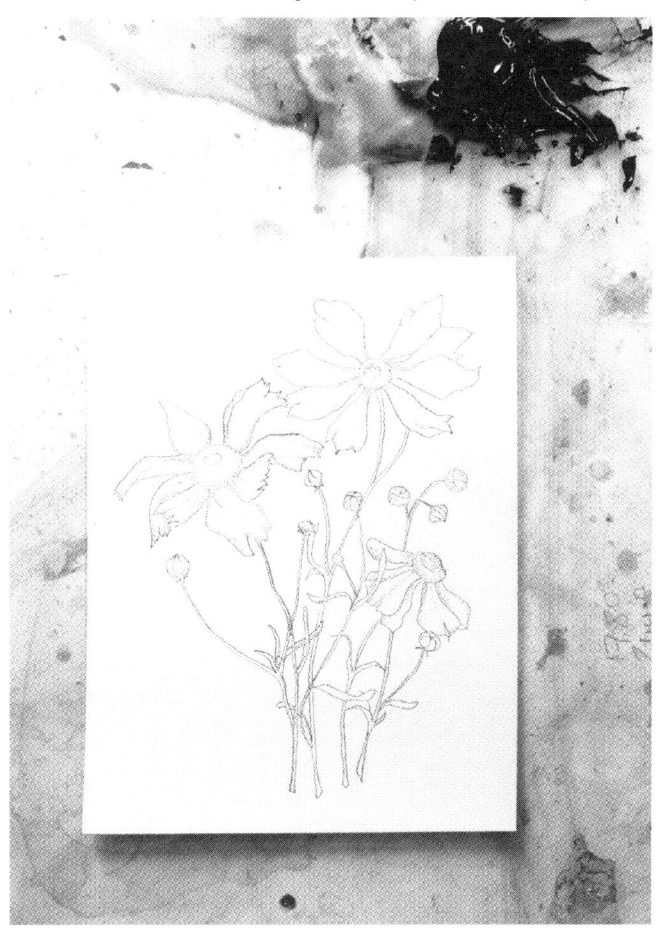

of how the ink might perform and how to control this will lead to better and better results. Handmade inks will also change each time a new batch is made, and different types of plates will require inks with differing qualities. The cardboard used here needs looser ink due to the delicate nature of the plate but a metal plate needs much thicker ink. Gaining an understanding and some experience of how to adapt and control inks is an important part of making your own and provides you with an added layer of knowledge and skill.

9. Finally, use a flat piece of tissue to remove any remaining ink from the upper surfaces of the plate. How much this is done depends on personal choice and how much plate tone is desired. Small areas can also be cleaned using a cotton bud to create highlights on the print. Wipe the edges of the plate to remove any extra ink.

10. The plate is now ready to be printed. Place it facing upwards on clean newsprint on the bed of the press, carefully place the dampened print paper on top, then a sheet of tissue to protect the press blankets.

11. Run the plate through the press and remove the print from the plate. The first print is a lesson in how the ink is performing and whether more or less wiping needs to be done on the next print. Don't expect to get a perfect print immediately.

12. If printing by hand, lay the plate onto a clean surface, add dampened paper and cover with a thin piece of felt or non-woven blanket. Apply pressure using the back of a spoon or a hand baren. Ensure all parts of the plate are reached. The progress can be checked by carefully lifting the edge of the dampened paper to check.

13. Any remaining ink should be scraped back into a container or covered for later use. Clean up tools and equipment using old rags and vegetable oil. Always wipe off any remaining oil with a clean cloth afterwards.

Troubleshooting

Ink is wiped away too easily – the ink is probably too thin and has too much light oil added. Thicken by adding more pigment (remember, the ink will need further mulling) or a little magnesium carbonate or calcium carbonate. Next time add more heavy oil rather than thin oil to start. It may also be that the pigment particles were too small as these are more easily wiped from the lines of the plate though this is not often a problem when making your own pigment.
Ink too thick to wipe – add a little light oil. Be very cautious with the amount and add a little at a time before mulling.
Ink is too slippery – the ink needs more tack. Add more pigment and heavy oil as needed.

Remember that different intaglio plates will require different types of ink and it is up to you to adapt the ink as required. Developing an understanding of how to adapt and improve ink to your personal requirements is part of the enjoyment of making your own ink.

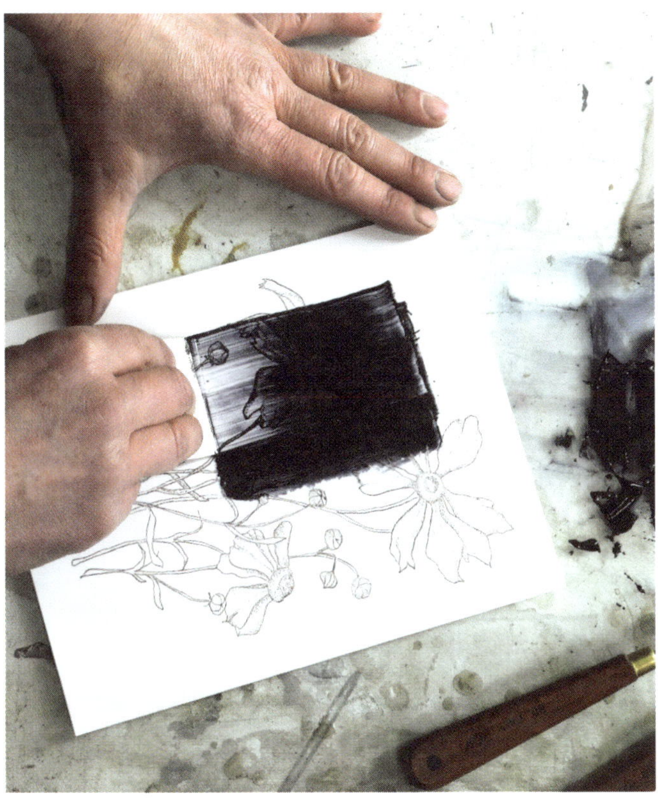

Ink should be applied to the complete surface of the plate using some mountboard, a squeegee blade offcut or something similar. The excess is removed using the same tool.

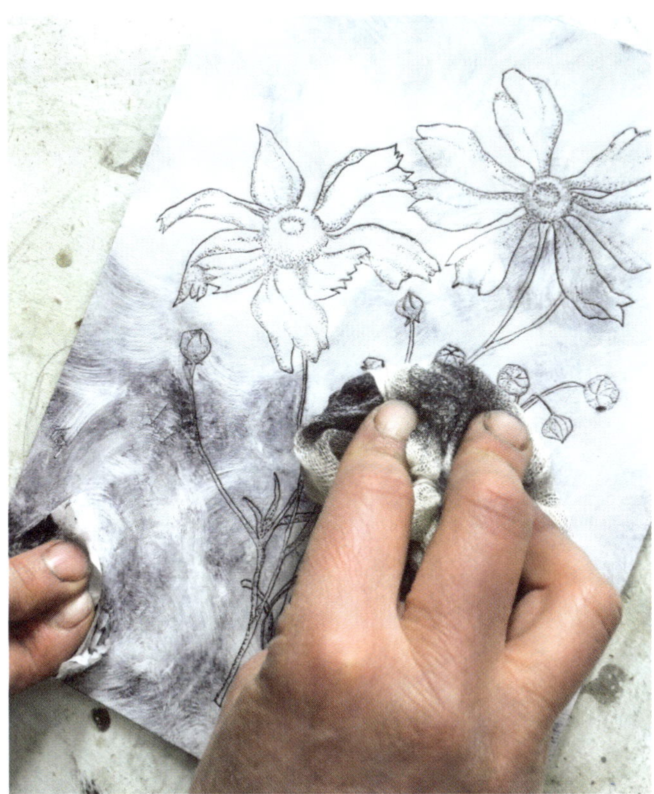

Scrim is used to remove more of the ink. The aim is to remove ink from the plate's surface but not from the indentations in the plate.

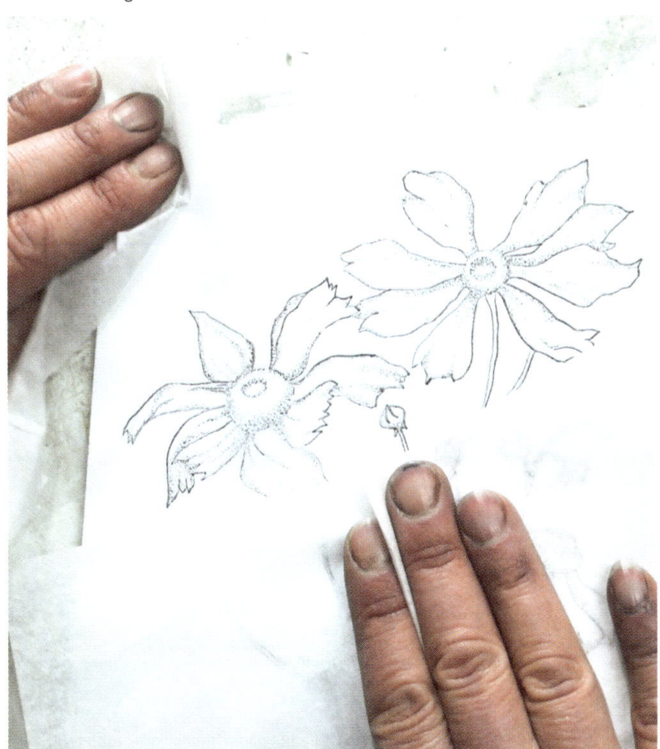

Tissue paper is gently rubbed over the surface to remove any remaining unwanted ink. Hold the plate in place with another piece of tissue.

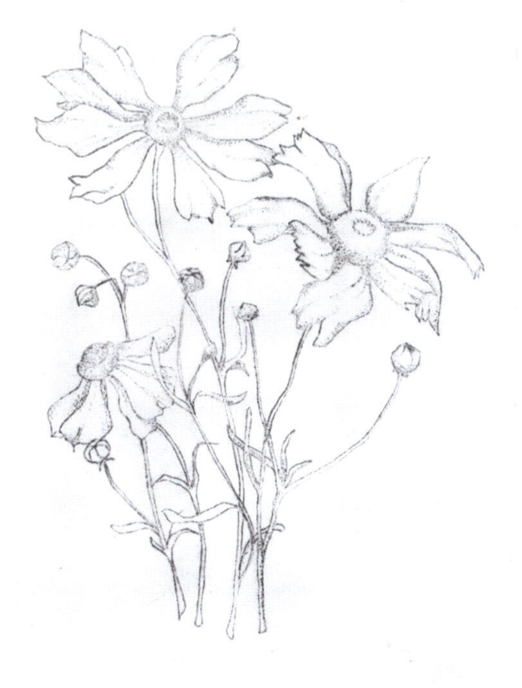

The first print provides vital information and feedback about the ink, the amount of ink-wiping done, plate tone and the plate itself. It will likely take several prints to get the inking up as required.

NATURE PRINTING

Nature printing is a method of printmaking whereby natural objects are used to directly create an impression. Rather than creating a depiction or representation of the object, it is the object itself that creates the image. There are numerous approaches to doing this, from creating a plate of the natural object to directly inking the object itself. Whilst lots of different natural items can be used for nature printing, plants and specifically leaves lend themselves perfectly to the discipline and provide beautiful detail and patterning that is hard to achieve any other way. The flat and fairly tough structure of most leaves also make them ideal for use with a printing press or hand baren to transfer the image onto the substrate.

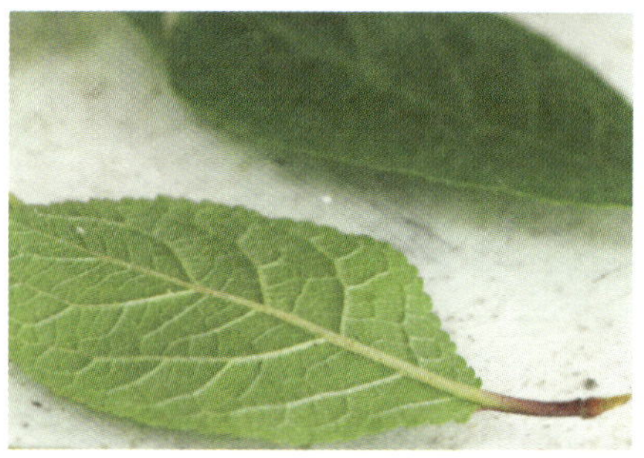

The back or underside of leaves are usually the best side to print as they have more details and veining.

There are advantages and disadvantages to many different types of leaves, although the best ones to start with are ideally hairless, not too succulent or fleshy, have detailed veining and are a fairly simple shape. Leaves from trees are particularly suitable for printmaking, including oak (*Quercus spp.*), silver birch (*Betula pendula*), cherry (*Prunus spp.*), aspen (*Populus tremula*) and hazel (*Corylus avellana*). Leaves from trees such as beech (*Fagus spp.*), ash (*Fraxinus excelsior*), alder (*Alnus glutinosa*) and rowan (*Sorbus spp.*) are harder for beginners to work with but make attractive prints. The majority of leaves have more detailing on the underneath or 'back' side, where the veins and stalk protrude slightly. This is the best side to print with and by simple observation mixed with a little bit of experience, you will quickly be able to choose leaves that will print well and produce effective leaf patterns.

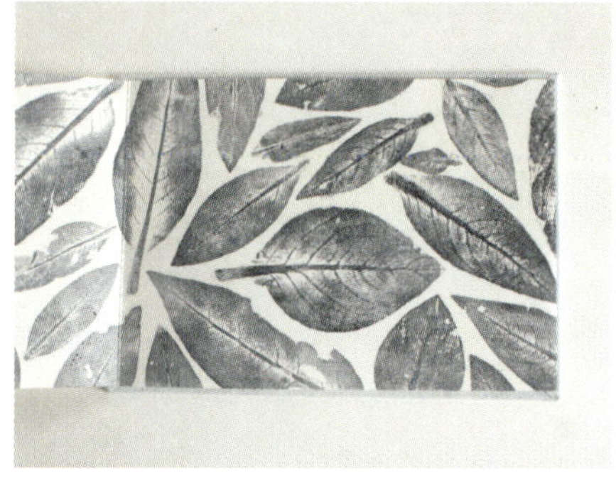

An Indigo Sampler. Concertina book printed with *Persicaria tinctoria* leaves using indigo oil-based ink. The covers are made from indigo-dyed paper.

Garden plants also create beautiful prints but most are delicate and will tear easily. Extra care is needed when manipulating the leaves, applying ink or moving them around ready for printing. Recommended plants include hardy cranesbill (*Geranium sylvestris*), rose (*Rosa spp.*) and yarrow (*Achillea spp.*) but try anything to see if it will print. Leaves that really don't work are the very smooth and waxy types such as laurel (*Prunus laurocerasus*), holly (*Ilex aquifolium*) and ivy (*Hedera helix*). They have hardly any raised veining which makes for a disappointing print.

Specific dye plants that have suitable leaves to print with include Japanese indigo (*Persicaria tinctoria*), woad (*Isatis tinctoria*), madder (*Rubia tinctorum*), coreopsis (*Coreopsis tinctoria*), saw-wort (*Serratula tinctoria*) and goldenrod (*Solidago spp.*).

Be prepared to work quickly or have easy access to the outside so the leaves can be left on the plants until needed. Plants in pots are especially useful as they can be brought into the studio and picked as required. Mid to late season tree leaves will last a lot longer but some will still wilt, which makes them harder to print with. Consider keeping sprays of leaves in water until ready to use.

The project below is an introduction to nature printing, encouraging the new ink-maker to create lake pigments from specific plants, make ink with them and then use the leaves from these plants to print with. It is an interesting method of recording site-specific plants and creating work made of and about place.

FACING PAGE
Nature printing uses natural objects to directly create impressions.

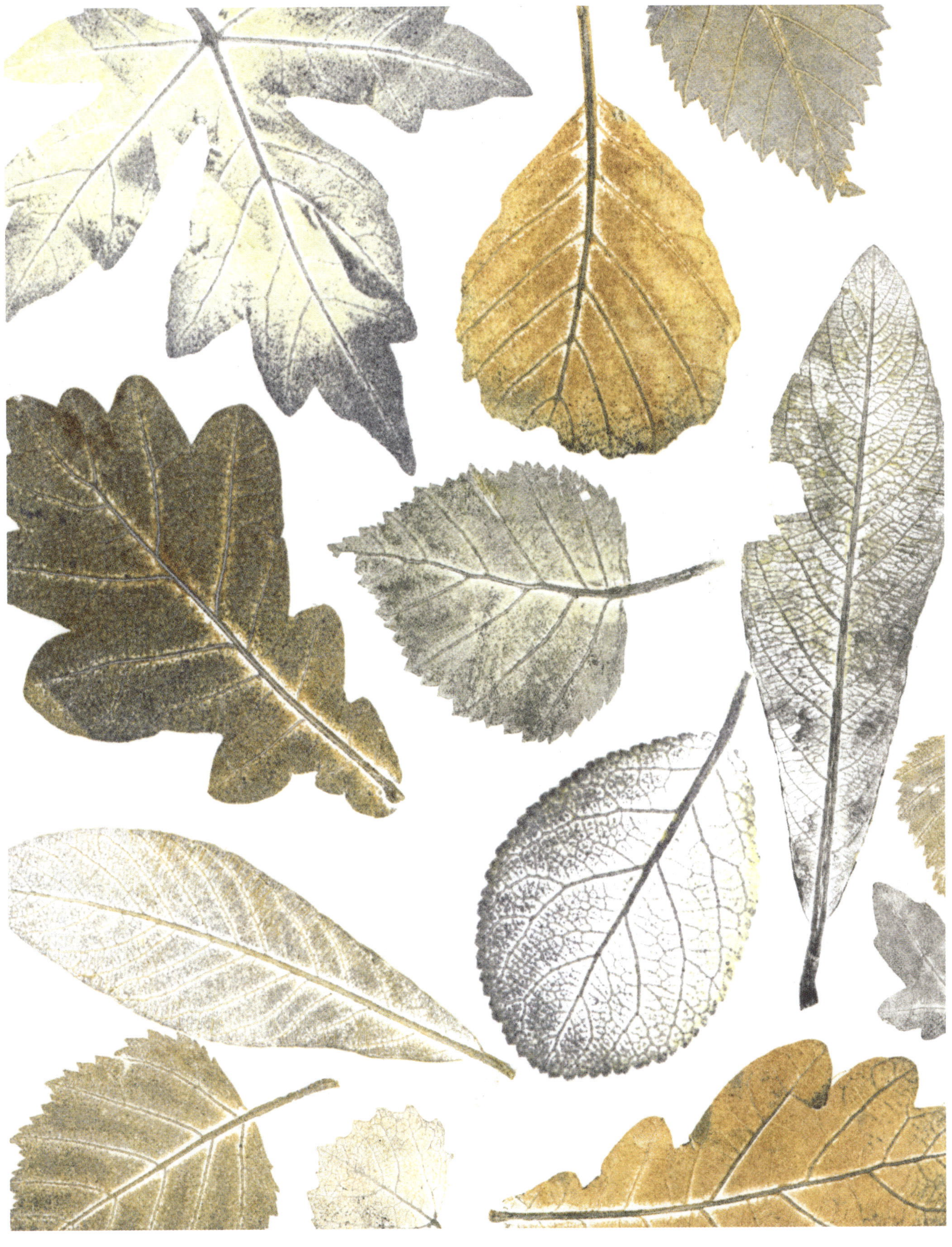

YOU WILL NEED:

- Glass slab for inking
- Soft shore rollers (brayers)
- Small crank-handled spatulas/painting knives
- Leaves
- Tweezers
- Tissue
- Newsprint
- Intaglio press or hand baren or similar
- Small offcut strips of paper
- Vegetable oil and rags for cleaning
- 3 × 10g (approx.) of sieved pigment (follow the recipe in Chapter 4 to make the lake pigments – any plant can be used but it is recommended to start with plants containing high levels of colourant)

METHOD:

1. Make the inks following the recipe in Chapter 7. It is best to make them on the day of use or the day before use. Inks can be stored but I have found using freshly made ink gives better results.

2. Take a toothpaste-sized blob of each ink and place at the top of the glass inking slab. Allow enough space between them to roll out without mixing. Using the roller, start rolling the inks out into a square, roughly the width of the roller. Don't just roll backwards and forwards with the roller – repeatedly pick the roller up and return to the top so the roller becomes completely covered in a smooth layer of ink. The aim is to get a thin and even layer of ink on both the roller and the glass slab, with no striations on either surface. The roller should make a light hissing sound when rolling it backwards and forwards on the ink, rather than a wet sticky noise.

3. Choose the first leaf to be inked and lay it down with the underside facing upwards. It is often easiest to have the stalk pointing away from you. This can then be held down with a free hand whilst ink is applied. Roll ink on from the top to the bottom, lift and roll again. Apply more ink to the roller as required and keep applying until the leaf has a light covering of ink. Try inking either side of the stalk to ensure as much coverage as possible.

4. Apply a different colour to the veins and stalk by lightly rolling ink on rather than applying a lot of pressure. This adds detailing and gives a three-dimensional impression when printed. Now a choice can be made; print just this one leaf and then repeat the process or put the leaf to one side, apply ink to another leaf and build up a number of them before printing the whole lot at once. This will likely be determined by the method of printing.

5. If using a hand baren or other hand tool, it is best to print each leaf individually. Inking them one by one allows for hands and muscles to take a rest but more importantly, placement and colour can be decided on as the work progresses. Place the leaf face down onto the paper (it can help to use tweezers), cover with a small piece of newsprint or greaseproof paper and apply pressure.

6. Carefully peel back the newsprint to check progress and if the leaf has printed, remove the paper and any leaf debris before repeating with the next leaf. Continue this way until the print is complete.

7. If using a press, it is satisfying to ink all the leaves to be included in a print at once. Once the leaves are inked, place the paper to be printed onto a sheet of newsprint on the bed of the press (so it won't need to be moved), lay the leaves out face down in a design (use tweezers if needed), cover with a layer of newsprint and put through the press.

8. To reveal the print, carefully peel back the newsprint and remove the leaves with tweezers if necessary. I sometimes place another piece of print paper on the top of the leaves when printing in this way as the other side of the leaves can create an attractive impression.

In intaglio printmaking, the inked plate (or object) is usually placed facing upwards and the paper to be printed on is then placed on top. I have found that reversing this (so that the paper to be printed on is underneath the leaves) is more beneficial as the three-dimensional nature of the leaves means that they can move as they come into contact with the press. It is easier to see and manage this when not trying to manipulate a thick piece of printing paper out of the way.

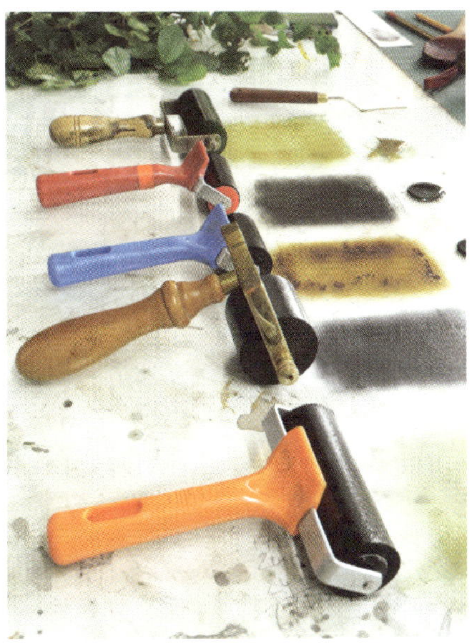

Weld, willow charcoal, alder cone, indigo and indigo/weld inks rolled out on the inking surface.

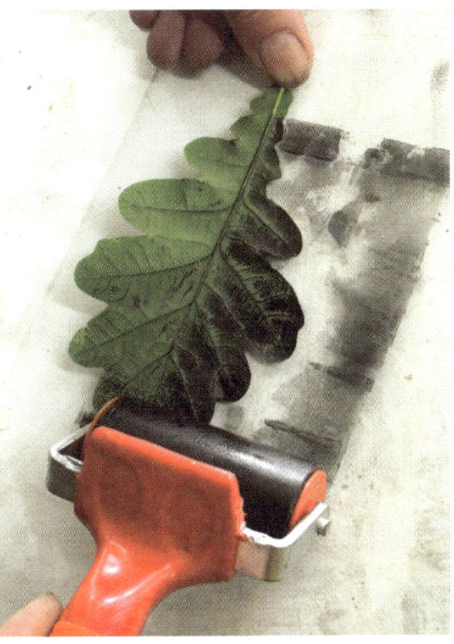

Inking an oak leaf using a willow charcoal oil-based ink.

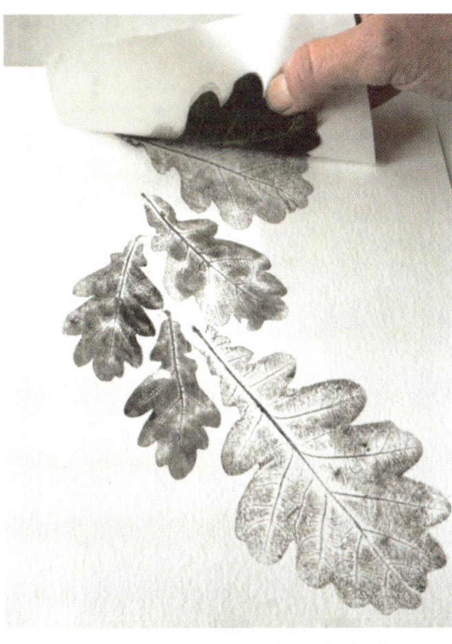

Revealing the hand-burnished oak leaf print.

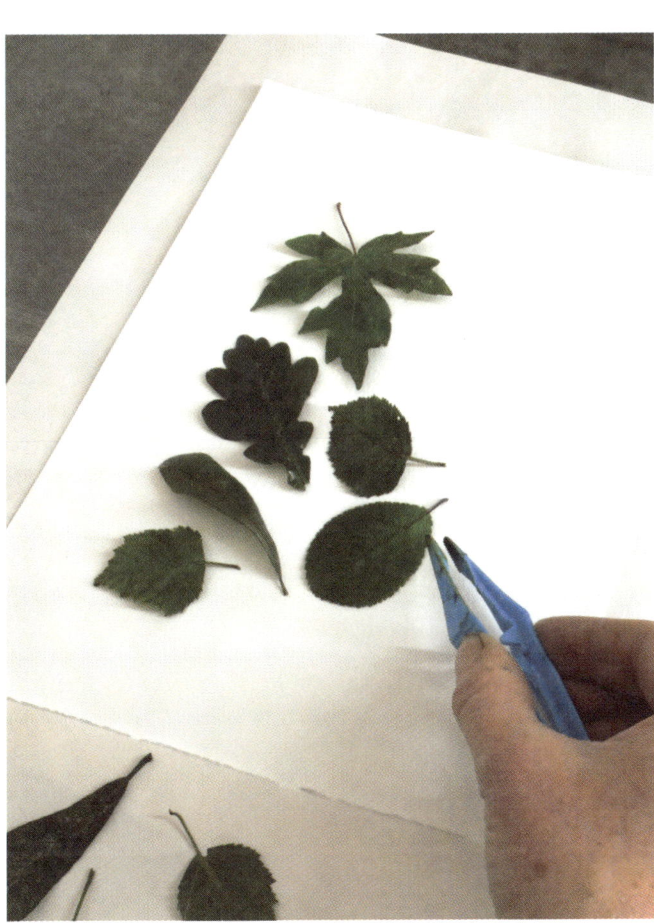

Placing inked leaves carefully onto the print paper using tweezers.

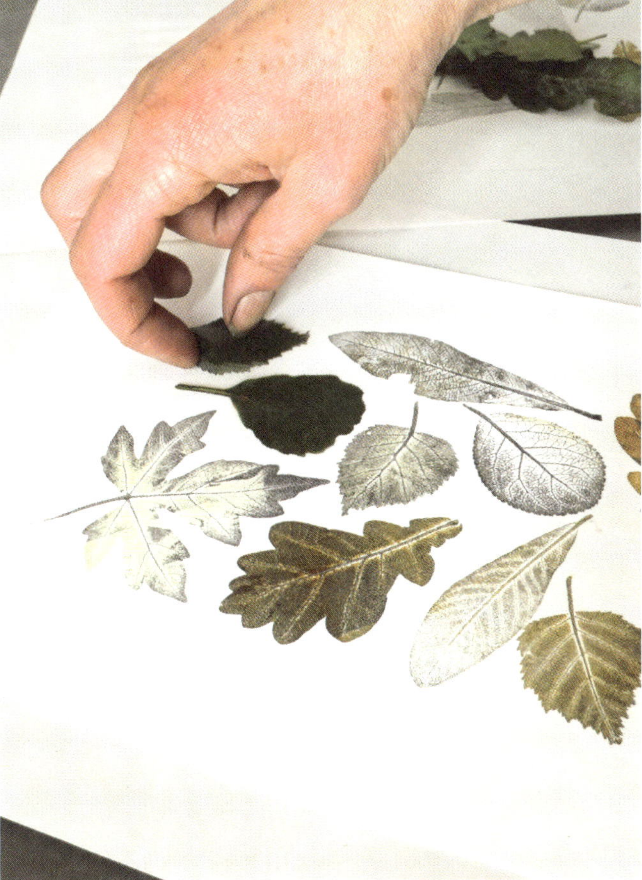

Removing leaves from the print. Further leaves can be inked and printed to fill remaining gaps or create overlays of leaves and colour.

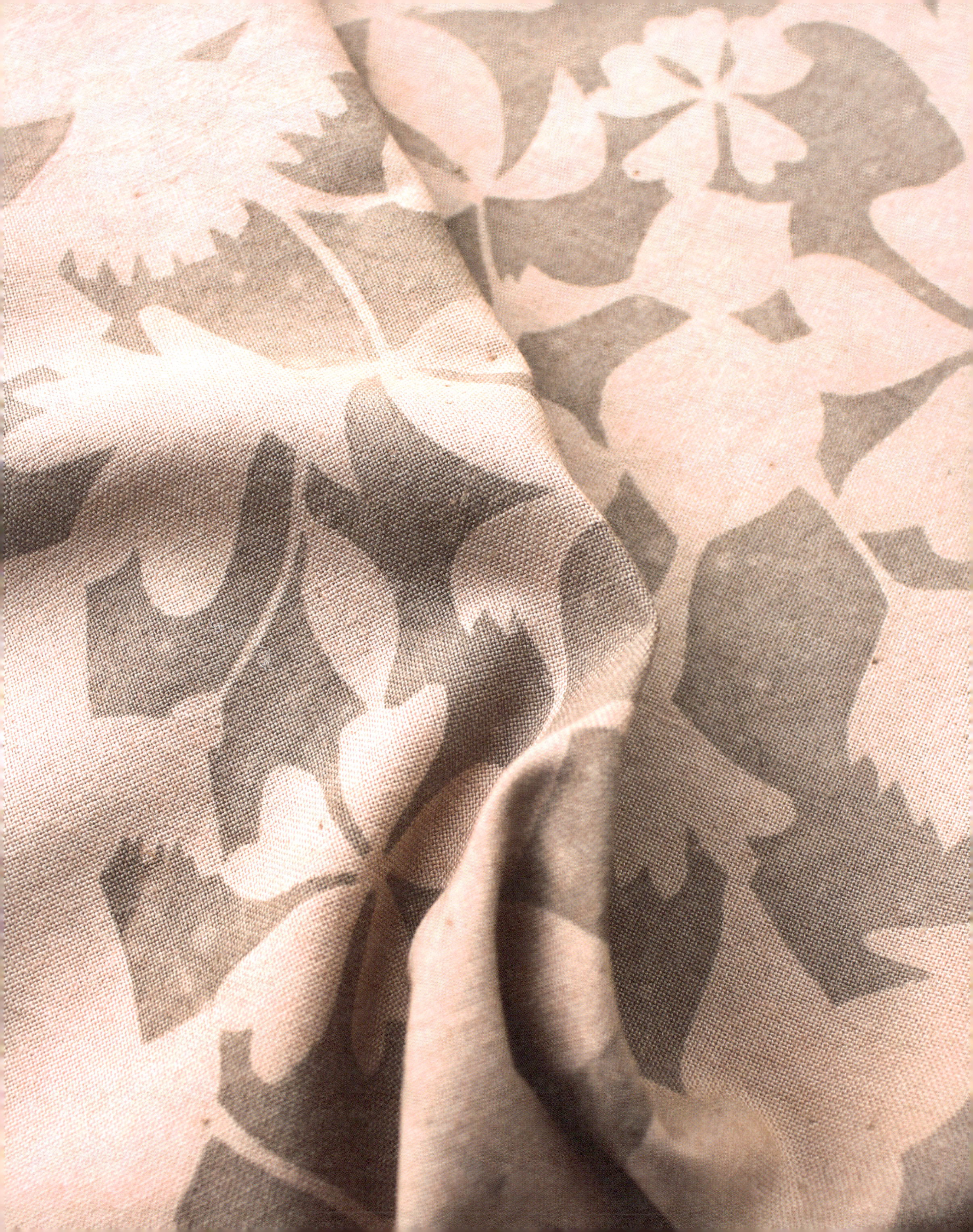

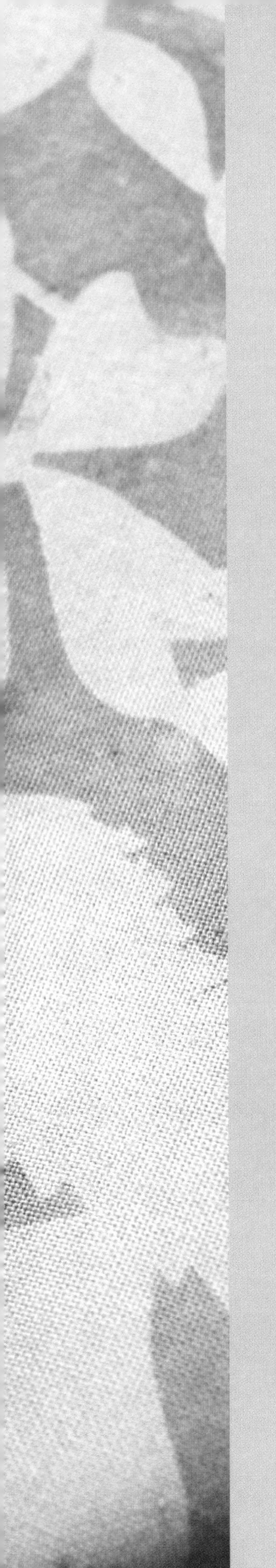

A Few Final Thoughts

Just before submitting my manuscript of this book to the publishers, I printed a plant-dyed piece of fabric (which had long since lost its dye identification label, although it was possibly dyed with a mix of madder and coreopsis) with a citric acid discharge paste. This had a minimal effect on the colour.

Disappointed, I washed it thinking I'd try again but because I had an iron/tannin complex bath on the go, chucked it (literally) into this pot. I've had good results discharging colour from iron-modified fabrics and I thought I might try this after dyeing it in the iron/tannin bath. A few days later, I checked the bath (it was just sat outside in the garden) and removed an unexpectedly coloured piece of fabric. The areas where the discharge paste was applied had gone darker. A completely unanticipated outcome!

A quick (very non-scientific) internet search revealed that iron is attracted to citric acid (possibly), so I can only guess that the areas where the discharge paste had been applied attracted more iron than the areas where it hadn't been applied, even though discharge paste applied post-dyeing will reduce the colour of iron.

My rather long-winded point is that the discipline of printmaking with plant-based colour is a constant surprise, a never-ending learning process and a lesson in never becoming complacent. Just when you think you might have a handle on a technique or process, something happens to set you straight or you get an unexpected result or even, sometimes, a lovely surprise.

What a way to keep you on your toes and excited about the day ahead…

FACING PAGE

Using plant-based colour provides an endless source of inspiration, experimentation and unexpected results. This naturally dyed fabric was screenprinted with a discharge paste before being immersed in an oak gall and tannin bath.

Bibliography

Adam, Robert and Robertson, Carol (2003) *Screenprinting: The Complete Water-Based System*. London, UK: Thames and Hudson Ltd.

Bancroft, Edward (1813) *Experimental Researches Concerning the Philosophy of Permanent Colours; and the Best Means of Producing Them, by Dyeing, Calico Printing, etc Vol. 1 & 2*. London, UK.

Banister, Manly (1969) *Practical Guide to Etching and Other Intaglio Printmaking Techniques*. New York, USA: Sterling Publishing Co.

Bechtold, Thomas and Mussak, Rita (2009) *Handbook of Natural Colorants*. Chichester, UK: John Wiley & Sons Ltd.

Bégun, André (2000) *A Technical Dictionary of Print Making*. Paris, France: Estampe.

Bersch, Josef (1901) *The Manufacture of Mineral and Lake Pigments, Containing Directions for the Manufacture of All Artificial Artists and Painters Colours, Enamel Colours, Soot and Metallic Pigments*. Second, revised edition. London, UK: Scott Greenwood & Co.

Bosence, Susan (1985) *Hand Block Printing & Resist Dyeing*. New York, USA: Arco Publishing Inc.

Boutrup, Joy and Ellis, Catharine (2018) *The Art and Science of Natural Dyes*. Atglen, USA: Schiffer Publishing Ltd.

Bridgewater, Alan and Bridgewater, Gill (1983) *Printing with Wood Blocks, Stencils & Engravings*. Newton Abbott, UK: David & Charles.

Cardon, Dominique (2007) *Natural Dyes: Sources, Tradition, Technology and Science*. London, UK: Archetype Publications Ltd.

Cave, Roderick (2010) *Impressions of Nature: A History of Nature Printing*. London, UK: The British Library.

Cliffe, Nicola (2024) *Printing with Natural Dyes*. Marlborough, UK: The Crowood Press Ltd.

Coles, David (2018) *Chromatopia: An Illustrated History of Colour*. London, UK: Thames and Hudson Ltd.

Dean, Jenny (2018) *Colours from Nature: A Natural Dyer's Handbook*. Second, revised edition. Findon, UK.

Dean, Jenny (2010) *Wild Colour*. Second Edition. London, UK: Hachette UK.

Delamere, François and Guineau, Bernard (2000) *Colour: Making and Using Dyes and Pigments*. New York, USA: Harry N. Abrams Inc.

Duerr, Sasha (2020) *Natural Palettes: Inspiration from Plant-Based Color*. New York, USA: Princeton Architectural Press.

Eastaugh, Nicholas; Walsh, Valentine; Chaplin, Tracey and Siddall, Ruth (2008) *Pigment Compendium: A Dictionary and Optical Microscopy of Historical Pigments.* Abingdon, UK: Routledge.

Ginsburg, Madeleine (1991) *The Illustrated History of Textiles*. London, UK: Studio Editions Ltd.

Griffiths, Antony (1996) *Prints and Printmaking: An Introduction to the History and Techniques.* Second Edition. London, UK: British Museum Press.

Hofenk de Graaff, Judith (2004) *The Colourful Past*. London, UK: Archetype Publications Ltd.

Hoskins, Steve (2004) *Inks*. London, UK: A&C Black Ltd.

Kafka, Francis J (1959) *Batik, Tie Dyeing, Stenciling, Silk Screen, Block Printing*. New York, USA: Dover Publications Inc.

Kirby, Jo; van Bommel, Maarten and Verhecken, André (2014) *Natural Colorants for Dyeing and Lake Pigments*. London, UK: Archetype Publications Ltd.

Knecht, Edmund and Best Fothergill, James (1912) *The Principles and Practice of Textile Printing*. London, UK: Charles Griffin & Company Ltd.

Lumsden, Ernest (1962) *The Art of Etching*. London, UK: Constable and Co. Ltd.

MacDonald, Lauren (2023) *In Pursuit of Color*. Los Angeles, USA: Atelier Éditions.

Marshall, John (2018) *Singing the Blues*. Covelo, USA: St. Titus Press.

McLaren, Keith (1986) *The Colour Science of Dyes and Pigments*. Second edition. Bristol, UK: Adam Hilger Ltd.

Murashima, Kumiko (1993) *Katazome: Japanese Paste-Resist Dyeing for Contemporary Use*. Asheville, USA: Lark Books.

Nakano, Eisha (1985) *Japanese Stencil Dyeing*. New York, USA: Weatherill.

O'Neill, Charles (1862) *A dictionary of dyeing and calico printing: containing a brief account of all the substances and processes in use in the arts of printing and dyeing textile fabrics.* London, UK: Simpkin, Marshall & Co.

Osborne, Roy (1980) *Lights & Pigments: Colour Principles for Artists*. London, UK: John Murray Ltd.

Petit, Gaston and Arboleda, Amadio (1977) *Evolving Techniques in Japanese Woodblock Prints*. Tokyo, Japan: Kodansha International Ltd.

Plowright, Charles (1901) *On Woad as a Prehistoric Pigment*. London, UK: Spottiswoode & Co. Ltd.

Ragab, Menna; Hassabo, Ahmed and Othman, Hanan (2022) *An Overview of Natural Dyes Extraction Techniques for Valuable Utilization on Textile Fabrics.* Journal of Textiles, Coloration and Polymer Science, Vol 19, No. 2, pp 137–154. (Accessed 2 January 2024).

Räisänen, Riikka; Niinimäki, Kirsi and Primetta, Anja (2016) *Dyes from Nature*. London, UK: Archetype Publications Ltd.

Recker, Keith (2019) *True Colors: World Masters of Natural Dyes and Pigments*. Colorado, USA: Thrums Books.

Redfern, Margaret and Shirley, Peter (2011) *British Plant Galls*. Second Edition. Telford, UK: FSC Publications.

Robinson, Stuart (1969) *A History of Printed Textiles*. London, UK: Studio Vista Ltd.

Rothwell, Charles Frederick Seymour (1897) *The Printing of Textile Fabrics: A Practical Manual on the Printing of Cotton, Woollen, Silk and Half-silk Fabrics*. London, UK: Charles Griffin and Co. Ltd.

Russ, Stephen (1964) *Fabric Printing by Hand*. London, UK: Studio Vista Ltd.

Sandberg, Gösta (1997) *The Red Dyes: Cochineal, Madder, and Murex Purple*. Asheville, USA: Lark Books.

Savvidis, George et al (2014) *Ink-jet printing of cotton with natural dyes*. Review of Progress in Coloration and Related Topics. Vol. 130 (3). Available at: https://www.researchgate.net/publication/261602845_Ink-jet_printing_of_cotton_with_natural_dyes (Accessed 10 January 2024).

Silver, Michal and Burns, Sarah (2018) *Barron and Larcher: Textile Designers*. Woodbridge, UK: ACC Art Books Ltd.

Stijnman, Ad (2000) *Oil-based printing ink on paper: Bleeding, browning, blanching and peroxides*. Papier Restaurierung Vol. 1, Suppl pp.62–68. Available at https://cool.culturalheritage.org/iada/pr00jb_l.pdf. (Accessed 23 June 2024).

Storey, Joyce (1978) *The Thames and Hudson Manual of Dyes and Fabrics*. London, UK: Thames and Hudson Ltd.

Storey, Joyce (1992) *The Thames and Hudson Manual of Textile Printing*. Revised Edition. London, UK: Thames and Hudson Ltd.

Vejar, Kristine and Rodriguez, Adrienne (2020) *Journeys in Natural Dyeing: Techniques for Creating Color at Home.* New York, USA: Abrams.

Westergaard, Sue (2020) *Screenprinting on Textiles: The Complete Guide.* Marlborough, UK: The Crowood Press Ltd.

Index

First published in 2025 by
The Crowood Press Ltd
Ramsbury, Marlborough
Wiltshire SN8 2HR

enquiries@crowood.com
www.crowood.com

British Library Cataloguing-in-Publication Data
A catalogue record for this book is available from the British Library.

For product safety-related questions, contact:
productsafety@crowood.com

ISBN 978 0 7198 4522 2

Typeset by maru studio G.K.
Cover design by Sergey Tsvetkov
Printed and bound in India by Parksons Graphics

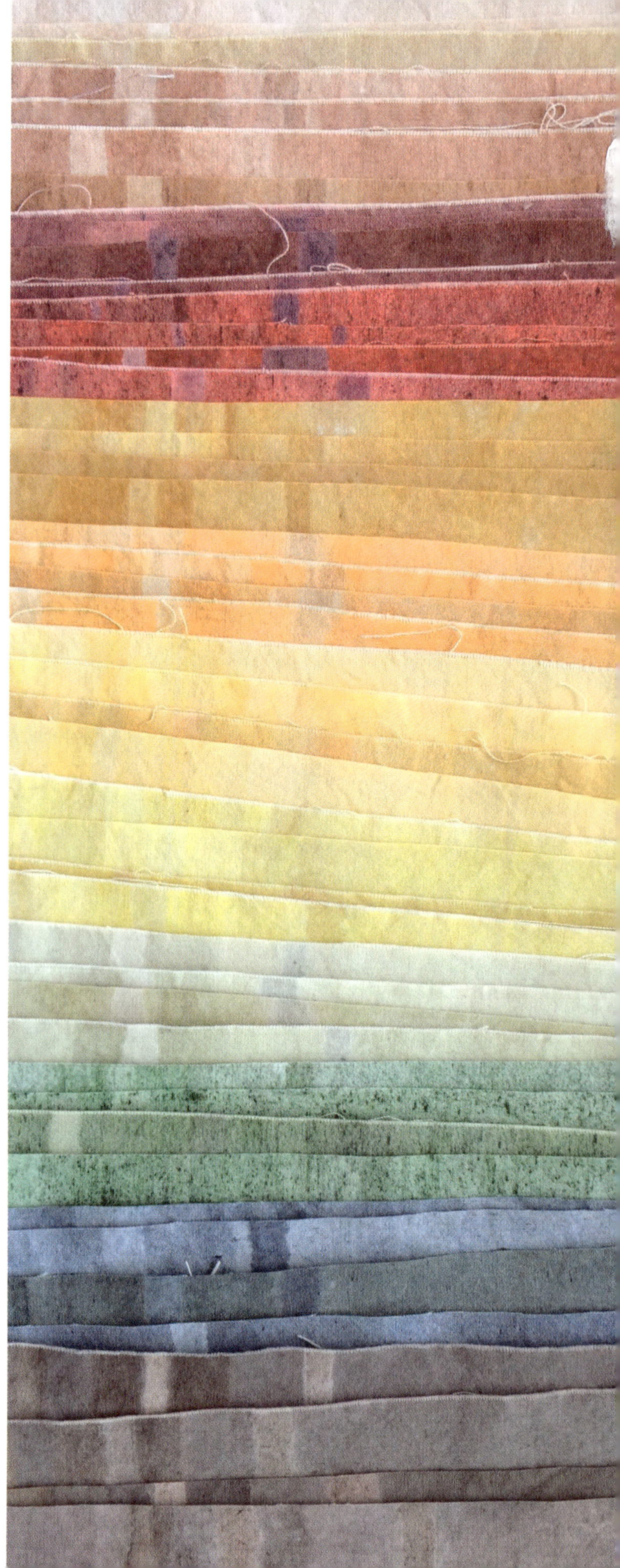

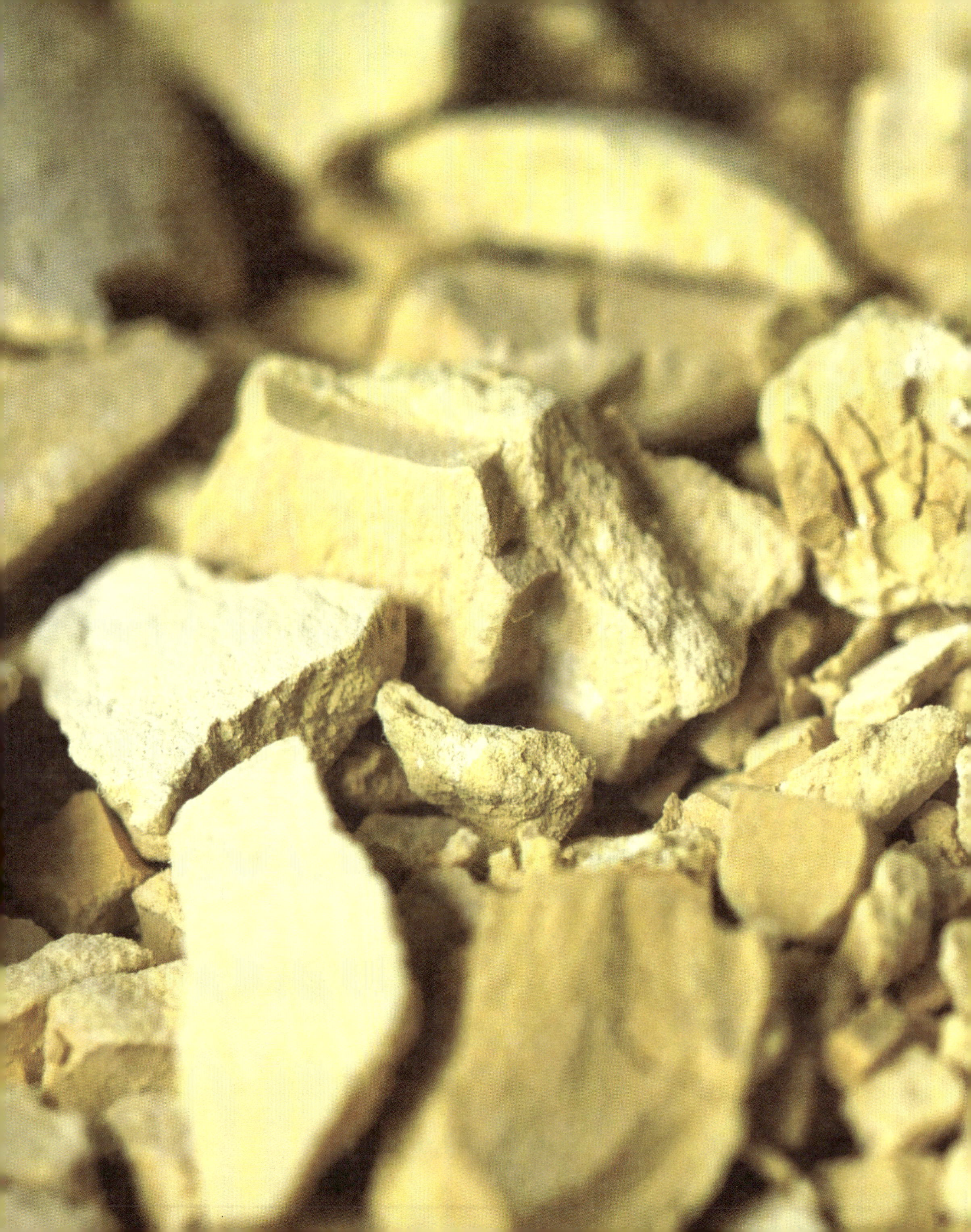